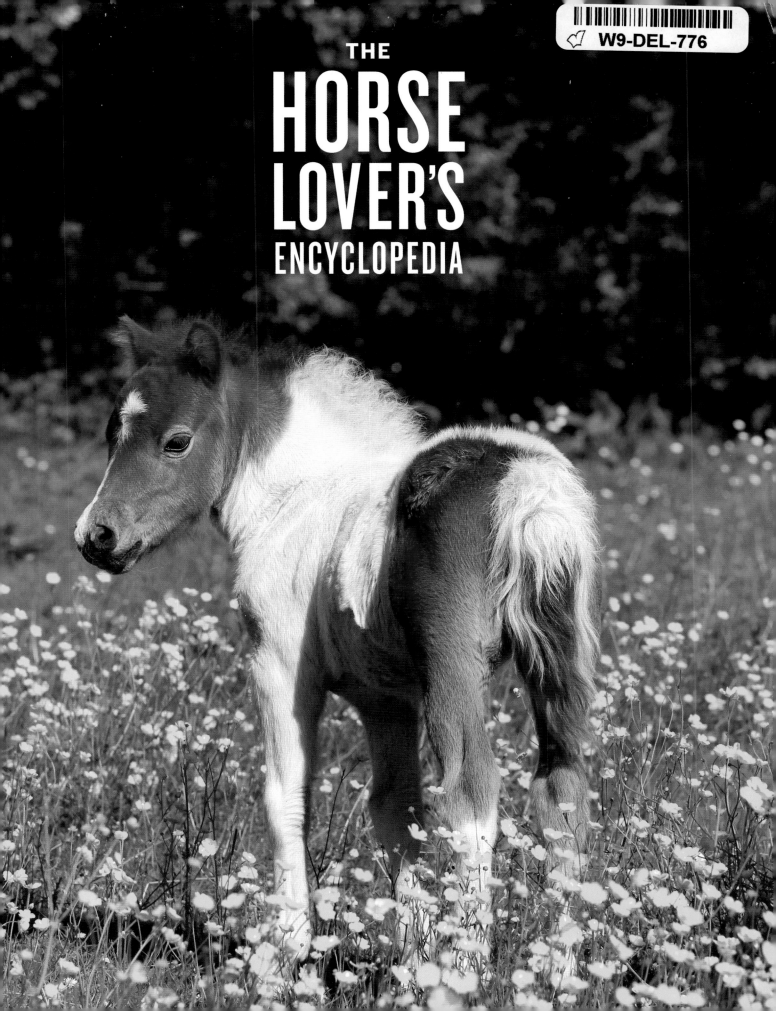

THE
HORSE
LOVER'S
ENCYCLOPEDIA

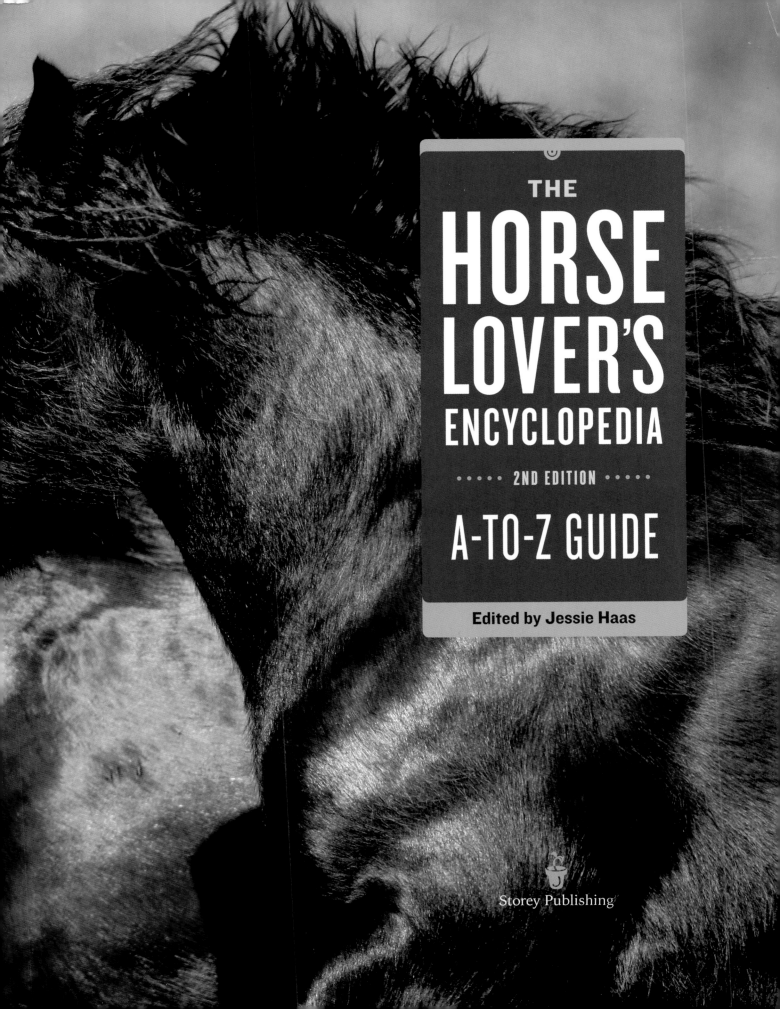

THE
HORSE
LOVER'S
ENCYCLOPEDIA

····· 2ND EDITION ·····

A-TO-Z GUIDE

Edited by Jessie Haas

Storey Publishing

The mission of Storey Publishing is to serve our customers by publishing practical information that encourages personal independence in harmony with the environment.

Edited by Deborah Burns and Lisa H. Hiley
Book design by Stacy Wakefield Forte
Indexed by Susan Olason
Text production by Erin Dawson

Cover photography by © Carol J. Walker (front) and © Bob Langrish (back)

Interior photography by © Bob Langrish, i–xii, 2, 3, 5 r., 7–11, 14 t., 15, 21, 22–24, 28 l., 29, 32 b., 33 t., 34–46, 48–53, 55, 58–60, 63, 70–73, 76, 77, 80–82, 87, 88 r., 90–93, 95, 96, 100, 101, 107–113, 116, 117, 119 b., 121 b., 122–126, 127 b., 129 t., 131–134, 138, 140, 141, 144, 145, 149, 150, 151 b., 152, 153, 159, 165, 175, 177, 179 b., 181–189, 191–195, 197, 198, 201, 205–210, 215–217, 219–221, 223 t., 241 t., 224–236, 240, 242–250, 253–256, 259, 261, 265, 267–270, 275, 276, 278, 280, 281 r., 282–284, 287, 291, 293, 298–302, 305 r., 307, 317, 320 t., 321, 322, 324, 325, 327 m., 331, 332 b., 334, 335, 338–346, 350, 351 b., 352, 355, 359, 360, 362 t., 368, 376, 389, 392, 395, 403–405; © Cheryl Rivers, 47 t., 64; © Dusty Perin, 4, 5 l., 12, 14 b., 17, 20, 26, 28 r., 32 t., 33 b., 47 b., 54, 57, 61, 66, 74, 75, 78, 79, 83, 84, 88 l., 89, 94, 99, 102, 106, 114, 118, 119 t., 121 t., 127 t., 128, 129 b., 136, 139, 143, 146–148, 151 t., 155, 157, 160–164, 167, 171, 178, 179 t., 180, 190, 196, 199, 202, 212–214, 218, 223 b., 239, 241 b., 251, 252, 258, 263, 266, 271, 273, 277, 279, 281 l., 286, 288–290, 292, 295, 303, 304, 305 l. & m., 310–315, 318, 319, 320 b., 323, 326, 327 t. & b., 328–330, 332 t., 336, 347, 348, 351 t., 356, 361, 362 b., 364–367, 370–375, 378–386, 390, 391, 394, 396–400

Illustrations by Alison Kolesar, 154; Chuck Galey, 313, 316; © Elayne Sears, 30, 86, 98, 110, 162, 169, 204 t.; Ilona Sherratt, 111, 195; Jim Dyekman, 25, 69, 192, 308 t.l., t.r. & b.m.; Joanna Rissanen, 6, 13, 16, 22, 24, 35, 45, 59, 71, 72, 75, 85, 103, 104, 130, 135, 137, 158, 171, 172, 182, 183, 200, 204 b., 238, 243, 247, 257, 278, 285, 287, 297, 302, 308 b.l. & b.r., 337, 340, 353, 361, 383, 401

Storey Publishing
210 MASS MoCA Way
North Adams, MA 01247
storey.com

Printed in China by R.R. Donnelley
10 9 8 7 6 5 4 3 2 1
Library of Congress Cataloging-in-Publication Data
Names: Haas, Jessie, editor.
Title: The horse-lover's encyclopedia / edited by Jessie Haas.
Other titles: Storey's horse-lover's encyclopedia.
Description: 2nd edition. | North Adams, MA : Storey Publishing, 2017. | Revised edition of: Storey's horse-lover's encyclopedia / edited by Deborah Burns. c2001. | Includes index.
Identifiers: LCCN 2016036407 (print) | LCCN 2016052545 (ebook) | ISBN 9781612126784 (pbk. : alk. paper) | ISBN 9781612126821 (hardcover : alk. paper) | ISBN 9781612126791 (ebook)
Subjects: LCSH: Horses—Encyclopedias. | Horsemanship—Encyclopedias. | Horse breeds--Encyclopedias.
Classification: LCC SF278 .S76 2017 (print) | LCC SF278 (ebook) | DDC 636.1003—dc23
LC record available at https://lccn.loc.gov/2016036407

For all the horses I have loved

It has been my great pleasure to work with the Storey team again, especially Deb Burns and Lisa Hiley. My friend Cheryl Pratt Rivers has been an inspiration and a great source of information.

CONTENTS

PREFACE TO THE 2ND EDITION

GROWING UP ON A SMALL FARM IN VERMONT, I wanted a horse from the time I could first articulate a wish. When I was six, Scamper came into our lives. A Morgan-Welsh cross, he specialized in rolling in anything that could stain his brilliant white coat: manure, green grass, or the soot and ash left over from a brush fire. He instantly put know-it-all young riders in their places, but when the saddle slipped and an old man and little child fell under his feet, he stood like a rock. He never shied that can I remember. Running away, balking, bucking, biting? Yes. But he took us on trails and to gymkhanas, skidded firewood, and pulled the hay fork when we put up loose hay. Unfortunately, though my parents had grown up working with draft horses, they didn't understand the differences between a large horse and a pony.

In hindsight it's easy to see that Scamper had equine metabolic syndrome. He foundered on grass and corn-stalks, and suffered episodes of lameness throughout his life. He also got heaves. If I could time travel with this book in my hand, we'd do better by Scamper. I hope somewhere he knows that.

In seventh grade I got a weanling filly. I managed to raise and train her, mostly out of books. Josey was beautiful, domineering, and fundamentally unsound, a heartbreaker of a horse who absorbed all my mistakes and lived to be 34. She taught me a great deal about lameness of all sorts. But at her best she was a thrilling ride—fast, powerful, and smart. She shied! In fact, she was more like a sling-shot than anything else, until I got myself a deep-seated dressage saddle.

As a kid my daily life with horses was all about challenges I barely met, battles I couldn't win. Meanwhile I devoured books about kids who trained wild stallions and won countless ribbons, and were "natural horsemen." Eventually I started writing stories about kids like me—struggling, overwhelmed, dedicated horse-lovers who learned the hard way. Thirty-five books later, naughty Radish in *Runaway Radish*, opinionated Bramble in the Bramble and Maggie series, and Beware in the Beware the Mare series have lured many horse-lovers into finishing their first book with chapters. I've also written a world history in poems about horses, a book about safety with horses, and two adult histories that feature horses on the covers.

Along the way, planning to breed Josey, I drove into a Vermont farmyard and saw the magnificent Morgan stallion Portledge Steven prancing in a pen. It was love at first sight. Realizing that it made no sense to breed an unsound mare, I bought the youngest and most affordable Steven son, a month-old colt I named Atherton.

He became a handsome, sweet, lovable horse, but our life together truly blossomed when I discovered clicker training. At last I could explain to him—with treats, the Morgan's native language—exactly what I wanted. We finished every ride excited and happy, each thinking that the other was extremely smart. He was my dream horse, until I lost him at 18 to a surgical colic.

Within a few months, I owned his three-year-old niece, Robin. She has matured to a pony-sized, sweet, and challenging friend. She bites and kicks out while being saddled, despite everything I've tried in the way of training, but becomes instantly cheerful and willing once I've mounted. She likes tricks and will let me know if too much time has passed since a clicker training session. I didn't want to need another horse, but I would hate to have missed Robin.

These horses have taught me so much, and editing *The Horse-Lover's Encyclopedia*, I've learned even more. If I could reach back and put it into my own hands at certain times in my past life, it would save me and my horses some trouble and some heartache. When we love horses we owe it to them to know everything we can, and the sum of what we can know keeps expanding. Advances in medicine, genetics, and materials have changed much of what horsemen do in the years since this book came out. And there are so many new sports one can do with horses, from working equitation to mounted archery. The California *vaquero* tradition is making a comeback, and people do agility with horses. The horse world is vibrant and exciting, and there's a place in it for everyone, whether as a spectator, a participant, a learner, or a humble schlepper of muck buckets and bags of carrots.

Or a breeder. My latest horse, the broodmare Woodgate Martha V., was purchased with the idea of breeding her to Robin's sire. Pregnancy did not result, but Martha V. has also won my heart. She came to Vermont from Kansas, arriving in a December snowstorm. Wracked with guilt at having subjected this poor horse to a 30-hour trailer ride, I drove up to see her the next morning. Martha was out playing in the snow-covered ring as if the trip, the snow, and the five-degree temperatures were no big deal. Her ears are always pricked, her spirit is friendly, and she's ready to start a new career, being valued for herself and not just her babies. I'm sure she has a lot to teach me.

— *Jessie Haas*

PREFACE TO THE 1ST EDITION

PERHAPS THERE'S A HORSE who recognizes your step and welcomes you with a soft nicker, his breath warm and steamy on a frosty morning. Or perhaps you have just started riding, and your pleasure in the sport has quickly turned into a passion. Or perhaps you are a seasoned competitor and know the thrill of partnering with a horse to pursue a goal. Whatever the reason, you are a horse lover: You exult in the grace and spirit of horses, and you are not alone.

In my case the passion for horses began before I can remember. Every week my father took my sister and me riding at a nearby stable. We started in the ring on the most amiable of horses, learned quickly, and soon went out on the trail. Over time we graduated to more challenging mounts. We refined our skills at camp and as teenagers took care of friends' horses during summer vacations. Trail riding was our favorite activity. We eventually knew every hiking trail and logging road in our part of the Berkshire mountains in northwestern Massachusetts.

For a couple of summers I took care of a plucky buckskin mare named Missy. She and I often climbed the wooded, long-abandoned, 18th-century Boston–Albany Post Road to the top of the Taconic Range that divides Massachusetts and New York. Emerging from the woods we would gallop north along the Taconic Crest Trail through blueberry meadows, high above the world. Below on our right were the thickly forested mountains of Massachusetts. On our left, the hills of New York rolled west to the Hudson River and the Catskill Mountains. Missy was willing, responsive, and eager to explore. My memory of her is forever linked with a sense of sunlit freedom and adventure. We were companions, seeking our fortune, and we were on top of the world.

The air of heaven, says an Arabian proverb, is that which blows between a horse's ears. Now an editor of horse books, I have met many people who would agree that paradise can be found on a horse's back. *Storey's Horse-Lover's Encyclopedia* is meant to celebrate this magnificent animal and help readers become more knowledgeable. I hope you will keep this book on your tack-room shelf and refer to it often.

After all, the horse world is vast and growing, with dozens of disciplines and hundreds of breeds. It contains numerous sub-worlds, or galaxies, such as jumping, barrel racing, polo, and endurance riding, which have developed completely different riding styles, tack, attire, and language. People in one discipline can be completely isolated from, and ignorant of, what is going on in other disciplines.

Yet at the center of all these worlds stands one creature: the horse, with its eloquent eyes, burnished

coat, arched neck, delicate legs, soft muzzle, and sweeping mane and tail. The horse has the same beauty and nobility whether it is carrying jockeys, rodeo team-ropers, Russian Cossack trick-riders, or Olympic three-day-eventers. The instincts of a horse are the same whether the horse is an Arabian, a mustang, a Morgan, or a Percheron. The potential health problems of a horse are the same. The ways one speaks to and cares for a horse are the same. Most of all, the profound bond between horse and human is the same, no matter what the breed or riding style.

Around the globe, horse people of diverse backgrounds have recently begun to come together to share their knowledge of horses: insights, training secrets, solutions. This wonderful development will enrich our relationship with horses. A champion Western reiner, for example, may have an insight that will solve a problem for someone training in dressage. One purpose of this encyclopedia is to facilitate communication between the various equestrian galaxies, to make it easier for us to understand and learn from one another by defining words and phrases.

Over the centuries of partnership between horse and human, an enormous amount of wisdom and general lore has accumulated. Modern "horse sense" has evolved from the experience of horse people of many cultures, including Arabian and Native American trainers; British Thoroughbred breeders; the cowboys and herders of Spain, Mexico, and the American Southwest; the military horsemen who laid down the fundamentals of precise horsemanship that later became dressage; and countless other breeders, trainers, and instructors. Every horse lover can benefit from studying equine history, physiology, and psychology.

In the end, however, the very best way to learn about horses is to spend time with them, in and out of the saddle. Find an hour just to watch your horse as he grazes, interacts with other horses, works in the ring, or simply dozes in the sun. Take long relaxed rides. Savor the moments when you are grooming your horse, talking to him, braiding his mane. This is when the true and precious bond between you and the horse is built.

Horses bring out the best in us. No matter what the rest of our lives are like, with horses we learn to be sensitive, courageous, responsible, and honest. Horses are sensitive, honest beings with whom we can share deep experiences, as I was fortunate enough to share joyous explorations with Missy on a mountain top.

We at Storey Publishing wish you a fair road and a willing steed!

— *Deborah Burns, Equestrian Editor*

ARABIAN

AAEP
➤ *See American Association of Equine Practitioners*

above the bit When the horse brings his head up to avoid contact with the bit while being ridden or driven.
➤ *See also on the bit*

abscess An inflammation surrounding a concentration of pus. Abscesses can occur anywhere in the horse's body, but are most common in the hoof.
➤ *See also hoof; gravel, in hoof*

acepromazine/acetylpromazine maleate
A tranquilizer, often abbreviated to "ace," that is sometimes used before stressful situations such as transportation by trailer. Injected intramuscularly, it takes effect in less than half an hour and lasts several hours. Ace does not actually relieve anxiety; it merely mutes the horse's physical responses. Unethical dealers may give a horse ace to make him appear well-mannered and calm.

Available at feed stores, ace is frequently administered by horse owners to solve behavioral problems that would be better addressed with training. It has no effect on pain sensation and should not be administered to horses who are bleeding or in shock. It causes involuntary erection in males, which may lead to penis damage. Using ace on an excited horse may actually make him more upset.

action The way a horse moves. Different breeds and disciplines emphasize different types of action. American Saddlebreds, for example, should exhibit sparkling, animated action, with elevated knees and hocks. Dressage horses display forward, supple, balanced movement. Western pleasure horses should move in a natural, relaxed style that is comfortable to ride, while the action of gaited horses like Paso Finos may incorporate a lateral swing that would be considered a grave fault in other breeds.
➤ *See also individual breeds*

acupuncture An ancient Chinese healing art that uses thin needles to stimulate certain external points (called acupressure points) on the body in order to stimulate the flow of energy or release blocked energy. Acupuncture may be beneficial when treating painful or chronic conditions that have not responded to standard medications, such as chronic colic or heaves. In addition to needles, weak electric currents, cold lasers, and ultrasound may be used to stimulate the points. A veterinarian may combine acupuncture with traditional medicine to maximize benefits to the horse. Horse owners can learn to massage acupressure points to relieve certain conditions.

"Adopt a Pony" programs Programs offered at some stables, in which a sponsor pays for purchase and upkeep of ponies to give lessons to young people who otherwise could not learn to ride.

African horse sickness (AHS) An equine disease endemic to much of Africa and parts of the Middle East that is transmitted by biting flies and mosquitoes. Symptoms include a high fever lasting several days and clearly apparent discomfort, with swollen eyelids and jugular veins. The disease can be fatal.

age The average life expectancy for a horse is 25 to 30 years; many horses, with good care, can live to be well past 30. Horses reach their prime at varying ages, depending on genetics, training, treatment, and a variety of other factors. Many show horses, including dressage horses, hunters, and polo ponies, are at their best when they are at least 10, and some compete or perform for many more years. Older, experienced horses can be valuable teachers, helping young riders develop their skills.

A 15-year-old family horse, for example, can help children learn to ride safely. For an adult, a calm, sensible middle-aged horse can be the perfect partner. However, if you intend to ride regularly, avoid buying a horse older than 20; you will likely have only a few years of riding before you have to retire him. It is difficult to sell an old horse, so you will have to decide—before you purchase him—whether you can take care of him once he is retired.

How old should your first horse be? The golden rule is "The younger or less experienced the human, the older or more experienced the horse should be." *Never* pair an inexperienced or uneducated person with an inexperienced or untrained horse. Such a match could result in life-threatening injuries.
➤ *See also teeth and age*

aggressive horses Aggression is attempting to injure with intent; it can range from biting (not casual nipping, but the fierce, jaws-wide-open kind) to full-on attacks with front or hind hooves. Some aggression is natural between horses but relatively rare toward humans. Aggression can be created in a foal raised without a proper understanding of boundaries, or in a horse who has had painful and confusing experiences with people.

Most horse-training techniques operate on the assumption that the horse is not aggressive, and trainers work to establish submission and docility. A horse who comes at you with teeth and hooves, *on purpose*, is in a different category and should be handled by an experienced professional.

AI
➤ *See artificial insemination (AI)*

aids The rider's means of communicating cues to the horse. Natural aids are the seat (or weight), legs, hands, and voice. Artificial aids (whips and spurs) amplify the natural aids.
➤ *See also hands; seat*

aiken A jump used in hunter classes, constructed of vertical wooden posts topped by evergreen branches.

airs above the ground Advanced high school dressage maneuvers executed from a rearing position. In training the horse progresses from levade, a 45-degree-angle rear held for several seconds, through several stages of hopping on the hind feet—croupade, ballotade, courbette—to capriole, in which he leaps forward while lashing out full force with his hind feet. The airs above the ground are said to have been originally useful on the battlefield to scatter enemy soldiers. They require great collection and physical strength, and are performed mostly by baroque European riding academies, including the Spanish Riding School.
➤ *See also ballotade; capriole; courbette; croupade; dressage; levade; Spanish Riding School*

albino A horse lacking all pigment in skin and hair is sometimes called an albino. Although white horses do have pink skin, they are not true albinos, as they have blue or brown eyes, not pink ones.

AIRS ABOVE THE GROUND

AKHAL-TEKE

An ancient hot-blooded breed developed in Turkmenistan. The name (AK-hal Tech-ay) means "pure Turkmen." Beautiful and fast, with a soft gliding gait and legendary powers of endurance, Turkmen horses were highly valued in the ancient world, and were traded from North Africa to China. During the 1600s and 1700s many were imported to England, where they had a profound influence on the modern Thoroughbred; the Godolphin Arabian may have been part Akhal-Teke.

Ranging from 14.2 to 16 hands, and weighing 900 to 1,000 pounds (408–454 kg), Akhal-Tekes look like small Thoroughbreds, lean and long, with deep heart girths. Narrowly built, with little body fat, they cool efficiently; quick recovery time is a plus for Akhal-Tekes competing in eventing and endurance. They have a low resting heart rate, but a large stroke volume and great aerobic capacity. Their calm, alert temperament is helpful in dressage, where, though not currently a fashionable breed, individual Akhal-Tekes can excel with good training. The Akhal-Teke stallion Absent won the gold medal in Prix de Dressage in the 1960 Summer Olympics.

Many Akhal-Tekes exhibit a metallic gold or silver sheen to the coat, and black horses may have a blue or purple sheen, due to hair structure. The normal opaque core is small or absent, allowing the transparent hair shaft to bend and refract light. Add the blue or partially blue eye common among Akhal-Tekes, and you have a horse of arresting beauty. Despite this, numbers are low, with fewer than 1,000 annual registrations and a worldwide population under 5,000. **Livestock Conservancy status: Threatened**

alfalfa hay A high-protein, legume hay. Most horses love alfalfa hay, but it usually should not be fed alone because it is very rich and can cause weight gain, loose stools, mineral imbalance, or even colic. Alfalfa contains more protein than an average horse requires. Alfalfa is best fed in a blend, mixed with clover and grass. Third-cut alfalfa is usually the most nutritious but may contain blister beetles. A horse who has had an episode of laminitis should not be offered alfalfa.
➤ *See also blister beetle poisoning; colic; feeding and nutrition; hay; laminitis*

amble A four-beat gait resembling the pace. The hind and front legs on each side move forward together but land separately, so there is no moment of suspension. It is smoother to ride than the trot, beautiful to watch, and can be very fast.

This extra gait shows up naturally in certain breeds instead of or in addition to the trot or canter. The Icelandic horse has a natural amble called the tölt. The five-gaited American Saddlebred ambles at two speeds—the slow amble is called the slow gait, and the fast version is known as the rack. Paso horses have three gaits—a walk, a slow amble, and a fast amble; they do not learn to canter.

Tennessee Walking Horses have a special extended amble, in which the hind legs take particularly large steps. This "Tennessee walk" (also called a running walk) can be as fast as a canter, and is extremely comfortable for the rider. The American Saddlebred, Tennessee Walkers, and Mountain Saddle breeds have Spanish blood, which is thought to have contributed the extra gait.

The amble is not the same as a pace, in which the legs on the same side strike the ground together.
➤ *See also gaited horse; Mountain Saddle Horses; Paso Fino; Peruvian Horse; rack; slow amble/slow gait; tölt*

AMERICAN BREEDS

American Cream Draft Horse

The American Cream Draft Horse, the only draft horse to originate in the United States, can be traced to an unusually colored mare in Central Iowa in the early part of the 20th century. Her offspring consistently showed the pink skin, amber or hazel eyes, and light, medium, or dark cream color that became the breed standard. Standing 15 to 16.3 hands high, Creams have refined heads, powerfully muscled bodies, and sturdy legs. Like most draft horses, they are kind, willing, and trustworthy. **Livestock Conservancy status: Critical**

American Curly

Originally a strain of northern mustang with a thick, curly coat; a curly mane and tail; and even curly eyelashes. A breed registry was formed in 1971; in order to avoid inbreeding, Arabian, Morgan, Appaloosa, and Missouri Fox Trotter blood was introduced, based on similarities between these breeds and the original Curly type. A sturdy breed resembling the old-style Morgan, Curlies are good, all-purpose ranch and family horses; they are exceptionally hardy in cold weather. Some Curly horses shed the mane and tail annually.

Curly horses have long been touted as hypoallergenic, and new research appears to support this claim. In one test, 37 of 40 riders with documented horse allergies showed no signs of reaction after exposure to Curly horses, and the remaining 3 responded well to a single dose of inhaled medication. Additionally, allergic reactions to flat-coated horses diminished in some of the riders over the three years of the study, suggesting that exposure to Curly horses desensitized them to equine allergens in general.

➤ *See also Bashkir*

American Indian Horse

A collective description of all Native American horses. Individual tribes had types of horses they preferred, but many of the bloodlines were lost when tribal populations were decimated. The American Indian Horse Registry researched and combined the remaining tribal lines into one breed, though some tribal lines remain individual. The American Indian Horse is a small, tough horse of Spanish type. Every color is allowed. American Indian Horses are excellent for trail and endurance, and are shown at Western breed horse shows,

AMERICAN CREAM DRAFT HORSE

AMERICAN CURLY

AMERICAN INDIAN HORSE

where they compete at their own variation of Trail classes and Western games.

➤ *See also Appaloosa; Florida Cracker Horse; mustang; trail class*

American Paint Horse

A popular stock horse breed of pinto coloration, based on Quarter Horse and Thoroughbred bloodlines. In order to be registered as a Paint, a horse must have two registered Paint parents or one registered Paint parent and one Quarter Horse or Thoroughbred parent. Paints are found in most disciplines, including their own races, but they are most popular in the Western disciplines.

➤ *See also overo; tobiano; tovero*

American Saddlebred/American Saddle Horse

A North American gaited breed, developed to have a comfortable stride and the endurance to go all day. Saddlebreds and the closely related Tennessee Walking Horses combine the qualities of colonial ambling horses with the blood of Thoroughbreds, Morgans, and Arabians. With their beauty, good minds, and endurance, they were the mount of choice for officers during the Civil War.

Today's Saddlebreds are primarily show horses, though people also use them on the trail. They can make fine dressage horses and are also shown in harness. Saddlebreds come in two types: the three-gaited horse (shown at the walk, trot, and canter) and the five-gaited horse (which also performs the slow gait and the rack).

Saddlebreds usually stand around 16 hands high, with strongly arched necks and tails, and finely sculpted heads. All colors are permitted, including pinto and palomino, and splashy white facial and leg markings are common. Though generally good-natured, Saddlebreds have a reputation for being fiery.

➤ *See also amble; five-gaited horse; pace; rack; racking horse; slow amble/slow gait; three-gaited horse*

American Walking Pony

A large pony (13.2–14.2 hands high) developed by crossing Welsh Ponies and Tennessee Walking Horses. Walking Ponies are beautiful and versatile athletes; some are capable of performing seven gaits. They are used for pleasure, driving, jumping, and trail. The breed, which has existed only since 1956, is small in population.

AMERICAN PAINT

AMERICAN SADDLEBRED

American Association of Equine Practitioners (AAEP)

A nationwide organization of veterinarians specializing in the care of horses, ponies, mules, and donkeys. The AAEP website (aaep.org) has a search function that allows you to find a nearby veterinarian.

American Horse Shows Association (AHSA)

Former name of the United States Equestrian Federation (USEF).

➤ *See also United States Equestrian Federation (USEF)*

anemia

➤ *See equine infectious anemia (EIA)*

anestrus

Not cycling into heat. Mares are typically anestrus in winter, when days are short, and their estrus (i.e., heat) cycles begin again in spring as daylight lengthens.

➤ *See also diestrus; estrus*

Anglo-

A prefix designating a cross-bred Thoroughbred. Anglo-Arabs are Thoroughbred-Arab, Anglo-Morgans are Thoroughbred-Morgan, and so on.

anhidrosis

Inability to perspire; most likely to occur in hot, humid climates. If a horse overexerts or is confined in an airless stall during hot weather, his sweat glands can overwork and ultimately shut down. The horse will be very hot but dry to the touch; he may pant after exercise, become uncoordinated, or collapse.

ANATOMY OF THE HORSE

The structure of a horse; essentially the basic "map" of a horse's body parts. The term "anatomy" is objective, with no judgment of the correctness or quality of how those parts fit together. In contrast, a horse's conformation can be considered good or bad, depending on breed standards and the absence or presence of conformation defects.

➤ *See also conformation; hoof; judging*

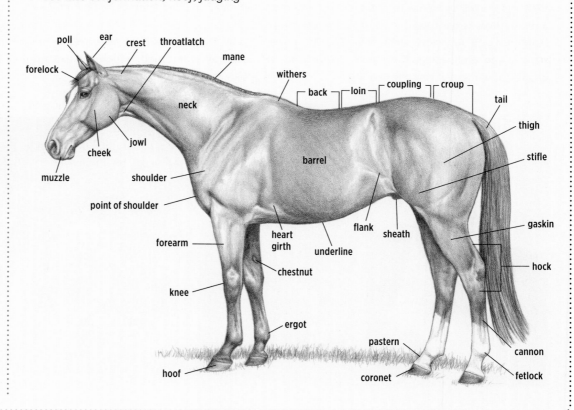

ANDALUSIAN

An ancient Spanish warhorse breed, later used as a stock horse and in the bull ring. Andalusians excel at dressage, working dressage, and doma vaquera; the latter two are newly popular sports based on Spanish stock horse training.

A handsome midsize horse, 15 to 16 hands high and 1,000 to 1,200 pounds (454–544 kg), the Andalusian has an elegant, straight or slightly convex profile and highly arched neck, short back, wide chest, and rounded croup. They have excellent feet and legs and profuse and often wavy tails. Most Andalusians are bay, gray, or black; chestnut is not an accepted color. They are spirited but exceptionally gentle, and they have great "cow sense." They are also called Pura Raza Española (PRE), or "Purebred Spanish," horses.

Signs of colic are also common. The condition can be fatal. The immediate remedy is to bring the horse's temperature down to normal—99.5 to 101.5°F (37.5–38.6°C)—by bathing him in cool water and placing him in a shady, cool spot. A fan may be necessary to cool him off.

Supplementing with electrolytes and amino acids is sometimes helpful; consult your vet. Anhidrotic horses may recover their ability to sweat in a cooler climate or season, but there is no cure; long-term management of the condition is essential.

anthelmintic Any of several medications used to treat horses and other animals for parasitic infections.
➤ *See also deworming; worming*

anticipation When a horse has learned a pattern (as in dressage or reining) too thoroughly, and performs the movement before the cue. To a judge, this reveals that the horse is working off memory, not paying attention to the rider or driver. To prevent anticipation, avoid drilling with actual patterns you will use in competition.

Appaloosa *(see next page)*

APPENDIX HORSE

A horse with one Quarter Horse parent and one Thoroughbred parent, as listed in the appendix of the Quarter Horse registry. An Appendix Horse may compete in all Quarter Horse shows. In order for the offspring of an Appendix Horse to be registered as Appendix Horse, the other parent must be a permanently registered Quarter Horse. Alternatively, if the horse has earned a certain number of points in Quarter Horse shows or races before being bred to a Thoroughbred, the foal can be registered as an Appendix Horse.
➤ *See also Quarter Horse; Thoroughbred*

APPALOOSA

A breed of athletic, dramatically colored and spotted horses developed by the Nez Percé Indians. Every Appaloosa is uniquely marked, but all share certain characteristics, such as mottled skin, mottling around the eye, and striped hooves.

LEOPARD SPOT PATTERN

The breed has two distinct genetic color patterns. Leopard Appaloosas are spotted all over, like their namesake. The background color of this horse's coat is usually white, and the spots may be brown, black, bay, chestnut, or golden. One or both of the horse's eyes may be blue (called a glass eye). On blanket Appaloosas, the spots appear primarily on the horse's rump, in a blanket-shaped area. The background color of the horse may be black, gray, red, dun, or palomino.

Appaloosas were nearly exterminated by the U.S. Army following the surrender of Chief Joseph in 1887. Hundreds were shot, stallions were gelded, and mares were deliberately crossed with draft horses. A group of breeders began working to save them in 1938, crossing Arabians and Quarter Horses with the remnants of Appaloosa stock. Modern Appaloosas strongly resemble Quarter Horses. Some breeders are working to reproduce the old type in the form of the Tiger Horse (from Spanish *tigre*, which refers to a patterned coat).

➤ *See also Pony of the Americas (POA), Tiger Horse*

BLANKET PATTERN

apple rump A short, round rump with a low tail head.

apron-faced
➤ *See bald-faced*

Arabization The crossing of Arabian blood into other breeds, and the selection for bigger eyes, prettier heads, a more dished profile, longer legs in proportion to body, and a higher tail set. These traits tend to win in show rings among all breeds. However, selection for them can mean selection against other traits that have been useful for horses and humans for centuries. Breeders with an interest in history and genetics have been working hard to preserve Spanish traits in particular, and to prevent Spanish-derived horses from becoming Arabized.
➤ *See also Spanish traits*

arena events Competitive events held in an arena; usually describes Western events.
➤ *See also breakaway roping; calf roping; cattle penning; cattle roping; team penning; team roping*

ARABIZATION

arena work Training in an enclosed pen or arena. Mounted and ground exercises performed in an arena improve riding and handling skills, facilitate communication with the horse, and provide a solid foundation for safe and effective horse-human interaction anywhere.
➤ *See also Arena Dimensions, next page*

ARABIAN

A hot-blooded breed developed for desert survival and for beauty by Bedouin peoples from Turkmen and Caspian stock beginning around 600 CE. Modern breeders have sometimes favored the latter at the expense of soundness and hardiness, but the Arabian (also called Arab) at its best is elegant and enduring. The breed is quite versatile, having international champions in a wide range of disciplines. Arabians dominate the sport of endurance riding.

Arabians are intelligent and like to be treated with respect, which has given them a reputation for being high-strung, but if handled well they make calm, reliable mounts. Traditionally, the Bedouin people treated their horses as family, and the horses responded accordingly.

A typical Arabian is small, 14 to 15 hands high and 900 to 1,100 pounds (408–499 kg). The head has a dished profile and large, expressive eyes. The neck is long and arched, the back short, the croup high and flat, and the tail set high and flagged when in motion. The skin is black, and the coat is fine and silky. All solid colors are permitted.

ARENA DIMENSIONS

Use	Size Required
Dressage (small size)	20 × 40 meters (66 × 132 feet)
Dressage (large size)	20 × 60 meters (66 × 198 feet)
Calf roping	100 × 300 feet (30 × 91 meters)
Team roping	150 × 300 feet (46 × 91 meters)
Pleasure riding	100 × 200 feet (30 × 61 meters)
Barrel racing	150 × 260 feet (46 × 79 meters)
Jumping (depending on type of course)	150 × 300 feet (46 × 91 meters)
Carriage driving (small size)	40 × 80 meters (131 × 262 feet)
Carriage driving (large size)	40 × 100 meters (131 × 328 feet)

Adapted from *Horsekeeping on a Small Acreage* by Cherry Hill

artificial gait A gait that the horse does not naturally display but must be trained to do, such as the Spanish walk.
➤ *See also gaits; Spanish walk*

artificial insemination (AI) Impregnation of a mare using collected semen. Some breeders choose this method when a mare is difficult to breed by natural service, or to extend the semen of a valuable or older stallion. It allows a stallion to service far more mares each season than he could naturally, since one collection of semen can often impregnate more than a dozen mares.

The easiest way to collect semen is to let the stallion mount either a mare in heat or a "decoy mare" (a breeding dummy designed for this purpose), and divert his penis into a specially designed artificial vagina.

AI is frequently used with Standardbreds and occasionally with Arabians and other breeds, but it is prohibited in breeding registered Thoroughbreds, with the intention of keeping Thoroughbred bloodlines natural and pure. Other breed associations also ban its use to preserve the integrity of their breed. The greatest fear is that the technology would allow a popular stallion, owned by breeders with strong financial resources for promotion, to flood the market, thus reducing genetic diversity for the breed.

ascarid (*Parascaris equorum*) A large parasitic intestinal worm also known as a roundworm. Unless numerous enough to cause intestinal blockage, the adult worms are rarely harmful. The migrating larvae cause the most damage. Adult females lay up to a quarter of a million eggs per day, which pass out of the body in manure and can withstand freezing and drying.

Treatment usually consists of oral anthelmintics, but this must be continuous and prolonged to be effective. Good sanitation will go a long way to reduce problems, with daily cleaning of stalls and holding areas, weekly pasture rotation, periodic raking or plowing and reseeding of pastures, and protecting the water and feed supply from fecal contamination.
➤ *See also anthelmintic; deworming; parasites*

aspiration pneumonia A type of pneumonia that develops when moisture or foreign particles collect in the lungs and cause an infection. A horse must never be tied so that he cannot lower his head to cough and relieve a blockage in the windpipe. Horses confined this way, such as in a trailer, are at risk of developing aspiration pneumonia.

ASTM/SEI The abbreviation for American Society for Testing Materials/Safety Equipment Institute. Riding helmets often carry a label stating that they comply with ASTM/SEI guidelines, indicating that they meet or exceed all ASTM/SEI safety standards.
➤ *See also helmet, safety*

asymmetry A condition in which the horse's body is different from one side to the other, rather than symmetrical. This may be genetic, or caused by faulty conditioning in which one side is developed more than the other. Many Thoroughbreds who race develop asymmetry, as they are trained to run only in a counterclockwise circle. This matters because most other sports require a horse to be laterally balanced. Off-track Thoroughbreds (OTTBs) often need a few months' rest at pasture to *lose* muscle development on their strong side before they are introduced to other work.

at the girth Describes a spot where the leg aid is used. "At the girth" means the rider who is sitting correctly uses the leg where it falls, directly beneath her.
➤ *See also behind the girth*

Australian cheeker A device designed to keep the bit high up in a horse's mouth and prevent him from putting his tongue over the bit. Also called the Australian noseband, it consists of rubber circles that fit around both ends of the bit, with strap extensions that join on top of the horse's nose and continue between the eyes and ears to the crownpiece.

aversive A cue or stimulus that the horse seeks to avoid. This can range from a whip to bit pressure, to even the mildest hand pressure; the exact definition is controversial. Aversives work with negative reinforcement. The aversive is applied, the horse responds, and the aversive goes away, rewarding and reinforcing the behavior.
➤ *See also clicker training; conditioning, as a training term; punishment*

azoturia/Monday morning disease/ tying up A condition characterized by severe cramping of muscles, more accurately known as exertional rhabdomyolysis or paralytic myoglobinuria. Azoturia occurred consistently when horses and humans historically worked a six-day week, appearing shortly after horses started back to work on Monday morning if the owner fed the same high-level ration on Sunday that was given on workdays. Azoturia is characterized by sudden onset of semiparalysis of the hind legs, usually occurring within 15 minutes of resuming work. The muscles of the hindquarters typically stiffen and become hard to the touch.

The condition is thought to be related to the buildup of glycogen in the muscles of an idle horse who is fed a high-energy ration. Upon exertion, this glycogen is used up rapidly and an increase of lactic acid in the muscles follows. This causes swelling and degeneration of the muscle fibers. Another theory is that the disease is related to a deficiency in selenium and/or vitamin C.

Treatment requires veterinary care and absolute rest.

AZTECA A modern breed developed in Mexico in the 1970s by crossing of the Quarter Horse, Andalusian, and Mexican Criollo. The goal was to produce a "gentleman's horse" that combined beauty, excellent temperament, and athleticism. Aztecas show strong Spanish character, with elegant heads, arched necks, and compact, well-rounded bodies. Mexican Aztecas must pass two rigorous tests before being added to the registry. The national Horse of Mexico, the Azteca is well suited for dressage, doma vaquera, working equitation, polo, pleasure riding, and Western sports.

back at the knee A foreleg condition in which the front of the knee is insufficiently extended, while the portion of the leg behind the knee appears over-extended. Also known as calf knees, this fault may be harmless in a pleasure horse but could lead to knee fractures if horse is used in high-stress events.
➤ *See also conformation*

back combing A technique of combing shorter mane hairs back so that longer hairs can be trimmed evenly.
➤ *See also grooming; mane, care of*

backing up Stepping backward; also called reining back or just backing. Horses back up at walking speed while raising and lowering diagonal pairs of legs, as in the trot.

Horses are often reluctant to step backward, as the area directly behind them is one of their blind spots. Training begins in hand, where the horse should be taught to back up lightly and smoothly. This can be built into the daily feeding routine. Establish a verbal cue as well as physical cues; this will help you transition to backing up under saddle or in harness. Every horse needs this skill, for ease of handling on the ground, getting out of trailers, and basic maneuverability. Backing up is part of many competitive disciplines, and can reveal holes in a horse's training.

back rail The section of the show ring that is behind a judge's back.

back to front Classical horsemanship emphasizes riding the horse from "back to front," meaning that the rider creates a flow of energy from the activated hindquarters, receives that energy, and then channels it through the bit. Even to slow down or stop, the rider uses her legs to create forward motion, which brings the horse to a stop with his legs squarely under him. The concept is also used in driving.

balanced conformation The horse has both vertical and horizontal balance. **Vertical balance** is determined by dividing the horse into three parts with two vertical lines, the first through the base of the horse's neck, the second through the point of the hip. The three parts should be relatively equal, with the shoulder area being the longest and the back being the shortest. (The neck is the horse's balancing arm; a short back is stronger and can support more weight than a long back.) There is little discrepancy between breeds with regard to ideals for vertical balance.

Horizontal balance is determined by drawing a line through the elbow and stifle joints, which should result in approximately equal upper and lower halves. The line should be roughly parallel to the ground. If it runs downhill in front, the horse will be heavy on its forehand and could be prone to tripping. Racehorses are more successful if they are "leggy," and cutting horses are more agile if they're "low to the ground."

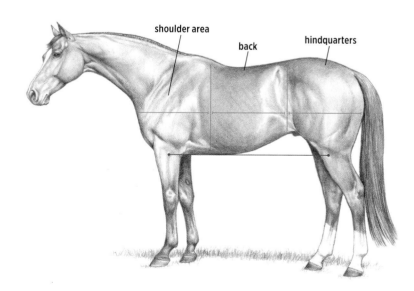

shoulder area

back

hindquarters

A horse with ideal conformation can be divided vertically into nearly equal thirds (blue lines) and horizontally into equal halves (red line).

BALD-FACED

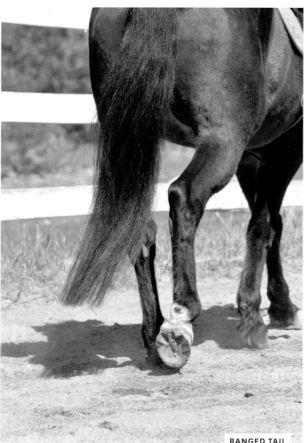

BANGED TAIL

balanced seat A fundamental approach to riding, wherein the rider's center of gravity is aligned with the horse's. The rider is balanced over her feet, which bear a considerable proportion of her weight; the position is as much like standing as it is like sitting. A vertical line could be drawn from the ear through the shoulder, point of hip, and back of heel. The rider can stand in the stirrups without affecting her leg position; she is upright but not stiff. The balanced seat is basic to most forms of riding.
➤ *See also seat*

bald-faced A horse whose face is predominantly white, usually including the eye area. One or both eyes may be blue. When the white doesn't cover the eyes but spreads over the lower half of the face, the marking is called "apron-faced." In a bonnet-faced horse, dark hair covers the ears and forehead, surrounding a mostly white face.
➤ *See also face markings; medicine hat*

balk To refuse to move forward, either on the ground or over a fence. A barn-sour horse balks when asked to leave the stable, for example.
➤ *See also barn-sour*

ballotade An advanced movement in Classical High School riding. From a rearing position, the horse leaps straight up, tucking his hind legs up to his belly and showing the soles of his hind feet.
➤ *See also airs above the ground; croupade; Lipizzan*

ball hitch, ball mount
➤ *See "Towing Hitches," page 366*

bandage
➤ *See shipping boots/wraps*

bandy-legged A term used to describe a horse who appears bowlegged when observed from the rear. The condition can adversely affect the horse's hip, hocks, and stifles.
➤ *See also conformation*

banging a tail To trim the tail evenly, usually just above the fetlocks. This style is seen in many disciplines, though some breed standards specify a natural

BARB

An ancient hot-blooded breed from North Africa. The Barb has a straight or convex head, powerful front quarters, a sloping shoulder and croup, and a low-carried tail. A product of the mountain deserts, the Barb is fast, agile, and tremendously hardy. This is a "taproot" breed, found in the pedigrees of many breeds, especially those of Spanish origin. Through the Irish Hobby and English Running Horse, it contributed greatly to the development of the Thoroughbred.

➤ *See also Andalusian; mustang; Spanish Barb; Thoroughbred*

tail. It is also a way to keep a very long tail from being stepped on.

➤ *See also tail, care of*

bar shoe A horseshoe that is connected at the heel; used to add support, apply pressure, prevent pressure, or stabilize the shoe or hoof.

bar stock Metal bar from which horseshoes are forged.

bareback bronc riding A judged rodeo event in which the contestant rides a bucking horse for eight seconds. The rider holds the bareback rigging (a form of surcingle) with one hand while spurring the horse's sides. Today's spurs are blunt, with rowels that roll easily, so the spurring is a matter of style. A rider who touches the horse, the equipment, or his or her own body with the free hand is disqualified. The rider is also judged on how well the horse bucks, so a good score is to some degree the luck of the draw.

➤ *See also bronc/bronco; rodeo; Western riding*

bareback pad A girthed pad made of suede or fleece used when riding without a saddle. Bareback pads equipped with stirrups are extremely unsafe. Without the structure provided by a saddle tree, a bareback pad with stirrups is prone to slip.

bareback riding Riding without a saddle. Many instructors believe that bareback riding helps beginning students gain a sense of balance and stability. It also offers riders a unique opportunity to move in concert with the horse and feel the action of the animal's muscles.

barefoot trimming Trimming a horse's hooves to be maintained without shoes. This involves removing flares, preserving or creating a good hoof angle, and beveling the edge of the hoof to make breakover easier and prevent cracking of the hoof wall. A bare hoof self-cleans more effectively, has better traction, and more readily maintains optimum moisture; bare hooves are also less costly to maintain and safer in case of kicks. While going barefoot is an option for a great many horses, some have particular issues that require shoeing for protection or therapy. Abrasive or stony ground may cause excess wear and soreness, and for some disciplines specialized shoeing adds necessary traction.

➤ *See also breakover; flare; hoof*

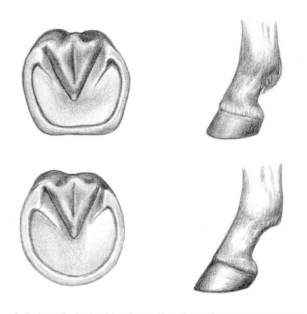

A "wild horse" trim (top) is a form of **barefoot trim** that has a shorter toe, with four points of contact with the ground. The breakover point is just 1 to 1½ inches (2.5–4 cm) from the point of the frog. A regular trim has a breakover point 2 inches (5 cm) or more from the point of the frog.

barley The first domesticated grain. Barley has been fed to horses for centuries, but it is now considered the least safe grain, due to low starch digestibility.

➤ *See also feeding and nutrition*

barn cameras Remote cameras that allow a horse owner to check on a horse without leaving the house. They are particularly useful for keeping watch on mares about to foal.

barns and facilities A stable and the out-buildings, pastures, paddocks, and other structures designed to meet the needs of horses and horsemen, whether owners or boarders. The word "barn" is also used to mean a building that houses animals and farm equipment. A barn can be a social scene; at a so-called show barn, for example, the boarders are interested in show ring competition, and a tenant who is interested in eventing, or not competing at all, may find herself out of step.

Horse facilities range from simple fenced pastures with run-in sheds to full-service training barns with multiple-stall stables, indoor and outdoor arenas, round pens, hot walkers, and even swimming pools for rehabilitation of injured horses. Every facility must meet a horse's basic needs:

- Fresh water 24 hours a day
- Food
- Shelter from inclement weather (including heat)
- Space for exercise outdoors
- Daily observation and, if needed, care by a knowledgeable person

In addition, every horse facility needs the following:

- A place to secure the horse indoors—a stall or shed with a door or gate
- A small, secure outdoor paddock with a strong, permanent fence
- Secure places to tie the horse, convenient to tack and supplies
- A secure place to store feed
- The ability to move the horse easily—gates and lanes

For safety and convenience, each horse should have a place where he can be securely shut in alone. This can be a stall, a run-in with a sturdy gate, or a small pen with a good permanent fence.

BARNS A typical horse barn consists of stalls, a tack room, a feed storage room, and a work area or center aisle. When building a new barn or assessing an existing one, here are some elements to keep in mind.

DRAINAGE. A barn should be situated on relatively high ground so that it won't become inundated with water after every storm or snowmelt. When constructing a new barn, you can build up the site so that it provides adequate drainage.

FLOORING. Dirt is usually considered the best barn floor. Packed dirt provides sure footing and, in most cases, adequate drainage. However, dirt can become dusty in dry conditions and a sea of mud in wet conditions. Concrete is less work to maintain, but it can become slippery when wet and provides poor drainage. It is also hard on the horses' legs. Wooden floors are softer, but they are high maintenance and can also become slippery. Rubber stall mats are recommended where you want better traction or an easier-to-clean surface, or

if your horse may be lying down frequently (such as a mare about to foal).

LIGHTING. Well-lit barns are safe and comfortable. Ideally, a light should be placed in each stall, at intervals above the center aisle, and above tack and feed areas, at least 8 feet (2.4 m) off the ground so that the horses cannot reach and break them. Wire cages around bulbs provide additional protection. Skylights, windows, large sliding doors, and roof panels and vents can be excellent sources of natural light. Because they reflect light rather than absorbing it, light-colored walls and ceilings take advantage of available light. Clear-span buildings made of translucent fabric offer the most natural light, and can make a pleasant barn environment.

STALLS. Ponies are comfortable in a space 10 feet (3 m) square, but full-size horses generally require a stall that is 12 feet (3.6 m) square; draft horses may need larger ones. For foaling or nursing mares, a double stall is recommended. Stallions also benefit from a large stall.

Stall walls must be durable to withstand the kicking, rubbing, and general abuse that horses inflict upon them. Walls should be at least 8 feet (2.4 m) high, with doors about 4 feet (1.2 m) wide. Partitions are commonly made of cement block, wood, or metal (but a horse can injure himself by kicking cement or by putting a hoof through metal). They must be smooth to prevent possible injury to the animal. Protruding splinters, nails, bolts, or sharp edges of any kind should be removed or covered.

If bars are used at the front or sides of the stall, the spaces between the bars should be no wider than 4 inches (10 cm) so that the horse cannot get caught in them. Bars keep horses from fighting with one another, but they also contribute to isolation. Ideally, the front of the stall should have an area that can be opened to let the horse put his head out, or closed for horses who abuse that privilege.

Stall doors can swing in or out, or they can be mounted on rollers. Rolling doors are the safest, as they can't block the aisle or the stall. Most important, a stall door should be wide enough to permit your horse to enter and exit without danger of injury.

VENTILATION. An average horse produces 50 pounds (23 kg) of manure and 10 gallons (38 L) of urine per day. Without ventilation, the barn air will become saturated with ammonia and other waste products. Along with dust and humidity, these pose respiratory threats to confined horses, but so can cold drafts. A barn must be well ventilated without exposing the horses to excessive drafts.

A window in each stall can simultaneously provide ventilation and light. Large, sliding doors at each end of a barn can do much the same. Roof vents and exhaust fans are additional ways of enhancing the exchange of air.

Horse barns do not need to be heated. While they may be more pleasant for humans, heated barns are an unnatural environment for horses and can cause them to become prone to respiratory problems and viruses.

FEED STORAGE. Barns typically include space for feed storage. Best practice is to avoid storing a large quantity of hay in a barn where horses are stabled. If stored in a loft above them, it can create unhealthy levels of dust, and it is a fire hazard. A separate hay shed is ideal.

Barns also include space for grain storage. Tight, lockable, horse-proof grain storage is a must. Breaking into stored grain and overeating is often fatal for horses. Good consistent protocol around securing the feed room can save a great deal of trouble and grief. Feed storage should also be mouse- and bug-proof, and spilled grain should be swept up to avoid attracting pests.

➤ *See also bedding; facilities; hazards; stall; tack room*

WATER In the stall, water should be provided in buckets or automatic waterers. Water in pastures and paddocks may be provided in troughs that are cleaned and filled regularly, or by clean ponds, streams, and rivers. In cold climates, water lines must be buried at least 3 to 5 feet (1–1.5 m) deep to prevent freezing. The hydrants and the pipe leading out of the ground to them can also freeze. Depending on climate, wrapping the pipe with insulating material might be enough; in some places, an electric heating element will be needed.

INDOOR ARENAS An indoor riding arena has a roof and solid walls that allow for working horses during bad weather or after dark; typically called "an indoor." Very popular in cold climates, indoor arenas are also useful for riding in hot weather, on rainy days, or after dark. An indoor arena needs to be safely constructed, with appropriate, well-maintained footing. It must be large enough for the particular discipline; a driving arena should be larger than a riding arena, unless the facility specializes in ponies. Prefabricated buildings are available, from the size of a small dressage arena to arenas that can accommodate a line of jumps.

OUTDOOR ARENAS An outdoor arena or ring may be fenced or marked out with stakes and tape; some sort of demarcation is needed. As with an indoor, an outdoor ring must be large enough to accommodate the disciplines practiced in it and the footing must be safe and appropriate. Grass can be slippery and is quickly worn down around the perimeter.

RUN-IN SHEDS Some horses prefer to live most of their lives outside. Some farms acquire extra horses who cannot be accommodated in the barn. And some farms offer field board. In all cases, shelter must be provided, and a run-in shed can be the answer.

These three-sided sheds should be large enough to accommodate all the horses living or grazing in the field, about 140 square feet (43 m²) per horse, which will give them room to jostle for position. Sheds should be built on high ground to allow for drainage, and the open side should be toward the south, to keep cold north winds out in winter. The roof should slope toward the closed back side so puddles do not form in front of the shed. If the shed is the only shelter, make sure it is possible to close all the horses you have inside it. That may mean dividing it into separate pens, and equipping the front with substantial gates. If grain is to be stored in or near the shed, it must be in a lockable room.

PASTURES AND TURNOUT

A good pasture is large enough to support the number of horses assigned to it without over-grazing. It should be uncontaminated with plants poisonous to horses. It should be checked regularly to be sure it is free of holes (from burrowing animals and other causes), sharp objects, and slick spots. Fences should be safe for horses and sufficient to keep them contained.

Not all facilities have enough acreage to provide pasture. Turnout paddocks may have little grass, but can still provide important exercise opportunities. Fencing needs to be strong, safe, and well maintained.

GATE GUIDELINES

Keep in mind these tips for best gates:

- Gates must swing freely and be light enough to handle.
- Gates must be around 4 feet (1.2 m) wide, or enough for a horse and human to pass through side by side.
- Avoid gates with narrow walk-throughs for humans; horses can get hung up in these.
- If your gate is heavy, rest it on a block at both its closed and open positions, to keep it from sagging and to take the weight off the hinges.
- Avoid flat metal gates with sharp corners and edges.

FENCING

The three requirements for fencing for horses are strength, safety, and cost-effectiveness. Also take into account the type of horses to be fenced in; for example, energetic, high-strung young horses need stronger, safer fences than older, retired horses. Draft horses are immensely strong and may not respect fences that easily hold saddle horses. Ponies can scoot under fences, and some individual horses are committed fence jumpers.

Common fencing materials include the following:

BARBED WIRE. Fencing wire consisting of two strands twisted together and armed with sharp points or barbs. Barbed wire is effective for cattle but should not be used to confine horses. It can inflict serious, even permanent, injury or death. If you are stuck with existing barbed wire, string electric fencing several feet inside it to keep horses away. This way, your horses won't be close enough to lean through the barbed wire and hurt themselves.

CHAIN-LINK. Mesh or woven-wire fencing that is highly effective at confining domestic animals while keeping other animals out. A chain-link fence can be used with horses; however, the sharp edges at the top and bottom should be covered to protect them from injury.

ELECTRIC FENCING. This is a charged tape, cord, or smooth wire that can keep horses on one side of it—if they are taught to respect it. However, when in a gallop or when frightened, a horse may simply run through an electric fence. And if the power goes off, there's no protection. Electric fencing is best used in conjunction with other types of fencing to prevent over-the-fence battles or to subdivide larger, more substantially fenced pastures into smaller paddocks; then, it would matter less if horses broke through it, as they would still be contained in the larger area by solid fencing. (See photo, page 99.)

NET OR DIAMOND-MESH. A safe, corrosion-resistant, and durable choice, diamond-mesh fencing can be stretched and braced between poles; using "no-climb" netting with small squares or diamond shapes will prevent even small horses and foals from getting a foot stuck in it. Often used to enclose paddock and pasture areas, it is sometimes called Kentucky wire fencing.

POLYVINYL CHLORIDE (PVC) TUBING, PLANKS, OR STRIPS. About twice the cost of wood fencing, PVC fencing is generally lower maintenance and longer lasting.

RUBBER OR NYLON TAPE. These strips are run through upright posts and then stretched. The tape may occasionally need restretching. The advantage is that when a horse runs into the fence, the tape is quite forgiving and inflicts less damage than other types of fencing. The disadvantage? Horses might chew the tape and get indigestible fibers lodged in the gut. Under the right circumstances, tapes can be cost-effective.

SMOOTH WIRE/HIGH-TENSILE WIRE. Barbless 12- or 13-gauge wire can be stretched between poles to make an adequate boundary fence. Though it lacks barbs, high-tensile wire can still inflict serious injuries on a horse who runs into it. Topping it with a rail or pipe, or running a strand of electric fencing inside it, makes smooth wire safer. To avoid life-threatening injuries, mark the fence in a manner visible to horses.

STEEL PIPE. More durable than wood, especially if coated with a rust-free paint, steel fencing needs fewer uprights than wood. But it has drawbacks. Steel pipe is unforgiving if a horse runs into or kicks it. And there have been a few cases of horses dying when they got their heads stuck between rails of pipe. Wherever you would like a fail-safe fence, though—at road boundaries or for stallion paddocks—steel pipe can be a good choice.

WOOD BOARD. Wood is a traditional type of fencing, particularly three- or four-board fences painted white, brown, or black. Wood is sturdy, durable, and aesthetically pleasing. Boards should be nailed to the posts on the inside of the post, facing into the paddock or pasture, making it harder for a horse to run through; the board would have to break rather than tear out by the nails. Horses can damage this fencing, though, by kicking, running into, leaning over, or chewing it. Running an electric fence wire inside the top rail of wooden fencing eliminates these problems. Wooden fences require a lot of upkeep, from replacing boards or posts to repainting and weatherproofing.

barn-sour A horse who is reluctant to leave the security of the barn or the herd.
➤ *See also herd-bound*

BARREL RACING

barrel The part of the body between the front legs and the loin, comprising the rib cage and abdomen.

barrel racing An extremely popular mounted game in which competitors ride a predetermined pattern around standing barrels. Various patterns exist, but the standard one is the cloverleaf pattern around three barrels. Barrel racing began as a women's sport; both boys and girls compete in youth divisions and at the collegiate level. Men may compete at events sanctioned by the National Barrel Horse Association, but the majority of adult barrel racers are still women.
➤ *See also mounted games; rodeo; Western riding*

bars

1. **In the mouth:** the toothless, gummed section of the horse's jawbone on which the bit rests.

2. **Of the hoof:** the portion of the hoof wall that angles in from the heel and runs parallel to the sides of the frog.

3. **Of a saddle:** the interior components of a Western saddle that determine the fit. Known as full quarter or semiquarter horse bars, the main difference is the angle of the bars and the width of the gullet.

bascule The arch of a horse's topline as he reaches down into the rider's hand; most frequently referenced in jumping, or when a horse works over ground poles.

BASCULE

BAROQUE HORSES

A group of breeds meeting the ideals of the European baroque period of 1550 to 1700: a square, uphill build; rounded musculature; a high arched neck; a short back; well-sprung ribs; a straight or convex profile; good bone; and great strength and agility. Baroque horses are intelligent, spirited, gentle, and highly teachable. They tend to form a strong bond with one person.

Baroque horses are neither hot bloods nor cold bloods. Sharing some of the characteristics of each, they are also emphatically not warmbloods as currently defined. They excel at classical dressage, particularly the collected movements. They are also naturals for Iberian-inspired sports like working equitation.

SOME EUROPEAN BAROQUE BREEDS

Andalusian and Lusitano (aka Pura Raza Española [PRE])

Friedriksborg

Friesian

Kladruber

Knabstrupper

Menorquin

Murgese

These breeds also have a claim to baroque status:

Azteca

Canadian

Gypsy Vanner

Morgan

Shagya Arabian

Spanish Barb

Spanish Mustang

Spanish Norman

➤ *See also individual breeds; classical dressage; doma vaquera; working equitation*

base-narrow, base-wide Seen from the front or the rear, a base-narrow horse has feet that are too close together; the defect is often accompanied by pigeon toes. A base-narrow horse will probably paddle when he travels, swinging his legs outward. The defect limits speed and agility and puts additional strain on pastern and fetlock.

A base-wide horse has feet that are too far apart and may have splayed hooves. This horse will probably wing inward when he travels, which places greater stress on inner part of limbs, often causing windpuffs, ringbone, or sidebone. Hooves wear excessively on inside edge.
➤ *See also conformation*

bathing horses For horses, baths are a mixed blessing. While they cleanse the animal and can help prevent infection, they also dry the hair and skin by removing oils. If not being shown or worked hard, a horse rarely needs a bath, especially if he spends time outdoors where rain can rinse him off.

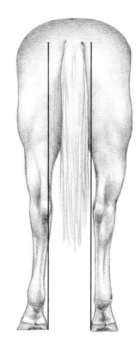
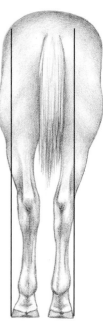

BASE-NARROW   BASE-WIDE

BASHKIR

An ancient Russian horse used for riding, draft, meat, and milk production. The Bashkir is a small, strongly built horse with high work and weather tolerance. The American Curly was once erroneously believed to descend from the Bashkir, and many people still use the name Bashkir Curly.
➤ *See also American Breeds, American Curly*

bay coloring A reddish brown body coloring with a black tail and mane and black points. The color may vary from tan to a deep brown. Red, or "blood," bays are a deep ruby-red brown. Mahogany bays are a very dark brown and may appear black. So-called wild bays may have smoky-white streaks in an otherwise black tail. Bay horses may also be dappled.

➤ *See also color, of horses; dapples; points*

bean

➤ *See diverticulum; smegma; sheath cleaning*

beat The sound a horse's hoof makes striking the ground; the number of beats per stride is one way of defining a gait. The walk is a four-beat gait in which each hoof strikes separately. The trot has two beats, with diagonal pairs of hooves striking simultaneously. The canter has three beats: one hind hits the ground, then the other hind and a fore, and then the other fore.

➤ *See also gait; stride vs step*

bedding Material placed on the floor of a stall or shed to provide a horse with a comfortable surface on which to rest. Bedding also preserves warmth in the stall, protects the horse from abrasions, and absorbs urine.

Bedding choices include straw, wood shavings and sawdust, pelleted sawdust, shredded newspaper, and sand. Peanut hulls are used in some southern areas, where they are available at a reasonable cost.

Each choice offers advantages and disadvantages. Deeply spread straw is soft, warm, and highly absorbent. However, it can be expensive and horses may eat it, which can cause colic. Pellets of compressed sawdust that expand when moistened can be more economical. Some hardwoods—particularly black walnut, but also oak and hickory—can trigger toxic reactions in horses, so shavings or sawdust made from them should be avoided. Sand can be ingested as horses feed, causing sand colic.

Whatever material is used, keep bedding clean and free of dust, mold, and sharp edges.

BLOOD BAY

DARK BAY

DAPPLE BAY

Research on the horse genome indicates that **bay** is the oldest horse color.

beet pulp The dry, fibrous remains after the sugar has been extracted from sugar beets. It is a high-fiber, low-sugar food for horses, and is commonly available in compressed pellets or flakes. Most people soak beet pulp before feeding.

behind the bit A term used to describe a horse who is attempting to evade the bit and forward driving aids by "sucking back" from contact.
➤ *See also on the bit*

behind the girth A leg position for a rider that is 2 to 4 inches (5–10 cm) back from the girth and the horse's center of balance. The behind-the-girth position is most often used when asking for lateral motion.
➤ *See also at the girth*

behind the leg A horse who does not respond, or responds sluggishly, to the rider's driving leg is said to be "behind the leg."
➤ *See also in front of the leg*

behind the vertical A head position in which the horse's face is behind an imaginary vertical line running down from his poll. It indicates improper longitudinal flexion, along the neck vertebrae instead of at the poll. A momentary positioning behind the vertical is not a serious fault. "Behind the vertical" is not synonymous with "behind the bit."
➤ *See also on the bit; rollkur*

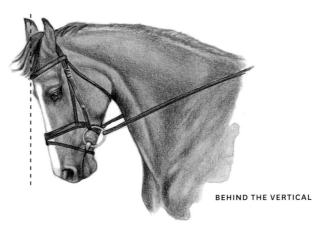

BEHIND THE VERTICAL

BELGIAN ❯ A popular, heavy-bodied draft horse known for its strength and patience. American Belgians, bred in the United States since 1866, are longer-legged and lighter than their European counterparts, with more action at the trot. Belgians are a favorite with American horsemen, as they are easy keepers with quiet dispositions. Most Belgians are chestnut or sorrel with a white mane and tail, white stockings, and a white blaze. Roaning and dappling are common. **Livestock Conservancy status: Recovering**

bell boot A boot, often made of rubber, that fits over the top of a horse's hoof. The boot protects the coronary band from injury when the horse is traveling or working, and is especially vital for horses who overreach.
➤ *See overreaching*

bench knees A conformation fault in which a horse's cannon bones are not centered directly under the knees. The defect, also known as offset cannons, can hamper the horse's knee movements and cause enlargement of the area where the splint bone attaches to the cannon bone.
➤ *See also conformation; leg, of horse*

bend The apparent curving of a horse's spine to the left or right, on a circle or through a turn. The horse's spine is incapable of flexing laterally, but the extension and contraction of muscles on either side of the spine do create an arc, which plays a role in proper balance.
➤ *See also flexion*

Betadine
➤ *See povidone-iodine solution*

Biothane
➤ *See synthetic tack*

bit A mouthpiece for a horse that aids a rider in controlling the horse. It rests on a toothless, gummed portion of the horse's jawbone known as the bars. Bits are typically made of metal but can be fashioned from rubber or plastic. There are three basic types of bits (and hundreds of variations): snaffles, curb bits, and combination (Pelham) bits.

Snaffles are considered the mildest. They apply direct pressure to the corners of a horse's mouth. Many snaffles are jointed at the center, but others feature multiple joints. Still others, known as straight snaffles or straight bits, are jointless.

Curb bits, used with shanks of varying lengths, apply leverage directly to the bars of the horse's mouth, as well as to the poll and chin. The longer the shank, the greater the leverage and the more severe the action. Curb bits are used in conjunction with a chain or strap designed to fit beneath the horse's jaw. The leverage action tightens the curb chain when the bit is used.

Combination bits (or Pelham bits), used with double reins, offer the rider the option of exerting pressure on either the corners of the mouth or the bars.

The width of the horse's mouth from corner to corner determines the width of the bit. The average is 5 inches (13 cm), but young horses and smaller breeds may need narrower bits, while large horses often need wider bits. As a general rule, a thicker bit is milder and more comfortable for the horse. However, excessively thick bits may not fit comfortably into a given horse's mouth. The texture of a bit can also greatly influence the bit's comfort.

bit guard Two flat rubber circles that fit around the ends of a bit between the skin and the bridle rings to keep the bit from pinching.

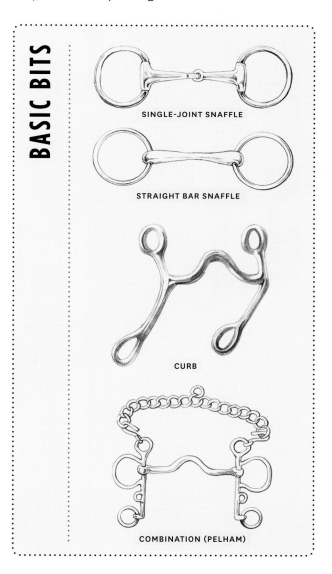

BASIC BITS

SINGLE-JOINT SNAFFLE

STRAIGHT BAR SNAFFLE

CURB

COMBINATION (PELHAM)

An advantage of a **bitless bridle** is that the horse can eat and drink while on the trail more easily.

bitless riding An increasingly popular fashion of riding horses without using a bit. Some people consider all bits inherently cruel and take pride in riding bit-free. Others come to bitless riding through owning a horse for whom it is difficult to find a bit that fits.

Bitless bridles range from the simple sidepull jumping hackamore to strong mechanical hackamores with shanks. Other types include the Dr. Cook and various versions of the Happy Wheel or flower hackamore, in which the reins and headstall are attached to metal wheels resembling the rings of a snaffle. Some riders do away with bridles altogether and ride with a neck strap or cordeo. Many Western horses are ridden in a bosal, a very old form of bitless bridle.

Aficionados of bitless riding feel that their horses perform more happily and willingly, and work through from behind more readily. It is possible to train and ride horses to a high level without ever using a bit, or to convert bit-trained horses to go bitless.

It can be difficult to find competitive venues for bitless riding. Currently, bitless bridles are permitted in dressage only in the Netherlands and Australia, but the Fédération Equestre Internationale (FEI) is frequently petitioned to change the rules, and it seems likely that it will someday happen. Bitless bridles are permitted in Western dressage.
➤ *See also bosal; cordeo; hackamore; sidepull*

bit seat An improvement made when an equine dentist smooths the front of the cheek teeth so the horse won't suffer discomfort from the bit.

bit wrap A sheet of latex or chamois leather that is wrapped around the bit where it rests on the bars. Some horsemen feel this gives a softer communication between mouth and hands. Others dislike the way it reduces the slipperiness of the bit in the horse's mouth.
➤ *See also bars*

black coloring To be considered black, a horse's entire body (except for white markings on the leg and face) must be colored true black, as opposed to very dark red or brown. Black horses may appear reddish if exposed to sunlight for long periods. True black coloring is uncommon.
➤ *See also color, of horse*

blanket clip
➤ *See clipping; "Common Clipping Terms," page 56*

blankets and blanketing Horses living outdoors year-round may never need blankets. In cold climates, they grow a thick winter coat that conserves heat and protects them against wind, moisture, and cold air. However, an outdoor horse who has been clipped or is in poor health will need blanketing. Hot-blooded breeds may feel the cold more, and may visibly shiver. Turnout blankets are recommended in such cases. These blankets are entirely waterproof, fit snugly, and are cut in a way that allows freedom of movement.

Stalled horses who are ridden in cold weather also benefit from winter blankets that help them cool down gradually after a ride. Any horse whose coat has been clipped must be blanketed if he will be exposed to cold or wet weather, and horses should be blanketed after they have been given a bath in cold weather.

Blankets are often used when trailering a horse to protect against drafts. However, overheating can occur in a closed trailer, so the horse's body temperature should be monitored. Blanketing the horse in two or more lightweight layers allows the handler to regulate the horse's temperature by removing or adding blankets one layer at a time. A blanketed horse can become dangerously hot, even in winter, if the day is warm or sunny or if the blanket does not wick moisture away from the body effectively.
➤ *See also cooler; saddle blanket; sheet*

blaze A white marking down the center of a horse's face that extends beyond the sides of the bridge of the nose. A blaze is wider than a stripe. If it extends around the sides of the face, the horse is said to be bald-faced.
➤ *See also face markings*

blind spavin Hock soreness without visible bony growth.
➤ *See also spavin*

blind spots
➤ *See vision*

blinders, blinkers Blinders are leather flaps used on a racing or driving bridle to shield the horse's vision from side distractions. Blinker, an older synonymous term, also describes the cloth hood worn by some racehorses.

blister beetle poisoning Several blister beetle species carry a substance in their bodies called cantharidin. If a horse ingests these beetles, cantharidin toxicity will result. Swallowing just one or two beetles (dead or alive) can cause severe blistering of the digestive tract. Ingestion of as few as three beetles can kill a horse.

The beetles feed on the pollen in alfalfa hay blooms, and horses may eat hay harboring these small flying insects. The symptoms of blister beetle poisoning are similar to those of colic, which can make the condition difficult to diagnose in a timely manner. Drugs and intravenous fluids can minimize absorption of the toxin if treatment is begun soon enough. The best preventive measure is to feed first-cutting alfalfa (because the beetles generally do not mature until midsummer) or hay that has been cut prior to the bloom stage. Blister beetles are native to the southern United States, and are most often found in alfalfa hay.

bloating When a horse tenses his stomach muscles, increasing the size of his barrel, as the girth is being tightened. It is not the result of the horse holding his breath, as is commonly believed. Bloating can result in a dangerously loose saddle. A bloating horse should be walked until he relaxes, not jabbed or kneed in the side. Horses bloat in anticipation of discomfort; to prevent a horse from forming this habit, always tighten the girth in stages, checking a final time before mounting.
➤ *See also girthy*

blocks, salt and protein Salt and protein blocks provide nutrients that supplement a horse's primary diet. Most horses benefit from unrestricted access to a trace mineral salt block. Molasses protein blocks are primarily useful for horses whose diets are unusually low in protein; access should be regulated. A horse who overindulges in protein blocks can be subject to colic, dehydration, or diarrhea. Horses can also benefit from calcium and phosphorus blocks, depending on their age and diet.
➤ *See also salt block*

bloodworms
➤ *See deworming; large strongyles; parasites; small strongyles*

BLINDERS

MINERAL AND SALT BLOCKS

blowout A horizontal crack in the hoof wall caused by an injury to the coronary band or a blow to the hoof wall.

blue hoof A hoof whose horn (the tough outer material) has a dense, blue-black color.
➤ *See also hoof*

blue roan coloring A body coloring that is an evenly distributed mixture of black hairs and white hairs. The head and legs of a blue roan horse are often darker than the remainder of the body.
➤ *See also color, of horse*

boarding stables Stables that rent stalls. In general, the more services provided, the higher the boarding fee. Because terms for boarding vary widely, horse owners should make sure they understand what is and is not included in any boarding arrangement before their horse arrives on the property. A written agreement, signed by both the property owner and the boarder, is advisable.

A SELF-CARE FACILITY (also called rough board) simply rents the owner a stall or pasture space. The owner must care for the horse in all respects—including, in some cases, providing water.

A FIELD-BOARD FACILITY (also called basic board) provides pasture area for a boarded horse. Basic services may be provided, and a shelter is generally available for the horse in times of emergency or bad weather.

A FULL-BOARD FACILITY offers a range of services, including water and food, but in many cases the horse owner remains responsible for grooming and exercising the horse. There may be an extra charge for special services such as medicating, bathing, and blanketing the horse.

A COMPLETE-CARE FACILITY attempts to meet all of the horse's needs, leaving the owner free to visit when he or she chooses. In addition, the stable may offer a range of amenities to the horse owners. Such facilities are generally the most expensive option.

bobsled A farm wagon with runners instead of wheels, for use on snow.

body brush A brush with soft bristles, used in long strokes to remove dirt from a horse's coat.
➤ *See also grooming*

body language, of horses

Horses communicate primarily through nonverbal cues and signals. Being alert to these signals is the best way to stay safe and to strengthen the bond between horse and rider. Because every horse is an individual, body language varies from one horse to the next. The best way to gain understanding of a horse's body language is to spend a great deal of time with that particular horse.

However, some expressions remain fairly constant. Squinted eyes and a pinched mouth indicate anger or resentment. A horse who flattens his ears and shows the whites of his eyes is probably feeling hostile. A horse who extends his ears and head forward is probably feeling friendly and curious. A horse who shakes his head while being ridden may be feeling playful or rebellious, or may be trying to rid himself of pesky flies.

HORSE TALK

Here are some common examples of horse body language and what they mean:

- Ears pinned back, head reaching toward you. "Stay back or I'll bite you."
- Ears forward, head high. "I wonder what that is over there?"
- Pawing with front feet. "I wonder if there is anything here to eat?" or "I want to get out of here!"
- Swishing tail (not at flies). "I'm irritated" or "My stomach hurts."
- Swinging hindquarters toward you. "I'm afraid" or "I'm getting ready to kick you."

- Lifting or stomping one hind leg (not at flies). "I might kick you" or "I have a stomach ache."
- Ears forward, head reaching toward you. "Hi, pal."
- Ears back toward you when you are riding. "I'm really concentrating and listening to you."
- Ears pinned back flat against the head. "I'm getting ready to buck."

From Your Pony, Your Horse by Cherry Hill

ALERT

RELAXED

ANGRY

bog spavin

➤ *See spavin*

bola or bolo tie
A narrow, braided string tie held in place with a decorative clasp or ornament, worn as part of Western attire.

bolting
When a horse runs away uncontrollably.

bone spavin

➤ *See spavin*

bonnet-faced

➤ *See bald-faced*

boots (for horse)
Protective coverings for a horse's lower legs. Boots come in many types, and each type is generally available several sizes, ensuring an adequate fit for most horses.

Fetlock boots and **hock boots** are named after the part of the horse's body they protect.

Splint boots use a reinforced plate or padding to protect the splint bones on the inside of the legs.

Rundown boots, also called skid boots, protect the rear fetlock area of a working horse from injury due to sudden stops.

Bell boots cover the upper portion of the hoof, encircling and guarding the coronary band.

Sport boots provide additional support to tendons and protect the inside portions of the legs. High-tech versions incorporate advanced carbon fiber for protection, with ventilation systems to keep the horse's legs cool; conventional boots and bandages hold heat against the tendons, which can contribute to inflammation and lameness.

For horses traveling in a trailer, **shipping boots** (also called traveling boots) protect the coronary band, the heel bulbs, the knees, and the hocks. The exteriors of these tall, durable, and thickly padded boots are often made of nylon.

Hoof boots can be used for riding a barefoot horse over harsh terrain, or when a shod horse has cast a shoe. They use hook-and-loop or cable fastenings and offer varying degrees of traction. Some accept screw-in studs for riding on ice and snow. Hoof boots can be used just on the front or on all fours. Some riders carry one hoof boot on trail rides in case a shoe is lost.

Treatment boots are used to protect an injured leg, joint, or hoof; keep it clean; and hold in medications (the latter are also called soaking boots). They are available in an ever-increasing variety of treatment modalities, including ceramic-infused fabrics, magnets, liquid titanium, vibration boots, ice or heat, and compression.

boots (for rider)
Boots with a heel, made for riding; the heel is intended to keep the rider's foot from slipping through the stirrup. Aside from the safety helmet, they are the most important items of riding attire. Boots that fit properly help secure the rider's feet in the stirrup, partly by limiting the range of motion of the ankles, and they prevent feet from becoming caught in a stirrup during a fall. They provide support for tired or weak ankles, helping the rider maintain proper posture and position. Steel shanks are common.

Tall English riding boots, which come nearly to the rider's knee, can be extremely difficult to pull on. They are available in styles that zip or lace. Higher-quality boots are contoured for a super-close fit, and are made of leather, with possibly some elastic stretch panels. Less expensive boots are made of rubber. Looser, insulated boots are recommended for winter riding. Ankle-high paddock boots are a more casual option, with or without half-chaps.

For Western riding, cowboy boots are most often the choice, ranging in height from 10 to 15 inches (25–38 cm). They can sport tooling, and some feature bright colors. Roper boots have a lower heel and shorter shaft than traditional cowboy boots. Western riders occasionally use a Western-style lace-up riding shoe, known as a chukka. Western boots are always made of leather.

➤ *See also half-chaps; sneakers (riding)*

borium
Tungsten carbide chips in a steel or brass matrix, used in shoeing. Blobs of borium can be applied to the toe and heel of a horseshoe to improve traction on hard surfaces like concrete, ice, and rock. They also increase the life of the shoe.

bosal A bridle with a rigid noseband made of plaited rawhide; also, the rawhide noseband itself. A traditional item of Western tack, a bosal should be carefully fitted so it doesn't chafe the jaw. The front part should be positioned about 4 inches (10 cm) above the nostrils, and the rear part should not touch the jaw at all. To keep it positioned correctly, a bosal is often tied to the horse's forelock or browband with a string. The term "bosal" is sometimes used to indicate any bitless bridle.

➤ *See also bitless riding, hackamore, Western tack*

BOSAL

bot block, bot knife A bot block is a coarse stone or fiberglass block used to remove bot fly eggs. A bot knife is a hook-shaped knife used for the same purpose.

➤ *See bot fly (Gasterophilus)*

bot fly (*Gasterophilus*) A hairy brown fly that resembles a bee. Bot flies lay eggs on a horse's legs; the horse ingests the eggs by licking or nuzzling itself. The larvae hatch in the warm, moist conditions of the horse's mouth. They lodge at first in the gums, and later emerge and are swallowed by the horse. After maturing in the stomach, they pass out in the animal's manure to become adult flies and begin their life cycle anew.

Infestations of the larvae can cause stomach ulcers, and a severe infestation may lead to unthriftiness, colic, poor appetite, and even death. Swarms of adult bot flies can agitate a horse into bolting, striking, or kicking at them, potentially endangering a handler.

BRABANT

A massive draft breed originating in Flanders. Standing 16.2 to 17 hands high and weighing up to 3,000 pounds (1,360 kg), Brabants are compact, with strong, short legs. Their heads are square and small. Brabants are known for their intelligence, kindly dispositions, great strength, and soundness. The American Belgian is a descendent but diverged considerably in type after World War I, when European imports ceased. Most Brabants are red bay, bay, blue, or strawberry roan.

➤ *See also Belgian*

botulism A serious illness caused by a spore-producing bacterium, *Clostridium botulinum*, which is found throughout the environment, particularly in soil. Horses become ill after ingesting spores while grazing or after eating contaminated food. Symptoms appear three to seven days later; they include paralysis and difficulty swallowing, breathing, and standing. Progressive paralysis causes death from suffocation. Unvaccinated horses almost always die, even with prompt treatment.

Botulism is endemic in central Kentucky, the mid-Atlantic states, California, and Florida, as well as parts of Europe. Horses living in or traveling to an area where botulism is prevalent should receive the three-shot initial series and annual booster shots.

bowed tendon An injury to one or both of the flexor tendons on the back of a horse's leg. This serious condition generally requires medical treatment, followed by an extended period of rest. The injury can happen during activity, but it can also be caused by incorrectly applied bandages.

box stall A stall, usually 12 feet (3.6 m) square, in which a horse can be turned loose to move about at will.
➤ *See also barns and facilities; tie stall*

boxy feet Narrow hooves with a small frog and a closed heel.

bradoon, bridoon
➤ *See double bridle*

bradoon strap A bit-hanger that passes over the crown of the horse's head and attaches to the bit rings, allowing a snaffle bridle to be converted to a double bridle.

bran, bran mash Bran is the outer coating of wheat, a by-product of milling. A bran mash—bran mixed with hot water and allowed to steep—was traditionally used as a moderate-calorie dinner for horses on rest days or sick days. However, bran is not as good for horses as was once believed. It is high in phosphorus and contains phytase, a compound that can bind calcium and make it unavailable. Though it is laxative in humans, there is no evidence that it is in horses.
➤ *See also feeding and nutrition; grains; mash*

branch One-half of a horseshoe, from toe to heel.

branding Marking an animal permanently with a hot iron or liquid nitrogen to identify the owner or breed. Branding was first practiced by the Egyptians in 2000 BCE. On Western ranches, horses and cattle are hot-branded with heated irons to mark ownership. In Europe, horses are branded once they have passed the rigorous testing qualifying them to called by a breed name and to be bred. Mustangs rounded up by the U.S. Bureau of Land Management (BLM), Standardbreds, and Arabians are freeze-branded on the right side of the neck, either with the registration number or a code that identifies the horse.

breakaway halter A halter with a crownpiece or fuse made of lightweight leather, designed to literally break away if the halter gets caught on something or the horse pulls back while tied. If you must leave a halter on a horse who is turned out to pasture, a breakaway halter can prevent injuries.
➤ *See also halter*

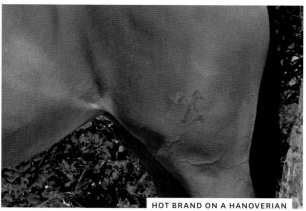
HOT BRAND ON A HANOVERIAN

FREEZE BRAND ON A MUSTANG

breakaway roping A timed calf-roping event in which the rider ties one end of the rope to the saddle with a length of string (called a breakaway rope). The rider ropes the calf as quickly as possible and stops the horse. When the slack goes out of the rope, the string breaks. A flagman signals time when the rope falls away from the saddle horn. A skilled breakaway roper can complete the event in as little as three seconds.
➤ *See also arena events; calf roping; roping; Western riding*

breaking

1. When a horse falls out of the desired gait. In harness racing, the term is used when a horse starts galloping, rather than trotting or pacing.

2. "Breaking a horse" is an old term, still in common use, for training a horse to a specific task. A horse may be described as "green-broke" (meaning he knows the rudiments of a task but needs seasoning), "broken to ride," or "dead broke" (meaning utterly reliable).

➤ *See also harness racing*

breakover The point in a horse's stride at which the hoof rolls forward onto the toe before leaving the ground. The hoof acts as a lever with the toe as the fulcrum. The longer the toe, the farther the force is from the fulcrum and the harder it is for the hoof to break over. Maintaining a long toe, as is common with shod horses, can create stress and hoof problems.
➤ *See also barefoot trimming; hoof*

breast collar A driving collar that fits across the chest rather than on the neck and shoulders. A brollar harness is a hybrid of the neck collar and breast collar. It allows maximum shoulder movement and is becoming popular for marathon driving.
➤ *See also driving*

breastplate, breastgirth In English riding, a strap that loops around the horse's neck and attaches to the saddle by straps on each side, and to the girth by a strap between the forelegs. The breastplate is designed to keep the saddle from slipping when riding uphill or jumping; it may also be used with a running martingale.

In Western riding, breastplates are Y-shaped and attach to the saddle and girth from straps centering on

BREAST COLLAR

a ring at chest level. Western-style breastplates also have a ring that may be used to attach a tie-down. They are most often made of leather, but may also be made of mohair, resembling a cinch.

A breastgirth passes around the breast, horizontal to the ground, and attaches to the girth on both sides. A strap crosses over the neck to keep the breastgirth from slipping downward.

A breastplate must be fitted properly to avoid interfering with the horse's way of going. A Y-shaped breastplate should be centered slightly above midchest level. It should be loose enough to allow a clenched fist to fit between the breastplate and the horse's body all over, including the top of the neck and under the chest.

breeches Comfortable pants for English riding. Breeches are stretchy for freedom of movement. Some feature reinforced suede or leatherlike patches on the inside of the calves; in full-seat breeches, the suede extends from below the knee all the way across the seat. These patches are grippy and help the rider maintain position, while enhancing the durability of the breeches.
➤ *See also chaps; jodhpurs*

breeching A broad strap on a driving harness that goes behind the horse's hindquarters. The breeching allows the horse to brace against, stop, and back the vehicle to which he is attached.
➤ *See also driving; harness*

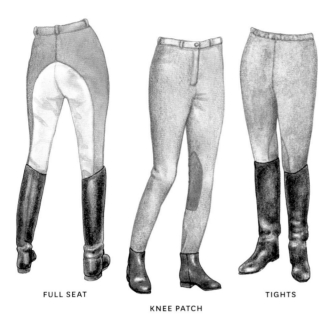

FULL SEAT

KNEE PATCH

TIGHTS

breed A group of horses with common ancestry and common inherited characteristics, including appearance, body shape, and/or coloration. Each breed has a standard to which animals are expected to conform, but enforcement of these norms varies widely. For many American breeds, simply having two registered parents suffices. Parentage was formerly certified under an honor system, but some registries—for example, the Morgan—have responded to widespread cheating among certain breeders by requiring that horses be blood-typed to be accepted.

Other breeds allow selected out-crossings to registered animals of certain other breeds. For example, the Quarter Horse registry accepts a certain degree of Thoroughbred out-crossing. Still other breed associations, especially in Europe, require young horses to pass a series of tests before being accepted into the registry and allowed to breed.

In some cases, the establishment of a breed depended on physical ability in a particular area,

Though fundamentally similar in shape, horse **breeds** vary tremendously in size, as demonstrated by the Clydesdale and Miniature Horse.

regardless of conformation or looks. For example, the term "Standardbred" originally applied to trotters capable of meeting the performance standard of 1 mile (1.6 k) in 2 minutes and 30 seconds. Any horse who could meet that standard could be registered; many Morgan bloodlines disappeared into the Standardbred registry, or in some cases horses were cross-registered.

Other breeds were carefully developed by crossbreeding high-quality horses, with the goal of combining the best qualities of each. When farmers in England began to cross the stout utility horse called the Old Norfolk Trotter with Arab blood, the result was the Hackney, which has a refined look and naturally high-stepping trot.

Many breeds can be traced to foundation sires, whose ability to pass along desirable traits created a new type of horse. Well-known examples include the Darley Arabian, Byerly Turk, and Godolphin Arabian for the Thoroughbred; Figure for the Morgan; Rysdyk's Hambletonian for the Standardbred; Black Allen for the Tennessee Walker. Though relatively unsung, the foundation mares had a great deal to do with the success of any breed.

➤ *See also breed standard; individual breeds*

breed association/breed registry

An organization dedicated to recording, promoting, and showcasing the virtues of a specific breed of horse, while maintaining the stud book, the official registry of all individuals in the breed. A breed association generally sponsors shows open only to horses of the breed it promotes. Many of these associations also offer programs and clubs designed specifically for young people. Most have excellent websites.

breeding

The practice of introducing a stallion to a mare in estrus for the purpose of mating. A mare in estrus may show signs including an open or relaxed vulva, "winking" of the clitoris, mucous discharge, a slightly raised tail, frequent urination, and an atypical degree of sociability. However, some mares are prone to "silent heats." These mares may be in estrus without giving any external signals. To determine whether such mares are in heat—and in some cases, to stimulate stronger heat—teasing is often necessary. Teasing involves exposing a mare to a stallion under controlled circumstances. A breeder can often determine whether the mare is in estrus by watching her behavior during the encounter.

BREEDING AT PASTURE

Breeding at pasture is the most natural method, requiring minimal intervention. It is particularly useful when one stallion is pasturing with a small group of mares. The stallion will approach, tease, and breed the mares at appropriate times, which enhances the likelihood of conception. A suitable stallion understands the need to be patient and cautious around the mares, minimizing the chance that he will be injured

BREED NAMES: GEOGRAPHY OR FUNCTION?

In the Old World, breeds were established on a foundation of native mares adapted to local conditions, crossed with stallions of a high-status type often brought to the area due to wars of conquest. Breeds in the Old World generally bear the name of a place or people.

Andalusian (from Andalusia)

Belgian (from Belgium)

Friesian (from Friesland)

Lipizzan (from Lipica)

In the New World, horse breeds were developed from a mix of Old World types to perform a specific job, and their names reflect that, though geography is also mixed in.

Quarter Horse (originally, Quarter Pather, or Quarter-mile Racer)

Tennessee Walker (originally Walking Horse or Plantation Walker)

Paso Fino

Missouri Fox Trotter

Standardbred

by an unreceptive mare. Injury to an unfamiliar or inexperienced stallion is the number one hazard of breeding at pasture. The method also makes it difficult to control which mare is bred and when conception occurs.

HAND BREEDING Hand breeding involves supervision of the mare, the stallion, and all aspects of the breeding process. The method requires knowledge of the mare's heat cycles, as ovulation typically occurs one to two days prior to the end of each cycle.
➤ *See also artificial insemination (AI); conformation; estrus; foaling; genetics; pedigree; stud farm; stud fee/ breeding fee; teasing*

breed standard
A set of criteria or standards that establishes the ideal characteristics for each breed, including physical traits and disposition (also called "mind").

BREEDING SUCCESS
Of all the mares bred in the United States every year, only 60 percent produce live foals. Reasons for this can include an unsuitable stallion, a stressful breeding situation, a uterine infection, or an abnormal estrus cycle.

bridle
A headstall, reins, and usually a bit, used to control a horse while riding or driving. English bridles include a cavesson, or noseband; some Western bridles don't. Others incorporate a light bosal and a mecate. Driving bridles usually include blinders.

A bridle should fit the horse comfortably and be free of cracks, loosened or rotted stitching, and other damage that could make it break during use. It should be suitable to the discipline for which the horse is used.
➤ *See also blinders; bosal; English tack; headstall; mecate; Western tack*

bridle horse
A Western horse trained in the California vaquero system. A finished bridle horse wears a bridle with a spade bit, as well as a light bosal. He works on a draped rein in a compact, collected framework, and is capable of great speed and maneuverability.

Trainers begin with a snaffle and progress to a heavy bosal, lightening the bosal as the horse learns to carry himself and respond to a touch on the rein. Gradually the horse progresses to a spade bit, a formidable-looking piece of hardware that rests against his palate. Though it looks harsh, the spade is a signal bit that is never deliberately pulled on. The rider steers with legs, weight, and light neck-reining. The horse learns to flex his neck at the third vertebra with his face vertical, a position known as "straight up in the bridle"; a finished horse is called a "straight up bridle horse."

The rule of thumb is that it takes five years to make a bridle horse. The training method has roots in Spain and was used on the great California ranches into the 20th century. Nearly lost, the system is being revived as people become interested in Western dressage, doma vaquera, and working dressage.
➤ *See also bosal; doma vaquera; spade bit; Western dressage; working equitation/doma trabajo*

bridoon
➤ *See double bridle*

brindle dun coloring
Dun (yellow or gold) body coloration with darker streaks on forearms and gaskins.
➤ *See also color, of horse*

broke
A "broke" horse is one who accepts being handled and ridden. He accepts the handler's leadership and responds in predictable ways to applied pressure from legs, hands, straps, or ropes.

broken crest
A heavy crest to the neck that falls over to one side; also called fallen crest.

BRIDLE HORSE

broke to tie
Trained to stand quietly when tied.

bronc/bronco

1. An unbroken range horse of western North America.

2. A horse used for saddle bronc and bareback riding in a rodeo.

Rodeo broncs live apparently rough lives, but their treatment in sanctioned rodeos is highly regulated and they have a low injury rate. Because they are expensive assets, worth $8,000 to $10,000 each, it is in the interests of the rodeo organization to treat them well. They work for only eight seconds at a time, a couple of days a week, and tend to have long careers, some only retiring in their twenties. Rodeo broncs who give up on the idea of bucking after a while may be moved on to another job, retired, or sold at auction.

➤ *See also rodeo*

broodmare
A mare used primarily for breeding.

➤ *See also breeding; foaling*

broom polo
An informal game often used to introduce riders to the fundamental concepts and techniques of polo. The game is played on horseback with a broom and an oversized ball that is generally 12 inches (30 cm) in diameter (basketball-sized). Riders form teams and attempt to hit the ball into their opponent's goal. Broom polo is often played at riding camps and vacation ranches.

brown coloring
A brown horse may appear black, but his coat is a mixture of black and brown hair. He typically has a brown muzzle, mane, tail, and legs. (Black points make the horse bay, not brown.) He may also have lighter coloring around the eyes.

➤ *See also bay; color, of horse; points*

brumby
The feral horse of the Australian outback. Brumbies are the descendants of horses who escaped from mining settlements during the Gold Rush of 1851. Hardy survivors, they are difficult to domesticate and now roam in large herds. In the 1960s they were the subject of a controversial culling program to reduce their numbers.

The name **bronco** comes from the Spanish word for "rough" or "wild."

Even draft horses will kick up their heels and give a good **buck** when feeling frisky.

brushing
➤ *See grooming*

brushing, in a horse's movement
Limb contact, when one hoof strikes another, or part of the leg, as the horse travels; a minor form of interference. Brushing of the leg will wear off the hair but not break the skin.
➤ *See interference*

brush races
Races over brush hurdles, rather than solid fences.
➤ *See also steeplechasing*

bucking
Springing into the air with an arched back, landing with stiff forelegs and lowered head. A defense mechanism for dislodging predators, bucking also quite frequently dislodges riders. A horse may buck when saddled for the first time, though modern training techniques tend to avoid this. Some horses buck because they haven't been properly trained. Others buck under saddle if they haven't had enough exercise; it's a good idea to let a horse like this work out the kinks on a longe line before mounting.

Bucking may also occur if a horse's tack doesn't fit properly, if it is stung by a bee, or if it is in pain or frightened. Sometimes a horse who has not been adequately warmed up will buck after a jump. Horses turned out after being cooped up overnight or after being ridden may run and buck as a way of blowing off steam and stretching their bodies.

bucking rolls/bronc rolls
Padded leather pouches retrofitted to a slick-fork saddle to act as knee-blocks do on an English saddle, or the swell on a swell-forked Western saddle. They are attached with leather strings or screws and offer the rider some security when working with a young horse.
➤ *See also Western tack*

buck knee
➤ *See over at the knee/buck-kneed*

buck rake
A rake that collects hay as it is pushed in front of draft animals, often used in conjunction with a beaver slide or an overshot stacker.

buckskin coloring
A tan, yellow, or gold coat with black coloring on the mane, tail, and lower legs.
➤ *See also "Buckskin or Dun?," next page; color, of horse*

buddy-sour
➤ *See herd-bound*

BUCKSKIN OR DUN?

Both are tan or golden horses with dark manes and tails. What's the difference, and how do you tell?

A BUCKSKIN IS PRODUCED BY A CRÈME DILUTION GENE acting on a bay base. Buckskins do not have dorsal stripes or zebra markings on the legs, though some may have a fuzzy-edged line of counter-shading down the back, and "wild bay" buckskins may have some mottling on the legs. Colors range from clear light yellow through tan, sandy, or dark cream with black points (mane, tail, legs, and sometimes the nose and the tips of the ears).

A DUN IS PRODUCED BY A DUN DILUTION GENE on a bay base. Duns have a dorsal stripe and may have zebra markings on the lower legs. Colors include yellow-tan with black points and a dorsal stripe; yellow-tan with non-black points; rosy with brown points (lilac dun); pale brownish red with brown points and stripe (muddy dun); washed-out red or yellow-red with brown, red, or flaxen points; and the legs and head darker than the body (claybank).

When a dun horse turns his neck inward, the darkly pigmented tips of the hairs come together, giving him a characteristic smuttiness of color. A buckskin may be similar in color, but his hairs have no concentration of pigment at the end, so his color is clear with no dark overcast.

BUCKSKIN

DUN

buggy A small, light four-wheeled carriage pulled by a single horse. Old-fashioned doctors' buggies have a top; modern show buggies do not.

bulb, of hoof The rounded protrusion at the back of the hoof where the frog and hoof wall merge with the skin.

bull pen A corral used to train horses.

bull snap A heavy-duty snap for a lead rope or trailer tie with a closing lever that pulls outward.

bun bag A bag strapped under the tail of a city carriage horse to catch manure.

Bureau of Land Management (BLM)
Federal agency with responsibility for managing wild horses on public lands. The BLM manages nearly all free-ranging herds in the United States. Periodically, the BLM rounds up wild horses and offers them for adoption, privately or through programs like Extreme Mustang Makeover.

burner A rawhide covering that protects the eye of a looped rope from excessive wear.

bustle A large leather pillow strapped under a horse's tail, to train the tail to remain elevated. This is done when showing Saddlebreds, Morgans, and other high-stepping breeds, and is an alternative to the now-illegal practices of nicking and gingering. It is done for aesthetic reasons.

bute
➤ *See phenylbutazone (bute)*

butt bar A bar placed behind a horse when the animal is being trailered or is in stocks. Rear-end contact with the bar encourages the horse to stay in place. A horse may also lean on the bar to maintain his balance while trailering.
➤ *See also restraints; stocks (as restraints)*

Buzkashi The national sport of Afghanistan; literally translated as "goat grabbing." Mounted teams of riders (from six to dozens on a side), called *chapandaz*, form a circle around the carcass of a goat or calf. At the signal, each rider tries to lean over, hoist the carcass from the ground, hitch it under his leg, and ride at a dead gallop away from the other players, who do their best to retrieve the goat. In the original game, the rider who kept the carcass away from the rest of the horde was the winner. A more complex version requires that the rider gallop around a distant flag and bring the carcass back to his team's scoring circle.

Buzkashi is a fast and furious sport that is played by tough, highly trained horses and expert riders. Riders wear thickly padded clothing and carry short leather whips, and although kicking and hitting opponents is not allowed, pretty much anything else goes, and the game can get quite rough. The carcass, which is sometimes filled with sand, usually winds up resembling a limp leather rag by the end. The winners receive great honor and acclaim, as well as prizes of money and fine clothes donated by sponsors.

cadence Expressive movement, with accentuated rhythm and tempo. Cadence is possible only in the trot and canter, which have moments of suspension.

calcium A mineral necessary, in combination with phosphorus, to maintain strong bones and teeth. Calcium deficiency can impair growth or lead to unsoundness in horses; excess calcium may affect the rate at which cartilage is converted to bone.

calf knee

➤ *See back at the knee*

calf roping A rodeo event in which contestants rope a running calf, dismount, flip the calf on the ground, and tie three of its legs together, usually in about the time it takes to read this sentence. A good roping horse will run directly behind the calf without directions from his rider, beginning to stop as soon as the rope is tossed. When the rider dismounts, the horse backs, keeping the rope taut. Once tied, the calf must remain down for six seconds.

➤ *See also breakaway roping; cattle roping; piggin string; team roping; "two wraps and a hooey"*

"NO JERKDOWN" RULE

In calf roping competition, rodeos and some associations have a rule to prevent the horse and rider from roping a calf and then stopping so suddenly that the calf flips over. The idea is for the horse to hold the calf at the end of the taut rope while the rider approaches. It's then up to the rider to throw the calf.

➤ *See also calf roping; cattle roping; team roping*

CALF ROPING

California-style bit A loose-shanked spade bit that allows riders to direct their horses with a light touch on the reins.

➤ *See also bit; bridle horse; off the bit; vaquero*

calk Projection on the bottom of a horseshoe designed to increase traction. Some calks are permanent; others screw into threaded sockets in the shoe and are removable. Also called studs.

calluses Thickened skin on the points of the hocks, caused from the pressure of lying down in a stall. The larger the horse, the harder it is to keep calluses from developing. In the wild, horses lie on grass, snow, and sand that has not been packed down. It is essential with heavy horses (drafts, warmbloods, and anything over 16.2 hands high with bulk), to keep the flooring well covered with bedding to prevent calluses from forming.

camped (conformation) Having legs that extend too far in a certain direction. A horse who stands with his front legs too far forward is "camped in front." If he stands with hind feet too far behind he is "camped out" or "out in the country." If his legs are too far under his body, he is "camped under." These terms may refer to the horse's actual conformation or to the way he is squared up (or not) for inspection by a judge.

cannon bone A long bone extending from the knee to the fetlock of a horse's foreleg, and from the hock to the fetlock of the hind leg. The cannon bone should be sizable enough to support the horse; it should also be

CAMARGUE HORSE

A breed of horse that runs semiwild in the marshy Rhone River delta of France. Camargue horses are small (13.1–14.1 hands high) and robust, with extremely good legs and hooves. All are born black or brown, and turn gray with maturity. Fast and agile, they make excellent riding horses. They are used locally to handle the black bulls of the region that are raised for provincial bullfights.

CANADIAN HORSE

A breed originating in colonial Canada, descended from French breeds and strongly influenced by the Morgan. As Canadian breeders preferred pacers, the Canadian is a source of "gaitedness" in the Standardbred, Saddlebred, and Tennessee Walker. Many Canadian Horses escaped from western settlements in Illinois and interbred with the northern mustang.

A small horse, usually black or brown, the Canadian resembles the old-style Morgan. They were used as farm horses, but by 1885 so many had been traded away that numbers were greatly reduced. Canada's government intervened, forbidding export, and the breed became essentially unknown in the United States. The population remains small, numbering around 2,000, but as the versatile Canadian becomes more well known, especially as a driving horse, the breed's future is looking brighter. **Livestock Conservancy status: Critical**

➤ *See also Morgan*

centered under the knee or hock to provide sufficient support to his body. An offset cannon will increase the amount of strain on the splint bones and knees or hocks; it can trigger the condition known as splints, in which hard, bony growths develop on the cannon itself.

An appropriately positioned cannon should make the leg appear wide from front to back—a desirable conformation known as **flat bone**. By contrast, **round bone** is a conformation fault. It occurs when a horse's tendon and cannon bone are positioned too closely together.

➤ *See also coffin bone; flat bone; leg, of horse; round bone; split bones/splints*

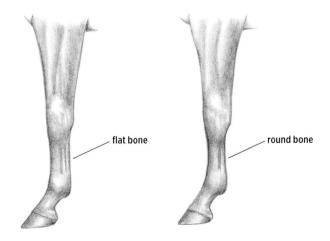

flat bone

round bone

canter A smooth, natural, three-beat gait that is faster than the trot. The typical speed of a canter is about 13 miles (21 km) per hour. The gait begins with one hind leg, continues with the other hind leg and the diagonal front leg, then finishes with the leading foreleg. When a horse is cantering, he places his leading front foot farther forward than his other front foot. Western riders refer to this gait as the lope.
➤ *See also gait; lead change*

cantharidin toxicity
➤ *See blister beetle poisoning*

cantle The wide, upward-projecting back part of a saddle's seat.

cap A hollow, deteriorated baby tooth that should detach from the gums when a horse's permanent teeth emerge. Retained caps, which do not properly release from the gums, can cause problems, including swollen gums, a sore mouth, sinus infections, and crooked or impacted permanent teeth.

capillary refill time A measure of blood pressure and hydration. Check a horse's capillary refill time by pressing a thumb against the gum above the upper incisors. The gum tissue will initially turn white from the pressure. By counting the number of seconds before the normal pink tissue color returns, you can evaluate the horse's status. A refill time of 1 to 2 seconds is considered ideal. A refill time that exceeds 3.5 seconds may indicate low blood pressure, circulatory impairment, dehydration, or shock.
➤ *See also shock*

capped hocks A condition in which the hocks (the joints above the fetlocks on the hind legs) have become thickened due to injury or a conformation fault.

capping
➤ *See tracking up*

capriole One of the airs above the ground. The horse leaps forward and up, and while airborne, flings his hind legs out behind him before landing.
➤ *See also airs above the ground; Lipizzan*

carbohydrates The sugars and starches that furnish most of the energy in a horse's diet. Oats, barley, and corn may contain as much as 60 percent sugar and starch. Molasses is another concentrated source of carbohydrates. The amount of "energy food" required by a horse varies according to his age, condition, reproductive status, and activity level.

Horses who consume a low-glycemic diet, mostly fiber, get the glucose they need through digestive processes. Digesting fiber does not elevate the horse's blood sugar or trigger insulin release. Diets high in simple carbohydrates (sugar and starch) lead to high blood glucose levels, which overload the glucose uptake mechanisms and may lead to equine metabolic syndrome, laminitis, or founder.
➤ *See also equine metabolic syndrome (EMS); founder; laminitis*

carriage

1. A four-wheeled horse-drawn vehicle, more substantial than a buggy. Carriages can be made of wood or metal, and may be formal or made for rough-and-ready action, like the combined driving marathon vehicle.

2. How a horse carries himself, especially his head, neck, and tail.

CAPRIOLE

CARRIAGE DRIVING

carriage driving Driving horses hitched to substantially built carriages, carts, or buggies in competitions; as distinguished from fine harness driving, in which horses pull light sulkies, "bikes," or four-wheeled show vehicles. Single horses, pairs, four-in-hands, and other configurations may be driven. There are two major divisions: Carriage Pleasure Driving and Combined Driving. Pleasure Driving classes cover reinsmanship, turnout, carriage dogs, and obstacle courses such as cones and Gambler's Choice.
➤ *See also combined driving*

carrier

1. An animal carrying a recessive gene that may affect its offspring.

2. An animal carrying a communicable disease without being affected by it.

➤ *See also genetics*

carrot stretches Stretches a horse can be taught to do by following a carrot or other treat. The horse may be asked to reach around toward his rib cage or hock, or between his front legs. Carrot stretches loosen the horse's muscles and thus strengthen the horse.

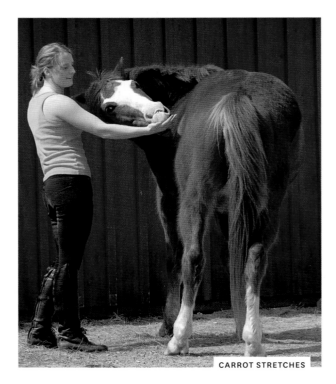

CARROT STRETCHES

cart A two-wheeled horse-drawn vehicle. Common types include easy-entry and Meadowbrook.

➤ *See also buggy; carriage; driving*

Caslick repair A surgical procedure in which the lips of a mare's vulva are cut and sutured, to prevent feces from contaminating the vagina. A Caslick repair is necessary if the anal sphincter is deep-set or if the vulva lacks normal tone. The lips subsequently grow together, reducing the size of the vaginal opening. The repaired vulva needs to be surgically opened before foaling, and closed again after the uterus heals. Widespread adoption of the Caslick procedure has greatly increased conception rate and live foal production.

cast horse A horse who is on his back in a stall or pen and unable to rise, often with his legs caught against a wall or fence. If a horse remains in this position for a significant amount of time, he may sustain intestinal, circulatory, or respiratory problems.

Approach a cast horse calmly and don't loom over him. If he's a short distance from the wall, he may just need to be pulled a little farther away so that he can get his feet back down. You may be able to pull his hindquarters by the tail, or his front end by looping a rope around his neck.

A horse who is up against the wall will need to be rolled over. Put on a helmet if you've got one handy. Loop a long rope a couple of times around one front pastern. Brace one foot high on the horse's neck, just behind his head, and push his head toward the wall as you pull his foreleg toward you. As soon as he starts to tip in your direction, move past his head, away from his thrashing legs. You want to be well out of his way as he lunges to his feet. Once he's up and calm, check him over for injuries.

CASPIAN HORSE

➤

A small, refined horse (10–12 hands high) that originated in Iran during the Stone Age. With a dished face; a vaulted forehead; a graceful neck; a short, straight back; and a tail set high on a level croup, the Caspian Horse strongly resembles the Arabian, its modern descendant. Caspian Horses appear pulling chariots in ancient Persian art going back to 3000 BCE, and were first mentioned in writing around 600 CE.

In the 1960s Caspians were rediscovered by an American woman, Louise Firouz, who gathered as many as she could find and exported a number to Europe. War in the region threatened the horse with extinction in its native land, but populations are slowly growing in the West. Not surprisingly, given their heritage, Caspians make superb driving ponies and are also excellent mounts for small children. The Caspian Horse is now considered a national treasure in Iran, and the breed's future is looking brighter. **Livestock Conservancy status: Critical**

➤ *See also history of the horse*

A horse who continually becomes cast may need a ridge of extra bedding around the edges of the stall to discourage him from lying near the wall. Or he can wear an anti-cast surcingle, a specialized piece of equipment with a heavy U-shaped bar over the withers which prevents him from rolling onto his back. In a pen, old tires can be placed along the fence where he tends to get cast. A horse who persistently gets cast may need the freedom of a pasture in order to remain safe and healthy.

castration
➤ *See gelding*

cataract
A medical problem in which the lens of the eye becomes cloudy or less transparent. Some equine cataracts can be surgically removed, but the condition often leads to blindness.
➤ *See also eye problems; vision*

catch rope
➤ *See lariat/lasso*

cattle penning/team penning
A rodeo competition in which three riders work as a team to herd three cows into a pen. The object is to accomplish the action in the shortest possible amount of time. In most cases, teams are allowed no more than 90 seconds to finish penning. A variation in which one rider herds one cow into a pen is known as one-on-one.
➤ *See also rodeo*

cattle roping/steer roping
A rodeo event in which a rider or team of riders uses a rope to capture a fleeing steer. The winners are those who rope the steer in the shortest amount of time. Entrants contribute part of their entry fees to a pot, which is divided among the winners.

cattle sorting
A penning competition in which a team of three riders separates cattle in numerical order. The team has 90 seconds to line up 10 cows in the correct sequence and drive them across the start line. The team with the most total cattle and least time wins. This combination of cutting and penning uses fewer cattle and puts less stress on them than cattle penning does.
➤ *See also cattle penning/team penning*

cavalletti
A series of parallel poles or rails placed on low supports, spaced apart at a predetermined distance roughly equivalent to a horse's trotting stride. Riding instructors use cavalletti to prepare their students for higher-level riding. Students gain control skills and awareness by riding in a straight line down this horizontal "ladder." Cavalletti are also used to regulate, confirm, or modify a horse's gaits; strengthen the back and develop a good bascule; and develop agility and proprioception.
➤ *See also ground poles/ground lines*

cavalry
An organized body of mounted soldiers. Horses enhanced the fighting capabilities of warriors for thousands of years until modern weaponry made cavalry units obsolete. From the fierce hordes of the central Asian plains, horses and riding techniques spread to the Greeks and Egyptians and into Europe, changing history and changing horses. By the Middle Ages, horses who had been bred for size and strength could carry a knight in heavy armor, though at the cost of maneuverability and speed.

As military technology advanced, cavalry techniques became more sophisticated. When armor was discarded, saddles became less bulky and horses were bred for agility and quickness. In the 18th century, French and Spanish riders developed methods of horse training based on reward and encouragement rather than pain and fear. These techniques form the basis of dressage riding as it is practiced today.

By the end of the 19th century, repeating rifles and machine guns wreaked havoc on mounted soldiers, and though many thousands of horses were used in World War I, the day of the cavalry was over. By the 1950s, both the U.S. and the British armies abolished their mounted units.
➤ *See also history of the horse*

cavesson
The noseband or nosepiece of a bridle.
➤ *See also bridle; longeing cavesson*

Celtic pony
A primitive pony that lived in the damp regions of what is now western Europe. In response to its wet, chilly environment, the Celtic pony evolved a water-resistant coat. This animal is the forerunner of many European pony and small horse breeds, including the Shetland and Icelandic.

Centered Riding

A system of riding developed by the late Sally Swift, based on changes in body awareness. Centered Riding emphasizes soft eye focus, awareness of the breath and center of gravity, and stacking the elements of the body—legs and feet, pelvis, rib cage, shoulders, head and neck—directly above the stirrups. It also uses visualization and encourages softness rather than a muscular approach. Teachers receive certification through Centered Riding Inc.

centerline

The imaginary line that runs lengthwise down the center of an arena.

➤ *See also arena work; "Arena Dimensions," page 10; quarter line; school figures*

center of gravity

The balance point of the body's weight. When a horse is standing still, his center of gravity is about 6 inches (15 cm) behind the elbow. If the horse is moving on the forehand, the center of gravity may shift forward; if the horse is working in collection, the center of gravity may shift backward.

For humans, the center of gravity is located within the abdomen, generally 1 to 2 inches (2.5–5 cm) below the navel. A rider should position her center of gravity as close as possible to the horse's center of gravity.

➤ *See also collection*

certificate of veterinary inspection (CVI)

A document that certifies the general health of an animal. The certificate of veterinary inspection (CVI) is prepared by a veterinarian after a physical examination has been conducted. Horse owners who transport their horses across state borders often need to present a recent CVI to state authorities or horse show organizers.

certified instructor

➤ *See instructor*

Certified Journeyman Farrier (CJF)

The highest level of certification awarded by the American Farriers Association.

➤ *See also farrier*

cervix

The neck of the uterus. A mare's cervix is tightly closed unless she is in estrus or on the verge of foaling. When the mare is in heat, her cervix opens as wide as ¾ inch (2 cm), allowing the sperm to enter the uterus.

➤ *See also breeding; foaling; gestation; uterus*

chain twitch

➤ *See restraints; twitch*

chair seat

A riding position in which the rider sits on the fleshy part of the buttocks, as if sitting in a chair. It is incorrect in many disciplines, but saddle seat riders and some Western riders do use the chair seat. In gaited riding the chair seat can help the horse find the correct body configuration that allows him to rack rather than pace.

chambon, neck stretcher, de Gogue

A group of training devices made of cords that connect from the girth through a crownpiece to the bit. They differ slightly in configuration, but all put

CHAIR SEAT

pressure on the horse's poll and mouth when he raises his head, and release when he stretches long and low. Devices like this are best used briefly, to show the horse that he can actually move with his neck stretched. Training exercises and good rider biomechanics can usually get the horse moving long and low without artificial devices.

champagne class
A class for easy-gaited horses in which the rider carries a brimming glass of champagne or another beverage, to demonstrate the smoothness of the horse's action.

change of lead
➤ *See canter; flying lead change; simple lead change*

chaps
Leggings of tough but supple leather or suede that protect the rider's legs and jeans from thorns and brush, or enhance grip on the saddle when schooling young horses. They come in three basic styles: batwings, chinks, and shotgun (or schooling). **Batwings** are wide, full-length chaps that drag on the ground and offer the most protection. **Chinks** fit loosely like batwings but come just below the knee and are usually fringed. **Shotgun chaps**, also known as schooling chaps, fit snugly around the length of the leg and are zipped into place; they can be fringed or not. English riders sometimes wear schooling chaps, though they more commonly wear half-chaps.
➤ *See also half-chaps*

charger
A horse ridden by a military officer.

chariot
A two-wheeled vehicle with spoked wheels, pulled by bitted horses and driven at a gallop or fast amble by a standing driver. Chariots were invented in the Eurasian steppes before 2000 BCE and were the first wheeled vehicles designed for speed. Chariots were used for racing at funerals (where a rich man's estate was divided among the winners) and for warfare. Imported to Egypt, war chariots determined the fates of ancient empires until around 600 BCE, when mounted warfare made them obsolete.
➤ *See also "Modern Chariot Racing," right; history of the horse*

MODERN CHARIOT RACING
A Western sport in which pairs of horses, usually off-track Quarter Horses, pull a chariot made of a 55-gallon (208 L) drum sawed in half and mounted on two bicycle tires. The horses race at a full gallop for 440 yards (402 m). Modern chariot racing derives from a winter race in which the horses pulled light sleighs called cutters.

check
An upward snap of the reins used to get a horse's attention.

check rein
A short strap that runs from the bit to the top of the bridle and back to the harness or saddle, used to prevent a horse from lowering his head.
➤ *See also overcheck*

cheekpiece
Straps on a headstall that connect the bit or noseband to the crownpiece.
➤ *See also bridle; halter; headstall*

chest bar
A chest-level bar placed in front of a horse in a trailer or stocks. Contact with the chest bar encourages the horse to stay in place while allowing him to lower his head.

chestnut
A tough, horny patch on the inside of all four legs. On the front legs the chestnuts are large and above the knee; on the back legs they are small and below the hock. Chestnuts are considered by most scientists to be vestiges of the ancestral five-toed foot. However, some scientists argue that they have a glandular origin, which may explain their strong, though not unpleasant, scent. The chestnut reflex, which prompts most horses to lift a foot when the chestnut on that leg is squeezed, is used by many horse people to cue the horse to pick up his foot.

LIGHT CHESTNUT WITH FLAXEN MANE AND TAIL

DARK CHESTNUT

LIVER CHESTNUT

chestnut coloring A coloration that includes various shades of red, ranging from bright red-gold to reddish brown or auburn. The manes and tails of chestnuts either match their coats or are lighter; they can even be flaxen with white hairs. A chestnut with a light mane and tail is often called a sorrel.

➤ *See also color, of horse; liver chestnut; "Red Horses," page 292*

chewing Horses rely on their molars and premolars to perform most chewing and grinding tasks. These flat-bottomed teeth appear in the back of the horse's mouth, behind the bars. With heavy use, they may become worn into sharp points that are not optimal for chewing. In these cases, the teeth can be filed using a tool known as a float.

Chewing also refers to the bad habit some horses develop of chewing on wood—including fences, stall doors, stall walls, and scrap wood. Lack of roughage in the diet can lead to chewing, but the habit is more often attributed to boredom. It is a difficult behavior to correct, so it is important to ensure that a horse who has begun chewing is not ingesting toxins, such as paint, along with the wood.

For trainers using correct natural horsemanship techniques, licking and chewing motions indicate that the horse is thinking and learning, and that he is ready to "join up," or accept the handler's directions. It can also mean that the horse is exhausted and thirsty and ready to give up and submit.

➤ *See also bars; cribbing; "join up"; natural horsemanship (NH)*

chin groove Area between the chin and the branches of the jaw where the curb strap of a bridle rests.

HORSES OF CHINA

China has a large population of horses, accounting for about one-sixth of the world population. There are over 30 breeds, most of which are completely unknown in the West. Many are small horses descended from Mongolian stock; they range from 12 to 14 hands high in China, but when moved to warmer areas with better feed, they increase in size.

Horses in southern China tend to be small and slender; in the north they are more massive, with heavier bone. Horses in China are used for work, not recreation, and tend to be extremely hardy and disease-free. Some Chinese breeds date back 4,000 years, while others are more modern.

The Chinese invented many important pieces of equipment still used in driving and draft work. These include the breast collar, the hame collar, the breeching strap, the single-horse vehicle with lateral shafts, and the practice of driving tandem. The Chinese claim the invention of the stirrup, though that is less certain.

chin spot A white spot or hairs below the lower lip, visible from the front.

chip off A Western riding and cattle-cutting strategy in which the rider works to isolate one cow from the herd.

chipping/chipping in When a horse finds himself too close to a jump and adds an extra, tiny step before taking off. This may make him knock down a pole, and can be difficult for a rider to sit. Also known as popping.

CHINCOTEAGUE PONIES

Chincoteague Ponies are small (typically around 12 hands high), tough, hardy inhabitants of Assateague, an island and national park off the coast of Virginia. They probably descended from horses who belonged to 17th-century colonists. Many, but not all, Chincoteague Ponies are pintos. They are the only wild pony in the United States.

The 1947 publication of the book *Misty of Chincoteague* by Marguerite Henry, followed in 1961 by the motion picture *Misty,* brought the ponies to the attention of a wider public.

On the last Thursday and Friday of July, the Chincoteague Volunteer Fire Department holds its annual Pony Penning Days, a roundup of the ponies and an auction of the foals and yearlings. The proceeds support the Fire Department.

chiropractic treatment Spinal adjustments used to relieve pain and stiffness. A horse's spine is relatively inflexible, even though it contains approximately 170 joints. The horse can experience pain and show symptoms if any of the vertebrae become misaligned or inflamed. Equine chiropractors use spinal adjustments to treat problems ranging from chronic back and neck soreness to lameness, stiffness, gait irregularities, and reluctance to be saddled.

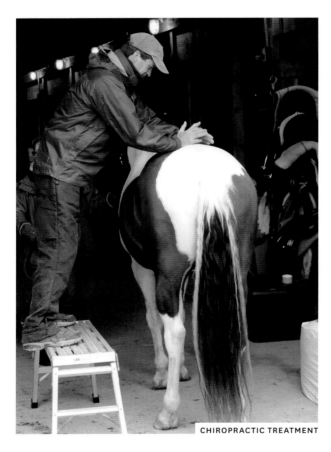

CHIROPRACTIC TREATMENT

choke A condition in which a chunk of unchewed food, a large wood splinter, or some other object becomes lodged in a horse's throat, blocking the esophagus. Symptoms of choke include straining to breathe, coughing, extending the head and neck, slobbering, and squealing. Although the condition is often self-correcting, it can lead to fatal complications such as aspiration pneumonia, so a veterinarian should be consulted when symptoms first appear. Keeping the horse calm and gently massaging the throat area may help resolve the blockage.

choker Collar of the shirt known as a ratcatcher, worn during hunter/jumper and lower-level dressage competitions.
➤ *See also ratcatcher; stock tie*

cholla A team roping game similar to polo, in which riders attempt to rope a six-pointed jack and drag it up and down the playing field through the goals of both teams. The jack itself is also called a *cholla* (pronounced *CHOY-uh*) after the desert cactus of the same name. It is usually made of leather or canvas stuffed with a filling material.

chop Hay that has been chopped, dried, and bagged for convenient storage. Chop provides roughage and can help prevent a horse from bolting his grain if added to his meals.

chorioptic mange
➤ *See mange*

chouse Cowboy term for pursuing cattle unnecessarily, often to the point of exhausting them.

chrome White markings on a horse, such as blaze, stockings, and so on; the term is most commonly used when a horse has a lot of white markings.

chronic obstructive pulmonary disease (COPD)
➤ *See heaves*

chute In cattle events, a fenced lane that contains a single cow behind a gate. Crew members open the chute's headgate to release the cow into the roping arena.

CID
➤ *See combined immune deficiency (CID)*

cinch In Western riding, the girth strap or band used to hold a saddle on a horse. Traditional cinches are made of mohair or other animal fibers, but they may also be made of nylon, cotton, rayon, neoprene, or leather. Back cinches are sometimes also used to hold the back of the saddle in place; these are commonly made of leather and must be connected to the front cinch.

circular pen

➤ *See round pen, round penning*

class An individual competition in a horse show; for instance, Equitation Class, in which the rider's correctness is judged, or Pleasure Class, in which the horse's gaits and performance are judged. A class may also be determined by the age and/or breed of the horse, or by the age, experience level, and/or gender of the rider.

Classical High School
The classical training of upper-level dressage horses, including the airs above the ground. Lipizzans are the best-known horses involved in Classical High School training, but there are Spanish and French centers of Classical High School training as well.

➤ *See also airs above the ground; dressage; Lipizzan*

classic fino A collected slow gait demonstrated by Paso Finos, in which the hooves move rapidly but take extremely short steps.

➤ *See also Paso Fino*

clean legs Legs without blemishes or unsoundness, especially from the knees or hocks down.

cleft of frog The V-shaped indentation in the center of the frog.

➤ *See also frog, of foot; hoof*

CLEVELAND BAY

The oldest established British horse breed; originally a pack horse. Cleveland Bays are always bay, 16 to 17 hands high, and extremely strong and powerful. They are excellent gallopers, a trait they pass on to cross-bred offspring. Their genetic distance from the Thoroughbred gives that cross great hybrid vigor. They have been widely used to improve other breeds, including the Oldenburg, Holsteiner, and Hanoverian, with a result that this once-common breed is now endangered; the British Royal Family has taken initiative to help preserve it.

There are around 1,000 Cleveland Bays worldwide, and about 180 in the United States. They make fine field and show hunters, and also excel at dressage and combined driving. **Livestock Conservancy status: Critical**

click

➤ *See nicking*

clicker training
A form of operant conditioning used to train animals, especially dogs and marine mammals, that has gained popularity in the horse world. Clicker training uses a sound (the click of a metal clicker, or "cricket") to mark a desired behavior. The click is followed by a treat or other form of positive reinforcement. Using successive approximation (small steps that build toward an ultimate goal), the trainer shapes a particular behavior progressively, first accepting a lower standard, then gradually raising the bar.

Clicker trainers teach the same behaviors as other trainers, but they reach the goal by a different route. They may train a horse to touch a target with his nose, then have him follow that target into a trailer; or they may teach him to stand on a mat, then ask him to stand on the mat in the presence of something frightening. Clicker training can be used at all levels of training.

➤ *See also aversive; conditioning, as a training term; punishment*

clinch
The part of a horseshoe nail (the sharp end) that is visible on the outside of the foot. This end is bent, or clinched, to hold the shoe on.

clinch cutters
A tool used to cut or straighten clinches and remove horseshoes.

clincher
A tool used to bend the horseshoe nail to form a clinch.

clinic
An organized session with a trainer or clinician. Clinics range in length from half a day to a week or more, and offer the opportunity for more intensive work than once-a-week lessons do. There are clinicians in all disciplines, and clinicians inventing new disciplines. Clinics may focus on unmounted work, mounted work, or a combination; they may be open to participants only, or may allow auditors. It is important to investigate a clinician thoroughly before committing the time and money to attend. Be sure that the methods used are humane, ethical, and in line with your training goals.

COMMON CLIPPING TERMS

Blanket clip: A body clipping pattern that shortens hair on the neck and underside of the horse, leaving the back, loins, quarters, and legs unclipped. This clip is suitable for horses doing medium to hard work in cold weather; it keeps the horse from sweating excessively during exercise and allows for a shorter cooling-out period, while retaining enough long hair to keep the horse warm and to protect the legs from brush.

Body clipping: Clipping all of the hair off the entire horse. Used most often in preparation for horse shows in spring; however, some people rely on body clipping to maintain a smooth coat throughout show season. Body clipping removes the natural oils from a horse's coat and requires fairly rigorous daily upkeep of the coat to prevent dry hair and dermatitis.

Bridle path: An area of clipped hair in the mane at the top of the neck, just behind the poll. The length of the bridle path varies with breed and discipline. It prevents chafing by the bridle's crownpiece and the development of painful ingrown hairs, which can cause headshyness. It also looks neat.

Hunter clip: A clipping pattern for horses who do heavy work and sweat a lot in cold weather. The hunter clip removes most of the hair, leaving the leg hair and a saddle-shaped patch of hair on the back to prevent soreness.

Show/sale clipping: Clipping is a major aspect of preparing a horse for competition and sale. In both cases, the goal is to make the horse look his absolute best. Clipping requirements and trends vary by breed and discipline, so it is best to learn these techniques from a knowledgeable professional.

Trace clip: A body clip that leaves hair on the horse's back, withers, and legs; so-named because it clips the area of the body where harness traces would run.

Stable clip: A clip that trims excess hair from the muzzle and fetlocks, along with the bridle path.

clip A metal extension on the outside rim of a horseshoe. Folded flat against the hoof wall, the clip helps stabilize the shoe.

clippers Haircutting tools used to trim horsehair. Heavy-duty clippers are suited for body and leg clipping. They can be used for extended periods because they are self-cooling. Light-duty clippers are suited for trimming around the head and for doing touch-ups. If used for removing heavy hair, the blades will dull and the motor may overheat and burn out.

In general, body clipping is done using #10 or #15 blades, which cut hair to about ¼ inch (0.6 cm) in length. Surgical blades (#30 or #40) will shave the horse bald. Clipper blades should be disinfected between use on different horses or if a horse shows signs of a skin infection.

clipping Trimming a horse's hair. Areas commonly clipped include the legs, exterior ear hairs, jaw, and the bridle path. Horsemen new to clipping should obtain assistance from someone who is confident and able to teach safe clipping methods. Horses can become quite nervous and potentially dangerous if handled inappropriately during clipping. And if you don't know what you're doing, you can render your horse unfit to be seen in public for a few weeks.
➤ *See also "Common Clipping Terms," facing page; grooming*

clipping a pasture Mowing a pasture to control weed growth and stimulate density of grass growth. The timing of this procedure depends on the life cycle of local weeds and grasses, so consult your Extension agent for advice.

closed reins In Western riding, reins that form a single loop from bit ring to bit ring, as opposed to reins that are individual, or split. Also called roper reins.
➤ *See also split reins*

close nail A horseshoe nail driven into the hoof close to the sensitive inner layer. A close nail may cause lameness.
➤ *See also hot nail*

MODIFIED HUNTER CLIP

closing the fingers To tighten the fingers on the reins, a subtle increase in contact.

clothing, for rider
➤ *See "English Show Attire," page 103; "Western Show attire," page 399*

clubfoot A condition in which the hoof-to-ground angle is atypically steep, creating a foot that is upright rather than angled. A clubfoot typically has a shorter-than-normal toe and a longer-than-normal heel.

Clubfoot can be triggered by an injury or unskilled hoof trimming, or it may be an inherited predisposition. The effects of the condition can be minimized through frequent corrective foot trimming, especially if the horse is not yet fully grown.

A breed of draft horse that originated in Clydesdale, Scotland. The Clydesdale is a heavy, big-boned horse known for its strength and its extravagantly feathered feet. Most Clydesdales are bay or brown, but roans are also common. Almost every Clydesdale has white markings on the face and feet; many have white on the belly.

A large horse (16.2–18 hands high) with a lively way of going, the modern Clydesdale is best known as a hitch horse, especially for the beer maker Budweiser, which maintains three traveling eight-horse teams.

The Budweiser look—bay with a wide blaze, stockings to the knee and hock, and tremendous feathering—has greatly influenced the breed. The population is at an all-time high in the United States, and there are about 5,000 globally. **Livestock Conservancy status: Watch**

➤ *See also feathering; hitch horses*

coach Someone who, unlike a trainer or instructor, takes a broad overview of a competitor's goals and strategies. She may point a rider or driver toward instructors and trainers, and she may occasionally do some teaching and training herself. She can help design a competition schedule, advise on the ins and outs of the discipline, mentor a competitor through the stress of the day, and give a wide array of horse help, including finding suitable horses and helping train them. A coach may or may not still be an active competitor.

A coach for an equestrian team is usually a medalist in that field, sometimes still an active competitor, sometimes on temporary leave from competition.

➤ *See also instructor; trainer*

coach horse breeds Breeds that were developed to pull coaches. These are European breeds, from areas that had a good system of roads during the coaching era. As motorized transport came in, coach breeds transitioned into riding horses; modern examples include the Holsteiner, Hanoverian, and Oldenburg.

Coach horse breeds and Thoroughbreds provide the foundation for the modern warmblood sport horse.

➤ *See also sport horse; warmblood*

coat The hair that covers a horse's body, as opposed to the mane and tail. The quality of a horse's coat is a good indicator of general health. It should be appropriately dense for the breed and season, lie smooth and flat, and exhibit a handsome gloss.

➤ *See also hair*

cob A stout, short-legged horse (usually less than 15.3 hands high), with heavy bone and muscle, a short neck, a round barrel, and close coupling. A good cob is energetic and a great weight carrier. Traditionally, cobs were mounts for the middle classes, an all-purpose animal that might work on the farm most days, be driven to market by the wife of the family, and be taken on a foxhunt by the husband. The best-known modern example is the Welsh Cob.

➤ *See also Welsh Pony*

WELSH COB

cobby Stoutly built and closely coupled.

coffin bone A bone, the distal phalange, located inside a horse's hoof. The coffin bone is comparable to the bone in the tip of human fingers and toes, but because the horse travels on its hooves, the coffin bone is one of the most important structures of its body.

If tissue surrounding the coffin bone becomes inflamed, the condition is known as laminitis. As inflammation progresses the coffin bone may rotate or sink downward; this displacement is a symptom of the serious, disabling condition known as founder. In extreme cases, the coffin bone may protrude through the bottom of the foot.

➤ *See also hoof; laminitis*

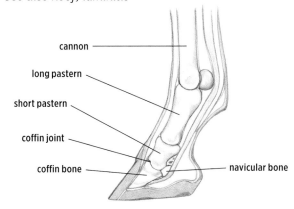

cannon

long pastern

short pastern

coffin joint

coffin bone

navicular bone

coffin joint The joint between the coffin bone and the bone above it, called the short pastern, or medial phalange. The joint also involves a third bone—the tiny, pyramid-shaped structure known as the navicular bone.

➤ *See also navicular disease; pastern; ringbone*

Coggins test, Coggins certificate A blood test to screen for equine infectious anemia (EIA), also known as swamp fever, a serious but now uncommon viral disease. A negative test indicates that EIA is not present and results in the issuance of a Coggins certificate, a document required when traveling or participating in horse shows.

A positive Coggins test indicates exposure to the virus; after a positive test, the horse is usually quarantined and retested. A horse infected with EIA will probably have to be euthanized.

➤ *See equine infectious anemia (EIA)*

cold-backed A horse who shows irritability on being saddled and mounted, particularly in cold weather. This is often due to the discomfort of tight muscles. Because they are in some degree of pain, cold-backed horses are prone to buck, and can be dangerous to ride. Usually the horse improves once the muscles are warmed up. Blanketing can be helpful, especially with a material that reflects the horse's body heat back to him. Using a quarter sheet can also be useful, as is lunging before riding.

➤ *See also girthy; "Types of Sheets," page 319*

cold blood
A type of horse that originated in cold climates; usually heavy-bodied, built for slow, steady work rather than speed. Cold-blooded horses have fewer red blood cells per unit of blood than other horses do, so they lack endurance for long-distance galloping. Air passages and lungs are proportionally smaller than in a light horse, so a cold blood has less "wind." The compact body, thick skin, long heavy hair, and layer of subcutaneous fat let a cold blood endure cold more easily, but all of these features make work in hot weather more stressful for the horse. A large head with small nostrils enables him to warm frigid air in his sinuses before it reaches his lungs, preventing damage. Breeds include all draft horses, Fjords, Haflingers, and the sturdier, shaggier ponies.

➤ *See also hot blood; warmblood*

cold shoeing
A shoeing method in which the shoe is applied cold, rather than being heated for shaping in a forge.

➤ *See also hot fitting, hot shoeing*

The Russian Heavy Draft is an example of a **cold blood** breed.

colic
A generic term for abdominal pain. The horse's digestive system couldn't be much simpler, but it is nevertheless subject to a variety of difficulties and breakdowns. These problems are often collectively described as colic, which is not a single disorder but a term that covers a range of abdominal discomfort. Symptoms of abdominal pain include poor appetite, listlessness, rapid pulse, repeatedly lying down and getting up, foot stamping, sweating, squatting, issuing groans or squeals, straining as if trying to urinate, biting or kicking at the belly or sides, and rolling.

Treatment depends entirely on the type of colic. Types of colic include the following:

FLATULENT COLIC. Excess gas in the intestine; it can be caused by an intestinal obstruction or from eating too much lush green feed. Walking can be helpful.

IMPACTIONS. Eating dry food without drinking sufficient water may cause manure to become hard and dry, creating constipation. Other causes include ingesting something indigestible, such as rubber or twine, or developing an enterolith (a calcium buildup around an indigestible object). The first symptom is usually constipation and loss of appetite. Gas builds up, causing even more pain. Surgery may be necessary, but early repeated treatments with hydration, lubricants, and medications often resolve the condition and soften the material enough to get it to pass. Thereafter, it is essential that the horse has water sufficient to keep his stool soft.

INFLAMED INTESTINES. The technical term is enteritis. Equine enteritis can be triggered by ingestion and accumulation of sand or gravel, a poisonous plant or chemical, an infection, or parasites. Signs include pain and diarrhea. Fluid replacement is important.

SAND COLIC. This results when the horse has ingested sand or small gravel over a long period. This can happen if the horse eats hay on sandy ground, or if his pasture is sandy and sand clings to the roots of plants he eats. Because it is heavier than the horse's feed, the sand settles in the cecum, the lower part of the intestine, and may obstruct other material trying to pass through. Sand accumulations are best cleared from the large intestine with a combination of psyllium powder and Epsom salt. Epsom salt draws water into the colon,

Colic is always an emergency. It can be fatal if it involves blockage, shock, or twisted intestines. Colic can also be relatively minor, but it's imperative to consult your veterinarian whenever your horse displays symptoms.

acting as a laxative. Psyllium powder swells when wet, trapping the sand and moving it out of the gut. Your vet may also administer mineral oil.

SPASMODIC COLIC. This may come from overexcitement, nervousness, spoiled or moldy feed, a sudden change in the diet, or a big drink of cold water when the horse is too hot. The vet may administer Banamine to ease the pain. Expect properly diagnosed spasmodic colic to resolve itself in a few hours.

TWISTED GUT (also known as torsion colic). The intestine may become twisted as the horse rolls on the ground. Torsion colic also can be triggered by muscle spasms or excessive gas buildup; many vets now believe that the torsion precedes rolling. Surgery is required. If untreated for too long, endotoxic shock can result, making it difficult for the horse to recover even if surgery is performed or a relatively small length of bowel is involved. Any colic that is not relieved by 10 cc of Banamine should be considered a possible torsion.

➤ *See also deworming; digestive system; feeding and nutrition; water, for horses*

collar, for grooming or tying A collar, similar to a dog collar, that fastens around a horse's throatlatch and is used in place of a halter. Grooming collars are used when a horse's head requires meticulous grooming, as for a show. Collars are also occasionally used when tying a horse to a picket line. They should never be used to tie a horse to a solid object.
➤ *See also picketing/staking out*

collar, of a harness The part of a harness that fits around the horse's neck and rests on the shoulders. The collar allows the horse to push against weight, and greatly increases his efficiency with heavy loads. The modern collar used for heavy draft and carriage driving was invented in the first century BCE in China. It was introduced to the West following the Mongol invasions.

collection A state in walk, trot, or canter in which the horse is gathered together yet moving with energy. The strides are shorter and higher than in the working gaits, the topline becomes shorter from poll to tail, and the horse appears taller, with an arched neck and lifted back. The center of gravity is farther back, and the frame is markedly uphill. Collection cannot be achieved by mechanically setting the horse's head in a particular position. It is the work of months or years of physical development and training, as the horse learns to raise his back, balance the rider (or carriage), and move forward with energy and cadence.
➤ *See also on the bit*

COLORADO RANGERBRED ➤ A breed of Western horse developed in from an Arab and a Barb stallion given to President Ulysses S. Grant. Rangerbreds are midsize (14.2–16 hands high) with deep builds, good bone, and excellent cow sense. They frequently exhibit Appaloosa coloring.

BASIC HORSE COLORS

Color	Description
Bay	Tan to reddish brown to mahogany coat with black points
Black	Completely black hair except for white markings
Brown	Dark brown to black coat with brown muzzle
Buckskin	Tan to gold coat, with dark points, often with a fuzzy line of counter-shading down the back
Chestnut /sorrel	A reddish brown or reddish gold coat, often with a lighter mane and tail
Dun	Yellow or gold body with black or brown points, with a dorsal stripe; often has zebra markings on the lower legs
Gray	Gray or white coat with dark skin; may have dapples
Palomino	Yellow to deep gold coat with flaxen mane and tail
Roan	A mix of white hairs with red or black
White	White coat with pink skin and muzzle

➤ *See also individual colors; albino; "Buckskin or Dun?," page 40*

color, of horse Color in horses is genetically controlled, and can be an absorbing subject of study—and a frustrating one if your goal is to produce a foal of a particular color. Horses come in two base colors, red and black. "Red" colors include chestnut, sorrel, palomino, cremello, red dun, and red roan. "Black" colors include black, brown, bay, buckskin, perlino, dun, grulla, and blue roan. (Gray and white fall outside these categories.)

Color is determined by recessive and dominant genes. If a foal inherits the same dominant gene from each parent and two different recessive genes from them, his coat will be of the dominant color. However, if both parents pass on the same recessive gene for color, the foal will be that color, no matter what color the parents are. For example, if a bay stallion and a gray mare each carry a recessive chestnut gene, their foal will be a chestnut.

In the three major horse colors—bay, gray, and chestnut—gray is dominant over bay, and bay is dominant over chestnut. To be gray, a horse must always have one gray parent; the trait cannot skip a generation, as chestnut can. A chestnut bred to a chestnut can only produce a chestnut, because the two recessive chestnut genes are present. However, a chestnut can result from mating two bays or two grays, or one of each, if each parent carries the recessive chestnut gene.

BEYOND BASE COLOR Broadly speaking, horses with red points (lower legs, muzzle, tips of the ears, and mane and tail) are base-red. Horses with black points are base-black. Color is also affected by a gene for distribution of black, which produces black points on base-black horses.

Some colors happen because a recessive factor "dilutes" a more dominant gene. Dilution genes form the third and fourth layers of color modification. With the cremello gene, a bay becomes a buckskin, brown becomes red dun, and chestnut becomes palomino. When there are two recessive dilution factors, the bay becomes perlino, or almost white with rust-colored mane and tail. A chestnut becomes a cremello, creamy white with light mane and tail and blue eyes.

The dun factor dilutes both red and black pigment, producing yellowish or pinkish red horses and horses with dorsal and shoulder stripes and barring on the front legs in base-red horses. In base-black horses, it produces the grulla coloration.

In spite of their different coat **colors**, these youngsters are all base-black, as shown by their black points.

A fifth layer, the roan gene, mixes white hair evenly throughout the coat without affecting the color of the face and legs.

Other genetic layers produce the various Paint and Appaloosa patterns. And if a horse has the single dominant gray gene, the horse will be gray in adulthood.

BREEDING FOR COLOR In order to breed for color, you need to know if that color is dominant, recessive, or heterozygous (mixed). You may not know the genotypes of each parent, although you can get clues by seeing the colors of their previous foals and checking the colors of their ancestors; this will help indicate the presence of recessive genes.

Dominant colors are bay, gray, tobiano paint, blanket Appaloosa, and line-backed dun. Recessive colors are chestnut, perlino, and cremello. Mixed colors are white, roan, buckskin, and palomino. For black, there must be multiple traits present, and the color can occur even if the parents aren't black.

➤ *See also face markings; genetics; individual colors*

COLOR THROUGH THE AGES

It appears that bay, or bay dun, is the ancestral horse color, seen in cave paintings and in genetic testing going back 35,000 years. Other colors are more recent mutations. Black became common on the Iberian Peninsula between 5500 and 4950 BCE. Chestnut appeared in Siberia around 3000 BCE and spread rapidly; by the Bronze Age, 28 percent of horses carried the chestnut mutation.

colostrum The initial milk a mare produces after foaling.

➤ *See also foaling*

colt An uncastrated young male horse, from birth up to four years of age.

colt-starting competitions Competitions in which trainers are given a fixed period of time, from a few hours to a few days, to introduce an untrained young horse of riding age to saddle, and to performance in front of a crowd. The competitions generally use range-bred Quarter Horses off large Western ranches. The Road to the Horse is an example of a colt-starting competition.

➤ *See also training competitions*

combined driving A competitive sport that tests both horses and carriage drivers in a kind of triathlon. Participants compete in driven dressage, marathon (a cross-country course with obstacles), and cones (a tight course driven between sets of cones with tennis balls balanced on their tops). Combined driving was invented by Britain's Prince Philip to be the driving equivalent of eventing.

combined grazing A technique for the efficient utilization of pasture, in which horses and other animals (generally cattle) are allowed to graze together in the same area. Each species consumes different grasses, ensuring that maximum benefit is derived from the pasture.

COMBINED DRIVING

combined immune deficiency (CID)

A genetic disorder in which a foal's immune system fails to develop fully, leading to infections and death. CID is found in Arabian and part-Arabian horses. There is no effective treatment, but the disorder can be prevented by testing for the presence of the genetic defect through DNA analysis. Carrier horses can still be used for breeding as long as the mate is free of CID. However, this practice is discouraged, as a carrier can pass the defective gene to offspring.

combined training (CT)

➤ *See eventing*

command of preparation, command of execution

Verbal commands used by instructors to ensure that riders perform movements or drills in a co-ordinated manner. The "command of preparation" alerts riders that a movement is about to begin; the "command of execution" signals riders to begin the movement.

A half-halt is a command of preparation for a horse. A verbal half-halt, such as "and . . ." or the horse's name, serves the same purpose while longeing.

➤ *See also half-halt*

commands

Verbal cues used to initiate behavior. Horses respond most readily to concise commands issued in a firm, authoritative tone. Commonly used commands include the words "Walk," "Trot," and "Canter," as well as sounds like the "kiss" or "cluck." Perhaps the most critical command is the one that stops all motion, most frequently "Ho" or "Whoa."

Voice commands taught on the lead or longe line lay the foundation for leg cues that are used while mounted. Horses learn by conditioning. Applying leg pressure consistently while using a verbal command the horse has learned previously leads to a conditioned response, which ultimately makes the verbal command obsolete. Research indicates that most horses require 25 to 100 repetitions of such verbal/leg command combinations before they learn to respond *consistently* to leg cues alone.

➤ *See also clicker training; cues*

common

Having a plain, coarse appearance.

competitive trail ride

A timed, judged ride over a predetermined trail within a specified period. Both horse and rider are scored. Each horse starts with 100 points and is docked points over the course of the ride based 40 percent on condition, 45 percent on soundness, and 15 percent on trail ability and manners. The horse with the fewest penalty points wins. Riders are judged on horsemanship, including grooming, trail equitation, and trail care.

A competitive trail ride covers 15 to 40 miles (24–64 km) per day, and lasts one to three days. The primary goal of this long-distance event is to maintain each horse in good physical condition throughout the ride. There are events for riders of all skill levels, many conducted under guidelines established by the North American Trail Ride Conference (NATRC).

➤ *See also endurance riding; extreme trail/mountain trail competitions*

COMPETITIVE TRAIL RIDING DIVISIONS

Three types of trail rides are sanctioned by the North American Trail Ride Conference, and there are three divisions. Rides are designated as one-day (type B), two-day (type A), or three-day (type AA). Divisions are as follows:

- **Novice.** For new competitors (Junior, Lightweight, and Heavyweight classes)

- **Competitive/Pleasure (CP).** For more experienced riders (no weight restrictions)

- **Open.** For advanced riders, featuring longer distances and a faster pace (Junior, Lightweight, and Heavyweight classes)

In Lightweight classes the rider and tack combined weigh 100 to 189 pounds (45–85.7 kg).

In Heavyweight classes rider and tack combined weigh 190 pounds (86 kg) and up.

complete feeds Processed feeds with a high fiber content designed to provide most of the fiber a horse needs as well as the other nutrients. Complete feeds are useful for horses whose grazing time or hay intake is limited. For senior horses with bad teeth, they can be mixed with water to form a mash.

concentrates Dense, high-energy feeds, usually cereal grains.

condition of horse This term often refers to the fitness or physical abilities of a horse; however, it can also concern the amount of fat a horse's body contains. You can estimate a horse's condition (fat levels) by feeling his back, ribs, neck, shoulder, withers, and the area directly above the tail. *See also "Judging a Horse's Body Condition," facing page*

conditioning program A planned, gradual increase in a horse's activity level (both duration and intensity) over a specified period. Achieving a moderate level of muscle and respiratory fitness typically requires three to six months of regular exercise. Strengthening bone is a longer process that relies on prolonged, low-intensity activities.

conditioning, as a training term A process of accustoming an animal to a stimulus. "Classical conditioning" is the association of an unconscious physical response with a conditioned stimulus. Pavlov's dogs heard their dinner bell and began drooling, a response not under their control. "Operant conditioning" is the association of a consciously chosen physical response with a conditioned stimulus. A clicker-trained animal uses learned behaviors to "operate" the clicker and get a treat. "Habituation," the process of teaching a horse to ignore previously frightening sights and sounds, is also a form of conditioning.

➤ *See also clicker training; natural horsemanship*

The contrast is clear between the rescue horse on the left, which rates a 2 or 3 on the **body condition scale**, and the overweight Morgan on the right, which is a 7 or 8.

JUDGING A HORSE'S BODY CONDITION

This chart provides rough guidelines for determining body condition. Some fat is necessary, and the ideal score is 5 or 6.

Score	Description
1 Poor	Extremely thin with no fatty tissue to be felt; ribs, vertebrae, and withers project prominently; bone structure readily observed
2 Very thin	Emaciated; prominent ribs and vertebrae; faintly noticeable bone structure; very thin neck, shoulders, and withers
3 Thin	Ribs easily seen; slight fat cover over ribs, neck, shoulders, and withers but noticeably underweight
4 Moderately thin	Ribs only faintly visible; neck, shoulders, and withers not obviously thin; vertebrae along back prominent
5 Moderate	Ribs cannot be seen but are easily felt; withers are rounded; area above tail feels slightly spongy; back is level over loin; shoulder blends smoothly into body
6 Fleshy	Can barely feel ribs; area above tail feels spongy; slight crease down back over loin may be present
7 Fat	Individual ribs can be felt, but area between them is noticeably fat; crease down back over loin; fat obvious along neck, withers, area above tail, and area behind shoulders
8 Very fat	Difficult to feel ribs; neck is thick; fat can be seen on withers, area above tail, and area behind shoulders; positive crease down back over loin; fat deposited along inner buttocks
9 Obese	Can't feel ribs; bulging fat on neck, withers, area above tail, area behind shoulders, and along inner buttocks, which may touch; deep crease down back over loin; flank is rounded

Based on material developed by Don Henneke

conformation The shape and structure of a horse's body, compared to an ideal or standard of perfection. A horse whose physical characteristics approach the ideal has good conformation. Deviation from the ideal constitutes conformation defects or faults. Some conformation faults limit the horse's performance or lead to unsoundness. Others, such as a Roman nose, are simply considered unattractive.

Few horses have perfect conformation, so a buyer should have realistic expectations when selecting a horse. However, conformation should not be dismissed as merely a matter of aesthetics. It plays a critical role in how efficiently the horse performs, how comfortable he is to ride, and whether he is likely to remain sound over a lifetime of riding or work. Horses with poor conformation generally have higher maintenance costs due to special veterinary, farrier, and other care. Evaluating conformation is particularly important when selecting breeding stock.

Many conformation standards can be applied to virtually all horses (see chart). However, the standard for a specific breed or type may vary with respect to certain features. The term "breed standard" refers to the written standards that comprise ideal conformation within a particular breed.
➤ *See also "Anatomy of the Horse," page 6; balanced conformation*

conjunctivitis An inflammation of the conjunctiva, the mucous membrane that covers the front of the eyeball and lines the eyelids; also known as pink eye. It is generally caused by contact with flies or other environmental irritants.

A horse with conjunctivitis will commonly squint or develop swollen eyelids. Tears or yellow pus may be discharged from the eyes. The condition is readily treatable with eye drops or ointment, but early intervention is important; untreated conjunctivitis can lead to impaired vision. During times of heavy insect infestation, equipping your horse with a fly mask can help prevent conjunctivitis.
➤ *See also eye problems; vision*

Connemara *See page 70*

consignor A person who puts a horse up for sale at an auction or on a consignment basis.

constipation A slowdown or stoppage of fecal transit, sometimes called fecal impaction. Constipation

CONFORMATION: WHAT TO LOOK FOR IN A HORSE

Conformation standards vary by breed. They also vary according to the type of work a horse will perform. Features desirable in a pleasure horse, such as well-laid-back shoulders, may be drawbacks in a working draft horse. The characteristics on the following list are most useful in evaluating pleasure horse conformation.

Overall Structure

* Well-balanced body with weight distributed appropriately
* Muscling long and lean, not bulky
* Attractive general appearance

Head and Neck

* Head size proportional with the rest of horse
* Wide forehead to provide adequate cranial space
* Eyes large enough to provide good peripheral vision
* Head tapering to a small muzzle with wide nostrils
* Matching upper and lower jaws, with upper and lower incisors meeting evenly
* Long, flexible neck with a slight arch or crest to serve as balancing arm for horse
* Neck meeting well-defined withers

Body or Barrel

* Deep heart girth
* Rib cage wider than shoulders (wide barrel)
* Long, well-sloped shoulder; ideal shoulder slope is 45 degrees
* Withers prominent enough to help anchor the saddle in place
* Well-muscled, strong back; loin that is not excessively long
* Back running smoothly into strong, deep hindquarters with sufficient distance from point of hip to point of buttock
* Well-muscled hindquarters

Legs and Feet

- Strong, straight, well-placed legs
- Weight distributed evenly on all four legs when horse is standing square
- Distance between feet the same as distance between forearms at chest
- An imaginary straight line drawn from point of shoulder should go down through center of front legs
- Knees large, flat in front, and well proportioned
- Cannon bone centered under knee; appears wide when viewed from the side
- Hind legs straight when viewed from rear; an imaginary line drawn from point of buttock should go down through the center of the hind legs
- Large, sturdy hock joint that appears flat on the outside edge
- Pasterns of adequate length
- Proper angle between pastern and foot, namely, a 45- to 55-degree angle in the front legs and a 49- to 59-degree angle in the rear
- Well-shaped feet large enough to support the horse
- Feet pairs in exactly the same size and shape
- Center of foot directly under center of fetlock
- Toes of the front hooves pointing directly forward
- Hooves wide at the heel, not contracted
- When horse is in motion, legs and feet move forward in straight lines; hind feet travel same path as front

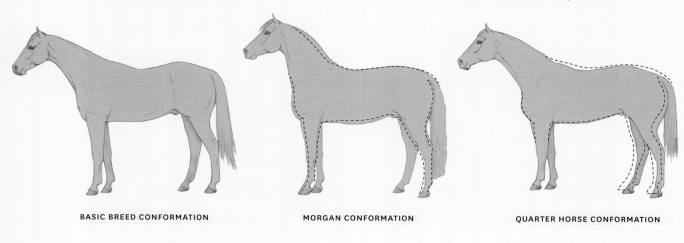

BASIC BREED CONFORMATION

MORGAN CONFORMATION

QUARTER HORSE CONFORMATION

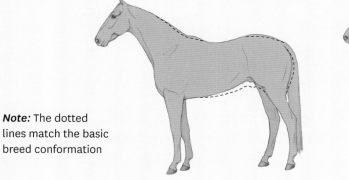

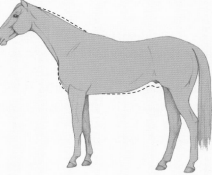

Note: The dotted lines match the basic breed conformation

STANDARDBRED CONFORMATION

THOROUGHBRED CONFORMATION

CONNEMARA

A popular Irish riding pony known for an effortless gait and jumping abilities. The Connemara descends from native ponies, later crossed with Arabians, Andalusians, and Welsh Ponies. The breed association has worked since the 1920s to keep the older bloodlines going and to breed the best to the best.

This relatively tall pony can grow to a height of 14.2 hands. The Connemara is a superb child's pony, jumper, and driving pony, and can even be used for light draft work. It is a staple of the pony hunter/jumper scene. Connemaras are predominantly gray or dun, but black, bay, or brown ones also occur.

often results in a lethargic horse who eats little or nothing. The horse may lie down for unusually long periods and may fail to pass normal amounts of manure and urine. Factors that can contribute to constipation include ingestion of bedding or dry feed, dehydration, and lack of exercise. Simple constipation can be cured by administering mineral oil through a stomach tube, followed up with plenty of drinking water.

contact The connection between the horse's mouth and the rider's hands, through the reins. A horse is said to be "on contact" when he reaches into the reins, stretching them between his mouth and the rider's hand to create a light, elastic connection. The rider does not create contact by tightening the reins; instead, she creates energy from behind and receives that energy as the horse reaches forward.

contest events
➤ *See mounted games*

contest horse A horse who has been trained to participate in contest events (mounted games). Speed, agility, and responsiveness are the key attributes of a contest horse.

contracted heel A heel that is atypically narrow. The frog, the foot's shock absorber, shrinks or shrivels, and the sole of the foot may become dished or concave. If left untreated, the condition can lead to permanent or long-term lameness.

Contraction of the heel is generally caused by injury, excessive dryness, or improper shoeing, including some cutting out of the frog when the horse is shod. The condition usually affects the front feet, but the back feet may also suffer.

Lengthening the toe, or front of the foot, also causes contracted heels because the extra length eliminates the slight expansion the entire hoof experiences when the foot strikes the ground. Lameness from other causes that alters the way the horse's feet strike the ground can also cause contracted heels. A certain amount of pressure on the frog is necessary for a horse's foot to grow the proper amount of heel.

The condition can be treated through corrective trimming and the use of special shoes, but recovery may take a year or more.

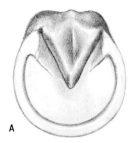 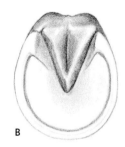

A   B

Unlike a normal foot (A), a **contracted heel** (B) is longer than it is wide.

cooler A light blanket draped over a horse to wick away moisture and keep him from getting chilled after a bath or vigorous activity. Coolers are frequently used between classes at competitions, where they help keep the horse clean and neat.

COOLER

cooling down, after exercise The process of bringing a horse to a normally cool temperature after exercise; also called "cooling out." A proper cool-down prevents lactic acid from accumulating in the horse's muscles and causing soreness.

Begin the cool-down by walking your horse for 10 to 15 minutes, either under saddle or in hand, even if he is breathing normally and no longer sweating. If the horse is hot, hose or sponge his legs, his belly, and the underside of his neck. Use cool (*not* cold) or lukewarm water, scraping off excess water until it feels cool. Let the horse's back cool off naturally; once his body temperature is normal, you can sponge off the saddle marks. Use a sweat scraper to flick excess water from his coat. On a sunny day, he can dry off on his own, either in the pasture or in his stall, but in cold weather you must make sure he is dry before you leave him.

After sponging the horse down, walk him until his body temperature is normal and he is dry enough to groom. You can rub him down with a towel or hay wisp to hasten the drying process, or you can drape a wool cooler over his back to help wick away moisture. Give a limited amount of cool (*not* cold) drinking water immediately after exercise if he is being walked, but wait until his body reaches normal temperature before providing him with free access to water and before feeding him any grain.

➤ *See also cooler; hay wisp*

COPD
➤ *See heaves*

cordeo A neck rope used instead of a bridle to guide the horse. A cordeo may be made of anything flexible—leather, rope, even baling twine. It should rest at the base of the neck like a breastplate, not higher up where it could press against the trachea. It is impossible to use a cordeo to compel a horse to do anything; rather it is a communication tool used to build a good relationship with the horse. In addition to building that relationship, however, long-term training is needed.

corium The blood-rich tissue that lines and nourishes the inside of the hoof.

corn (feed) A high-starch, energy-dense grain; also called maize. Because corn is low in fiber, it is easy to overfeed, making horses fat or "hot" (difficult to control). Corn is prone to mycotoxin contamination, which can be fatal to horses. It can cause orthopedic diseases in growing horses, and is being phased out of many commercial horse feeds. Corn may appear in feeds as a distillers' dried grain, a by-product of ethanol production, which increases protein and B-complex vitamins.

Corn is commonly fed in shelled form, but some horse owners feed it directly from the cob. Younger and older horses may have trouble chewing whole corn. In such cases, the corn can be served rolled or cracked. All corn should be dry and a year or more old before it is fed, to minimize the chance that a horse will consume mold- or fungus-infested kernels. However, because poisoning from spoiled corn can be fatal, it's wisest to avoid corn altogether.

➤ *See also concentrates; mold/fungi in feed*

corn (medical condition) A bruise at the buttress where the hoof wall curves to join the bars, usually caused by an overgrown shoe or wedged stone. It is often visible as a reddened area, and it may feel hot and tender. Corns can develop when the horse steps on a sharp object, but they are more often the product of poorly fitting shoes or shoes that are left on for too long. A severe corn can cause infection and lameness.

Treatment often simply involves removal of the shoe followed by a period of rest and healing. If the injury becomes infected, it should be treated as an abscess, by a veterinarian. The hoof will then need daily soaking and continued protection until the healing process is complete.

One reason to clean a horse's feet frequently is to detect corns before they become problematic. Corns are not always visible, even during trimming, but they are detectable with a hoof tester, an instrument that looks like a large pincers and is used to put pressure on the sole. If the horse flinches, you've found a corn—or something more serious, such as an abscess.

cornea The transparent front portion of the eyeball. A horse's cornea is susceptible to injury from tree branches or any other object that makes contact with it.

The result is significant pain for the horse and a possible infection. Although many corneal injuries heal without intervention, an infected cornea should be treated with antibiotic ointment.

➤ *See also eye problems; vision*

corner feeder A feeder for hay and/or grain, mounted in the corner of a stall.

➤ *See also feeding and nutrition*

coronary band/coronet band The area of soft tissue directly above a horse's hoof, where the hoof meets the leg. The hoof grows down from the coronary band; therefore, any injury or bruise to the coronary band will affect hoof development and can cause a horse to become lame. It is essential for a horse's foot health to keep the coronary band in good condition. If it is injured, veterinary attention is advised to prevent the formation of proud flesh, which could hamper hoof production and cause deformity and/or lameness. Horse owners often use bell boots to cover and protect this sensitive area, particularly when trailering.

➤ *See also lameness; proud flesh*

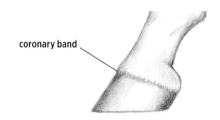

coronary band

corral A turnout area designed to confine horses while providing them with an opportunity for moderate exercise. Corrals are generally square or round, and are often attached to barns for convenience.

A corral should be more than an effective containment area; it should also be a safe, open place to romp. A durable perimeter fence 5 to 6 feet (1.5–1.8 m) high is standard, with no sharp edges or protruding nails. Size is also a factor; the possibility of injury increases as the size of the enclosure decreases. A typical corral is 1,600 feet (488 m) square.

➤ *See also paddock; pasture, horses on*

corrected feet Feet that have been trimmed and shaped to mimic ideal foot conformation. Owners of show horses sometimes engage in correction in order to make their horses appear more attractive. Some believe that corrective shoeing will fix certain leg and movement faults. However, this sort of alteration can impair the ability of the feet to absorb shock, and it may lead to chronically sore feet or even lameness.

corrective trimming Trimming performed on a horse's foot to change the shape, to alter the relationship between the toe and the heel, or to correct a significant conformational problem. Trimming can be quite helpful when it is done to correct a defect or help an injured foot heal. However, trimming done for purely cosmetic reasons can lead to foot problems.
➤ *See also barefoot trimming; hoof*

costume class A riding event partially judged on the horse and rider's costume. Arabian classes feature desert costumes, including colorful capes, coats, pantaloons, scarves, sashes, and headdresses. For Appaloosa events, riders don historical costumes from American frontier and settlement days, with special emphasis on the historic garb of the Nez Percé Indians. However elaborate the costumes, competitors are judged primarily on the skill of the rider and the performance of the horse.

counter-canter/counter-lope A balanced working or collected canter on the outside lead with proper counter-flexion. This is not the same as cantering on the wrong lead. Counter-canter work can significantly improve a horse's strength and balance.

MEDIEVAL COSTUME

NATIVE AMERICAN COSTUME

ARABIAN COSTUME

73

counter-flexion Flexing the neck of the horse toward the outside of the arena or circle. In general, a horse's neck and body should follow the arc of the circle he is traveling. Persistent counter-flexion is a sign of a balance problem. But some school figures such as renvers (haunches out) can be done with the horse flexed toward the outside of the arena.
➤ *See also renvers*

courbette One of the airs above the ground performed by high-level dressage horses. Balancing on his hind legs, the horse hops forward several times.
➤ *See also airs above the ground; Classical High School; Lipizzan*

course designer A specialist in the development of courses for horse shows and events. Designers must be licensed for rated or accredited competitions. Course designers must strike a balance between competitive challenge and the safety of horses and riders or drivers.

cowboy curtain A trail obstacle made of long strips of heavy fabric or nylon hung from an overhead rail.
➤ *See also trail trial*

Cowboy Dressage
➤ *See Western dressage*

cowboy mounted shooting A fast-paced Western sport in which competitors ride patterns while shooting at balloons with a pistol loaded with blank ammunition. The cartridges are loaded with black powder that can explode a balloon from a distance of 15 feet (4.6 m). Riders are scored on time plus penalties, which are given for faults such as missing a balloon, dropping a gun, riding off-course, or falling off a horse.

Tack and clothing are modeled on the American West of the late 1800s and only .45-caliber single-action revolvers similar to ones used from that time period are allowed. Women may compete in pants, skirts, or in period riding habits, and some women compete riding sidesaddle. Older-style Western saddles with a deep seat

COWBOY CURTAIN

COWBOY MOUNTED SHOOTING

A horse with good **cow sense** works cattle the way a herding dog works sheep.

and high cantle are used. Horses may be of any breed; speed, agility, and a tolerance for loud noises are key. Both riders and horses often use earplugs. There are divisions for all ages, as well as a therapeutic riding version.
➤ *See also mounted archery*

cow-hocked
A conformation fault in which the hocks are closer together than the fetlocks. The defect can stress the stifle and hip joints; if severe, it could cause calcified growths on bones in the hock joint and subsequent lameness. However, a mild case of cow hocks can actually be a virtue in working horses, since such conformation allows the stifles to clear the flanks.
➤ *See also conformation*

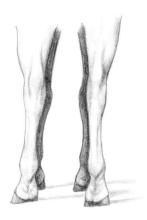

This is an acceptable degree of **cow hocks**.

cow sense
1. In a horse, an enthusiasm for working cows coupled with the assertive nature and know-how necessary to control their movements. A horse who has cow sense may be described as "cowy." Cow sense appears to be a heritable trait; it is marked in horses of Spanish origin like Andalusians and Quarter Horses.
2. In a rider, the ability to closely observe and anticipate the behavior of a cow.

crack
A separation or break in the hoof wall. Vertical cracks are referred to by location: toe cracks, quarter cracks, heel cracks. Cracks originating in the coronary band are called sand or coronary cracks, while those starting at the bottom of the hoof are called grass cracks. Surface cracks are shallow fissures in the hoof wall. A horizontal crack is called a blowout.

cracked heel
➤ *See scratches*

cradle
A collarlike device placed on a horse's neck to limit movement of the head, preventing him from chewing on wounds, bandages, or blankets.

crease nail puller A farrier's tool used to remove the nails that hold a horse's shoe in place; the tool reaches into the crease of the shoe and grabs the nail heads, allowing the farrier to pull out the nails.

cremello coloring Creamy white, with a light mane and tail and blue eyes.
➤ *See also color, of horse*

crest The topline of the neck, from poll to withers. A horse with a thick, arched neck is said to be "cresty." Stallions often have thicker crests than do mares.

crest release A maneuver in which a rider moves her hands forward along a horse's crest while the horse is jumping, to avoid using the reins for balance.

The heavy **crest** on the Bardigiano is part of this Italian breed's conformation.

CREST RELEASE

cribbing An equine bad habit, until recently thought to arise principally from boredom. New research associates it with stomach pain from excess acidity or ulcers. Cribbing involves biting on the edge of a board or clamping onto any solid object with the front teeth while simultaneously arching the neck and gulping air, producing a grunting or burping sound. Some people refer to this practice as "windsucking," and horses prone to the behavior are known as cribbers or windsuckers.

Although it sounds rather innocuous, cribbing is associated with problems that include indigestion, colic, excessive weight loss, and prematurely worn teeth. Once established, the habit is difficult to break. It becomes addictive, in part because the horse gets a bit of a high from doing it; research indicates that cribbing triggers the release of endorphins, which stimulates the pleasure center in the horse's brain. Cribbing may also relieve stomach pain.

Cribbing may have a genetic component, so adjusting the diet won't always stop it. To discourage cribbing, many people use a cribbing muzzle or a cribbing strap, a collarlike device that that prevents the horse from expanding his esophagus in order to suck air. Surgery, which involves cutting muscles in the throatlatch area, is the only long-term remedy. It is fairly effective if the habit is not well established, but some horses will relapse with time. Dietary measures, such as feeding a forage-based diet or adding antacids to the diet, may also be helpful.

CRIOLLO/ARGENTINE CRIOLLO

The Argentine version of the mustang; a robust horse descended from Barb and Andalusian horses of the Spanish conquest. Many of the Spanish conquistadores' horses escaped, and their descendants adapted to the extreme heat and cold of the Pampas.

A sturdy, thickset horse with heavy muscling and a straight or convex profile, the Criollo is outstandingly tough. It was crossed with Thoroughbreds to produce the highly valued Argentine Polo Pony.

➤ *See also polo*

crop A short riding stick or whip used to reinforce leg aids. A crop is usually made of flexible fiberglass, 16 to 25 inches (41–63 cm) long, with a leather loop or tongue on the end. A bat is generally a shorter whip with a wider leather piece that makes a popping sound when used. Under most circumstances, riders do not need to carry a crop. If one is necessary, it should be held in the palm of one hand and applied only if the horse does not respond to leg aids. A crop may also be used to lightly touch the shoulder to alert the horse to an upcoming jump. Some horses have learned to fear the crop and need to be habituated to it. For others, the mere sight of a crop in the rider's hand eliminates the need to actually use it.

➤ *See also whip (as aid)*

cross-bred A term that describes a horse whose parents are of two different breeds. Such a horse may be called a cross for short, as in the term "draft cross."

cross-breeding Intentionally breeding a horse of one breed to a horse of another. The production of an outstanding foal requires two parents who are themselves outstanding; however, the results are not entirely predictable. A thorough understanding of the traits and bloodlines of both parents is essential to achieving the desired results; even then, surprises happen.

cross-canter/disunited canter A canter in which the horse leads with one foot in the front and the opposite foot in the back. Cross-cantering is an undesirable habit created by stiffness in the horse's body; it is uncomfortable to ride.

cross-country riding The second phase of three-phase eventing; cross-country involves galloping a course through fields and woodland with natural or natural-looking jumps. The course may incorporate uphill jumps, downhill jumps, logs, fences, ditches, and streams, along with varied terrain. Over the past decade or so, cross-country courses have become shorter, with less emphasis on fitness and galloping, and more on technically difficult obstacles. Some in the eventing community have begun to push back against this trend, as it has resulted in an increasing death rate among upper-level horses and riders.

cross-firing An interference when the hind foot strikes the diagonally opposite front hoof; mainly a fault in pacers and long-backed horses.

cross-tying, cross-ties Tying a horse with two ropes, one on each side of its halter. The cross-ties should be attached to sturdy walls, rails, or posts, and the snaps should allow for quick release. A horse should never be cross-tied in a bridle; if he pulls back against the bit, he could injure his mouth.

Cross-ties are used while grooming or tacking up a horse in its stall or a barn aisle. By limiting side-to-side

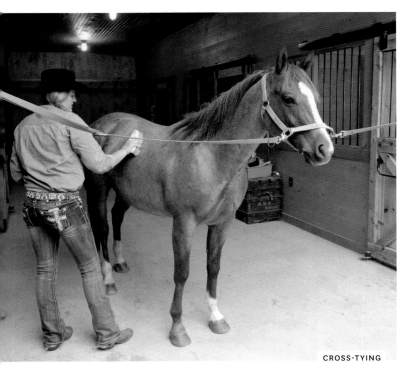

CROSS-TYING

motion, they diminish the likelihood of injury to both horse and handler and allow free access to both sides of the horse. Horses need to be taught to stand in cross-ties. Otherwise, the very motion-limitation that makes them so convenient may be frightening.

croup The top of the rump, corresponding to the sacral vertebrae.

croupade One of the airs above the ground, similar to the ballotade. In the ballotade the horse shows the soles of its hind feet; in the croupade it does not.
➤ *See also airs above the ground; ballotade*

crupper/crupper strap A strap that fastens under the tail, used to hold the saddle or harness in place. In driving, cruppers are standard. In riding, they are relatively rare, used mostly for trail riding in steep terrain or to stabilize a saddle on a round pony.

cryptorchid A male horse with either one or two testicles that did not fully descend into the scrotum; also called a ridgeling. Castration of a cryptorchid is a major surgical procedure. The medical term for the condition is "cryptorchidism."

cue A signal that a horse has learned, which tells him that a specific behavior is being requested. Cues may be verbal or physical; the word "walk," leg pressure at the girth, and a step forward taken by a handler on the ground are all cues for the horse to walk. Horses also respond to unconscious cues, generally physical signals we have built into our training routine without being aware of it. You may think your horse is disobeying or anticipating, when he is responding to a cue you don't know you are giving.

curb (of hock) Name given to swelling of and, later, a permanent enlargement or thickening of the calcaneocuboid ligament, which is found about 4 inches (10 cm) below the point of the hock on the inner side. The condition is commonly caused by a sprain that can result when a horse slips on wet ground in such a way that the hind legs slide forward under his belly. Horses with too much angle to their hocks, or sickle-hocked horses, are prone to this type of sprain. Treatment options vary, so contact your veterinarian.

curb bit A bit with shanks, used in conjunction with a curb strap or curb chain under the chin. Curb bits deliver signals to a horse via leverage pressure applied to the bars of the mouth, the chin, and to a degree the poll. The most common type of bit for Western riding, the curb bit is also used in English riding, usually as part of a double bridle.

➤ *See also bradoon; double bridle; snaffle; spade bit*

curry/currycomb To curry is to groom a horse's coat using a currycomb. The comb itself is a round or rectangular flat tool usually made of rubber or plastic. It has stubby, semipointed teeth that serve to loosen dirt, hair, and dander for later removal with brushes. The currycomb is applied with a vigorous, circular motion, which stimulates the oil glands, contributing to the health of the coat. It should not be used on sensitive areas such as the lower legs. Some people use it primarily to clean the other brushes every few strokes.

➤ *See also grooming*

Cushing's disease/Cushing's syndrome/PPID
A common metabolic disorder that primarily affects older horses; the scientific name for it is pituitary pars intermedia dysfunction (PPID). It is characterized by overactivity of the adrenal glands, frequently in response to a tumor of the pituitary gland. The adrenal glands are responsible for secreting hormones called corticosteroids; excessive secretion causes symptoms such as frequent urination, weight loss, persistent infections, laminitis, and a coat that fails to shed. Cushing's disease is not curable, but can be managed.

cutter

1. A rider who participates in the Western show event known as cutting; also, the first rider to enter the herd in the Western event called team penning. This rider "cuts" individual steers from a herd.

2. A horse who participates in cutting.

3. A lightweight single-horse sleigh. These are used in the West in cutter races.

➤ *See also cutting; team penning*

cutting A Western event in which a horse and rider demonstrate their skill at choosing and separating one

Having long hair in the summer, a pendulous belly, and a tendency to founder are all symptoms of **Cushing's disease**.

steer from a herd and successfully blocking its attempts to rejoin the herd. During this event, mounted helpers known as "herd holders" and "turnback riders" control the remainder of the herd and attempt to keep the cut steer facing the horse and rider. Each contestant performs for two and a half minutes. Cutting is a high-stakes competitive sport with a nationwide following and an active youth organization. Young cutters compete for college scholarships, adult cutters for prize money. Any breed can compete, but Quarter Horses dominate the sport; about 96 percent of cutting horses are Quarter Horses.

cutting teeth The somewhat painful emergence of first teeth in a young horse. While cutting teeth, the horse may seek to relieve gum soreness by chewing on materials including wood, metal, and rope. Many behavioral problems encountered while training young horses can be attributed to pain from cutting teeth.

CVI
➤ *See certificate of veterinary inspection (CVI)*

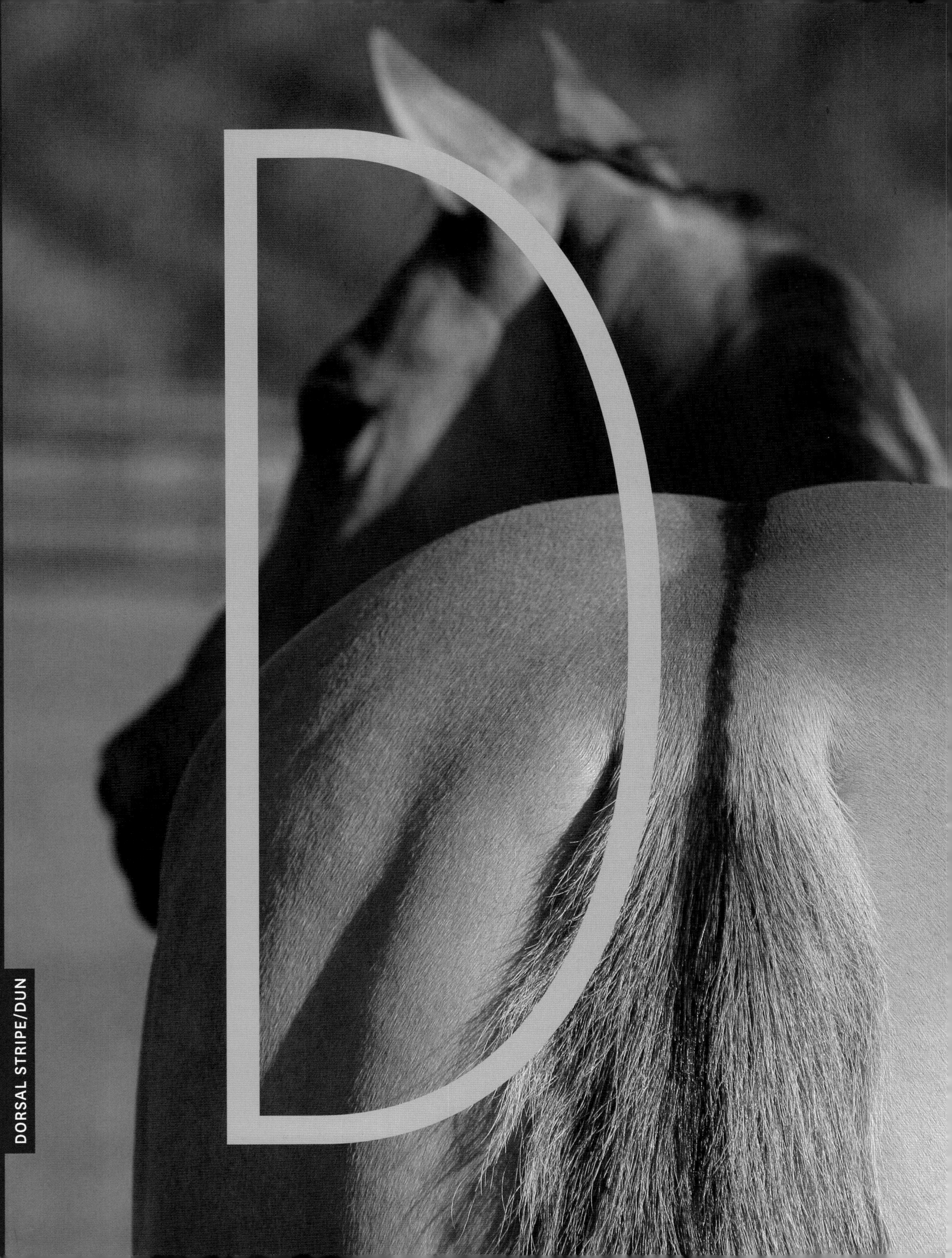

DALES PONY

A large pony (14–14.2 hands high), usually black or brown, native to northern England. Originally a pack pony, the Dales Pony is an excellent mover used today for dressage, hunting, and driving. The Dales Pony almost became extinct in the 1950s. The global population is small but rising. **Livestock Conservancy status: Critical**

dally To wrap the end of a rope around the saddle horn. Dallying is a technique often used by participants in cattle roping events.

dam A mother horse. Foals are described as being "out of" a specific dam.

dandy brush A stiff-bristled brush used to remove dirt, loose hair, and scurf from a horse's coat. The brush, sometimes known as a mud brush, is applied with short strokes and a whisking action. The bristles should be cleaned periodically with a currycomb.

dapples Rings or spots of color on the horse's coat that are a different color from the rest of the coat. Dapples are an inherited trait frequently seen on gray horses during the years when their coats are lightening toward white, but also seen on bays and sometimes chestnuts. Dapples appear after the winter coat is shed, and are brought out by good grooming and good nutrition.
➤ *See also color, of horse*

dark bay coloring A brown horse whose coat is so dark that it almost appears black; legs (above any white markings), mane, and tail are black.
➤ *See also bay; color, of horse*

dark horse A relatively unknown competitor that makes an unexpectedly good showing.

Though commonly associated with gray coloring, **dapples** may also appear on a bay or chestnut coat.

darkness, riding in When riding in darkness, you can't see obstacles, holes, changes of terrain, or protruding tree branches. Your horse can see them better than you can, but he may not share your concern for overhead hazards. If you're riding on a road, drivers will have difficulty spotting you, and your horse could be panicked by oncoming headlights. If you must ride in darkness, use reflectors and reflective tape, strap a headlamp on over your helmet, wear light-colored clothing, and stick to familiar territory.

DARTMOOR PONY

A small British pony breed (12 hands high), hardy, sure-footed, and gentle. Britain has had native ponies for more than ten thousand years. The rocky terrain and sparse grazing of Dartmoor, in southeastern England, produced a strong, agile pony that was used in the tin mines for centuries.

Dartmoor Ponies can easily carry an adult but also make excellent children's mounts, good jumpers, and fine driving ponies. They are usually bay, brown, or black, with minimal white markings. **Livestock Conservancy status: Threatened**

deadened tissues Tissues on a horse's body that have become numb. The condition is most often associated with a too-small halter or a bit trauma. Pressure can deaden tissues, reducing or eliminating the horse's ability to respond to cues.
➤ *See also mouth, hard or soft*

dead-sided A term used to describe a horse who does not consistently respond to leg cues from the rider. School horses commonly become dead-sided when they learn to ignore ineffective riders.

dealer A person who buys and sells horses on a professional basis. Reputable dealers are skilled evaluators of horses; they can be of service in helping buyers find horses appropriate for their needs. However, a comprehensive veterinary exam is recommended prior to any purchase.

deciduous teeth The "baby," or temporary, teeth that emerge in the first nine months of a horse's life. The horse's first deciduous incisor appears at birth. All of the temporary teeth have typically been shed by the time the horse is four to five years old.
➤ *See also dental problems*

deep digital flexor tendon A band or cord of connective tissue at the rear of a horse's leg. Like other tendons, this one serves to transmit the action of the muscles to which it is connected. It flexes the bones of the lower leg.

deep going Soft, wet ground, called deep going or heavy footing, can be dangerous for a horse. Be careful not to take your horse at high speed through terrain with deep going. If a portion of your pasture tends to be wet and spongy, you can add a layer of sand or gravel to firm it up.

deep seat Riding with long stirrups, with the seat bones in the deepest part of the saddle. The thigh is as vertical as is consistent with proper position, and there is more weight on the seat than in the light seat.
➤ *See also light seat*

deficiency diseases Health problems that are triggered or exacerbated by nutritional deficiency. These include, but are not limited to, colic, respiratory ailments, rickets, hyperparathyroidism, vitamin A deficiency, dehydration, anemia, and abortion. To minimize the possibility of deficiency-related disease, feed your horse a balanced ration. If your hay or pasture are poor, feed a

forage-balancing supplement. Be aware, however, that overfeeding a horse can also lead to health problems.
➤ *See also dehydration; feeding and nutrition*

dehydration
A condition in which body fluids are abnormally depleted. Horses need to drink 5 to 20 gallons (19–76 L) of water per day, depending on size, age, the condition of the horse, and prevailing weather conditions. Horses tend to drink less in cold or wet weather.

Under normal circumstances, you can avoid dehydration by allowing your horse free access to plenty of fresh drinking water. However, dehydration can happen quickly in certain circumstances. In hot weather a horse working hard can lose nearly 4 gallons (15 L) of water per hour. Also, many horses won't drink unfamiliar water, and often refuse to drink from a running stream. If your horse is fussy about water, truck a supply along with him to competitions. Trail riders can carry a collapsible pail for dipping water out of streams.

A severe case of diarrhea can dehydrate and kill a horse within a day. Consult a veterinarian if your horse begins producing watery manure.

Dehydration can be a particularly serious problem in a sick foal. The foal may stop nursing, which exacerbates the effects of the illness it is experiencing and further depletes body fluids. The early symptoms of foal dehydration include dullness, listlessness, and skin that has begun to lose its elasticity. As the condition

worsens, the foal's eyes begin to appear sunken and its skin will further lose elasticity, failing to spring back into place when pinched. Shock, kidney failure, and death will result if the loss of fluids is not quickly addressed.
➤ *See also diarrhea; water, for horses*

dental problems
Horses are not prone to cavities, but they can develop other issues with their teeth. Horses two to four years of age are prone to retained caps, wolf teeth, and impacted teeth. They should be examined two times per year, or three times if they are in training or give you cause for alarm. Mature horses can generally get by with an annual exam at the time of vaccination, although twice-a-year checkups may be recommended for elderly horses as well.

Uneven wear can cause teeth to develop sharp points or ridges. These can be removed by floating—filing the teeth with a rasp. If left untreated, teeth with sharp ridges or points can make chewing a painful and/or inefficient activity, leaving the horse susceptible to starvation, colic, and impaction.

As a horse ages, he may begin to lose teeth or wear them down to the gums. Tooth loss can also interfere with chewing and digestion. If your older horse begins

THE PINCH TEST FOR DEHYDRATION

To test for dehydration, pull a fold of skin on your horse's neck or shoulder area away from his body. When you release the skin, it should return almost immediately to its normal position flat against the body. If it remains markedly peaked for two to three seconds, some dehydration is probably present. A "standing tent" of skin that lasts five seconds or longer indicates moderate to severe dehydration that may require the attention of a veterinarian.

Adapted from *Stablekeeping* by Cherry Hill

FLOATING A HORSE'S TEETH

SIGNS OF POSSIBLE TOOTH PROBLEMS

- Bad breath
- Chewing with difficulty or eating slowly
- Drooling
- Quidding (dropping wads of food while chewing)
- Hay or grain remnants in drinking water
- Head tossing or other avoidance of the bit
- Loss of appetite
- Reluctance to turn in response to bit
- Tender tooth bump on lower jaw
- Weight loss

to lose weight or eat slowly, or if you notice quids— small wads of chewed forage—on the ground around your feeding area, consult a veterinarian.
➤ *See also age; caps; dentist, equine; float; impaction; teeth; wolf teeth*

dentist, equine A veterinarian who specializes in dental care for horses. General veterinarians know how to float (file down) sharp edges on molars, remove wolf teeth, and pull abscessed or broken teeth. For more complex problems, your vet should refer you to an equine dentist. Be sure to request credentials and references.

Many horsemen entrust dental care to a non-veterinary dental care provider (NVDCP). An NVDCP is nonlicensed and, by definition, does not have a veterinary education. He or she can't legally sedate a horse, and can only use a hand float unless supervised by a veterinarian.

Anyone can claim to be an equine dentist; there is no oversight body. Ideally, an equine dentist should be a licensed vet, with postdoctoral or advanced training in dentistry. Many equine dentists without veterinary training do provide excellent care, however, and will readily refer you to a veterinarian if they come across a situation they can't handle.
➤ *See also dental problems*

derby A race for horses of a specific age; in the United States and Great Britain, derbies are almost always for three-year-olds.

Hunt derbies, popular in Great Britain and recently introduced to the United States, are a jumping competition with two rounds, Classic Hunter and Handy Hunter. Classic Hunter is judged on performance, pace, jumping style, quality, and substance. Handy Hunter is judged on brilliance of pace and handiness. Obstacles are reminiscent of the hunting field. The Handy Hunter round includes options for tight turns, clever jump approaches, hand galloping, and trotting a fence. Scores in the two rounds are combined to produce a winner.

In combined driving derbies, drivers compete on a set course with a combination of marathon obstacles and cones. They are judged on time and penalties.
➤ *See also combined driving; futurities*

dermatitis Any swelling or irritation of the outer layer of skin. Equine dermatitis is commonly caused by parasites, such as mites; these parasites can also carry diseases. However, dermatitis may also be triggered by burns, allergies, tumors, and assorted irritants found in the environment. Symptoms typically include redness, swelling, or lumps; the horse may be seen scratching or rubbing against fences, walls, or similar objects. If you locate a possible problem area, have it checked by a veterinarian before washing, clipping, or brushing the area so that you do not end up destroying the evidence.
➤ *See also fungal infections; hives/wheals/welts; mange; mites; parasites; photosensitization*

DEWORMING

deworming Dosing with medications to kill internal parasites. Worms pose a serious, ongoing threat to the health of every horse. Young horses are particularly vulnerable. A successful deworming program combined with effective pasture management is the best way to minimize this threat.

It used to be standard practice to deworm horses every two months (once a month for foals), or to use a daily dose of pelleted pyrantel tartrate instead. However, as parasites have developed resistance to many deworming drugs, best practice now starts with fecal testing. Your veterinarian can do this, or you can use the kits available through many tack catalogs, and send samples to a lab. Horses who are not shedding large numbers of parasite eggs will need less frequent deworming. Consult your vet for a deworming program that makes the most sense for your particular situation.

For difficult horses, a bit is available that introduces deworming medicine into the bit cavity area. Using this device can ensure that your horse gets his full dose of medication.

Management of pasture areas also helps control parasites; larvae thrive and mature in the warm, moist environment provided by manure. Droppings can be removed and composted, or the clumps of manure can be spread out with a harrow.

➤ *See also bot flies; ivermectin; parasites; pyrantel tartrate/Strongid C; individual parasites and medications; worming*

diagonal

1. Front foot and opposite hind foot. A trotting horse's legs move in diagonal pairs, creating the steady two-beat rhythm of this gait. When a posting rider rises as the left foreleg moves forward, she is said to be "posting on the left diagonal." When riding on the rail in an arena, it is correct to post on the outside diagonal, that is, to rise with the foreleg nearest the rail. Similarly, when riding a circle or other pattern that requires bend, it is correct to post on the diagonal to the outside of the bend to help the horse maintain his balance.

2. During arena work, "crossing the diagonal" means crossing from one corner to the diagonally opposite one, in a straight line through the center.

➤ *See also posting trot*

The trot is a **diagonal gait**.

diagonal gaits Gaits in which diagonally opposite hooves (right front, left rear; right rear, left front) are picked up and set down simultaneously, or nearly so: trot, fox trot, trocha, pasitrote.

diagonal jump A jump of uneven height, with one end shorter than the other.

diarrhea Loose, runny, or liquid stool. In a horse, diarrhea is usually a minor, transient condition caused by overly rich forage, a dietary change, or some other factor; however, it can also be symptomatic of a more serious disorder. Copious watery diarrhea is always sufficient cause to contact a veterinarian, as it can rapidly lead to dehydration. Marked loss of bodily fluids can kill a horse within 24 hours.

Serious diarrhea may signify the presence of an infectious disease, so it is wise to separate a diarrhetic horse from others. Remember to clean your hands, clothing, and equipment after working with a sick horse, so that you don't carry the infection to other horses or prolong your own exposure.

➤ *See also dehydration*

diastema An abnormal gap between teeth. It is also used to describe the interdental space between the horse's incisors and cheek teeth where the bit rests, commonly called the bars.

dichlorvos An organic, phosphorus-containing compound that is used as a deworming medication. Dichlorvos is particularly effective against the larvae of small strongyles. Several treatments given at regular intervals are generally necessary. In some cases, dichlorvos can be effective in controlling worms that have become resistant to other drugs. It is also effective against bot flies.

diestrus The time in a mare's reproductive cycle when she is between periods of estrus (i.e., heat). For most mares, diestrus commences immediately following ovulation and lasts 14 to 19 days.
➤ *See also anestrus; estrus*

diet
➤ *See feeding and nutrition*

digestive system The esophagus, stomach, small intestine, large intestine (cecum and large colon), and small colon.

The horse's stomach is relatively small, with a capacity of just 2 to 5 gallons (7.5 to 19 L). The bulk of digestion takes place in the large intestine, which consists of the cecum—a pouch around 4 feet (1.2 m) long—and the large colon, which is about 12 feet (3.6 m) long. The cecum's function is to ferment and break down roughage; it can hold 5 to 10 gallons (19–38 L) of ingested material.

Processing and fermentation of the food are both accomplished by an array of microbes that inhabit the cecum and the colon. Bacteria, protozoa, and yeasts break down cellulose and other fibrous materials, transforming them into the nutrients that maintain a horse's healthy condition. These nutrients include fatty acids, amino acids, and B-complex vitamins. The process also generates heat, which is why feeding hay (not concentrates) to a horse on a cold day can help him stay warm.

The digestive system is one of the horse's major weaknesses. Digestive disorders cause more distress and mortality than any other system. Prevention consists of ensuring that horses are fed regularly and properly, never overeat, always have access to fresh water, and bear a low parasite load.
➤ *See also colic; deworming; feeding and nutrition; water, for horses*

digital artery A branched artery located on the outside and inside of a horse's leg, just above the fetlock. The digital artery is easy to find, and is a good place to take a horse's pulse.
➤ *See also pulse and respiration*

digital cushion A spongy area within the horse's foot, located above the frog, which helps absorb shock when the horse is in motion. Also known as the "plantar cushion."

digital extensor tendon A vertical band of connective tissue at the front of a horse's lower leg, used to extend the leg.

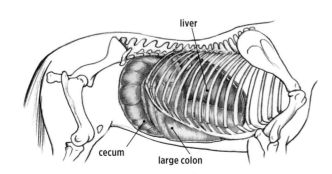

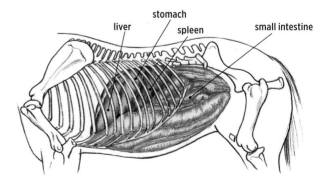

A simplified view of the equine **digestive system**

direct rein/leading rein/opening rein

A rein effect in which the rider moves the rein in the direction she wishes the horse to turn, without increasing backward pressure.

➤ *See also indirect rein*

dished face
A slightly concave profile below the eyes, often combined with a bulging forehead, a dainty muzzle, and large eyes; characteristic of Arabians.

DISHED FACE

dishing
The movement that results when a horse swings his forelegs inward when walking or trotting, rather than moving them straight; also called "dishing in" or "winging in." It arises from a conformation fault and may lead to interference.

➤ *See also interference; paddling*

dishonest horse
A horse prone to unexpected misbehavior, or one that takes advantage of a handler's lapses of attention.

dismount
To get off a horse.

➤ *See also emergency dismount*

disposition
The emotional characteristics, attitude, and "personality" of a horse. Many systems have been created to describe and understand horses' personalities, and these have their uses. But the most important assessment is personal. Does this horse have a good mind? Can I understand and get along with him? Can I make him mentally comfortable? Can I get done with him what I need to get done? The following factors influence the answers:

REACTIVITY. Does the snap of a twig send him sky-high, or does he glance mildly around in that direction?

BOLDNESS. When he sees something new, does he head over to investigate or hang back?

SOCIABILITY. Does he like people? Is he emotionally dependent on other horses?

DOMINANCE. How hard does he try to be the one in charge?

The ideal horse for an amateur might be sociable, bold, and only moderately reactive, with few dominance issues. But this may not make the best competition horse. In many show disciplines, an ability to channel excitement into elevated gaits or enthusiasm over jumps makes all the difference. Some of the best dressage horses have extremely difficult personalities. When buying a new horse, get the frank opinion of your coach as to whether you are up to dealing with your prospect's disposition.

Disposition is doubly important if you decide to breed the horse. Do not perpetuate a dangerous disposition, even if the packaging is pretty. A good mind can make up for many faults, but the ideal is a good mind in a sound body.

➤ *See also body language, of horses*

distemper
➤ *See strangles*

disunited canter
➤ *See cross-canter/disunited canter*

diverticulum/blind pouch
A small pouch near the tip of a male horse's penis, located adjacent to the urethral opening. Balls of smegma—a waxy substance consisting of dirt, skin cells, and fatty secretions—accumulate in the diverticulum. In some cases, these balls (or "beans") become large enough to affect urination, so the diverticulum should be cleaned once or twice a year.

➤ *See also sheath cleaning; smegma*

dock The upper part of the tail; the tail head. All tail hairs grow out of this area, so the dock and its underside should be carefully cleaned and rinsed when you shampoo a horse's tail. If itching develops, the horse may rub against fences or walls in attempting to quell the itch. This can cost him many tail hairs—and it may be the start of a tail-rubbing habit that is tough to break.

docking The practice of shortening a horse's tail by cutting the tailbone (dock) between the third and fourth coccygeal vertebrae. Docking was once common among carriage and draft horses not only to help keep the tail clean and create a look that emphasized the breadth of the horse's rump but also

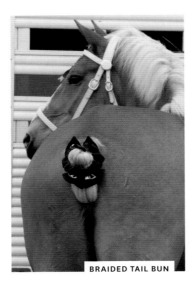

BRAIDED TAIL BUN

to keep the horse from getting his tail over the lines, which could cause an accident. It has become less common as people have come to consider it inhumane to remove one of a horse's main defenses against flies. To achieve the look of a short tail while allowing the horse to have his fly swatter when off duty, many horsemen now create a braided tail bun—a temporary, painless, and stylish solution.
➤ *See also tail*

dollar bill class A show-class contest, also known as "Sit a Buck," in which riders attempt to keep a dollar bill under their knee, seat, or thigh through the walk, trot, and canter. The winner is the rider who holds the bill there the longest. This class tests the effectiveness of the rider's leg position.

doma vaquera The Iberian stock horse equitation style, developed over centuries of working with aggressive bulls. Horses ridden *a la doma vaquera* work in a highly collected state, frequently at a canter

or gallop. They need speed, lightning-fast reactions, spirit, and animation yet must remain calm and perfectly controllable. This requires exceptional horsemanship and training, as well as a suitable horse. Pura Raza Española (PRE) horses have been bred for this work for centuries.

In Spain and southern France horses on working ranches are still ridden *a la doma vaquera*. Doma vaquera competitions are increasingly popular in the United States as well. After being vetted, and having their tack and clothing inspected to be sure it is correct and authentic, competitors enter an arena of 60 x 20 meters (197 x 66 feet) and ride an 8-minute freestyle test, performing all the maneuvers needed to face a fighting bull, including an explosive gallop from a standstill, skid stops, sidepasses, and canter pirouettes. The walk is also emphasized; horses are expected to halt square from a canter or gallop, then

DOMA VAQUERA

Primarily kept for pleasure in North America, **donkeys** in many other countries work as they have for more than five thousand years.

go into a strong, purposeful walk. Judges like to see the *mosquera* (fly fringes on the bridle) swinging rhythmically. Tests are leveled for basic, intermediate, and advanced horses.

Doma vaquera also employs the *garrocha*, a 13-foot (4 m) wooden pole used for working bulls. Its use has evolved into a beautiful art form in which the rider rests one tip of the pole on the ground while cantering and pirouetting under, over, and around it in an elegant dance, set to Spanish guitar music.

Doma vaquera competitions are held at Andalusian-Lusitano shows in the United States. A third form of competition, doma trabajo (working equitation), combines doma vaquera freestyle, the *garrocha*, trail obstacles, and cow work.

➤ *See also Andalusian; Lusitano; working equitation/ doma trabajo*

dominant gene/dominant trait

➤ *See genetics*

donkey The domestic ass (*Equus asinus*). Hardy and gentle, donkeys are affectionate companions for people and other animals, and can serve as alert guardians of a flock of sheep, goats, or llamas. With their friendly nature, they are ideal for children and make good mounts for therapy programs. They are strong and sure-footed, making them ideal pack animals. However, like mules, they will often "discuss" your request with you, wanting to know exactly why you want them to do it.

Donkeys are not classified by breed, but range in size from miniatures standing under 36 inches (91 cm) to mammoths that can be 14 hands high and up. Colors are gray, dun, roan, black, brown, and even spotted. Donkeys are fairly easy to keep but need regular inoculations and foot trimming, just like horses.

➤ *See also mule*

dorsal stripe A dark stripe along the back of a horse or donkey exhibited by primitive horses, including Przewalski's horse, and by modern dun horses.

DORSAL STRIPE

double To bend or turn a horse sharply. Doubling can be an effective means of stopping a runaway horse. Establish a secure seat, loosen one rein, and use strong pressure on the other to bring horse's head around toward your knee. In bad footing or among trees, doubling may be more dangerous than just hanging on; you don't want to make the horse slam into something or fall.

Natural horsemanship and some clicker trainers teach horses to yield their hips in response to a light rein and leg cue, which can make life easier when a horse spooks. Doubling is then a learned behavior, and can be used before a situation becomes too dangerous.
➤ *See also pulley rein*

double bridle A bridle that uses two bits: a curb bit, and a small snaffle bit called a bradoon. The bradoon lifts the head, and the curb aids in flexion. These bridles are most commonly used on highly trained dressage and saddle seat horses.
➤ *See also bridle; Pelham bit*

double-judged Horse show events that are evaluated or scored by two judges.

double-rumped A desirable trait in a draft horse, in which a groove running down the center of the horse's hindquarters creates a heart shape when viewed from the rear.

doubletree On a wagon, carriage, or farm implement, two singletrees attached to a bar, called an evener, that keeps a pair of horses pulling evenly, and also attaches them to the vehicle or implement.
➤ *See also harness; singletree*

down command A voice command used by handlers in conjunction with fingertips pressed down on the top of a horse's head. It signals the horse to lower his head. Lowering the head is calming to the horse, and makes grooming and bridling easier. It is a skill every horse should acquire.
➤ *See shying*

downhill balance Conformation in which the croup is higher than the withers. A horse with downhill balance is front-heavy, and usually does best at straight-line activities such as racing. Many sprinters have downhill balance.

downhill riding Riding downhill can challenge the balance of inexperienced riders and horses alike. When riding downhill, sit upright in the saddle. Keep your upper body at the same angle as any trees or tall weeds growing on the slope, and your knees and thighs firm to hold yourself in place. Horses have a natural tendency to speed up when going downhill; use checks and releases to maintain control. Unless the slope is treacherous or has an established diagonal trail, head straight down instead of attempting a diagonal descent. If you encounter a hill that seems too steep for you, dismount and lead your horse, staying to one side of him if possible to avoid being hurt if he falls.

draft cross A horse who is a cross between a draft horse and a smaller breed. They are popular on dude ranches to carry heavier riders.

draft horse A heavy, muscular horse traditionally used for farmwork, logging, mining, and hauling freight. "Heavy horses" date back to early medieval times, when they were developed to carry knights and their armor into battle. When the horse collar was introduced to Europe, the knights' chargers found new jobs. They were the backbone of farming and freighting until the internal combustion engine replaced them.

Draft horses are considered cold-blooded. Many weigh considerably more than a ton. They are as intelligent and trainable as any other type of horse, and have a tendency to be more placid, though individual temperament varies widely. Drafts eat more, and exact more wear and tear on facilities, than smaller horses. It can be difficult to find a farrier willing to work with a large draft horse.

Widely used by the Amish community, draft horses are experiencing a resurgence in popularity among many small-scale farmers. A horse farmer can often work her land early in the spring, while her neighbor using a heavy tractor must wait for the ground to dry. The fuel a draft horse uses—hay, grain, grass—can be grown on the farm, and the waste he produces—manure—can go back on the land as fertilizer. Big horses can diversify a farmer's income stream; she can sell young stock, or offer hay and sleigh rides.

Draft horses are also used for logging. Horse loggers pride themselves on their low impact in the woods. Hooves do far less damage to the land than tractor tires.

Draft horses are also found pulling carriages in major cities, and on some police forces. Many experts on policing believe that an officer on a draft horse is both safer and a better deterrent to crime than an officer on a smaller horse.

Ponies and miniature horses of draft type can also be useful on the small farm or homestead. They can pull roughly twice their own weight, and so can bring in a significant amount of firewood or hay, and power garden tractor equipment.

➤ *See also Belgian; Brabant; Clydesdale; Percheron; Shire; Suffolk*

For heavy farmwork, **draft horse** breeds of 1,600 pounds (726 kg) or more, standing at least 16 hands high, are most suitable. The best known are the Belgian, the Clydesdale, the Percheron, the Shire, and the Suffolk Punch (shown here). Smaller draft breeds, such as the Haflinger and the Norwegian Fjord, are ideal for hilly farmwork, and miniature horses can do anything a garden tractor can do.

draft pony A heavy pony, often produced by crossing a draft horse with a pony. Draft ponies can be useful on a small farm, and have their own highly competitive division in pulling contests.

drag

1. In a cattle roping event, when a cow plants all four feet and refuses to move after being roped.

2. To "ride drag" is to position oneself at the rear of a column of riders or a herd of cows.

drag hunt A cruelty-free form of foxhunting, in which a scent lure is dragged for the hounds to follow.
➤ *See also foxhunting*

dress
➤ *See "English Show Attire," page 103; "Western Show Attire," page 399*

dressage The French word for "training"; a formal English riding discipline that has its roots in the teachings of the Greek master Xenophon, and in the riding schools of the European Renaissance. It can be defined as the practice of "classical horsemanship," and as the systematic art of training a horse to perform precise exercises in a balanced, supple, athletic, and responsive manner. At the highest level, riders in formal attire put their horses through routines or tests, using aids so subtle they are all but invisible.

Dressage initially reflected the training of horses for military purposes. The first equestrian academy was established in 1532 by the Italian master Federico Grisone. The Spanish Riding School in Vienna, Austria, where the baroque art of Classical High School dressage is famously performed, was established in 1572. Dressage as a competitive discipline dates only from the end of the 19th century. It was introduced as an Olympic event at the Stockholm games in 1912.

Horses and riders of nearly all backgrounds can benefit from learning the exercises and movements that constitute dressage. Ideally, horses become well conditioned both physically and mentally, and are able to fulfill their athletic potential. Riders experience a horse who is a joy to ride and benefit from their own greatly improved riding skills. Over the course of time—and this can take a number of years—horse and rider become a highly skilled team, riding in harmony with seemingly effortless coordination.

Dressage students begin with the execution of relatively simple exercises such as figure eights and circles. They practice lateral (sideways) movements and learn to make correct transitions from one gait to another. As these are mastered, the exercises become progressively more difficult. In competitive dressage, the upper-level tests include the piaffe (a trot on the spot) and passage (an elevated trot with moments of hesitation between footfalls). In Classical High School dressage, upper-level movements include the airs above the ground—levade, ballotade, croupade, capriole, and courbette.

LEVELS OF COMPETITION Horses and riders begin competing in dressage at the Introductory or Training Level, progressing to First Level, Second Level, Third Level (medium difficulty), and Fourth Level; only then do they graduate to intermediate levels. The highest level of accomplishment is the Grand Prix, which is the standard applied at the Olympics and at world championships. Dressage is one of the phases in three-phase eventing.

Dressage competitions take place in an arena with a pastern-high rail around it. The standard arena is 20 meters (66 feet) wide and 60 meters (197 feet) long. Horse and rider enter the arena alone, halt facing the judges, and salute. Then they ride a prescribed pattern, or test, suitable to their level. Memorization of tests is an important strength, but at many levels it is permissible to use a reader or caller who reads the test aloud to you.

WESTERN DRESSAGE A relatively new form of Western competition that is increasingly popular in many different breed organizations. Western dressage is a progressive training system with six levels of tests. Introductory tests take place at the walk and jog only. Later tests include lengthened and collected work at all three gaits, as well as shoulder-in, leg-yield, and half-pass. The goal is to produce a responsive, willing, and calm horse with light, pure gaits. The discipline rewards smaller horses of stock and pleasure types who may not excel at regular dressage.

GRAND PRIX DRESSAGE COMPETITION

DRIVEN DRESSAGE   Driven dressage transfers the values of ridden dressage—forward, light, flexible movement and precise execution of figures—to carriage driving. Drivers in elegant turnout execute figures at walk, trot, and canter, with the apex of difficulty being one-handed canter circles. Collection and extension as well as working gaits and rein-backs are part of the tests. Dressage is one-third of combined driving.
➤ *See also airs above the ground; combined driving; eventing; Classical High School; rollkur; Spanish Riding School; Western dressage; Xenophon*

dressing room   The front part of many horse trailers are equipped with walk-in dressing rooms that may double as tack rooms. The typical dressing room adds about 4 feet (1.2 m) to the length of a trailer. It provides a handy, secure place to store essential supplies—and, of course, a private dressing space.

drills, mounted   Riding performances that allow teams of riders to demonstrate team horsemanship skills such as precision, timing, cooperation, and coordination. Drills may be directed by voice, hand, or whistle signals, and they are often performed to music. Anywhere from 4 to 20 or more horse-and-rider pairs complete a choreographed routine. Equestrian drill teams perform at venues like fairs, rodeos, and expositions; in addition, the United States Equestrian Drill Association sanctions nationwide competitions. Common drills include the Figure Eight, the Crossover, the Snail, and the Tricycle.

driving   Driving today includes day-to-day transportation for the Amish, city carriage rides for tourists, pleasant jaunts down country roads, pleasure driving at shows, and the complex sport of combined driving. Vehicles used in driving range from a single-passenger cart and one miniature horse to a coach with a four-in-hand of elegant warmbloods to a large wagon pulled by a team of two to twelve draft horses.

Pleasure Driving classes are judged on the manners and performance of the horses. In Turnout classes, participants are judged on the appearance and appropriateness of their harness and attire. In Reinsmanship classes, judges assess the skill and talent of the driver.

In combined driving, the driving equivalent of three-day eventing, entrants do driven dressage, a cross-country course, and a cones course.

Driving can be a great alternative for horsemen kept from riding by physical limitations or age. Drivers, or whips, at the upper level of combined driving include many women over 60. That doesn't mean driving is easy or free from hazards. A shying or runaway driving horse tows a large projectile behind him, and can do a lot of damage. Good training is essential for horse and whip.
➤ *See also combined driving; whip*

driving bridle
A bridle designed for use when driving horses. Driving bridles have stiff cheekpieces, a browband, a crownpiece, a throatlatch, and a gullet strap (a strap connecting the throatlatch to the noseband under the horse's jaw). This helps make the bridle secure and difficult to rub or pull off. A secure bridle is important; a driver in a cart pulled by a suddenly bridleless horse is in an extremely hazardous situation.

Traditionally, blinders were added to driving bridles, and shadow rolls (pieces of sheepskin) were added to the nosebands of harness racing horses. Both devices limit a horse's field of vision (shadow rolls prevent the horse from seeing his shadow), minimizing the possibility of shying, which is particularly dangerous when a horse is harnessed to a vehicle.
➤ *See also blinders, blinkers*

driving pony
A pony used to pull a cart or wagon. Most pony breeds are well suited for this purpose, and a person with a beloved but outgrown riding pony can enjoy learning to drive.

driving seat
Rider position with assertive seat aids and the upper body vertical or slightly behind the vertical. The driving seat is used in dressage to encourage the horse to move strongly forward.

drop noseband
A noseband that sits lower on the horse's nose than an ordinary cavesson, and fastens beneath the bit rings. It is meant to keep the horse's

The Morgan, like many breeds, is as well suited for **driving** as it is for riding.

mouth closed and quiet, but must allow for light mouthing and chewing. A drop noseband is trickier to adjust than a flash noseband, and can damage the sensitive nasal bone. If you need to use one, be sure to ask a qualified instructor to check the adjustment.
➤ *See also flash noseband/flash attachment*

dropped sole
Sole that protrudes downward and has become convex rather than concave.

dropping

1. Releasing a horse too early in attempting a jump. Dropping can cause the horse to fail to jump and the rider to fall backward.

2. In a male horse, allowing the penis to extend out of the sheath.

drop the shoulder
A rider error that involves leaning excessively to the inside while making a turn.

Duckett's dot
On a horse's hoof, the point at the center of the sole.

dun coloring
A yellow, gold, or tan body with black or brown points; often confused with buckskin.

DUN COLORING

A dun always has a dorsal stripe (a line of darker hair down the spine) and may also have stripes on the legs and/or withers.
➤ *See also buckskin coloring; "Buckskin or Dun?," page 40; color, of horse*

dun factor
The gene that produces dorsal stripes, shoulder stripes, and front leg barring on dun horses.

Dutch collar
An alternative to the neck collar, the Dutch collar is designed to fit over a horse's chest. Variations include the breast collar or heart collar. The collar is a primary part of the driving harness.

dwarf horse
As distinguished from a miniature horse, a genetically deformed animal that is abnormally proportioned. For example, its head may be too big for its body. Such deformity is heritable.

DRUGS AND HORSES

Appearance- or behavior-enhancing drugs are sometimes given to horses by unethical dealers or horse show competitors. The drugs may temporarily calm an unruly horse or make a sick or lame horse appear healthier.

Many horse show associations attempt to deal with this difficult problem by conducting random drug tests and penalizing dishonest exhibitors. Competitors should familiarize themselves with the list of banned substances for their sports, and be aware that some treats and herbal medicines may "test"—that is, show a false positive for a drug.

Horse buyers should insist on a veterinary exam that includes the analysis of a blood or urine sample prior to purchase.

ear nets Fabric or net sleeves that fit over a horse's ears to keep insects away. Ear nets range from inexpensive crocheted bonnets to personalized versions with monogramming and Swarovski crystals. Plain or fancy, ear nets can make rides much more pleasant during bug season, and for sensitive horses they can be absolutely essential.

➤ *See also fly masks*

earplugs Devices placed in the horse's ears to reduce loud sounds. Earplugs can help a nervous horse react more calmly in an unfamiliar environment. They may be made from sheepskin, foam, or various combinations of fabric and sponge. Riders and drivers of many disciplines use them, but they are especially important in cowboy mounted shooting. Use earplugs when your horse needs them, but don't use them every day, or you risk creating a dependency. Your horse should develop the ability to cope with unexpected sounds.

➤ *See also cowboy mounted shooting*

ears A horse's ears are both receptors and communicators. In addition to channeling sound, the ears communicate much about how the horse is feeling and what he may be thinking.

EAR ANATOMY The inside of a horse's ear consists of an ear canal at the base that descends in a straight line for about 2 inches (5 cm). The canal then turns sharply and extends to the eardrum. This bend keeps debris away from the eardrum. The inner ear also contains fine hairs that filter out debris and insects. These hairs play an important protective role. If you remove them as part of grooming for showing, it is incumbent on you to keep the horse stabled or otherwise protected from flying insects.

The outer part of the ear is controlled by ten muscles, which allow it to rotate in every direction, to funnel in sounds and express emotions. Visually prominent, ears play an important role in horses' communications among themselves, and can tell us much about their inner state.

HEARING Horses can hear higher frequencies than we do. They sense lower frequencies as well, through their ears, and their hooves and teeth while grazing. They can hear over greater distances, up to several miles depending on wind. It is believed that they sense lower-volume tones than humans, and that they are more sensitive to loud noises.

Sounds often worry horses. Much of the stress of trailering comes from the rattling of the rig and the sound of traffic noises; travel may be less stressful with earplugs. The sound of clippers, which resembles that of a swarm of insects, may cause concern. Wind, which is noisy in itself, masks the sounds the horse may be using to tell him about what's going on nearby and may bring in sounds from a considerable distance. Humans may fault the horse for reacting to "nothing," but he has access to information we lack. Horses often hear storms coming long before humans do, and may know about other impending events as well.

EAR PROBLEMS The primary problems that affect equine ears are injury to the eardrum, internal infections, and minor external problems. Damage to the eardrum will result in hearing impairment or deafness. The eardrum is well protected under normal circumstances, but penetration of the ear by a sharp object (such as a tree branch), blows to the head, and middle-ear infections can cause damage.

Middle-ear infections are caused by bacteria or viruses that enter the ear via the bloodstream or the eustachian tube, the canal that extends from the throat to the ears. The infection may develop in the guttural pouch in the wall of the eustachian tube. The salivary gland below the ear might also become inflamed from infection. Symptoms of infection include fever, head tossing, ear rubbing, an accumulation of discharge in the ear, pain upon chewing, drooping ears, and reluctance to have the ears handled. The horse might also carry his head in an odd position.

Horses are more commonly subject to external ear problems, but these conditions tend to be relatively minor and do not result in hearing loss. Insect infestations, frostbite, warts, skin infections, and small tumors are among the problems. Consult your veterinarian anytime your horse evidences ear discomfort or you discover unusual lumps, inflammation, or fluid discharge.

➤ *See also body language, of horses, "Ear Talk," next page*

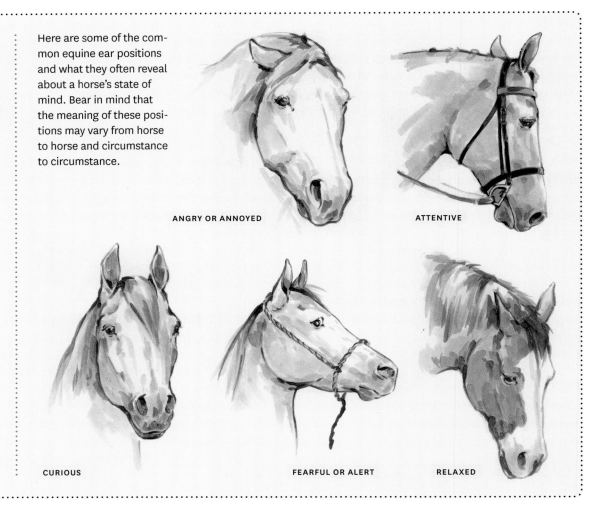

EAR TALK

Here are some of the common equine ear positions and what they often reveal about a horse's state of mind. Bear in mind that the meaning of these positions may vary from horse to horse and circumstance to circumstance.

ANGRY OR ANNOYED

ATTENTIVE

CURIOUS

FEARFUL OR ALERT

RELAXED

eastern equine encephalitis (EEE)

➤ *See equine encephalitis*

easy entry cart A low-slung two-wheeled cart that is entered in front of the wheel, rather than from behind the seat or over the wheel.

easy gaits Gaits that are comfortable to ride and faster than an ordinary walk, but slower than a canter or gallop; also called intermediate gaits. The easy gaits include flat-footed walk, running walk, fox trot, broken or stepping pace, saddle rack, and true rack. An easy-gaited horse is one for whom one or more of these gaits is natural.

easy keeper A horse who maintains weight on little feed. Easy keepers are less expensive to feed than hard keepers, but they need careful monitoring. They develop laminitis and/or metabolic problems more easily than other horses. Morgans and pony breeds are notable easy keepers.

edema An abnormal accumulation of fluid within, or surrounding, connective tissues; also known as fluid retention. The most common location for edema in horses is in the lower half of the hind legs of idle horses or those with scratches, or around the udder of pregnant mares. The best prevention and/or treatment in either situation is mild exercise. Exercise increases circulation, which helps the fluids diffuse and allows the tissues to regain normal tone.

➤ *See also scratches*

egg bar shoe An oval horseshoe connected at the heels, used to support weak hooves and legs. Egg bar shoes provide support beneath the heel, which is especially beneficial when a horse has navicular disease, collapsed heels, underrun hooves, or flat soles. Egg bar shoes are also used to give more support on soft ground. However, if your horse is wearing these shoes, do not turn him out into a muddy area. Mud, manure, straw, and other debris easily collect inside the egg bar shoe. For this reason, it is especially important to clean the horse's hooves daily.
➤ *See also lameness; horseshoes*

EHV
➤ *See equine herpes virus (EHV)*

EIA
➤ *See equine infectious anemia (EIA)*

eight-up Four pairs of driving horses hitched one in front of the other.

electric fencing
➤ *See barns and facilities*

electric horse walker
➤ *See hot walker*

electrolytes The "salt" molecules or minerals normally found in the bloodstream, including sodium, potassium, calcium, and magnesium. Electrolytes, which are essential to maintaining normal body functions, are lost in sweat when horses are working in hot, humid conditions.

Horses need 0.1 percent sodium in the diet, increased to 0.3 percent when working or pregnant. Since horses like salt, most will consume all they need from a free-choice salt block. Potassium is well supplied, sometimes oversupplied, in forage, and should not be included in supplements or electrolyte mixes.

Electrolytes cannot be stored in the body, so must be supplied in feed or water.

Electric fencing comes in a variety of widths. Horse owners can combine wide tape, which is good for visibility, with thinner strands that are less expensive and somewhat easier to work with.

elk nose/moose nose A sagging muzzle, with the top lip overhanging the lower one. Elk nose occurs in older horses as nasal cartilage softens.

emergency dismount A method of dismounting while the horse is moving, used when a situation has become unsafe. Riders can be hurt while dismounting in motion; it's worth learning this skill from a knowledgeable teacher in a controlled situation and practicing it in a ring.

encephalitis
➤ *See equine encephalitis*

endorphins Natural morphinelike chemicals that are produced in the brain. When released, they reduce pain, decrease heartbeat, and create calm. A twitch is an effective restraint because it causes a release of endorphins.
➤ *See also twitch*

It's a good idea to practice doing an **emergency dismount** in an arena before you need it in real life.

endo-tapping A relaxation technique developed by horseman J. P. Giacomini, in which the horse is rhythmically tapped with a rubber ball on the end of a semirigid fiberglass stick; a ball fitted on the handle of a dressage whip will also work. The horse becomes habituated to the tapping, and is said to go into a state of deep relaxation, in which he is much more trainable. The reason this works is not understood.

endotoxemia A condition in which endotoxins released by pathogenic bacteria in the intestines seep through the intestinal wall and enter a horse's bloodstream; triggered in many cases by a uterine infection or overconsumption of grain. The poisons damage blood vessels, depriving body tissues of needed oxygen. Because the ends of the arteries in a horse's hooves are particularly vulnerable, endotoxemia can quickly lead to laminitis (or founder) or to endotoxic shock, organ failure, and death. Broad-spectrum antibiotics can be used if endotoxemia is suspected.
➤ *See also laminitis*

endurance riding A trail riding competition, with worldwide championship events sanctioned by the Fédération Equestre Internationale (FEI), in which horse and rider cover a predetermined course within a maximum time; there is no minimum time limit. The winner is the first to cross the finish line while meeting horse soundness guidelines, making endurance riding both a race and a test of the horse's conditioning. Riders generally cover about 50 miles (80 km) per day, with a maximum 3-day ride of 150 miles (241 km). Veterinarians examine the horses every 10 to 15 miles (16–24 km).

Endurance riding is one of the most grueling horse sports. In early days riders rode until their horses dropped, which brought the sport into disrepute. Even now, though the sport is sanctioned and there is careful monitoring, horses do occasionally die during competition, generally of colic. Rigorous conditioning is essential. Novice endurance rides of 25 to 30 miles (40–48 km) are offered for less experienced riders and/or horses.

In North America and Great Britain, Arabian horses have dominated the sport of endurance riding due to their stamina, speed, and heart. But endurance riding is open to all breeds, and Quarter Horses, Morgans, Appaloosas, Akhal-Tekes, Moyle Horses, Fox Trotters, and mustangs have all done well.

ENDURANCE RIDING

engagement A way of going in which the horse flexes his hocks, reaches deeper under his body, and carries more of his own weight with his hindquarters, rather than pushing his body ahead of his hind feet like a wheelbarrow. Engagement lowers the hindquarters and loads them so that they produce a powerful thrust; it is necessary for impulsion and then collection. An engaged horse has a rounded topline, lowered croup, and flexed abdominal muscles. Engagement demands great strength, and the ability to work in engagement must be developed gradually.

➤ *See also collection; movement, conformation and*

English riding Broadly speaking, most European riders and the majority from the East Coast of the United States ride English. Modern English riding is characterized by riding on contact with the reins in both hands, in a saddle without a horn or rigging. Riders usually post to the trot, though a sitting trot is required for some classes and disciplines. The horse exhibits more forward energy than in most Western show classes. Styles vary widely, with hunt seat encouraging ground-covering gaits; saddle seat encouraging high-stepping gaits; dressage concerning itself with impulsion, flexibility, and collection; and sports like polo, steeplechase, flat racing, and jumping very much about getting the job at hand done efficiently.

English riding evolved from 17th-century cavalry riding, in England and in western Europe. As Thoroughbred and Thoroughbred-type horses became popular, ambling horses fell out of favor. Cavalrymen, who now spent many hours at the trot, began to post. English foxhunting was also a strong influence. Speed across country and an ability to jump were paramount; however, what we now consider to be the most efficient seat for hunting and jumping, the forward seat, was invented by an Italian cavalry officer, Federico Caprilli, in the early 20th century.

DISCIPLINES Because of its genesis in military and aristocratic life, English riding tends to be more formal than Western, mimicking the ways horses were ridden in former, some would say more elegant, times. Disciplines under the general heading of English riding include the following:

BALANCED SEAT. The riding style of pleasure and trail riders, balanced seat most closely resembles the seat used in dressage or Western riding, with moderately long stirrups and an all-purpose saddle that can be used for either jumping or dressage.

AN ENGLISH RIDER USING A BALANCED SEAT

DRESSAGE. Dressage, which originated with the training done with cavalry horses, is ridden in a deep-seated saddle, with much longer stirrups than hunt seat. Jumping is not part of the discipline, which focuses on lightness, flexibility, and the ability to transition smoothly between collection and extension.

HUNT SEAT. Anyone who rides in a close-contact or all-purpose English saddle is riding some form of hunt seat, a descendant of the old way of foxhunting. Hunter classes may include jumps. The horse is judged on way of going, manners, and jumping form. Jumper classes (ridden in hunt seat style) are judged purely on time and faults; the horse who gets over the jumps quickest, with the fewest faults, wins.

POLO. Invented in India, polo is played on small horses called ponies (though they may be taller than an actual pony) in modified English tack.

SADDLE SEAT (also called park seat). Saddle seat originated in European riding in city parks, a means of exercise and display for the upper classes. The rider uses an extremely flat, so-called cut-back saddle, which places the center of gravity well back toward the loins. This works against the horse raising his back as desired in dressage and hunt seat, and promotes high-stepping gaits. Saddle seat horses are ridden in a double bridle. The emphasis is on flashy motion, though good manners are also important. Saddle seat riders generally show in formal attire resembling a tuxedo.

STEEPLECHASE AND FLAT RACING. Racehorses are all ridden in English tack, in the forward seat invented by Caprilli.

PREFERRED HORSE BREEDS For hunt seat riding a predominantly hot-blooded riding horse is the preferred type. Thoroughbreds and Thoroughbred crosses are the classic hunters, with many Quarter Horses of the longer, leaner type fitting the bill as well. Other common breeds include Morgans, Appaloosas, warmbloods, Connemaras, and other riding-type ponies. You might also see Selle Français horses, a light Thoroughbred-type horse from France, or even a draft horse-Thoroughbred cross. No matter the breed, the horse should look, act, and move as if he could jump and follow hounds.

For dressage, warmbloods are currently favored, although any breed, including gaited horses, can be taught dressage. Polo ponies are small, sturdy, quick horses of any breed. Saddle seat breeds include the gaited breeds, Morgans, and Arabians.

SHOWS Almost all English shows are open shows; that is, your horse need not be of a particular breed to compete. Breed associations also hold shows in which any English discipline may be included, as may Western disciplines and events particular to that breed alone.
➤ *See also dressage; endurance riding; "English Show Attire," below; foxhunting; polo; saddle; saddle seat; sidesaddle, riding; steeplechasing; warmblood; Western riding*

ENGLISH SHOW ATTIRE

Refer to the rule book for a specific show for exact details, as fashions and rules change.

Dressage

Lower levels of competition: Black hunt coat; white breeches; white shirt with white stock tie or choker; hunt cap, bowler, derby hat, or helmet; black gloves; black hunt boots with dressage top; spurs optional
Fédération Equestre Internationale (FEI) level: Formal coat with tails; top hat or helmet; white gloves; spurs mandatory; otherwise same as at lower levels of competition

Hunter

Conservatively colored coat; light-colored breeches or jodhpurs; white or pastel shirt with white stock tie or choker; tall black hunt boots; helmet

Jumper

Black or (in FEI classes) scarlet coat; light or white breeches; otherwise same as hunter

Saddle Seat

Three-piece suit in conservative color; dress shirt with tie; top hat or helmet in formal or evening classes; derby, snap brim, homburg, or helmet in less formal classes; jodhpur boots; gloves; whip and boutonniere optional
(different breeds may have different requirements)

English tack The saddle used in English riding; also called a flat saddle. English saddles are generally smaller than Western saddles and have no saddle horn. Beyond that they vary widely, in style and even color—dressage saddles are often black, whereas most other saddles are manufactured in shades of brown leather. Some English saddles are made of synthetic materials.

ALL-PURPOSE SADDLES are for general riding; they usually have a deep to medium-deep seat and flaps that extend moderately forward.

DRESSAGE SADDLES have a deep seat and flaps that come down almost straight, with external knee blocks to help position the legs.

JUMPING SADDLES have a shallower seat, and flaps that extend well forward.

PARK SADDLES have a cut-back pommel to accommodate a high neck carriage, flat, shallow seats, and wide flaps, enabling the saddle seat rider to sit far back in the saddle.

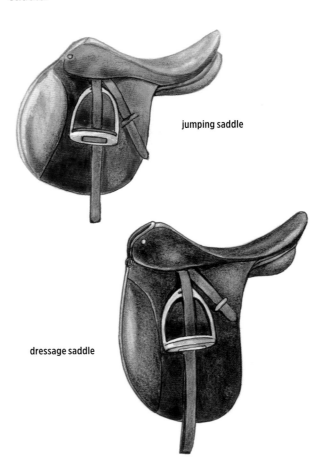

jumping saddle

dressage saddle

BRIDLES English bridles come in two basic types. The **snaffle bridle** is a simple bridle with a browband and noseband. The standard noseband is not meant for control and does not need to be used; however, the snaffle bridle can be used with many styles of noseband for greater control. It can also accommodate a Pelham bit and double reins.

A **double bridle** has a second headstall, made of thinner leather, which carries the bradoon (thin snaffle). It should be fitted with a basic cavesson noseband, to avoid interfering with the action of the curb bit. It is always used with two sets of reins.

English bridles may also be bitless.

➤ *See also bitless riding*

enteritis Inflammation of the intestines. Enteritis is one of the serious conditions that falls under the broad umbrella of colic, and merits the prompt attention of a veterinarian.

➤ *See also colic; diarrhea*

enteroliths Stones that develop when layers of minerals accumulate around a foreign object in a horse's intestines. An enterolith can become quite large without causing any apparent problem, but it must be removed surgically if it is located in an area where it obstructs the digestive tract. Feeding bran or bran mash on a regular basis may increase your horse's likelihood of developing intestinal stones. Enteroliths are more common in areas where calcium and magnesium oxalates concentrate in alfalfa hay. In these areas, such as the Central Valley of California, avoid feeding local alfalfa hay; rely on grass hay.

entire Term used to describe an uncastrated horse.

Eohippus The precursor of the modern horse, *Eohippus*, also known by the name *Hyracotherium*, was a dog- or deerlike animal, probably yellow, with four toes on each front foot and three toes on each back foot. It was a mere 14 inches (30 cm) high at the shoulder and weighed as little as 12 pounds (5 kg). It appeared in North America some 60 million years ago but disappeared from the continent sometime after the Ice Age, crossing to Asia and Europe via land bridges. It became extinct on all continents, but its descendants in North America evolved into modern horses.

➤ *See also evolution of the horse*

epiphysitis Common (but incorrect) term for physitis.

➤ *See also physitis*

EOHIPPUS

FITTING AN ENGLISH SADDLE

- The saddle should rest on the horse's ribs, not on his spine, and must accommodate the width of his withers.

- The gullet is the "spine" of the saddle, which keeps the weight of the saddle off the horse's spine. You should be able to see through the gullet when the horse's head is down.

- When the horse raises his head, the withers should not press against the pommel.

Beyond this, saddle fit is an immensely sophisticated topic. It is difficult to know if a saddle causes discomfort to a horse, and if so, where. Professional saddle fitters can make an evaluation using gauges, gel-filled impression pads, or a computerized pressure monitoring system. Be aware that some saddle fitters may have an interest in selling you something, and that saddle fit may be subject to fads. The ultimate judge is your horse. If he performs willingly and does not display signs of a sore back, it's safe to assume your saddle fits.

EPM

➤ *See equine protozoal myeloencephalitis (EPM)*

equine-assisted activities and therapies (EAAT)

➤ *See therapeutic horsemanship*

equine dentist

➤ *See dentist, equine; teeth and age*

equine encephalitis/encephalomyelitis

A disease of the central nervous system that can affect humans as well as horses; also known as "sleeping sickness." The disease is contracted through viruses carried by mosquitoes. In North America there are four strains: Eastern (EEE), Western (WEE), Venezuelan (VEE), and West Nile virus (WNV). EEE occurs primarily east of the Mississippi into southern Canada and in central South America; WEE occurs west of the Mississippi into southern Canada and throughout South America; VEE occurs in the southern states and throughout central South America; and WNV is found throughout the United States and most of Canada. Mortality rates are 100 percent for EEE, 25 percent for WEE, and up to 90 percent for VEE. WNV is rarely fatal but can be debilitating and difficult to treat.

Equine encephalitis is transmitted primarily during peak mosquito season. Symptoms include fever, loss of appetite, fatigue, poor muscular coordination or staggering, partial or complete blindness, brain swelling, and paralysis. Currently there is no cure, but close medical attention can reduce mortality in some strains. Vaccination is essential.

equine herpes virus (EHV)

A virus that causes the disease known as rhinopneumonitis. The EHV-1 strain of the virus is known to cause abortions in broodmares; the EHV-4 strain induces respiratory illness, particularly in young horses. All horses who travel or have contact with breeding animals should be vaccinated annually.

➤ *See also rhinopneumonitis*

equine infectious anemia (EIA)

An incurable, potentially lethal viral disease that ravaged the U.S. horse population in the 1960s. EIA, also known as swamp fever, is now far less common. The virus is transmitted by biting insects, but a significant contributing factor in the past was infection transmitted via unclean needles and syringes. Although disposable medical equipment and heightened awareness of the need for proper sanitation have reduced the incidence of EIA, the disease has not been eliminated.

EIA is most commonly seen in horses who graze in wet pasture areas, where blood-sucking insects thrive and may transmit the virus. The disease can then spread from one horse to another, because the virus is present in the blood and all secretions of an infected horse.

The symptoms of an acute attack include fever, loss of appetite, anemia, depression, excessive sweating, and watery discharge from the nostrils. However, the chronic form of EIA is more common. An episode may involve intermittent low-grade fever, anemia, irregular heartbeat, muscular weakness, staggering, and unexplained weight loss. A horse with the chronic form of the disease may be symptom-free for extended periods but is subject to relapses and is always a carrier of the virus.

There is no effective treatment for EIA at this time, but a blood test known as the Coggins test has become a powerful tool in detecting and halting the spread of the disease. All horses should have a Coggins test before being trailered off the home farm, and the Coggins certificate should accompany the horse. A Coggins certificate is *required* for interstate and international travel, and for participation in every sanctioned competition. Following strict sanitation procedures and quarantining or destroying infected horses are also necessary preventive measures.

➤ *See also Coggins test, Coggins certificate*

equine influenza

A highly infectious virus that affects a horse's upper respiratory tract. Symptoms include fever, dullness and depression, coughing, weakness, lack of appetite, runny nose, swollen eyelids, and watery eyes. Equine influenza can become serious if a horse is subjected to heavy activity or significant stress during the early stages of the disease. It is spread by inhalation, and the virus can be carried on the wind.

The recommended treatment regimen involves providing absolute rest, a nourishing diet, and good ventilation in the facility where the horse is recuperating. Antibiotics may be administered; these are not effective against the virus, but they help prevent secondary bacterial infections such as pneumonia and strangles.

A vaccine is available, and is particularly useful for horses who have been exposed to infected horses. However, the vaccine provides only short-term protection that lasts three to four months. By contrast, a horse who has recovered from equine influenza will develop built-in immunity that lasts for at least a year.

equine metabolic syndrome (EMS)

A syndrome in which the horse becomes less sensitive to insulin, causing blood glucose levels to remain high. EMS may be caused by chronically high levels of sugar and starch in the diet; ponies and easy-keeper breeds, like Morgans, are particularly susceptible. EMS may also be caused by low intake of minerals, or there may be other factors. It is not yet completely understood. The syndrome shares some symptoms with Cushing's disease.

Symptoms associated with EMS include the following:

- Chronic low-level laminitis, white line disease, hoof rings, or strange growth patterns in the hoof.

- Obesity, which may include abnormal fat pads on the neck, shoulders, and around the tail head. The fat pads will be very hard and inflexible to the touch.

- Blood tests showing high concentration of circulating glucose and insulin; insulin is slow to clear following a meal.

Diet management and regular exercise are essential for EMS horses; consult your veterinarian regarding treatment.

➤ See also carbohydrates; Cushing's disease

equine protozoal myeloencephalitis (EPM)

A neurological disease that affects a horse's spinal cord and nervous system. EPM is caused by a protozoan, Sarcocystis neurona, that is carried by opossums and certain birds. Horses typically contract the disease by eating feed or drinking water containing opossum feces. Once inside the horse, the protozoan migrates to the spinal cord, resulting in inflammation and nerve damage that can be crippling.

Early diagnosis and treatment is key to minimizing the damage caused by EPM. Subtle symptoms that may indicate the presence of the disease include slight changes in the horse's stance, gait, movements, or coordination. Later symptoms include hind-end lameness, muscular weakness or atrophy, noisy breathing, seizures, leaning to one side, and drooping ears and lips on one side of the face. The diagnostic process should include a spinal tap, and treatment can be both lengthy and expensive. However, the majority of horses recover well enough to resume normal activities.

Preventive measures include buying heat-processed feed (heat destroys *S.neurona*), keeping your supply of grain covered at all times, and making sure possums can't get into your feed room or water supply.

equine recurrent uveitis (ERU)

A chronic, recurrent form of uveitis (inflammation of the iris and related structures in the eye); also called moon blindness, iridocyclitis, or periodic ophthalmia. Repeated bouts of inflammation can lead to cataracts; the first recurrence is usually within a year, and recurrences occur progressively sooner after that, eventually leading to blindness. The disease is thought to be linked to infection with leptospira, a bacteria spread in the urine of rats. Good hygiene is the best preventative, especially the use of sealed feed bins and automatic waterers.

Aggressive treatment with anti-inflammatories is the usual treatment, but surgery is also possible and can be successful. If the eye is blind and painful, it should be removed.

➤ See also uveitis

equine veterinarian

A specialist in the care and treatment of horses. Equine veterinarians are represented in the United States by the AAEP.

➤ See also American Association of Equine Practitioners (AAEP); veterinarian

Vaccinations, usually given annually, can prevent many equine diseases, and giving them provides an opportunity for an equine veterinarian to examine a horse while he's healthy.

equine viral arteritis (EVA) A viral disease of the arteries, of special concern to breeders as it causes abortion in broodmares when transmitted through the semen of an infected stallion. EVA is also conveyed through other means of direct, horse-to-horse contact, and is highly contagious. However, it is not generally life-threatening in nonpregnant horses.

Symptoms often resemble those of a mild attack of influenza, including fever, coughing, nasal congestion, and short-term respiratory infection. Swelling can occur in the muzzle, legs, and eyelids, and stallions may suffer swelling of the sheath and scrotum. In severe cases, a horse may become weak and unable to stand. These cases require intensive treatment, particularly in foals and older horses. A horse who recovers from EVA is no longer contagious and benefits from immunity to the disease that lasts for several years; however, infected stallions continue to spread the virus in their semen.

A vaccine is available that effectively limits outbreaks and protects susceptible broodmares. Breeding stallions who are not infected can be vaccinated so they do not contract the disease from an infected mare. However, because the vaccine contains a modified live virus, it is not risk-free. Consult your veterinarian to determine if vaccination is appropriate.

"equitating" "Looking pretty" in the saddle; indicative of a common view that equitation is all about the aesthetics of pleasing a judge. In reality, good equitation depends on proper biomechanics to create an effective seat that helps the rider control her horse.

equitation The formal art and practice of riding horses. Skilled equitation involves maintaining a body position that is both effective in controlling the horse and correct for the type of riding you are doing. Equitation also demonstrates the mental composure necessary to control the horse and correct any mistakes he may make. It is an art that takes years to master.

Equitation classes are competitions in which the rider, not the horse, is judged. However, the horse must be well trained and capable of performing the required movements. Equitation classes in all but the smallest shows are divided between English and Western; English is usually further divided between hunt seat and saddle seat. Hunt seat equitation may include small jumps.

Riders are judged on their form in the saddle, the turnout of horse and rider, and correctness. Prompt response to the ringmaster's commands and demonstrated knowledge of the proper way to reverse direction and perform other figures is crucial.

JUNIOR EQUITATION CLASS

Equus caballus The scientific name for the modern horse.
➤ *See also feral horses*

ergot

1. A fungus that can grow on grasses, including wheat, rye, barley, bluegrass, red top, brome, and reed canarygrass. A horse who consumes ergot regularly with his feed may develop circulatory problems that cut off the blood supply to extremities, such as the ears, tail, and feet. In severe cases, gangrene can develop and the horse may die.

2. The horny growth found at the rear point of the fetlock on all four legs. Some horses have virtually no ergots; others have large, readily visible growths. Scientists consider ergots to be the evolutionary remnants of footpads. Ergots can be removed (generally for aesthetic reasons) by peeling them off immediately after a bath, when they are soft and somewhat pliable.

estrus
The period when a mare is in heat, which may last 1 to 10 days. Mares' estrous cycles vary widely, from 1 to 10 days, with a period of diestrus (i.e., no heat) in between. Ovulation occurs about 24 to 48 hours before the end of heat. Mares may not be consistent over their lifetimes. One year, a mare may have 5-day cycles; the next, 10-day cycles.

Signs of estrus in a mare include increased interest in stallions and geldings, sometimes demonstrated by aggressive behavior such as kicking or nipping, rubbing against the male horse or against a fence, squatting and urinating frequently, elevating the tail, and "winking" the clitoris. However, some mares experience "silent heat," meaning they are in estrus but do not exhibit the behavior or symptoms associated with heat.

Most mares in the Northern Hemisphere have a period of anestrus (i.e., no cycles of heat) in winter. About the time of the vernal equinox, March 21, many mares begin to cycle again, but the exact season depends on the climate in the mare's home location. The first few cycles are less fertile than those later on, as the summer solstice, June 21, approaches. During first cycles, a mare may be bred, but she probably won't become pregnant. If you must breed early, work closely with a knowledgeable veterinarian.

Mares in heat may be difficult to work with. In some performance horses the difficulty is considered so great that they are given drugs to suppress heat while in training. Some horse owners find that supplements such as magnesium, raspberry leaf, and chasteberry are effective in smoothing out a mare's moods.
➤ *See also anestrus; breeding; diestrus; foal heat, breeding at; silent heat*

euthanasia
The practice of humanely ending the life of a horse who is critically injured, terminally ill, in chronic pain, or unable to function. The decision to put down a horse rather than prolonging his misery is likely to be the most emotionally difficult one a horsekeeper will face. Sometimes the choice is obvious, but other times, as with an older horse who is having difficulty getting around but is otherwise enjoying life, it can be a tough call.

Owners weighing the euthanasia decision need to realistically assess whether they will be available on a regular basis to help the horse if he gets into trouble, how much expense they want to go to maintain the animal, and his quality of life. If the body will be buried, this must be done in unfrozen ground; this may dictate putting the horse down before the ground freezes, rather than waiting for a crisis.

INJECTION BY A VETERINARIAN Horses are typically euthanized by injection, by a veterinarian. The body needs to be disposed of promptly, either by burial or by being taken away by a knacker, as the drug used can poison dogs or other animals that may be tempted to feed on the body.

HUMANE USE OF A FIREARM The decision to humanely end a horse's life is never easy. Most of the time we are lucky enough to be in a location where a veterinarian can handle the situation for us. However, it is actually quite important that horse owners become familiar with using a firearm to end their horse's life. For example, if a horse is severely injured as a result of a trailering accident, the most humane decision might be to end his life as quickly as possible.

Even if you don't carry a firearm in your vehicle or are uncomfortable handling one, you can save your horse pain and suffering if you know how to talk a police officer or rescue person through the process of using a firearm to end the horse's life. Without proper guidance, an inexperienced person may have to make several attempts before the animal dies. Talk with your veterinarian about the steps for ending a horse's life so that you are prepared if ever faced with this difficult decision.

EVA
➤ *See equine viral arteritis (EVA)*

evasion Action taken by the horse to avoid the effect of the aids, such as coming above the bit, getting behind the bit, or ducking the back away from weight aids.

eventing Combined training that incorporates three riding disciplines: dressage, cross-country, and stadium (or show) jumping; also called three-day eventing, three-phase eventing, or horse trials. Eventing is an Olympic event, but competitions exist for riders of all skill levels.
➤ *See also cross-country riding; dressage; show jumping*

Michael Jung of Germany won individual gold in **eventing** at the 2012 Olympics in London, riding La Biothesque Sam.

evolution of the horse

Equids (horses, asses, and zebras) are a highly evolved family of ungulates (hoofed animals) most closely related to tapirs and rhinoceroses. Their evolution began in North America some 60 million years ago with an undersized ancestor commonly called *Eohippus* (Dawn Horse); the proper scientific name for this deerlike forest animal, which stood 14 inches (36 cm) tall, is *Hyracotherium*. It had four toes on each front foot, three toes on each hind foot, caninelike pads on the bottoms of its feet, a small brain, and small teeth suitable for chewing only the tenderest of browse. *Eohippus* migrated out of North America via a land bridge and evolved in dozens of directions over the next 50 million years before dying out.

Meanwhile, in North America pre-horses *Mesohippus* and *Miohippus* became somewhat larger, and three-toed, with most of the weight borne on the middle toe. The toes still had pads behind the small hoof, suited for traveling of soft ground.

During the Miocene epoch, as grasslands spread, equids evolved to exploit the ecological niche of poor-quality vegetation. They developed an organ called the cecum, a large pouch connecting the small intestine and large colon. Similar to a ruminant's four-chambered stomach, the cecum ferments food matter and extracts nutrients. It is less efficient than ruminants' stomachs, extracting only 70 percent as much energy from a given amount of food, but it allows the horse to eat more poor-quality food, and eat it faster. Per unit of *time*, a horse gets more energy out of low-nutrient forage than does a cow. This allowed equids to coexist with enormous herds of ruminants, and to extend their range into drier, colder areas where ruminants would not survive.

The poor-quality diet also pushed equids to become larger. The larger an animal is, the less proportional surface area it has, which conserves body heat. This allowed equids to expand their range northward.

LARGER AND FASTER

With size came speed. The outer toes disappeared, and equids began to run on their middle toes. The toe structures elongated, making the whole leg longer and lighter, with fewer muscles and a restricted range of motion, mostly forward and back. This made the cannon bone susceptible to injury—with only skin, ligaments, and tendons to protect it—but allowed for much greater speed and efficiency. The "springing foot," an arrangement of tendons that allows elastic energy to be stored and reapplied with each stride, contributed greatly to that efficiency, and is also what makes the horse so rideable. The leg does the work while the back stays relatively level. The horse runs efficiently, an adaption in response to its need to travel vast distances to find food and water.

Further increasing the basic energy efficiency of the horse is the "passive stay" apparatus by which the tendons and patella lock into the bones and allow the horse to stand without expending muscular effort. Studies show that horses actually burn about 10 percent less energy standing up than lying down; with cattle and sheep it is the opposite.

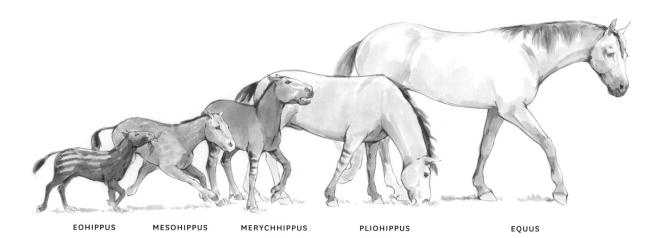

EOHIPPUS   MESOHIPPUS   MERYCHHIPPUS   PLIOHIPPUS   EQUUS

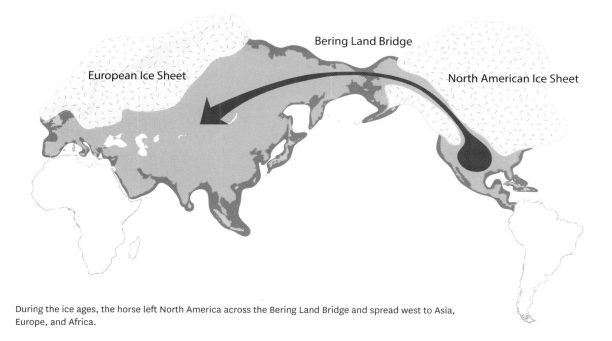

During the ice ages, the horse left North America across the Bering Land Bridge and spread west to Asia, Europe, and Africa.

Grazing required tough teeth to deal with the cellulose and silica in grass. The jaw became longer and stronger. Teeth became higher crowned, covered with cementum, and ever-growing. Grazing also required an elongated head, so the eyes could see over the top of the grass. The eyes migrated to the sides of the head, allowing equids to watch the horizon in nearly 360 degrees.

The first recognizably "horselike" horses appeared about 15 million years ago in North America, developing into four primary groups. *Pliohippus* began as a three-toed horse but gradually lost its side toes, becoming the first one-toed horse. It resembled the modern horse, but had curved teeth and a dished face with concave depressions on the sides.

Another one-toed horse, *Dinohippus*, appeared in North America about 12 million years ago. Its teeth, skull, and feet bore a striking resemblance to the modern horse, and there is evidence of a gradual transition over time from *Dinohippus* to *Equus*, the modern horse genus.

MODERN TIMES Several equine species crossed the Bering land bridge into Eurasia 1.8 million years ago at the beginning of the Ice Age. They had stocky, zebralike bodies; short heads; short, rigid tails; and manes that stood straight up. They rapidly populated the plains and deserts of the Old World, evolving into zebras in Africa, and into ass and horse subspecies in Europe, Asia, and the Mideast. The modern horse, *Equus caballus*, was present in central Europe 1 million years ago. From there it spread and diversified, adapting to local conditions.

In northern Europe, the Draft subspecies developed in response to cold winters, bogs, and wet snows. This horse was thick, with heavy limbs, large feet, and long hair. On the Continent it was fairly large; on the British Isles, trapped by rising sea levels, it became smaller, resembling the many British pony breeds. The Draft subspecies is ancestral to modern draft horses and most ponies of draft type.

In central Europe, a warmblood type evolved, becoming slightly mooselike as its grassland environment reverted to forest. There was also a smaller, more ponylike wild horse, the tarpan. Both these types contributed to modern European breeds.

Far to the east, the sturdy, tundra-adapted Przewalski's horse survives to this day in small numbers. It is emphatically a modern horse, not an ancestor, going back only about 200,000 years, and does not appear in the bloodlines of other modern horses.

In Iran, the Oriental horse acquired long limbs, a narrow body, short fine hair, and large frontal sinuses to moisten incoming air. Very early, a small Oriental corresponding to the Caspian Horse was present in that area. The Caspian is probably an ancestor of the Arabian and other Oriental breeds.

Przewalski's horse is the last example of the horse as it evolved without human influence. It branched off from the modern horse several thousand years before domestication. While not an ancestor of the domestic horse, it is closely related.

SOCIAL STRUCTURE Equine social structure continued to evolve. Where food supply was abundant and consistent, equids like Grevy's zebra and the African asses became solitary and highly territorial. Horses, evolving in areas of sparse food supply where constant migration was necessary, evolved to form harems of one stallion, a group of mares, and their offspring. Harems move as a unit, sometimes long distances as they follow good grazing. Maturing colts and fillies are driven off and form their own bands. The stallion defends his mares against other stallions, while the lead mare tends to make decisions about when to go to water or move to fresh pasture.

Herd structure requires the instinct to form social bonds. These hold the herd together and help modern horses make friends with stablemates. The social instinct also helps create the horse-human bond, and is one of the factors that made domestication possible.

EXTINCTION AND DOMESTICATION The horse could thrive on low-protein, high-fiber forage that would starve a cow. His digestive system allowed him to keep on the move, rather than resting for hours to chew a cud. He was large, fast, migratory, curious, adaptable, and social.

All this worked well on the grasslands in competition with ruminants, and 1 million years ago there were vast populations of equids throughout the world. But during the Ice Age, grasslands in North America were squeezed out by glaciers and evergreen trees. Horse habitat shrank to small pockets, and humans, new on the continent, began hunting horses. By 10,000 years ago horses were extinct in both North and South America.

In Eurasia horses were also in trouble. Superbly adapted to grassland, they did less well in areas that were becoming forested, such as western Europe. As human population increased, so did hunting. Though Paleolithic art depicts a few horses in captivity—wearing halters, or staked out—this seems to have been rare and isolated. Horse populations dwindled, with nearly all subspecies approaching extinction as of 6,000 years ago. But at the last minute, humans in Ukraine invented riding, and horse populations rose dramatically all across Eurasia.

➤ *See also breed;* Eohippus; *history of the horse; Przewalski's horse; tarpan*

ewe neck A conformation fault in which a horse's neck is thin, weak, and affords little or no flexion at the poll, characterized by a concave line from poll to withers. A ewe-necked horse may carry his head and neck quite high, which can limit his ability to see what is beneath him.
➤ *See also neck*

exercise wrap A bandage used to provide support for a horse's lower leg tendons during exercise. The bandage is wrapped around the legs, extending from the middle of the cannon bone downward to the fetlock.

exertional rhabdomyolysis
➤ *See azoturia/Monday morning disease/tying up*

extension A pace in which the horse lengthens his outline and stride to their utmost while maintaining balance, cadence, and contact. Walk, trot, and canter may all be extended. Extended gaits are required in the upper levels of dressage, both driven and ridden.

EXMOOR PONY

An ancient pony breed native to Great Britain. Exmoor Ponies descend from a similar pony found between 45 and 50 degrees north latitude 100,000 years ago, which may have evolved while trapped behind an Alaskan ice barrier for many generations. The Exmoor shows jaw development similar to fossilized bones in North America, unlike any other living breed of horse.

Other adaptations are a two-layer winter coat, with fine springy hair next to the skin, and a greasy, water-repellant outer coat; hair that forms ideal drainage patterns, with the whorls shunting water rapidly off the body; the "ice tail," a fanlike growth of hair at the top of the tail that also facilitates drainage; and an ability to digest roots, which other breeds cannot tolerate.

Exmoors have lived wild on the moors of southwest England for at least 5,000 years. They nearly became extinct during World War II, when the area was used for troop training. Some ponies were shot during target practice, and many were eaten. Following the war, preservation efforts began. The breed is still small in number, but Exmoors are well regarded as children's and driving ponies. Recently, a herd of Exmoor Ponies was exported to Czechoslovakia, to run wild in a former army zone that is now a wildlife sanctuary. The ponies' role is to stop the spread of invasive grasses. The worldwide Exmoor population is fewer than 800, mostly in England.
Livestock Conservancy status: Threatened

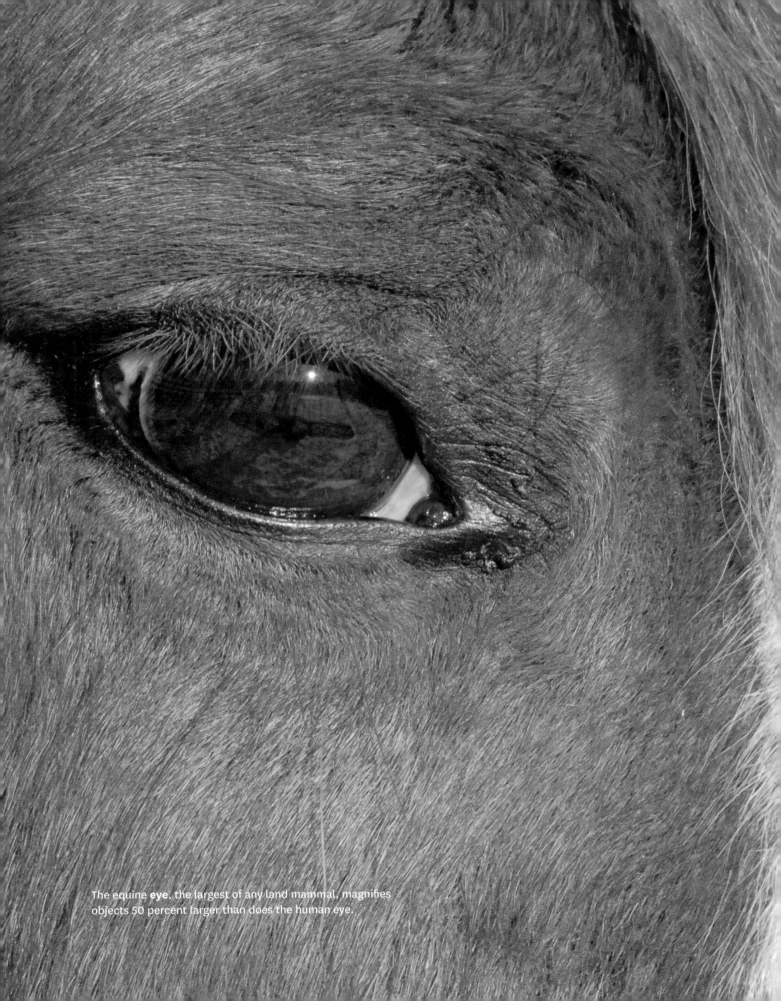

The equine **eye**, the largest of any land mammal, magnifies objects 50 percent larger than does the human eye.

extreme trail/mountain trail competitions

➤ See "Extreme (Not Your Mother's) Trail Class," right; versatility trail competitions

eye color

➤ See iris

eye problems
Horses suffering from impaired vision may be skittish in response to environmental stimuli or simply unable to see and avoid hazards. However, many visually impaired horses adapt successfully. Some handlers believe that "pig-eyed" horses—horses with small eyes—are more likely to be high-strung or difficult to handle because of diminished peripheral vision.

A horse's eye is protected from many potential injuries by a fatty cavity that lies behind it, allowing the eyeball to retract inward in response to a blow or an impact. However, this protection is not absolute, and injuries to parts of the eye are not uncommon. Torn eyelids result when a horse rubs his face against sharp objects, such as nails or barbed wire. Ulcers can form on the eye as the result of irritation from embedded slivers or seeds. An eye that is struck by a tree branch, whip, or the tail of another horse can develop a corneal injury that may require treatment with an antibiotic ointment.

Common equine eye problems include conjunctivitis, moon blindness, night blindness, and cataracts. All eye problems are potentially serious. Even minor problems, if left untreated, can develop into conditions that could result in impairment or even blindness. Inspect your horse's eyes regularly, and contact your veterinarian at the first sign of problems.

➤ See also cataract; conjunctivitis; equine recurrent uveitis (ERU); night blindness; vision

eyes

➤ See vision

EXTREME (NOT YOUR MOTHER'S) TRAIL CLASS

Trail classes were once sedate events where you might back through an L-shaped obstacle, open and close a gate, and perhaps pop over a small jump. Today's trail and versatility competitions offer much more variety, emphasize speed as well as smoothness, and constitute a training challenge that results in a horse you can do almost anything on.

Though the word "extreme" is used in the names of a couple of these competitions, their ethic emphasizes smoothness and correctness. The idea behind these sports is to treat horses well and broaden their scope.

EXTREME COWBOY RACE

A competition created in the early 2000s by horseman Craig Cameron, who wanted to challenge horsemen to develop horses like the old-time, all-around ranch horse, emphasizing trail skills, versatility, and willingness. Extreme Cowboy competition has divisions for everyone from children ages 7 to 11 up to people older than 55. It incorporates elements of trail, ranch, jumping, barrel racing, cutting, and reining, along with shooting and other skills.

Challenges may include mounted archery, backing up or down hills, bareback riding, blindfolding and leading a horse, sorting and roping cattle, and log pulling. In one challenge, horse and rider pull a pallet stacked with 350 pounds (159 kg) of hay bales, with a 5-gallon (19 L) pail of water balanced on top.

Competitions are both judged and timed. The judging emphasizes work on a loose rein, with soft transitions and correct leads. Extreme Cowboy competitors use Western or Australian tack.

➤ See also doma vaquera; versatility trail competitions; Western riding; working equitation/doma trabajo

FOAL

face brush A small, very soft brush that allows dirt to be removed from the tender sides of the face, beneath the forelock, the backs of the ears, and along the front of the face down to the nostrils, as well as from the deep groove under the chin. Although this brush is soft, it should not be used near the eyes. Both the corners of the eyes and nostrils should be gently wiped with a soft, damp cloth.
➤ *See also grooming*

face flies Flies that resemble houseflies and feed on the secretions of a horse's eyes and nostrils and on the blood from other fly bites. Use fly repellent on the horse's face to keep face flies at bay; horses who are badly affected might require a fly mask for protection when outdoors in summer.
➤ *See also pest control*

face markings White (or, rarely, black) markings on the face, from a small snip on the nose to a blaze that covers both eyes. They add to a horse's individuality, and are used as part of official identification on forms such as breed registry certificates and Coggins tests.
➤ *See also "Leg Markings," page 204*

facial expression
➤ *See body language of horses*

false pregnancy When a mare fails to come back into heat even though she is not pregnant. Up to 15 percent of mares with confirmed pregnancies lose the embryo before the 100th day. Losing the embryo doesn't make all mares return to their prepregnancy state. Many will continue to produce progesterone, the hormone that maintains pregnancy, which may keep the mare from coming back into heat for several months. False pregnancy can be convincing; an ultrasound may be needed to determine what is going on.

FALABELLA

A breed of miniature horses, named after the Argentine family that developed it. The smallest known Falabella was a West Virginia–bred horse named Sugar Dumpling; she stood only 20 inches (51 cm) high. Falabellas descend from Criollo horses left to run wild on the Argentine Pampas. In the mid-1800s, small Criollos were crossed with small Thoroughbreds and Shetlands. They breed true to type and size, and are gentle and strong far beyond their stature. They frequently live into their forties.
➤ *See also miniature horse*

farrier A professional horseshoer. Farriers also trim hooves. There are many levels of practicing farriers, ranging from self-taught people with basic skills to thoroughly educated, high-tech farriers. Though some states require licensing, there are many farrier associations with differing standards, and testing is erratic.

The greater the performance demands placed on your horse, the more precise his shoeing needs are. If you do a specialized sport, find a farrier who thoroughly understands that sport. Ask people who do the same things you do, with the same kind of horse, and ask a prospective farrier for references.

➤ *See also hoof; horseshoes; way of going*

FARRIER

fats All horse feeds contain some fat, derived from the grains—oats, millet, barley, and corn—generally found in them. The fat will usually range between 2 and 4 percent, a good level for maintenance. Some horses need more, though; horses who are insulin-resistant, who work hard, or who become fat or overly frisky on too many carbohydrates can benefit from added fat in the diet, up to 10 percent. Added fat will also increase coat gloss.

The easiest and least expensive way to add fat to a horse's diet is to feed whole flaxseed (also called linseed). Other good sources of fat are stabilized rice bran and whole roast soy. It's best to avoid corn oil, which tends to increase inflammation after exercise.

fault Penalty points in a competition. Many competitions are judged on time and faults. Points may be deducted for doing a pattern in the wrong order, touching an element such as a jump or hazard, knocking down a jump or hazard, having the wrong equipment, and other mistakes.

fear (in horses) As a prey species, the horse flees for survival; he survived and evolved by listening to his fears, and they remain with him. What often sets off flight is the sight of sudden, fast, unfamiliar movement. It doesn't really matter *what* is moving; sometimes a candy wrapper will do it. The horse's genes tell him to move first, and find out what the thing is when he's at a safe distance. Evolutionarily, there's no downside to this strategy.

The horse may also be afraid of anything that smells like a carnivore, from pigs to humans. He may fear any object that looks like a predator crouching to spring. He may be afraid of snake-like ropes or wire. In addition, he may fear wet spots, standing water, streams, and mud; in the wild, these areas could keep him from escaping predators. Most horses will also be startled by loud or unexpected noises.

Horses used for pleasure or work purposes cannot flee as can a horse on the open plains. If he is not able to flee to avoid what he perceives as danger, a horse may resort to other means of protecting himself, including kicking with his hind feet, striking with his front feet, or biting. Or the horse may crowd you uncomfortably while seeking protection.

PREVENTION The best way to deal with a horse's fears is to prevent them. A horse's first experience of any new stimuli should be positive. That can best be accomplished by a calm, short introduction. The first mounting, the first drive, the first trailer ride should all be brief and pleasant, something the horse won't mind repeating.

Fear may also be prevented through positive reinforcement training, which often means clicker training. Positive reinforcement fires a seeking system in the brain, one of curiosity, playfulness, and happy expectation that inhibits the fear system. A horse operating on

Most horse-related accidents are caused by horses shying in **fear**—a strong reaction to the sight of something unexpected. A good seat helps this rider stay firm in the saddle.

the seeking system will be less likely to panic, because his brain is operating differently. Using positive reinforcement, you can teach him that new stimuli are fun, and a source of good things.

feathering The long hairs at the backs of the pasterns of draft horses such as Clydesdales and Shires. Many breeds will develop some feathering in winter, even if it is not typical of or desirable in their breed. For pleasure and show horses, the feathers are removed with electric clippers to show off the horse's conformation. Some people also clip feathers to keep dampness and mud from collecting there and causing diseases, such as scratches. However, evidence suggests that feathering actually helps drain water off the legs, away from the skin and pasterns.
➤ *See also Clydesdale; fetlock; pastern; scratches; Shire*

FEATHERING

fecal balls
➤ *See manure, as indicator of health*

fecal screening Examination of a fecal sample by a veterinarian or veterinary lab, to determine parasite load. Fecal screening is recommended to determine a deworming schedule.

Fédération Equestre Internationale (FEI) A global organization that establishes rules and regulations for international equestrian sports, including the Olympic Games. The FEI has also developed a set of standardized aids; if you ride any well-trained horse in the United States, Germany, or France, he should respond to the same aids, which makes it easy for instructors to work with horses and riders from many national backgrounds.

feedbag
➤ *See nosebag*

feeding and nutrition A horse's feed and nutrition have an enormous impact on his ability to do the job he is trained to do, on his mental attitude, and on his longevity. Because a horse has only one stomach and a cecum (rather than the four stomachs of a cow, for example), he must be fed so that his simple digestive system is not overwhelmed, which can result in a dangerous colic or other health problems.

Feeding horses is a large and complex topic, but the following are some simple constants.

DIET SHOULD BE FORAGE-BASED — PASTURE OR HAY. Horses evolved to eat more or less continuously, and are happiest and healthiest when they have lots of time to graze. Pastures should be kept in good condition, but for easy keepers, it may be a mistake to improve pasture too much. It is harder to keep horses from overeating on rich pasture than to supplement poor pasture.

A WORKING HORSE NEEDS MORE and higher-quality feed than a nonworking or retired horse. An idle horse weighing 1,000 pounds (454 kg) needs about 25 pounds (11 kg) of hay daily to maintain his weight and normal bodily functions. (This may vary from individual to individual.) A working horse will need more hay, and should be fed a concentrate as well. Some horses also require supplements of vitamins and minerals; if your horse loses condition or weight, ask your vet to recommend a diet and supplements to help.

FEEDING CHANGES AS HORSES AGE. Older horses, especially those in light work, may need supplements to maintain condition and weight. Very old horses may need special soft food, as their teeth may be worn down.

MINERALS ARE KEY TO HEALTH. The essential minerals for horses are calcium, phosphorus, magnesium, sodium, chlorine, and potassium. Horses need trace amounts of iodine, cobalt, copper, iron, zinc, manganese, and selenium. Various soils provide, through hay and grasses, many of these minerals in varying quantities. In some regions, supplements are needed for one or another mineral; in other regions, supplementation would cause overdose. Veterinarians can help determine specific needs in your area.

HORSES NEED VITAMINS, TOO. Horses can obtain virtually all the vitamins they need if they are kept on good pasture and not worked beyond the limits of the energy found in their diet. If a horse is partially pastured and partially fed grain and hay (particularly if he does a substantial amount of work), it is necessary to analyze his rations and his condition to decide if any supplemental vitamins are needed and which ones.

SALT IS ANOTHER ESSENTIAL ITEM. Grasses do not provide it; usually, it is added to commercial feeds. Because excess salt is simply flushed from the system, as long as the horse has sufficient water available, it is safe to provide free access to salt. Usually, blocks are hung in a rack in the stall or just set on the floor for the horse to lick at will. Large salt blocks can be used in pastures for field-boarded horses.

OVERFEEDING CAN BE WORSE THAN UNDERFEEDING. A horse who breaks into the grain bin, or even one put out too suddenly on rich pasture, can rapidly develop a life-threatening situation with colic or founder. A fat horse has more weight to carry, which can damage his joints.

FEED QUALITY IS CRITICAL. Moldy or spoiled feed can cause serious illness, and rodents and opossums getting into feed can spread disease. Store grain and pellets in rodent-proof containers with tight-fitting lids, or in metal-lined bins that close tightly. Wherever you store grain, keep the area safe from horses by using horse-proof latches.

WATER IS VITAL FOR EQUINE DIGESTION and metabolism. Horses will generally drink water periodically while grazing, and must have free access to water if stalled. A horse eating hay and concentrates needs even more water than a horse on grass. Giving free-choice access to clean water is one of the best ways to prevent colic.

RATIONS SHOULD BE WEIGHED rather than measured or eyeballed. Feeding flakes of hay is tricky because not all hay is created equal; some balers bale tightly, and their flakes weigh more than flakes from a loose baler. A minimally active horse needs about 25 pounds (11 kg) of hay, in two or three feedings per day.

NOT ALL GRAIN IS EQUAL. A bushel of corn weighs nearly twice as much as a bushel of oats. Weigh each new feed mixture, whether homemade or commercial, to see how much your standard measure of *that feed* weighs, and then calculate the volume of that feed needed to supply what your horse requires. Each time you change your formula or change commercial rations, weigh again to determine how many scoops equal the pounds needed for good health.

➤ *See also calcium; digestive system; float; hay; individual minerals; pelleted feed; phosphorus; protein; salt (sodium chloride); supplements; vitamins; water, for horses; weighing feed*

feet
➤ *See hoof*

FEI
➤ *See Fédération Equestre Internationale (FEI)*

fences
➤ *See barns and facilities; jumps*

fence walking
➤ *See pacing*

fender
The rectangular or triangular panel of leather that hangs down from a Western saddle. The fender holds the stirrup and protects the rider's leg.
➤ *See also Western riding; Western tack*

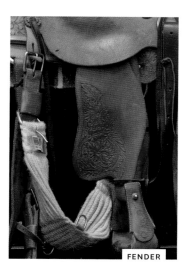

FENDER

Feeding and nutrition: These Konik horses, like all horses, evolved to not only survive but thrive on grass alone. Forage should still provide the bulk of any horse's diet.

FELL PONY

A large British pony (13.2–14 hands high) originally developed as a pack pony. Tough and versatile, Fell Ponies make excellent riding and driving ponies, and are large enough to carry adults. The breed has seen some resurgence recently. **Livestock Conservancy status: Watch**

feral horses Free-running horses who have escaped from farms and ranches, or their offspring. The mustang of the American West is a feral, rather than a wild, horse. Technically, all modern "wild" horses except Przewalski's horse are feral, as all are descended from domesticated horses. One scientific term for modern feral horses is *Equus ferus*.

fertility
➤ *See infertility*

fescue grass A pasture grass (*Festuca elatior syn. Festuca arundinacea*) that can cause mares to abort and other horses to become ill. It's not the grass itself, commonly called tall fescue, that causes problems but rather *Neotyphodium coenophialum* (also known as *Acremonium coenophialum*), the fungus that grows on much of it. Pregnant mares should not be fed fescue hay, which can cause retained placenta, failure to produce milk, and even abortion. In other horses, fescue toxicity manifests as low thyroid, stiffness, reluctance to work, and poor muscle development. Horses may show remission if fed hay made from other grasses, or if given thyroid and iodine supplements.

fetlock The hair growing on the back of the fetlock joint.

fetlock joint The rounded, bony, bulblike structure on a horse's leg just above the pastern. Technically called the fetlock joint, the term is almost always shortened to fetlock. It corresponds to the joint attaching a human's fingers to the long bones of the palm, and the toes to the long bones of the foot (joining metacarpals and metatarsals to proximal phalanges).

fiador A lightweight rope or cord tied to the bottom knot of a bosal and fastened around the horse's neck and head, to hold the bosal in the correct position. A fiador is not intended to be used for leading or tying.
➤ *See also bosal; hackamore; mecate*

fields, riding in Horses associate fields with freedom, so riding in fields requires skill and knowledge. A horse will probably be more easily distracted in a field than in an enclosed riding ring. There's more to look at—birds, insects, maybe deer or other animals nearby. Open spaces may trigger the urge to run. If your horse is distracted or nervous, give him a job to do to get his attention. Ask for a few well-known but somewhat exacting figures like small circles, and execute them precisely. As your horse does this work, he'll be absorbing the scents and sights around him, and should begin to relax.
➤ *See also pasture, horses on; trail riding*

field trialing Hunting birds with dogs from horseback. Field trial horses must be fit and gun-wise. Tennessee Walkers are the traditional breed, but the McCurdy Plantation Horse was developed for field trialing and is gaining a following. Nonhunters may observe a hunt on horseback. Known as "the gallery," they must know field trial etiquette, and all horses must be absolutely safe for dogs to be around.

figure eight A schooling pattern used in many disciplines: two circles that join in the middle to form an eight. It can be executed at a walk or trot/jog while riders learn how to maintain and change bend by using leg/hand/body coordination. At the canter or lope, it becomes a more serious test of riding ability. Riders must maintain proper bend and symmetry in both circles, and achieve a proper change of lead in the middle. Riders learn first how to perform a simple change of lead, which is done by asking the horse to come down to a trot, walk, or halt prior to signaling for the new lead. Once this is mastered, riders learn how to perform a flying lead change, in which the change occurs midstride without any break of gait.

figures
➤ *See school figures*

filly A female horse up to four years of age.

finished horse A horse who is fully trained for the job at hand; the opposite of the "green" horse. The same horse could be "finished" as a riding horse but be "green" as a driving horse.

A finished horse may not be suitable for a novice. In some disciplines the horse may have a far more refined understanding of the aids than the inexperienced rider or driver is capable of, and this can lead to frustration on both sides. Also, playing the "school horse" role may dull some of a finished horse's responses.

fistula of the withers An infection of the withers that can develop into a life-threatening injury. It has many causes; most commonly an ill-fitted saddle causes bruising. If left untreated, infection might develop under the skin, draining painfully between the horse's shoulder blades and spine. Infection can eventually open up a hole through the skin and into the muscle below that is large enough to fit a man's fist. Cures, at this point, are difficult and slow; often, the horse must be put down.

Fistulous withers can also be caused by tack bumping the withers repeatedly and causing bruising, or by cuts in the area further aggravated by bumping or by unclean saddle pads.

fitness
➤ *See conditioning program; interval training*

five-gaited horse Any breed that performs other gaits in addition to walk, trot/jog, canter/lope, and gallop; the breed most commonly associated with the term "five-gaited" is the American Saddlebred. These horses are born with the ability to perform two additional gaits, the rack and the slow gait.
➤ *See also amble; American Breeds, American Saddlebred; pace; Paso Fino; Peruvian Horse; rack; racking horse; tölt*

FJORD/NORWEGIAN FJORD

A breed of small, sturdy horses who look remarkably like Przewalski's horse, with the same dun coloring and dorsal stripe; the likeness is accentuated by the common practice of roaching the mane so it stands erect. Rarely exceeding 14.2 hands high, Fjords are sometimes classified as a horse, sometimes a pony.

Fjords have been bred in Norway since the time of the Vikings, with little alteration except increased size. They invaded western Europe along with their Viking owners, and are present in the bloodlines of all modern draft breeds. A strong-willed but pleasant character and a willingness to work make these horses popular as family horses. They are used for trail riding, dressage, jumping, and driving, and they make excellent small draft horses.

➤ *See also Przewalski's horse*

flagger In roping events, a mounted rider who holds a flag with his outstretched arm until a competitor successfully ropes the cow. At that time, he drops his arm and the flag.

flag race A timed competition in which riders pick up one or more flags and place them in cans or buckets while riding a prescribed pattern.
➤ *See also mounted games*

flank The area on a horse's side between the thigh and the barrel.

flank cinch The back cinch used on many Western saddles.

flanking In roping, a Western event, seizing a calf by its flank and leg and placing it on its side.

flare A concave outward bend at the side of the hoof; a hoof wall that is flared is weaker than a straight wall. Most hooves develop flares as they grow out, but they can be kept in check if the farrier trues up the hoof wall with a rasp periodically.

flash noseband/flash attachment

A two-part cavesson. A regular cavesson fastens around the horse's jaw. The flash attachment, fastened to the midpoint of the cavesson by a loop, wraps around the horse's chin, below the bit, and fastens snugly to keep the horse's mouth closed. It is used only with a snaffle.

➤ *See also drop noseband*

flat bone A desirable conformation trait in which the tendon lies well behind the cannon bone, with tissue intervening. The cannon bone appears wide and flat when viewed from the side, and has greater circumference than a cannon with round bone. Flat-boned legs hold up better under stress, as the tendon is subject to less wear.

➤ *See also cannon bone; round bone*

flat feet An inherited or man-made condition (due to poor hoof care) in which the sole of the hoof is not concave, so that there is no natural way for the horse to avoid bruising the sole on rocks. Shoeing with pads added between hoof and shoe can help, as can toughening the sole by applying iodine to it. If you use iodine, avoid the hoof wall (iodine dries it out) and other tissues that iodine will burn.

flat-footed walk

1. A true four-beat walk used by most horses in pleasure and competition.

2. In gaited horse parlance, an energetic yet relaxed walk, 4 to 6 miles (6–10 k) per hour, with longer steps and increased overstride. Horses nod their heads more than in an ordinary walk, and back motion is less. Also called "flat walk" or "slow paso llano."

flat racing Thoroughbred (and other breed) racing on the flat, as opposed to over fences.

From the ancient Greeks to the Romans to the Anglo-Saxons, horse racing and hunting on horseback have been popular sports. King Charles II, who ruled from 1660 to 1685, around the time the English Thoroughbred was being formed, is known as "the Father of the British Turf." He founded the Royal Stud and developed a small racecourse at Newmarket into the famous center for racing that it remains.

FLAT RACING AT CHURCHILL DOWNS IN KENTUCKY

In the United States, racing followed the colonists, whose informal races at short distances led to the development of the Quarter Horse, which can outrun a Thoroughbred in a sprint. The first American oval track was created on Long Island in 1665. Racing survived the disruptions of the Revolutionary and Civil Wars to become firmly entrenched in the American sport scene. The advent of the mechanized gate and the photo finish simplified the process of getting the race started and determining how it finished.

➤ *See also harness racing; speed, of horse; Thoroughbred; Triple Crown*

flatulent colic

➤ *See colic; feeding and nutrition*

flat work Riding that does not incorporate jumps.

RACING TERMS

BACKSTRETCH: The long section of the track on the far side of the racecourse.

BLINKERS (OR BLINDERS): Patches (or hoods) attached to the bridle to restrict the horse's vision and reduce his inclination to shy at objects coming up behind him.

BREEDER'S CUP: The annual racing championship, consisting of eight races held at a different track each year and offering total of $13 million in prize money.

CLAIMING RACE: A race in which the horses may be purchased by preregistered buyers at previously set prices.

CLASSIC: A traditionally important race. Also refers to the length of a race; an American classic is 1¼ miles (2 k), while a European classic is 1½ miles (2.4 k).

CUPPY: A term that describes a dry, crumbling track surface.

DAILY DOUBLE: A wager in which the bettor must select the winners of two consecutive races (often the first and second of the day).

DAILY RACING FORM: A paper containing statistics about races, horses, and jockeys.

EXACTA: A wager in which the bettor must select the first two finishers, in order.

FURLONG: One-eighth of a mile, or 220 yards (about 201 m).

HANDICAP: A race with weights assigned according to each horse's previous performances or the process of selecting horses (frequently for the purpose of placing bets) based on past performance.

HOMESTRETCH: The straight section of track between the last turn and the finish line.

IN THE MONEY: A term describing a horse who places first, second, or third in a race.

LENGTH: In a race, the distance of about 12 feet (3.6 m), which a Thoroughbred covers in ⅕ of a second.

MUDDER: A horse who races well on a muddy track.

OTB: Off-track betting.

PLACE: To finish second.

SCRATCH: To withdraw a horse from a race before it starts.

SHOW: To finish third.

SILKS: The brightly colored shirts and caps worn by the jockeys. Each owner or stable has its own colors and design.

STAKES: A race for which the owner must pay a fee to enter.

flehmen response A behavior in which the horse curls his upper lip and raises his head in order to draw air across the vomeronasal organ, a specialized organ located in the roof of the mouth. It can be a reaction to odd tastes or smells in the environment, or an effort to obtain the scent of a mare in heat. It's often called a "horse laugh," and horses can be taught to produce it on cue. (The German word *flehmen* means "to curl the upper lip.")

FLEHMEN RESPONSE

flexion When the horse yields his jaw and poll, moving his head slightly, longitudinally (toward his chest) or laterally (to one side or the other).
➤ *See also flexion test; hock; stifle*

flexion test Part of a prepurchase exam performed by a veterinarian to determine whether the horse is sound for the purposes you intend to use him for. It can also be used to find lameness in horses. The veterinarian holds the hock or other leg joint in a flexed position for an extended period of time. When it is released, a helper jogs the horse away and the veterinarian assesses whether or not the horse has regained normal use of the stressed joint within the appropriate length of time.

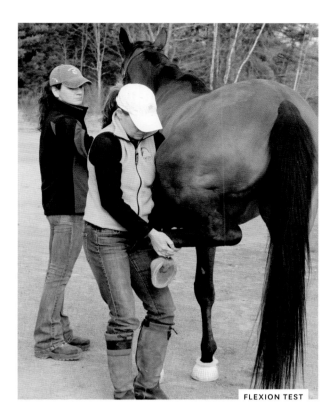

FLEXION TEST

flexor tendon The tendon in the leg that allows the horse to pick up his hooves.

flies

➤ *See bot flies; face flies; horseflies/tabanids; parasites*

flight instinct

➤ *See fear (in horses)*

float

1. To rasp a horse's teeth to remove sharp points. The equine dental rasp is called a float. After the age of two, horses should have their teeth checked at least once a year and floated when necessary.

2. To cut away part of the hoof wall at the heels so that the heel does not bear weight on the horseshoe.

➤ *See also dental problems; hoof*

FLORIDA CRACKER HORSE

A gaited horse that traces back to the Spanish conquistadores, the Florida Cracker Horse was later bred to herd and pen half-wild cattle. A strong, tough horse with great endurance and a well-developed herding instinct, the Florida Cracker naturally exhibits either a running walk or an amble.

Free-roaming herds have been introduced into a couple of state preserves by the Florida Department of Agriculture and Consumer Services. The breed's unusual name is taken from sound made by the long whips used by cowboys to gather cattle.

flu/influenza

➤ *See equine influenza*

flukes Parasitic flatworms that live in freshwater snails and spread Potomac horse fever (PHF).
➤ *See also Potomac horse fever (PHF)*

flying lead change

Changing from one canter lead to the other in the space of a single stride. In a flying lead change, the horse changes lead midstride at the canter or lope without breaking out of the gait. Bringing the horse back to a trot or jog to make the change is called a "simple change."

USES OF LEAD CHANGES IN JUMPING Horses negotiating the tight corners and turns of a jump course, and approaching a jump, must be well balanced. The leading foreleg must hit the ground just prior to takeoff, or the horse will jump from too far back or too close; the leading hind leg must be able to push the weight off the ground.

USES OF LEAD CHANGES IN WESTERN RIDING Many Western horsemanship pleasure events use a serpentine pattern requiring eight lead changes. Pole bending competitions also demand that horses change leads easily as they weave around the poles. Pole benders often train their horses to change leads on voice command alone. Reining horse competitions also require numerous well-executed lead changes.
➤ *See figure eight; lead (canter); tempi changes*

fly mask Fine-woven mesh protective gear that fits over a horse's eyes, and sometimes his ears and muzzle. Masks are usually held securely under the chin with Velcro strips, with a padded strap around the ears to secure them from above. The horse can see through the mesh,

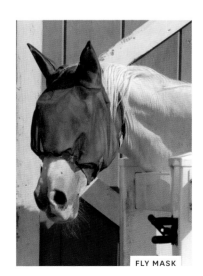

FLY MASK

but the flies cannot get in to feed on the discharge from the horse's eyes. These masks are appropriate for any horse grazed outdoors in daylight during fly season (they are taken off when the horse returns to his stall), especially horses who are particularly bothered by flies.

foal The offspring of a mare and a stallion. A male foal is a colt; a female is a filly.

foal heat, breeding at

The mare's first heat after foaling, usually within 3 to 12 days. The nursing foal may experience minor diarrhea at this time. Some breeders believe in rebreeding on the foal heat; others believe strongly that it is a bad idea, as the mare may harbor minor infections from foaling.

foaling Mares have been foaling in the wild for thousands of years, and most mares conceive, carry, and birth a foal without much need for involvement from humans. When they give birth under the artificial conditions in which we keep and raise them, however, intervention may be called for.

Gestation may vary between 305 and 395 days, averaging 340 days (11 months and 1 week). Light breeds tend to have longer gestation periods than do heavy breeds. Also, some stallions customarily sire foals that are carried a longer or shorter time than usual. As a general rule, mares with first foals often have shorter gestation periods than those who have borne foals before.

EARLY LABOR The mare's udder enlarges during the last month of gestation. A dry, waxy substance that is normally inside the mammary ducts begins to push through the teats as milk replaces it. This process, known as "waxing," is a classic sign that the mare will likely foal soon. The first stages of labor may last anywhere from 3 hours to 72 hours. Mild uterine contractions position the foal for birth, with his head and front legs pointing toward the birth canal. The mare may go to a faraway spot in the field, or stand with a distant look in her eye. She may be restless, pacing and nibbling a few bites of food.

ACTIVE LABOR Once a mare enters active, or second-stage, labor, the water sac breaks, after which the foal should be born within 30 minutes (perhaps a

Foaling is usually a normal process that unfolds without need for human intervention.

little longer for a first-time mother). A foal should emerge from the dam front feet and head first. Anything other than this position signifies a malpresentation, which must be corrected immediately if the foal is to be born live.

After a foal is born, the mare usually remains lying down for 10 to 20 minutes, allowing the blood from the placenta to pass to the newborn through the umbilical cord. When she stands up, the umbilical cord breaks naturally and she should expel the placenta with a few more contractions.

NURSING A healthy foal will be on his feet and nursing within two hours of his birth. It is crucial that he nurse within several hours, as that is when he is most able to absorb the antibodies provided by the mare's colostrum. Antibodies are the components of a mammal's blood that enable it to fight off bacterial, viral, and fungal intruders in the system. Foals are born without antibodies and must quickly obtain them by nursing on colostrum, which is produced by the mare only in the first few days after giving birth.

➤ *See also nurse mare; orphan foal; weaning*

Foals are the **nursing** champions of the farm. While calves nurse only about 4 times in each 24-hour period, foals nurse 48 times—every half hour on average! After a few weeks, the foal's hunger can be satisfied by hourly nursing. Later on, the foal's nursing will drop to a mere 18 times in 24 hours.

129

foot care

➤ *See hoof*

foot flight
The path a foot takes from the time it leaves the ground until it lands.

forage
High-fiber plants such as grass or legumes, in fresh or hay forms. Forage should form the bulk of most horses' diets. If the forage is low-quality or deficient in nutrients it may need to be supplemented with a forage balancer, a commercial mix of minerals, vitamins, and protein.

➤ *See also hay*

forage poisoning

➤ *See botulism*

forecart
A two-wheeled cart used to pull a piece of farm machinery while providing a safe seat for the driver. Some forecarts include an engine, which can be used to power large machines. Other machines have a ground drive, a system that uses the turning force of the implement's wheels to create the power to run the implement.

forehand
The horse's head, neck, shoulder, and front legs; the part of the horse in front of the rider's hands and legs.

forelock
The part of the mane that grows from between a horse's ears and hangs down the face.

forging
Hitting the sole or shoe of a forefoot with the toe of a hind foot. It can be caused by conformation problems, such as sickle hocks, or a square frame (ideal conformation is a longer underline than topline). Young, tired, or poorly conditioned horses may forge, as may those whose toes have grown too long and need trimming.

➤ *See also overreaching*

fork

➤ *See pommel; slick-fork saddle*

forward seat
A style of hunt seat riding in which the rider inclines her torso a few degrees in front of the vertical during all work above a walk. Irons (stirrups) are usually one to two holes shorter than in balanced seat, creating a deeper bend in the knee. This seat is also balanced—that is, the rider's weight is distributed behind the withers of the horse and in line with the horse's center of gravity—but the balance is achieved through an S curve rather than the more static position of balanced seat.

Balanced seat riders most often shorten their stirrup leathers one or two holes when jumping big fences to allow their buttocks to clear the saddle as the horse jumps up and rounds his back. (Horses rarely round their backs over low fences.) Forward seat riders generally carry the same stirrup length over fences and on the flat.

➤ *See also balanced seat; center of gravity; two-point seat*

founder
A structural change in the hoof in which the coffin bone rotates or sinks downward, as a result of laminitis. Many people use the terms "founder" and "laminitis" interchangeably, but founder is the extreme condition resulting from laminitis.

➤ *See also laminitis*

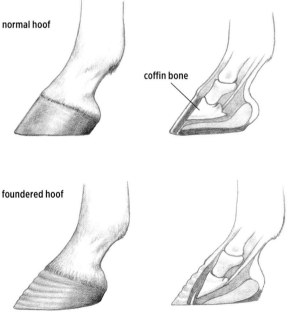

normal hoof

coffin bone

foundered hoof

FOUNDER

"four-beater" A horse with a four-beat canter or lope. The canter is a three-beat gait. In a four-beat gait (also called a "trashy lope" by Western riders), the horse will set his front hoof of the second beat down before he has completely pushed off the hindquarters. The gait makes for an uncomfortable ride, at best, and is frowned upon by show judges.

4-H A program for young people in the United States and Canada, run by states or provinces. Since the early 1900s, 4-H has taught young people about agriculture, livestock, and home economics. As of 2015, more than 6 million youths ages 5 to 19 were involved in 4-H with projects ranging from horses and livestock to communications and expressive arts. The programs are administered primarily through Cooperative Extension Service offices of land grant universities within the United States and Canada. The 4-H Horse Project focuses on horsemanship education rather than just riding skills. Members learn the wide range of skills required to become responsible horse owners and/or managers. These skills include the following:

- The skills needed in horseback riding
- Safe horse-handling and management practices
- How to have fun with horses through games, shows, and clinics

four-in-hand/four up Two teams of horses hitched and driven one in front of the other. "Four-in-hand" is the carriage-driving term; "four-up" is the draft term.

FOUR-IN-HAND

foxhunting A sport that was developed in England for a bona fide agricultural purpose: ridding farms of foxes, which killed small livestock and were a general nuisance. A pack of hounds is used to scent and pursue a fox, and riders follow the hounds, until the fox loses them or loses his life.

Humans have been hunting on horseback for thousands of years, though foxhunting as we know it today is a more recent development. The first mounted hunters were after large meat animals such as deer, boar, and other horses. In medieval France and England, the hunt evolved primarily as a sport of the nobility. The French influence is still felt in some hunting terms, such as "Tallyho!" (from the French *Ty a hillaut*, meaning that the quarry is in view and running).

The first mention in print of chasing foxes for sport appears during the reign of King Henry VIII. By the 17th century, foxhunting had become a popular pastime for gentlemen, merchants, and farmers as well as lords and ladies. It was also useful to farmers; without rabies to thin the population, foxes multiply rapidly, and are considered vermin in Britain.

Hunting came to America with the first settlers and became firmly established, especially in the eastern United States. The goal of American hunters is to send the fox to ground, not to kill him, as American fox populations are fewer. Coyotes, where common, are also hunted, and as they kill unacceptable numbers of sheep, they are more frequently killed. Americans also participate in drag hunts; the United States Pony Club plays a large role in educating future foxhunters.

Legend has it that the famous "pink" jackets commonly worn by hunt staff and some members (which are actually red) are named for the tailor who designed them, rather than the color itself. Evidence for the existence of such a tailor is scarce, but the term persists.

Live foxhunting was banned in England in 2004; however, enforcement is not strict and in some districts hunting continues. Foxhunting is also an American sport; live foxes or coyotes may be hunted, or riders may chase after a "drag," a fox-scented object drawn over the land before the hunt. For horsemen, hunting offers the thrill of an unpredictable ride across country, with many kinds of fences to jump.

➤ *See also hunter*

fox trot One of the easy gaits. The defining trait of the fox trot is its rhythm. One front foot touches the ground a split second before the diagonal rear foot; there is then a pause, followed by the other front foot and finally the other rear foot a split second later. This rhythm has the same cadence as the phrase "a chunk of meat and two potatoes."

➤ *See also Missouri Fox Trotter*

frame The posture in which a horse carries himself while working; usually refers to his degree of rounding up and compression from back to front, or to his headset.

free-choice feeding Keeping hay available to horses at all times, usually in round bales. Free-choice feeding is less work for the horsekeeper, and may suit some horses well. Others eat too much in this situation and need to be fed individually.

NATIVE HORSES AND PONIES OF FRANCE

France has been home to horses since prehistoric times. Many of the ancient cave paintings of horses are in France, as is Solutre, a site where Stone Age humans hunted horses by driving them over a cliff. The modern French raise many fine horses and engage in horse sports. They are also one of the countries in the world where horsemeat is often eaten. Some prominent native breeds include the following.

The **Merens pony**, also called Ariegois, has lived in the Pyrenees since prehistoric times. Black with an Oriental head, rather straight shoulders, and a long, strong back, it is used for riding and light draft work. The **Landais** is an elegant pony, 11 to 13 hands. Like the Merens, it runs wild, but when tamed makes an excellent children's riding pony. The **Pottok**, an ancient small horse of the Basque Pyrenees, stands 12 to 14.2 hands, and is a rugged pack and riding pony.

The **Boulonnais**, a midsize gray draft horse, stands 15.1 to 15.2 hands and has a very Oriental head. It is energetic yet gentle, and is used for work and meat.

The **Breton**, an ancient draft breed from Brittany, comes in three types; draft, small draft, and cob. The Breton has airy, beautiful gaits, including an amble, and strongly influenced the Canadian horse. It is used for work and meat. The **Comtois** is a sturdy draft horse known since the fourth century. Very sure-footed, they are excellent for mountain logging and vineyard work, and are also used for meat.

➤ *See also Camargue horse; Percheron*

LANDAIS

BRETON

FRIESIAN

An elegant black baroque breed from Holland. Friesians stand 15 to 17 hands high, and have a regal bearing, with long, noble heads; graceful necks set upright on well-sloped shoulders; and well-balanced bodies. Mane and tail are abundant, as is the feathering on the lower legs. Friesians carried knights in the Middle Ages and influenced many breeds, including the English Fell and Dales Ponies, the Standardbred, and the Canadian Horse. The breed was influenced in turn by the Andalusian, and is one of the few European breeds with no Thoroughbred crosses.

The breed standards are exacting; mares and stallions are rigorously tested before being accepted for breeding, and a stallion and his offspring continue to be tested until he is 12. This results in great consistency, soundness, and good temperament within the breed.

Friesians have bold, crowd-pleasing action, and are used for dressage, driving, and pleasure riding; for many people, they represent the ultimate in equine elegance. They are also popular as circus horses and, because of their black coloring, are still used in the funeral business.

freedom of movement A horse's ability to perform the movements or gaits asked for by a rider in a strong, supple manner, without restriction in any of his muscles or joints. Restriction is usually most obvious when watching a horse trot. Horses with conformation faults of the hips, shoulders, or legs, or those experiencing pain, will often appear stilted in their movement. An obvious example of restricted movement is when a horse with early stages of laminitis or navicular disease appears to be tiptoeing around the arena, trying to avoid bearing normal weight on its painful front feet.

freestyle In dressage or reining, a choreographed routine set to music, incorporating various mandatory elements and meeting a specified time limit. Musical freestyle is a creative art form, and is a spectator favorite. Freestyle tests are performed in dressage from First Level up. In reining, riders often perform their 4-minute routine in costume. Tack is optional.

free walk In dressage, a walk on a long rein in which the horse does not necessarily maintain contact with the rider's hands. The objective is to have the horse relax and stretch outward and down with his head and neck, with an elongated outline. It is required in tests at the lowest level.

frog, of foot A V-shaped structure beginning at the heel and extending into the sole about two-thirds of the length of the foot. The frog is the shock absorber for the hoof.
➤ *See also hoof*

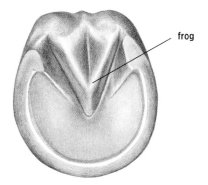

frog

full pass
➤ *See sidepass*

fungal infections Infections caused by a fungus, such scratches or thrush.
➤ *See girth itch; mold/fungi in feed; ringworm; scratches; warts*

fungi in feed
➤ *See mold/fungi in feed*

furlong One-eighth of a mile, or 220 yards (about 201 m); a distance measurement used in flat racing.

Fusarium moniliforme A fungus that produces deadly toxins and is the factor in moldy corn poisoning. It lives in soil and is commonly found on moldy corn stalks or corn that has been rained on or stored wet. Small doses make horses lose weight and stop eating. They may appear listless. Large doses are usually fatal.
➤ *See mold/fungi in feed; toxic substances*

futurities Competitive events sponsored by a variety of breeds and disciplines—including Thoroughbred and Quarter Horse racing, cutting, reining, and barrel racing—in which breeders are confident enough in the offspring of certain crosses that they are willing to gamble nomination fees to the event beginning while the foal is in utero. Nearly every major breed in the United States sponsors futurities that range from halter competition with a few hundred dollars paid to the winner, to international performance competitions with tens of thousands of dollars paid to the winner.

gag bits A group of snaffle bits designed to be used with two reins. They raise the horse's head by raising the bit in his mouth, as well as acting on the corners of the mouth and the poll, similarly to curb bits but without a curb strap. Some gag bits (Balding, Cheltenham) have holes in the bit rings, one on top and one on the bottom. Rounded cheekpieces pass through these holes, and the reins are attached to them. Severity is determined by bit ring size; the larger the rings, the more severe the bit.

The American gag or elevator bit has shanks, like a Tom Thumb snaffle. The Dutch gag has cheekpieces consisting of three stacked rings.

Gag bits are popular for strong horses being ridden cross-country, and are most often seen in polo, eventing, show jumping, and cross-country hacking. They are not permitted at any level of dressage.

➤ *See also bits*

gait A particular sequence of foot movements. The horse has four legs and, theoretically, 100 possible ways of sequencing them; the combination of sequence and speed defines the gait. In reality, when not cantering, the horse uses one of nine clearly defined symmetrical gaits. The natural gaits, which are passed down genetically, are listed here in English, along with the most common non-English names used for them in the United States:

- The ordinary walk; all horses have this gait.

- The flat-footed walk, also called flat walk (slow paso llano)

- The running walk (paso llano)

- The pace (skeið, flug skeið, huachano)

- The broken or stepping pace, also called the amble (skeið-tölt, sobreandando)

- The saddle rack, sometimes called the singlefoot (slow tölt, fino, corto, largo)

- The true rack (true tölt, fast largo)

- The trot

- The fox trot (brokk-tölt, trocha, pasitrote)

Artificial gaits are not passed down genetically but are developed by special training methods. An example of an artificial gait is the Spanish Walk.

➤ *See also artificial gait; canter; five-gaited horse; flat-foot walk; fox trot; gallop; jog; lope; pace; pasitrote; paso llano; running walk; skeið; sobreandando; Spanish walk; three-gaited horse; tölt; transition; trot; walk*

WALK SEQUENCE

TROT SEQUENCE

CANTER SEQUENCE (LEFT LEAD)

The Missouri Fox Trotter is one of a number of **gaited horse** breeds that naturally perform a smooth gait that typically falls between the trot and the canter.

gaited horse A horse who naturally performs gaits other than walk, trot/jog, and canter/lope. The gaited horse is esteemed for the smoothness of its gait. The predisposition to gait is genetically inherited. Generations of breeding will strengthen this tendency, and it will crop up unwanted from time to time in horses with gaited breeds in their ancestry. Many Morgans, for instance, will singlefoot, though this is frowned on by the breed registry.

➤ *See also amble; American Breeds, American Saddlebred; Andalusian; Missouri Fox Trotter; pace; Paso Fino; Peruvian Horse; rack; Rocky Mountain Horse; running walk; slow gait; Standardbred; Tennessee Walker*

GAITED BREEDS: WHO THEY ARE AND WHAT THEY DO

There are at least 80 breeds worldwide that are gaited. Here are a few of the most common.

- American Saddlebred (slow gait, rack)
- Florida Cracker (flat walk, running walk, amble)
- Icelandic (tölt, flying pace)
- Kentucky Mountain Horse (singlefoot)
- Mangalarga Marchador (*marcha*, a trot or amble with moments of three-leg support)
- Missouri Fox Trotter (fox trot)
- Paso Fino (paso fino, paso corto, paso largo)
- Peruvian Horse (paso llano, a form of running walk)

GAIT SEQUENCES

Horses move in a greater variety of ways than any other quadruped. They can move two legs at once, on the same side or opposite sides. They can move one leg, then two, then one. They can move one leg at a time. They have two-, three-, and four-beat gaits.

Of the commonly known natural gaits, the slowest is the walk, a four-beat gait in which the horse moves one foot at a time forward, in this sequence: left hind, left fore, right hind, right fore. Next is the two-beat gait known as the trot, jog, or pace. In trot and jog, paired diagonal feet leave the ground simultaneously and, before the first pair touches down, there is a moment of suspension with all four feet off the ground. In the pace, lateral pairs move forward in turn, also with a period of suspension.

In the canter or lope, a three-beat gait, one hind leg pushes off, then the opposite hind and its diagonal foreleg create the second beat; and the final beat occurs when the opposite foreleg (diagonal to the first beat) reaches out and strikes the ground. Again, there is a moment of suspension, which accounts for the sensation of flying that many people feel when they ride. The fastest gait, the gallop, is like the canter but with four beats, as the second hind leg and first foreleg strike the ground separately.

Each horse has a cruising speed at each gait, at which he moves most efficiently. He will automatically transition to the faster or slower gait when asked to change speed out of his comfort zone; he may break into a trot when asked to speed up the walk, or trot faster rather than breaking into a canter. Extending his range in each gait is a matter of training and balance.

Gait Rhythm

Tapping the rhythm of the gaits out with your fingers will give you a better feel for them.

Walk	1-2-3-4, 1-2-3-4
Jog/trot	1-2, 1-2, 1-2
Pace	1-2, 1-2, 1-2
Lope/canter	1-2-3, 1-2-3, 1-2-3
Rack	1-2-3-4, 1-2-3-4
Gallop	1-2-3-4, 1-2-3-4, 1-2-3-4

gallop The horse's fastest gait; speeds can reach 18 miles (29 k) per hour and more. The gallop is a four-beat gait, with a moment of suspension when all four feet are off the ground.

➤ *See also gaits*

Galvayne's groove A groove that usually appears on a horse's upper corner incisors when he is about 10 years old.

➤ *See also age*

To an observer, it may seem that a horse is pitching forward at the **gallop**. However, to a rider, the canter and gallop are smooth gaits, because there is less concussion, and three to four sliding beats are easier to sit to than two concussive ones.

GALICEÑO

A small horse (12.2–14.2 hands high) descended from horses brought to the New World by the Spanish conquistadores. Galiceños were found running wild on the Yucatan peninsula, and several groups were imported to Texas. This is a strong horse with a natural, ground-covering running walk. Capable of carrying adults, the Galiceño excels as a cutting and reining horse. Galiceños are exceptionally gentle and intelligent, with a strong herd dynamic. Stallions can be kept together, as they are not aggressive with each other. **Livestock Conservancy rating: Study**

gas colic

➤ *See colic*

gaskin
The muscle in the horse's upper hind leg, between the hock and the stifle, comparable to the human calf muscle. The tibia and fibula are the bones associated with the gaskin. Weak or underdeveloped gaskins can lead to problems with drive or impulsion.

gasterophilus

➤ *See bot flies*

gelding

1. The act of castrating.

2. A castrated male horse. Geldings are far easier to care for than stallions, and are much safer for the average horse owner. They are less prone to injury and usually have a consistent attitude, unlike mares, who may have hormone-driven mood swings. Geldings can usually share turnout with other geldings, and many are perfectly compatible with mares.

➤ *See also stud colt*

gender terms
A young female horse, from foal to age 4, is a **filly**; a male is a **colt**. The father of a foal is the **sire**; the mother is the **dam**. An adult female is a **mare**, while an adult unneutered male is a **stallion**. A neutered male is a **gelding**.

genes Chemical codes that transmit various traits of a living creature. Genes are located inside chromosomes. In genetics, the term "zygosity" refers to an individual's hereditary traits in terms of gene pairing in the zygote from which it developed:

HETEROZYGOUS refers to the inheritance of a mixed pair of genes, one recessive, one dominant. The foal will show the dominant gene, but it can pass on either gene to its own offspring.

HOMOZYGOUS DOMINANT means that an animal inherited two dominant genes together and both expresses that trait and will pass it on to its offspring; indeed, a homozygous dominant horse can pass on no other trait to its offspring but the homozygous dominant one.

HOMOZYGOUS RECESSIVE is when two recessive genes come together in the foal to create a homozygous recessive animal. This horse expresses the trait and passes on the recessive gene to his offspring.

genetic disorders When some genes are doubled up, they result in a fetus whose organs are improperly formed. Some genetic disorders are apparent, such as the lack of an anus or eye sockets, or water on the brain. However, the most common lethal gene is that for white coloring. It may produce roans and whites that die soon after conception; it may also produce a white overo pinto that dies soon after birth because of a faulty intestinal tract, which accompanies the white gene. The lethal white situation occurs when two horses carrying the gene (two true roans, for example) are mated.
➤ *See also combined immune deficiency; hyperkalemic periodic paralysis (HYPP)*

genetics The science of heredity; the scientific study of the differences and similarities among related individuals. An understanding of genetics is a vital key to breeding success, regardless of the size of the program. Skilled breeders can produce animals with traits

A bay sabino mare and palomino sabino foal. The **genetics** of the sabino coloration are not well understood; indeed, all pinto colorations other than tobiano are still being studied.

desirable to the breed ideal, marketplace, and/or show arena—and can even change the direction of an entire breed. Unfortunately, many breeds have been negatively influenced by uneducated breeders who crossed individuals with highly heritable faults.

Two primary concepts to understand in genetics are phenotype and genotype. Phenotype is the expression of genes that can be observed by the human senses: color, conformation, movement, and so on. Genotype is the actual genetic makeup of an individual as determined by its genes: you can't see it when you look at a horse, but it is inherited from the horse's ancestors and passed along to its descendants.

You can view photos or even videos of a horse's ancestors, and determine what characteristics are consistently passed on from one generation to the next. Nothing in breeding is foolproof, however, and parents may carry recessive genes for an undesirable trait that simply hadn't been paired up before. One recessive gene will not result in that trait being present in the foal, but two will.

CROSS-BREEDING
Breeding individuals of different breeds to combine the best traits of each, and to produce hybrid vigor (heterosis).

DEFECTS
Defects often run in families, although mutations and poor pre- and postnatal care can be responsible for many problems. Inbreeding is risky unless you are certain there are no bad recessive genes in the family that will cause a defect when doubled.

DILUTION FACTORS
Recessive genes that produce nothing alone but that affect other color genes to create variations in coat color, including buckskin, red dun, palomino, perlino, cremello, and grulla.

DOMINANT TRAITS
A trait that is produced by a dominant gene. A dominant trait will always be present in a foal instead of a trait controlled by a recessive gene.

INBREEDING
The mating of two closely related animals—sibling to sibling or parent to offspring. Over time, inbreeding dramatically decreases the genetic variation within a bloodline, concentrating both good and bad genes. If undesirable genes are present, inbreeding offers a greater chance of birth defects. It also reduces genetic diversity within the breed.

DEADLY COLORS

White and roan horses are rare for the simple reason that if dominant genes for those colors are present, it is lethal to the embryo. For a live foal of those colors to result, the colors must be produced by the pairing of a recessive and a dominant gene.

LINE-BREEDING
A breeding technique that attempts to fix certain traits by mating relatives descended from a particular outstanding horse. The undesirable traits of the ancestor and the breeding partner should be assessed to be sure undesirable traits are not being fixed as well. To distinguish it from inbreeding, use this rough rule of thumb: inbreeding is the mating of sibling to sibling, or parent to offspring. Line-breeding is the mating of cousin to cousin, or aunt/uncle to nephew/niece.

OUTCROSSING (OUTBREEDING)
The mating of unrelated individuals within a breed; often, because their genetic makeup is more varied, the offspring are of superior quality.

PEDIGREE
The lineage of the horse; the family tree showing all his ancestors.

PREPOTENCY
The ability of a stallion to produce foals that look like him, no matter what type of mare he breeds. The stallion Justin Morgan, foundation sire of the Morgan breed, is an outstanding example of a prepotent horse.
➤ *See also color, of horse*

genome
The horse genome was mapped in 2006, with the goal of finding ways to improve horse health care. A Thoroughbred mare named Twilight was the first horse sequenced. Seven additional horses from different breeds were also sequenced.

gestation
The length of time it takes for a fertilized egg to become a foal. Gestation varies widely, between 305 and 395 days, with an average of 340 days (11 months and 1 week).
➤ *See breeding; foaling*

When two individuals produce an offspring superior to what would be expected by their mating, it is called *nicking*. This is indeed a lucky phenomenon that occurs through an inexplicable combination of genes.

get (of sire) A stallion's offspring. In Get of Sire classes several offspring of a stallion are entered as a unit, and judged on their quality and uniformity.
➤ *See also produce (of dam)*

gingering Ginger or ginger extract inserted into the rectum, causing a burning sensation that makes it uncomfortable for the horse to lower his tail. It was once common to ginger Saddlebreds for the show ring, to produce a high tail set. The procedure has become less common since animal protection groups began policing competitive horse events. It is not allowed at shows sanctioned by the United States Equestrian Federation (USEF).

gingivitis An irritation of the gums caused by rough feed, taps between the teeth, injuries and bruises, ill-fitting bits, improperly cared-for teeth, twitching and lip chains, and weakness in the tissues of older horses. Gingivitis can lead to other dental conditions, including problems in the underlying bone. It is treated by cleaning and antibiotic washes.

girth The English term for the leather, cotton, or synthetic strap that buckles around a horse's belly and holds the saddle in place on his back. Leather girths are highly durable, if well maintained. Synthetic girths, such as those made of breathable neoprene, and cotton girths cost less and are often cooler, absorbing less sweat.

Different disciplines and types of saddles call for different types of girths. Racing girths are elastic, to allow for maximum rib cage expansion at a gallop. They are often combined with racing surcingles, which cross over the top of the saddle for extra safety if the girth breaks. A dressage girth is shorter than the average girth, because the dressage saddle has more depth and many have longer billets.

Some dressage riders use very wide, padded girths that eliminate pressure points, allow for chest expansion, and reduce stress. So-called anatomical girths are contoured to reduce pinching at the elbows. A wide belly area on jumper girths protects the horse from injuring himself with the studs in his shoes when he tucks up his front legs.
➤ *See also cinch*

girth itch A fungal disease caused by the girth or cinch rubbing the skin raw. If left untreated, the skin may peel, leaving widening, sore, inflamed spots and making the horse unrideable. The spores of the fungus can persist in brushes and tack, spreading the problem throughout the barn. Disinfecting and using different tack and equipment for each horse helps diminish the problem.
➤ *See also fungal infections*

girthy Objecting to having the girth or cinch tightened. A girthy horse might pin his ears, bare his teeth, move restlessly while being saddled, or even try to bite or kick. It's important to fasten the girth loosely at first and tighten it slowly while avoiding overtightening it.
➤ *See also bloating; cold-backed*

ENGLISH GIRTHS

glass eye
➤ *See iris*

gloves, use of
Many competitive disciplines require the use of gloves. Gloves also increase safety when handling horses, preventing rope burn and increasing grip strength if a horse startles and pulls.

For showing, read the rules and study prevailing fashion in your discipline. For schooling and recreational riding and driving, you can wear any glove that is flexible and grippy enough. Garden gloves with nitrile palms offer a great combination of grip and feel, and are inexpensive. Requirements for winter riding will vary with the severity of the weather, but there are many options.

goat tying
A timed Western event in which the goat, with a collar around its neck, is staked at one end of the arena. The competitor starts at the other end and gallops her horse toward the goat, halting as close to it as possible. The competitor then dismounts, flips the goat on its side, and ties any three legs with a leather thong or braided nylon goat string.
➤ *See also rodeo*

GOATS MAKE GOOD COMPANIONS

Horses are herd animals and like to have another of their species nearby. If it is not possible to keep two horses, a goat will often make an acceptable companion. Particularly sociable horses may even benefit from having a goat share not only their paddocks but also their stalls.

grab strap
➤ *See hand-hold strap*

grade horse
An unregistered horse of uncertain parentage. Even a horse with known parentage is a grade horse if you do not have his papers. While lack of papers will not prevent you from participating in open shows in your discipline, you will not be able to show your horse in breed shows hosted by a breed registry.

grains
Concentrate feeds; also, cereal grains fed to horses. The four major horse grains are oats, barley, corn, and sorghum (milo). Crimping, rolling, or steaming cracks the outer covering of grains, making them easier to chew and digest. The food/energy value often rises when grains are processed in these ways. The proof can be seen in manure: When whole-kernel grains are fed, many kernels pass through in their entirety, without having released full nutritional value.
➤ *See also individual grains*

Grand Prix
A competition at the highest levels of dressage or jumping. Grand Prix jumping competitions often carry substantial prize money for the top six finishers. These events are judged on speed and accuracy: that is, not knocking down fences or landing in water jumps.

Grand Prix dressage is an international sport; the makeup of tests is decided by the Fédération Equestre Internationale (FEI) rather than the United States Equestrian Federation (USEF), which determines the content of tests up to Fourth Level. Grand Prix tests typically include passage, piaffe, canter pirouettes, and tempi changes.
➤ *See also dressage; Fédération Equestre Internationale (FEI); stadium jumping/show jumping; United States Equestrian Federation (USEF)*

granulosa cell tumor
A tumor in a granulosa cell, which is part of the ovary and produces the female hormone estrogen. A granulosa cell tumor causes reproductive problems but is usually not malignant, although it can rupture. If it has become cancerous, signs may include personality change, irritability, or aggressive or vicious behavior. The mare may also exhibit stallionlike behavior around other mares, especially those in heat, because the tumor alters her hormonal balance.

GOTLAND

An elegant midsize pony (11.2–13.2 hands high) native to Sweden; also called Skogsruss. The Gotland is an ancient breed, used by the Goths by around 1800 BCE to pull their chariots. Today's Gotland—with its pronounced withers, well-sloped shoulder, and strong, straight back—is an ideal child's mount. Gotland Ponies were imported into the United States in the 1950s as part of a therapeutic riding program. After nearly becoming extinct, the breed is in better shape today, with over 100 individuals in the United States. **Livestock Conservancy status: Watch**

grass clippings, feeding Grass clippings should not be used as horse feed. Because they are soft and easily swallowed, the horse may overeat and experience an impaction. Clippings also spoil and ferment relatively quickly, so a horse should not be grazed on lawns that have been recently cut. If a horse does get into grass clippings, watch for signs of colic.
➤ *See also colic*

grass hay Hay made from grasses; it is often less dusty than legume hays. When growing grass to make hay, good choices are timothy, smooth brome, and intermediate wheatgrass. (Downy brome, or cheatgrass, should not be used as hay.) In general, dry-land grasses are preferable to swamp grasses, as the latter are usually coarse.
➤ *See also hay*

grass toxicity Although most grasses are natural feeds for horses, some can cause problems. The following is a list of problem grasses and their effects:

- Buckwheat, when dried, can cause photosensitization.

- Perennial rye grass can cause photosensitization.

- Sorghum and Sudan grass, common in southern pastures, are dangerous particularly after a frost or drought, which changes glycosides in the plant into cyanide. An affected horse, starved for oxygen, breathes heavily, grows weak, falls into a coma, and dies within a few hours.

- Tall fescue causes abortion, retained placenta, and failure to produce milk in mares. It is not the grass itself, but the fungus *Neotyphodium coenophialum* (also known as *Acrimonium coenophialum*), that infests much of this grass and causes the problems.

- Torpedo grass, abundant in the South and in Florida, causes severe and often lethal anemia.

gravel, in hoof

A term for when an abscess works its way up and out of the hoof through the coronary band instead of coming out through the bottom of the foot.

➤ *See abscess; hoof*

gravel, in turnout area

If you use gravel as a surface in pens and turnout areas, be sure it is ⅜ inch (1 cm) in diameter or smaller. This is small enough that it will not catch in horses' shoes and will not be scooped up when shoveling manure.

grazing muzzle

A muzzle that limits the amount of grass a horse can eat. Grazing muzzles can reduce a horse's grass intake by 30 to 80 percent, enough to keep an easy keeper from gaining excess weight and reduce the risk of laminitis, while allowing the horse to move around naturally at pasture. Check your horse frequently to make sure he hasn't removed the muzzle; some horses are quite adept at that. Various types are available, some

GRAZING MUZZLE

GREAT HORSE

A forebear of today's draft horse, particularly the Shire, the Great Horse was developed in England in the 12th century by crossing French and Friesian heavy horses with lighter native stock. Initially used to carry armored knights, Great Horses transitioned to farming and hauling after armor became obsolete, and the introduction of the horse collar made horses more practical for plowing. The Great Horse stood 16 to 17 hands high and weighed over half a ton.

that are complete units and some that attach to halters. With the latter, use a breakaway halter for safety.

grease heel/greasy heel

➤ *See scratches*

green horse

A horse lacking experience and training. Some consider a horse with *no* training to be green, while others consider a horse who has only had basic training under saddle to be green. A green horse requires an experienced, confident rider until he has reached a more finished level.

➤ *See also finished horse*

grid

➤ *See jumping grid*

grooming

Cleaning and brushing a horse. The massage afforded by grooming increases circulation and relaxes the horse's mind, gives his coat a shine, and builds trust between horse and handler. Grooming also gives a horse owner a chance to assess a horse's condition and make needed changes in his feeding.

Grooming removes dirt, sweat, glandular secretions, dead skin cells, and loose hair. It also brings natural oils, which protect the horse from weather, to the surface of the skin. Grooming gives you an opportunity to closely inspect the skin, head, mane, tail, legs, and hooves. During grooming, you can find ticks and bot fly eggs adhering to the hair or skin, and you can discover small nicks and cuts before they become bigger problems.

➤ *See also clipping; hay wisp; mane, care of; tail, care of*

Many horses enjoy a good **grooming** that reaches itchy spots they can't reach themselves.

ground driving

➤ *See long lining*

ground poles/ground lines

1. Poles placed just in front of the vertical elements of a jump in order to help the horse judge the takeoff point. A "timing pole" is a ground pole placed a canter stride away from a jump; it is used to help novice jumpers learn when to prepare the horse and themselves for the jump.

2. Poles placed on the ground for the horse to cross over. A common exercise is to place three or more poles a stride apart, like cavalletti, and ask the horse to trot over them.

➤ *See also cavalletti; jumping*

Working over **ground poles** is useful at any level of training.

GROUND-TIE

ground-tie A trained behavior in which the horse stands still when the lead rope or reins are dropped on the ground. Start by teaching your horse to stop and stand while you hold a lead rope, then a longer line. When he has that behavior solidly mastered, move to dropping the reins while you work around him, staying close enough at first to catch and correct him if he moves. Being able to ground-tie is part of a continuum of stopping and standing, an essential part of every well-trained horse's repertoire.

ground work
➤ *See in-hand training*

growth plate closure A sign that the horse's skeleton has matured; it usually takes place between the fourth and fifth years, but may be delayed till age seven in large warmblood horses. Bones are lengthened by laying down cartilage at their ends, known as growth plates. Eventually, the cartilage turns to bone and growth ceases. Working a horse too young can cause

inflammation and predispose the horse to lameness and deformities.

grulla/grullo coloring A variant coat color of black or brown caused by a genetic dilution factor; pronounced *grew-ya*. The actual color ranges from bluish gray to brownish gray.
➤ *See also color, of horse*

gullet, of a saddle The hollow channel down the underside of a saddle. English saddles tend to have narrower channels; Western saddles have wider ones. Some synthetic and leather saddles come with a changeable gullet system, allowing the saddle width to be changed to fit different horses.
➤ *See also bars, of a saddle; English tack; Western tack*

gullet strap, in driving A strap running under the horse's jaw that connects the throatlatch to the curb strap, preventing the bridle from being rubbed off. Loss of a bridle is one of the biggest hazards in driving.
➤ *See also driving; harness*

gum problems
➤ *See dental problems; gingivitis; teeth*

gut sounds A healthy horse has a variety of gut sounds, with short spans of silence between them. You can listen for sounds with a stethoscope, or with your ear pressed directly to his side. Listen to your horse's gut frequently when he is healthy and eating normally so that you will get a sense of what sounds are normal for him. If you hear a constant rumbling, the horse's gastrointestinal tract may be overactive. If you hear none, there could be blockage or a shut-down gut. This is part of the information you can give a veterinarian if you call with a suspected case of colic.

guttural pouch Sacs located in the walls of the eustachian tube, directly below the ear, connecting with the nasal passages and throat. Guttural pouches are unique to horses, and their function remains a mystery. Their location allows them to become infected; trouble signs include nasal discharge, nose bleeding, or swelling in the throatlatch region.

Bacterial infections, which frequently occur following an upper respiratory infection, are treated with

Grulla horses may be mouse-, blue-, dove-, or slate-colored, with dark or black points and no white hairs mixed into the body hairs; genetically, this is a different color from gray. Grullas usually have dorsal and shoulder stripes, and many have leg barring.

antibiotics, irrigation of the pouches with a catheter, and occasionally surgical drainage. Prognosis is usually good.

Fungal infections in the guttural pouches are more serious. They can damage the carotid artery and cranial nerves. Treatment is daily infusions of medication through a nasal tube; if the carotid artery is involved, it must be repaired surgically to prevent a fatal hemorrhage. Prognosis is only fair, due to the difficulty of treatment.

In foals, air may enter the guttural pouches, causing difficulty breathing and a snoring sound while nursing. The treatment is surgery, and the prognosis is good.

gymkhana A program of competitive mounted games, usually with a timed element. Events may be for individuals or teams. Also called o-mok-see or omoksee.

➤ See also mounted games

gymnasticize To systematically develop a horse's strength and suppleness, through exercise that may include ground poles, hacking or trail riding, hill work, galloping, and jumping.

habronemiasis

➤ *See summer sores*

hackamore

A bitless bridle; however, not every bitless bridle is a hackamore. In modern parlance the word "hackamore" usually refers to a mechanical hackamore, a bitless bridle with shanks that uses leverage to put pressure on the nose, poll, and chin groove. This can be a harsh bridle, and is not allowed in certain sports. A jumping hackamore is a noseband with rings for rein attachment, used as a sidepull bridle.

➤ *See also bitless riding; bosal; sidepull*

hacking

Pleasure riding outside an arena. Hacking can be a relaxing break from schooling for horse and rider.

HACKAMORE

HACKNEY HORSE/HACKNEY PONY

A show-ring harness horse of British origin, once popular for pulling carriages. The Hackney Horse stands about 15.3 hands high. He may be any solid color, although some white markings are allowed. He has brilliant action that appears effortless.

The Hackney Pony, which shares the stud book with the Hackney Horse, measures 14 hands high or less, is courageous, has great stamina, and exhibits the same high-stepping action and brilliance. The Hackney Pony is popular in the United States, while the Hackney Horse numbers about only 3,000 globally, with fewer than 200 in the United States. **Livestock Conservancy status: Critical**

A breed of strong, sturdy chestnut horses from the Austrian Tyrol. All Haflingers have a white or flaxen mane and tail. The Haflinger descends from native mountain ponies crossed with Arabians, most recently in the 1870s. Haflingers work easily on steep slopes, can be ridden or driven, and also make excellent small draft horses. They are not usually worked until they are 4 years old, but can remain active and healthy to age 40 and older.

hair Horses' bodies are covered with a coat of hair, thinner and finer in hot-blooded breeds, thicker and coarser in cold-blooded breeds. Horses grow a long winter coat as the days shorten in the fall, and begin to shed that coat as the days lengthen in the spring. As they shed the old coat, they grow a new, short summer coat. The horse experiences a loss of proteins as the hair falls out, and a metabolic challenge as he grows new hair in spring. This is a large demand to make at a time when nutritional levels may be low, due to months without green fodder. For this reason, older horses frequently lose weight in the spring.

It's important to groom your horse often in spring to encourage the shedding of old hair and the growth of a sleek summer coat. A thick mat of winter hair is a perfect environment for organisms that cause skin problems, especially in wet conditions. Also, that heavy coat in warm weather is like being in a sweater you can't take off.

If your horse is slow to lose his winter coat, check that he is eating a balanced diet with enough protein and sufficient mineral intake. Parasites, illness, and stress also delay shedding, as does hormonal imbalance. Older horses may have Cushing's disease, which is a tumor in the pituitary gland that interferes with hormone levels.

In early fall, horses shed their fine summer coats as they begin growing the longer coat again. This rarely affects weight and health, as the horse is typically well-nourished after a summer on pasture.

Horses with heavy coats may need to be clipped when in work. Failure to shed in the spring is a sign of a health problem, probably Cushing's disease.

CURLY HAIR A few breeds (American Curly, Bashkir) have dense, curly coats, with curls in the ears and curly eyelashes. Their manes and tails are also wavy. Some annually shed and regrow their manes and, more rarely, their tails. Recent research now supports the long-held belief that curly-coated horses are hypoallergenic.

EARS AND MUZZLES A horse's muzzle hairs are feelers, and help him find objects in his blind spot. Similar hairs help protect the eyes from injury by signaling when his head is too close to an object. The hair inside his ears helps keep out the cold in winter and flies and gnats in summer. Fashion dictates clipping ear and muzzle hairs for showing. Be aware that when you do, you are slightly handicapping your horse's ability to care for himself. It is your responsibility to make up for this by keeping him safe and protected from insects.
➤ *See also clippers; clipping; cold blood; cooler; Cushing's disease/Cushing's syndrome/PPID; feathers; grooming; hot blood; shedding*

LEG HAIR Horses with cold-blooded ancestry have longer hair on their legs, ranging from the modest fetlocks of ponies and Morgans to the voluminous feathering of Shires and Gypsy Vanners. These locks, and some of the whorls that decorate horses' coats, channel rainwater off the body and keep it from penetrating the coat.

MANES AND TAILS All equine species have long, usually upright, hair on the crest of the neck. Around the time when they were domesticated, horses developed longer manes, which hang down the sides of their necks. The mane has always been seen as beautiful, and is also quite useful for riders using a minimum of tack.

Mane styling has long been used as a social signal, and it remains key in creating the right look for particular sports. Long, flowing manes belong to baroque sports; driving and other English sports favor the neatness of braids; and in Western sports, manes may be clipped, thinned, or banded. In old California, manes were cut in different ways to signify the degree of the horse's training. Customarily, the mane is trained to hang on the right side of the neck, which keeps it out of a handler's way.

Horses differ from other equines by having long hair over the whole tail, rather than just a tuft at the end.

Cold-blooded, winter-adapted horses have heavier tails and manes, which help buffer wind and snows.

half-breed
A horse produced by breeding a purebred with a horse of different breeding. A half-breed registry is an organization that registers, transfers, and maintains official records of half-breed horses.

half-chaps
Knee-length leggings used to protect and support the rider's calves when the rider is using short boots. Half-chaps are made of leather, suede, or synthetic material; most fasten with zippers, though some use Velcro. Half-chaps mimic the look and function of a tall boot but are much easier to put on and take off than tall boots are.
➤ *See also chaps*

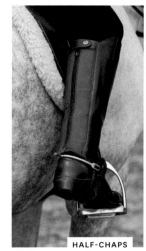

HALF-CHAPS

half-halt
A momentary rebalancing of the horse, through brief application of the halt aids. The rider essentially calls the horse to attention by increasing contact with the lower legs while simultaneously increasing the rein contact ever so slightly. This creates a contained form of energy that can then be put to a variety of uses, such as transitioning from one gait to another.

half-pass

1. In Western riding, a lateral movement often performed along the rail, with the horse's forefeet and hind feet on two different tracks.

2. In dressage, a lateral movement in which the horse travels forward and sideways at the same time, with his body bent in the direction he is traveling. The outside legs pass in front of the inside legs. The half-pass is more advanced than the leg-yield and is a variation of haunches-in (or travers).

➤ *See also leg-yield; travers*

half-seat

1. In Western riding, rising up out of the saddle with the weight in the stirrups.

2. In English riding, either:

   - Lightening the seat by pushing more weight down into the heel and slightly inclining the body forward (but not so far that the rider is in a two-point, or jumping, position)

   - A position used for the hand gallop, a speed faster than canter. It allows the horse's back to move more freely under the rider. The rider's weight is not shifted entirely to the irons, but rather is distributed along the inside thigh and the calf.

Some instructors use the term "half-seat" interchangeably with "two-point seat" or "jumping position." However, in the half-seat, the seat bones maintain a light contact with the saddle.
➤ *See also jumping; light seat; two-point seat*

halt When the horse, responding to the aids, comes to a complete stop. Ideally he stands square, with weight distributed evenly over all four legs, and remains motionless, on the bit, looking straight ahead. He should be alert, focused on the rider, and ready for the next instruction, but should not move until that instruction is given.

halter Bitless headgear used to lead and tie a horse. "Haltering" is putting on a halter.

Halters may be made of leather or nylon web strapping, with buckles for adjustment; they can also be made of knotted rope.

Grooming halters are made of leather, and have only a crownpiece and a noseband, to minimize straps in a groom's way. Shipping halters have sewn-on sheepskin covers on all surfaces, to protect the horse's head while traveling.

Avoid leading horses even a short distance using a halter alone; it's too easy for a horse to pull away. Always attach a lead rope, which gives you leverage and allows you to get out of the horse's way without setting him loose.

Halters should not be left on pastured or stalled horses. The horse can catch the halter on things—including his own shoes—and injure himself, and pasture mates often bite at each other's halters in play. Also, the constant movement of a grazing horse's jaws against the halter can wear his hair off.

If you must leave a halter on a pastured horse in order to catch him, make sure it has a breakaway leather crownpiece or fuse; if the horse catches the halter on something, the leather will break. Never leave a halter on an unsupervised foal.
➤ *See also rope halter*

EMERGENCY HALTER

In a pinch, a single length of rope can serve as a halter, and will be far more effective in controlling a horse than the same rope looped around his neck.

Begin by tying a loop in one end, using a nonslip knot such as a bowline.

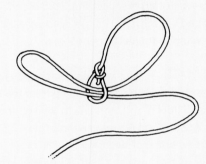

To catch the horse, hold the loop in your hand, and pass the other end of the rope over the horse's neck. Grab the rope under his jaw, make a loop in it, and push the loop through the first loop you created. Pull the second loop over the horse's nose, and use the tail end of the rope to lead him.

To release the horse, simply slip off the nose loop and pull. The rope will drop off his neck.

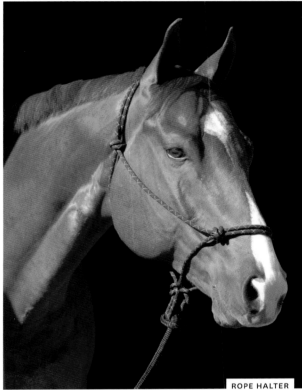

ROPE HALTER

LEATHER HALTER

hand, as unit of measurement The standard unit of measurement for horses. One hand equals 4 inches (10 cm). The measurement is derived from the ancient practice of using the width of the palm of a man's hand to determine how tall a horse was. If your horse measures 61 inches (1.5 m) at the withers, the highest point on his back where it meets his neck, he is 15 hands and 1 inch (2.5 cm) high. This measurement is written as 15.1 hands high (hh). It is spoken as "fifteen-one."

hand-breeding

➤ *See breeding*

hand gallop A gait that falls between a canter and full gallop; it is a three-beat gait.

hand-hold strap A sturdy strap that can be buckled to the stirrup bars of an English saddle, to give the rider something to hang on to; also called a grab strap or SOS strap. Often used for therapeutic riding or longe-line lessons, hand-hold strap is also useful for beginners, especially when learning to post, as it allows the rider to steady herself without putting weight on the bit. A rider working on steady hands might also loop just her pinkies around the grab strap rather than hanging on to it with her whole hand.

handling horses Leading, administering health care, and generally working around horses. Establishing good ground manners and paying attention to details is important. In your relationship with your horse you must be the dominant partner, but becoming your horse's leader should not involve harsh treatment or physical punishment; these are ultimately counterproductive. The other aspect of establishing leadership among horses is trustworthiness—yours. Be the one your horse can rely on, for food, water, good decisions, and calm in frightening moments. Avoid unnecessary shouting. Don't ask your horse to do unsafe things, and demonstrate that you won't force him to do anything but rather will teach the correct response.

BODY CONTACT The horse must always know where the handler is, so he doesn't become frightened and spook. Speak quietly, and keep a hand on his back—not a ticklish flank—as you move around him. Horses generally prefer firm, smooth contact, and stroking rather than the friendly slap on the neck we often give them. They accept firm pressure on the neck, back, and rump but may squirm away from pressure on the belly, sides, and head.

BRIBERY Tempting a horse to do something by showing him, and then giving him, treats. It is not the same as treat-based training, which rewards the horse after he makes a step toward your goal. With bribery, you are helpless to get the behavior unless you have a treat handy. With training, you work on establishing the behavior, then fade the use of treats.

CHAIN RESTRAINT A chain over the nose or under the chin gives greater control by inflicting painful pressure on sensitive areas of the face. The chain might injure the horse, so it must always be used with restraint. However, when it is essential that a horse not be able to break free—that is, when injury or death could result—a chain can be useful. A chain can also help a small person control an excited horse, often without the need to use force. The presence of the chain alone focuses the horse's attention. A chain restraint is not a long-term substitute for training, but it may be a short-term stopgap.

CONSISTENCY Always giving the same cue for a behavior; always responding in the same way to the horse's wanted or unwanted behaviors. Every interaction with your horse is a training session. You may want to indulge him at certain times, but the horse doesn't have a grasp of situational appropriateness. He has no idea that today misbehavior "doesn't count," or that the words "whoa" and "stop" mean the same thing.

DISTANCE, MAINTAINING Your personal space, when handling a horse, should be determined by the amount of space that makes you and your horse comfortable. On average, that space is about 18 to 24 inches (46–61 cm) around your body. If the horse pushes into that space, quickly and firmly correct him. This is an area where it's easy to be inconsistent, and "suddenly" find that you have a horse in your lap. In reality, you didn't notice when he reduced the space to 16 inches (41 cm), and then 13 (33 cm). You didn't correct him, and he figures that the rules must have changed.

GROUND RULES

Establishing clear ground rules for handling defines your expectations for your horse and for anyone else who is allowed to handle him. The rules should include the following:

- The horse must respect your space. He's not allowed to crowd you, walk into you, or rub against you at any time.
- The horse is not allowed to nip or bite, even if it might be interpreted as a playful gesture.
- The horse must respond to basic commands without hesitation.
- The horse must stand quietly when asked, whether being led or ridden, without excessive fidgeting or fussing.

DOMINANCE In herds, horses maintain a dominance hierarchy. In a domestic setting, the rider/handler must be the dominant "horse." This requires being clear and consistent in your expectations of the horse, being aware when he missteps, and consistently correcting the situation. Some horses, especially youngsters, test daily to see if there has been a change in hierarchy. Your job is to say, firmly but pleasantly, "No, I'm still the boss."

HARD-TO-CATCH HORSES The hard-to-catch horse may succumb to treats and grain taken to the field, but then he will only come if there are treats. A better method is to catch him by waiting for him to come to you out of curiosity, no matter how long it takes, and then rewarding him with a treat when he is where you want him to be. This approach is tedious, but it's the only way to get over the problem for good. It's best to start this training in a small enclosure, rather than a large field.

If you want a horse to remain catchable, regularly catch and halter him for purely pleasant reasons—supper, a treat, a nice scratching. A horse with confirmed bad habits should be turned out in a very small paddock or pen. Catch him for everything—feed, water, grooming—until he understands that he is dependent on you for those good things and is eager to come to you to get them.

HOLDING A HORSE Begin with a properly fitted halter, or add a chain over the nose if more control is needed. Choose an open location with nothing nearby for the horse to bump into; or, if he must be perfectly still, hold him next to a wall or solid fence. You can also back him up against a fence or wall; but be aware that a horse who feels too confined may react by plunging forward.

When holding a horse for a farrier, vet, or saddle fitter, stand on the same side as the professional is working. This allows you to monitor any dangerous reactions.

LEADING A HORSE Walk beside the horse's left shoulder, a foot or so away. Grasp the lead rope or reins a few inches below the chin with your right hand. Pass the lead or reins across your body loosely, and fold the remaining rope or reins in your left fist. Never wrap the rope or reins around your hand. The lead rope should be slack unless you need to change directions or stop. When handling an untrained or difficult horse, remember that you'll have a lot more stopping power if you step out at an angle from him.

RIGHT OR LEFT?

It is customary to lead a horse from his left side; most people are right-handed, and this gives control to their stronger arm. Most horses expect to be led from the left, and may be confused if you try to lead them from the right. It's a good idea, though, to teach a horse to be led from either side.

When leading a horse along a road, always walk in the same direction as the traffic, on the right side of the road, keeping yourself between the vehicles and the animal.

TURNOUT Some horses bolt into the pasture, often bucking and kicking, as soon as the lead is unsnapped or halter removed. This is a very unsafe situation. Make him stop and wait before releasing him. Another technique is to drop a treat on the ground, making sure your horse sees you do this. Remove the halter and walk away while he's eating.

hands, rider's A rider's hands are one of the primary ways of communicating with the horse—but to have good hands, a rider must have an independent seat, so she is not using the reins to help stay on the horse, or transmitting unconscious signals. The hands must be able to deliver sensitive, varying amounts of pressure to the reins, and to feel the horse's mouth and movement through them. Generally, the hands should be the aid of third resort, following the weight and legs.
➤ *See also aids; reins; seat*

hand twitching
➤ *See restraints*

Hangbahn training A form of arena training in Germany and Scandinavia that uses sloping ground; a slope between 6 and 10 degrees is best. Hangbahn training is usually practiced once a week. Riders focus on a different figure every week, such as ovals, figure eights, and transitions. Working on a slope uses different support muscles, and causes the muscles of the back and hindquarters to fire differently. It is excellent for suppling and strengthening, and for improving proprioception.
➤ *See also hill work*

hard mouth
➤ *See mouth, hard or soft*

harness The system of straps that attaches a driving or draft horse to the load he is pulling. Harnesses may be made of leather or synthetic material. Styles include single or team draft harness, carriage harness, fine harness, and racing harness. Harnesses include the following:

- A headstall and bit

- A breast collar or neck collar, a surcingle or belly-band, and traces to secure the vehicle to the horse

- Breeching or tugs to aid in stopping the vehicle (optional in some settings)

- A crupper to help prevent the harness from being pulled too far forward on the horse's body

harness, foal Harnesses for foals are often safer and more humane than halters. They place pressure on the sturdy shoulders and chest rather than on the fragile head. You can purchase a foal harness, or you can use an adult horse halter, put on upside down, as a harness for young foals.

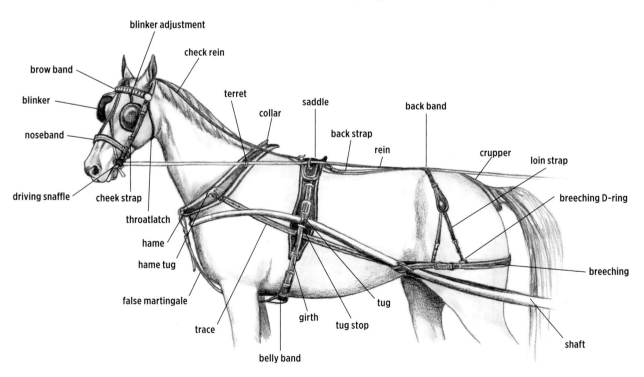

harness racing

Racing horses harnessed to light sulkies around an oval track. Although chariot racing was one of the original Olympic events (around 1000 BCE), harness racing as a sport is a peculiarly American tradition. From its origins on country roads and at county fairs, harness racing garnered legions of new fans when Roosevelt Raceway opened on Long Island in 1940. Today many cities in the Northeast and Midwest have harness tracks, and the sport is also popular in Florida, California, and Canada. It has also migrated to Europe, where it is popular in France and Scandinavia. Harness racing is considered a sport of the people, not the elites. Horses tend to be less expensive than racing Thoroughbreds and to have longer careers. Amateur owners can actually drive and train their own horses. There is also a minor sport of harness racing for ponies.

Both trotters and pacers vie for wins in their own Triple Crown races. Pacers race in the Cane Pace (the Meadowlands, New Jersey), the Messenger Stakes (Yonkers, New York), and the Little Brown Jug (Delaware County Fair, Ohio). The trotters compete in the Hambletonian (the Meadowlands), the Yonkers Trot (Yonkers Raceway), and the Kentucky Futurity (Lexington's Red Mile).

➤ *See also flat racing; pace; speed, of horse; Standardbred; Trottingbred Pony*

haunches-in

➤ *See travers*

hay

Grass and legumes preserved by drying. Hay has less than 20 percent moisture content, and pound for pound has three-quarters more nutrition than the same plants fed fresh, as pasture plants have 80 to 86 percent moisture content.

Horses need forage as the mainstay of a healthy diet. Grass is ideal, but good hay is a fine substitute when horses are stabled or pastures are poor—and hay is a necessity in winter.

The average mature horse consumes 2 to 2.5 percent of its bodyweight in feed each day. At least half of that should come from hay or pasture for optimum growth and development. Mature horses who are not working or being used as breeding animals can actually thrive on high-quality forages alone. However, horses who are still growing, who are being used as breeding animals, or who are in athletic training programs usually require supplementation with grains and other concentrates to maintain optimum health.

NUTRITIONAL VALUE Hay provides many nutrients. The exact nutrient value of any given sample of hay can be determined only through forage testing, which is available through your local Cooperative Extension Service. Generally, hay is high in calcium and low in phosphorus. It often contains high levels of potassium and vitamins A, E, and K. If it is dried in the sun rather than via chemicals, it likely will have high levels of vitamin D. The protein content of hay varies almost too much to generalize, but legume hays (such as alfalfa or clover) can provide as much as 20 percent crude protein and grass hays (such as timothy or bromegrass) average about 10 to 15 percent protein and can dip as low as 3 percent.

TYPES OF HAY There are two main types of hay with which most horsemen are familiar. These can be fed singularly or in a mix known simply as "mixed hay."

LEGUMES. A family of plants having root nodules that produce nitrogen; they also have stems that leaf out into leaflets, as is typical of the clover plant. Legumes are high in protein, calcium, beta-carotene, and vitamin E. Some believe legumes are also the most palatable of hays. This is why many horsemen prefer alfalfa or alfalfa-mix hays over grass hay for growing, breeding, or highly athletic horses. Still, their high protein content makes legumes potentially dangerous to feed to mature, idle horses.

GRASS HAY. There are many varieties of grass hay. A few of the most common ones fed to horses are timothy, Bermuda grass, bromegrass, bluegrass, ryegrass, and orchard grass. Grass plants grow with tall stalks and long, slender leaves that often wrap around the stalk, rather than branching out the way legumes do. This makes grass hay dry faster; as a result, mold is less of a problem. Grasses also don't have problems with blister beetles like alfalfa can, which means grass hay is often a better choice for horses with compromised breathing. The lower protein and nutrient density actually makes grass hay more desirable as a feed for mature and idle horses who aren't used for breeding.

MIXED HAY. A combination of legume and grass varieties into one crop. Mixed hay provides the best of both types of hay. It is more appealing to horses because they often prefer the smaller leaves of legumes.

➤ *See also feeding and nutrition*

hay bag/net/feeders **Hay nets** are bags made of rope netting; most are intended to be filled with hay and hung from a wall or cross-bar, but there are also nets intended to hold a whole bale fed on the ground, or to cover an entire round bale.

HAY BAGS are made of solid or mesh material, with openings in the front through which the horse can eat. Hay bags have the advantage of neatness, as there is only one opening; this makes them better for use at shows, where competitors need to keep public areas clean. Many designs also hang flatter than a traditional hay net, taking up less space, and so may be better for use in a trailer. Bags are easier to fill than nets; have a neater, more upscale appearance; and are correspondingly more expensive.

Nets and bags of all sizes are available in small-mesh, slow-feeder styles, which reduce wasted hay and increase the time the horse spends eating. This reduces boredom and keeps the stomach more constantly full, mimicking natural grazing and possibly preventing ulcers and colic.

Another form of hay bag is intended purely for neat transportation at shows; it zips around a whole bale, so no wisps of hay fall from it. An empty feed sack works just as well for a few flakes of hay.

The simplest way to fill a hay net is to stack the flakes you want to bag on a solid surface, open the net wide, and work it down over the stack. Then flip the bag and pull it tight. You can also hang the bag so that you can hold the opening wide, or fit it into a clean muck bucket before filling.

HAY FEEDERS are boxes filled with hay, which is eaten through a metal, plastic, or webbing grid. They keep a barn or turnout area neat, prevent hay waste, and are available in slow-feeder styles.

ORCHARD GRASS

hay bank The horse equivalent of a food bank; a supply of hay established by a network of farmers and horse rescue organizations that can be drawn on by horse owners who face a life emergency. Horse rescue organizations will know if there is a hay bank in your state. If there isn't, and you are in a position to do so, you may want to start one.

HEAT ENERGY FROM ROUGHAGE

More body heat is created in the horse by digestion of roughage than grain. If it is extremely cold outside, increase the ration of hay, not grain. As a rough guide, a 1,200-pound (544 kg) horse should eat a minimum of a half to a full bale, or 20 to 40 pounds (9–18 kg) per day. Add an extra 10 percent for every 10 degrees below freezing.

hay, soaking Hay may need to be soaked if it is dusty, if a horse is highly reactive to hay dust, or if nutrient content must be reduced as part of treatment for certain medical conditions. One easy method is to fill a hay net; immerse it in a tub filled with water for 15 minutes; drain the water; and then feed the hay directly from the tub, or hang the net.

Or in cool weather, cut the bale strings, run abundant cool water over the hay, especially between the flakes, and let the bale stand a few hours; don't let the flakes fall apart, but compress them together. The hay will brighten and soften, and dust is virtually eliminated. In warmer weather this method encourages mold growth, so don't allow the hay to stand wet for more than a couple of hours.

A hay steamer is an insulated sealed box that will hold up to a whole bale of hay. High-heat steam is infused in the box, killing fungal spores and bacteria and creating dust-free hay.

The smaller mesh of the **hay net** on the left slows feeding and minimizes waste. All hay feeders should be tied with a quick-release knot and hung high enough that the horse can't catch a hoof in the rope if he paws.

hay wisp A grooming tool made of hay, used for giving a stimulating massage. Using a hay wisp can be a nice addition to your grooming routine. Holding the wisp flat, smack it vigorously against the larger muscles (neck, shoulders, hindquarters) and then whisk it along the direction of the hair growth. This causes the horse's muscles to contract, then relax. The contraction and relaxation of the muscles acts as a massage does, carrying waste products from the muscles and nutrients to them.

➤ *See also grooming*

head, of horse "You can't ride the head," the old saying goes, meaning that a pretty head is useless without a functional body. But a horse's head is important in our impression of him. The shape of the head is often prominently described in breed standards as expressive of the character of the breed. The head needs to be in proportion to the body, and the way it is carried helps the horse balance himself. A good horse can have a common head and still perform well; a better horse will have a head appropriate to his type and the capacity to perform better.

➤ *See also conformation; individual breeds*

head bumper A flat, padded, leather or neoprene cap that attaches to a halter and protects the horse's head while he is being trailered. If the horse rears or is bounced up to the top of the trailer, the bumper will protect his poll.

WEAVING A HAY WISP

1. Fluff up a couple of flakes of soft, long-stemmed hay or straw and dampen it well. Take a 2-foot (61 cm) length of twine and tie it to a wall, leaving about 6 inches (15 cm) hanging on one side. Starting with the longer end, twist a handful of hay onto the twine; keep adding handfuls as you go. You'll have to use both hands to keep the twist tight. You'll run out of twine, but continue to twist hay until you've got about 9 feet (2.7 m) of "rope." It should be about ¾ inch (2 cm) thick. Twist another length of twine into the end of the rope for about a foot.

2. You'll need a second person to help with the rest of the process. Detach the end of the rope from the wall and maintain the tension on the twisted hay. Lay the twine into a rough pretzel as shown. The short end of the pretzel should have about 6 inches (15 cm) of twine left free.

3. Take the longer end of the rope and begin to weave it behind one loop and in front of the other.

4. When you reach the top of the loops, run the end through both loops twice.

5. You should have a woven pad of hay with two ends of twine hanging out. Tie the twine into a handle (custom fit to your hand).

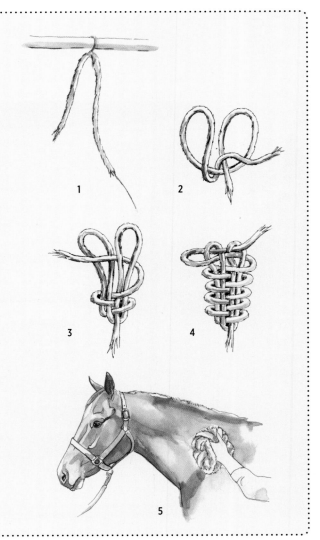

header

1. In Western riding, a roper who brings down calves by settling the catch rope over the animal's head.

2. In driving, a person who stands by the head of a horse during idle times to help keep the horse calm.

headshaking

➤ *See photic headshaking*

headshy A term used to describe a horse who will not let you handle or groom his head, face, or ears. Often, the behavior is a result of trauma, either purposeful or accidental. Most headshyness can be cured through repetitive gentle retraining and by gaining the horse's trust.

HEADSHY

headstall The straps that form a bridle and hold the bit in place.

hearing

➤ *See ears*

heart girth Circumference of the horse's body just behind the elbow.

heart rate A horse's resting heart rate should be around 38 to 42 beats per minute (bpm). The higher the fitness level, the lower the heart rate, as low as 26 bpm for an exceptionally fit horse. A pulse between 75 and 105 bpm following moderate work is average; extreme exertion can raise it above 200. Excitement, pain, and illness will also increase heart rate.

A healthy horse should return to 60 bpm after 10 to 15 minutes of rest; in an out-of-condition horse, recovery may take 45 minutes. If the rate falls to 44 to 50 bpm within 15 minutes, the horse is in top shape and can take on more intensive training. If his pulse fails to drop below 72 bpm in that amount of time, he has overexerted. Back off to a level of training where the horse can recover properly; then gradually increase the workout.

If the horse recovers to his resting heart rate within 10 minutes, the current level of training will only maintain, not improve, his condition. To increase fitness, increase the workload.

heat cycles

➤ *See estrus*

heat (in hoof and leg) Usually a symptom of an injury or infection. Heat can also contribute to degradation of the hoof and leg due to extreme exercise. People who use horses in high-speed activities pay a lot of attention to effectively cooling the foot and leg after exertion. Heat that accumulates in a horse's lower leg tissues can eventually lead to damage and lameness. Familiarity with how your horse's legs feel when he is sound and cool can help you locate injuries.

➤ *See also hoof; lameness; leg, of horse*

heat stroke/hyperthermia An abnormally high body temperature, often caused by exertion on a hot or humid day. Symptoms of heat stroke in a horse include reluctance to move; trembling; weakness; quick, shallow breathing; flaring, reddened nostrils; and even collapse. A resting heart rate that doesn't fall below 60 beats per minute, respiration above 40 breaths per minute, a temperature above 104, and dark red or purple-tinted gums are signs of emergency heat stress. Excess heat can lead to colic or laminitis, so it should be addressed immediately.

The quickest way to cool a horse off is to hose the lower surfaces of the neck, the chest, the belly, and the legs with tepid water. Cold water can cause the blood vessels to restrict, which is counterproductive. Pay special attention to the lower legs while hosing. Heat can accumulate in the tendons day to day, and lead to a breakdown.

After hosing for a short time, some people prefer to quickly scrape off the water with a sweat scraper, and hose again; some research indicates that the film of water on the horse's body can actually trap heat. Other horsemen believe in continual hosing. Let experience, and a rectal thermometer, be your guide. If possible, wait until the horse has cooled off before moving him.

heaves A disease characterized by loss of ability to perform, constant or intermittent cough, wheezing associated with exhalation, and a watery discharge from the nostrils; also known as recurrent airway obstruction (RAO), a term many veterinarians now prefer over the formerly used term "chronic obstructive pulmonary disease (COPD)." Heaves interferes with a horse's ability to breathe by constricting air passages, thus also limiting the horse's stamina and activity level. Like asthma in human beings, heaves is often triggered by dust or allergies. Horses kept indoors or fed dusty hay are susceptible.

As the condition worsens, the horse may lose weight because he is using so much energy to breathe; it often causes breeding problems in mares. Heaves is not curable by antibiotics because it is caused by dust and mold; after the first attack, there will probably be relapses of varying severity. The condition is generally controlled through the use of antihistamines and medications that clear the air passages. Horses suffering from heaves should also be kept in environments that are free of dust and mold.
➤ *See also hay, soaking; pelleted feeds*

heeler In Western riding, a roper who brings down steers by roping the steer or calf's hind leg.

height, measurement of Many competitions have Pony and Horse divisions; some Pony divisions are further divided between small, medium, and large ponies. Height determines what division these equines are eligible to show in, so they must first be measured. The measurement is made in hands, inches (or centimeters), and fractions of inches (or centimeters); a small difference in shoeing can determine which division a pony shows in.

Height is most accurately measured with a horse measuring stick. It is possible to make an approximation with a weight tape from the feed store, or an ordinary measuring stick, but these are subject to interpretation.
➤ *See also hand, as unit of measurement*

helmet, safety A protective helmet designed specifically for riding horses; it is the first item of equipment a rider should buy. Be sure the helmet meets the current standards established by the American Society for Testing Materials (ASTM) and the Safety Equipment Institute (SEI). These standards do not guarantee that a helmet will prevent head injury; however, if properly fitted and secured, a helmet greatly reduces the risk. Approved helmets are constructed of expanded polystyrene, which crushes on impact and absorbs the energy of the fall, cushioning the head. Bicycle helmets are not

A measuring stick is a handy tool for **measuring the height** of a horse; the animal must be standing on level ground. Measuring height this way is sometimes called "sticking a horse."

recommended for horseback riding, because they are too shallow and do not cover the head adequately.

Inexpensive helmets, if ASTM/SEI approved, are just as safe as expensive ones. The variations are chiefly a matter of style and ventilation. Some have longer brims to improve sun screening; this can also be accomplished by buying a separate helmet visor.

Helmets are fastened with a nylon or leather harness; many have a dial system in the back to ensure easy tightening. Always fasten and tighten the harness of your helmet before mounting.

WESTERN
Periodically, helmet makers attempt a helmet that looks like a Stetson, but these have never been widely adopted. Some current Western helmets are traditional English-style helmets embellished with Western motifs; others resemble the traditional polo helmet, with a leather covering. Avoid the Stetson-shaped construction hard hat; in an accident, it can cause severe injury or death if the rigid brim digs into the ground.

SAFETY FIRST
There can be considerable social pressure to wear that Stetson in barrel racing, or a fancy hat with feathers in a driven cones class. However, almost every horse show association now endorses rules that make protective headgear acceptable in

THREE-POINT HARNESS

every class of competition. Riders and drivers no longer have to risk their safety for the sake of fashion or tradition.

Horse activities cause far more concussions and deaths annually than does football. As more upper-level competitors begin to wear helmets, protective headgear will cease seeming odd and begin to look professional.

COVERS AND ACCESSORIES
Helmet covers are available to sport your stable colors; to make a schooling helmet look more formal; to protect your helmet from rain; to make you more visible after dark or during hunting season; and to keep your head warm.

Helmets can also be fitted with global positioning system (GPS) devices or cameras. These should be attached with an exterior hook-and-loop band, not by

drilling into your helmet, which could compromise its ability to protect you. Check the rules for any competition you enter to be sure helmet cams are legal.

You can also wear a headlamp on your helmet to shed extra light for night-time riding or chores; there are many available with adjustable straps.

hemionids
While hemionid means "half-ass" in zoological terms, these animals are not crosses between an ass and another equid. They have features of both horse and ass, as well as distinct characteristics of their own, most notably extremely long lower leg bones. Examples of hemionids include the Mongolian kulan of Central Asia and the onager (also known as the "wild ass" of biblical times), which is still found in the Middle East and Asia.

hepatitis
There are two kinds of hepatitis: infectious hepatitis and noninfectious hepatitis.

INFECTIOUS HEPATITIS
Infectious hepatitis, also called serum hepatitis or Theiler's disease, is caused by using contaminated needles and syringes. Onset of symptoms is sudden, and the horse is almost always violent, deranged, and impossible to catch. He will usually run into walls or fences. Ninety percent of horses with infectious hepatitis die, despite treatment with antibiotics, glucose electrolyte solutions delivered intravenously, and B-complex vitamins.

Hepatitis and/or death of liver tissue is often caused by vaccination, especially if the serum has been derived from equine tissues. The disease may occur one to three months after the injection; a delay of six months is not unheard of. Vaccines that have caused hepatitis include encephalitis serum, tetanus antitoxin, pregnant mare serum, and anthrax antiserum.

NONINFECTIOUS HEPATITIS
Noninfectious hepatitis is caused by poisons in the body and can be acute or chronic. The acute form comes on suddenly and is often fatal because liver damage is so severe. Causes can be toxins from poisonous plants or contaminated feed, or from an unrelated bacterial infection that produces liver-damaging toxins. The horse may have stomach pain mistaken for colic. He may stagger or drag his feet, and he may deteriorate mentally. He may stand with feet wide apart and head drooping, or he may walk into trees or

fences. He may have muscle tremors, and he may become photosensitive. In some cases, the horse becomes violent and unmanageable. If no irreparable damage has been done, removing the source of the toxin and then providing nursing care can help the horse recover.

herbal therapy Many herbal remedies and supplements are available for horses, and there are books of varying degrees of sophistication on the subject. If you want to use herbal treatments for minor maladies, take the precaution of consulting several sources before proceeding. Horses are herbivores, and herbal medicines may be especially compatible with their diet if chosen with care. There is wide acceptance of herbs, including valerian for calming horses, raspberry leaf and vitex for smoothing out the bumps in a mare's personality, and yucca and devil's claw for joint problems.

Be mindful that some of these substances can test—that is, they resemble banned drugs, or are themselves forbidden. If they show up in a blood test at a competition, you may be eliminated. Be conversant with the rules, and find out which herbs may cause a problem.

herd-bound A term used to describe a horse who is dependent on the companionship of other horses, and creates trouble when separated from them. A herd-bound horse may continually run a fence line trying to see other horses, call after them incessantly, or paw or weave in his stall. If he is turned out with others, he may be difficult to catch and bring in alone. In lessons, he may call to other horses and dash to the gate. It may be impossible to ride him away from

HERB AND SPICE TREATS THAT TEST

Some treats may result in a positive drug test. Avoid giving your horse any of the following if you plan to compete with him:

- Caffeinated drinks, including sodas
- Cinnamon
- Chocolate
- Nutmeg
- Persimmon
- Sassafras
- Willow leaves

the stable, and a herd-bound horse who appears well trained at home may unexpectedly act up in competition at a strange place.

The herd-bound horse must be retrained. This often begins with separating him from his buddies so he learns he can actually survive on his own. Some trainers break the herd bonds and create a new bond with themselves by keeping the horse in solitary confinement 23 hours of the day. His only company is the trainer, who supplies him with all good things. Since horses are social animals, this usually creates a strong bond, though the attraction to other horses will remain strong.

A less drastic, but effective way to retrain the herd-bound horse is by increments; out on a trail ride, part from your companions and ride the other way around a bush. Even this may be difficult for the herd-bound horse, but in a moment he and his friend are reunited. Repeat this until he's relaxed about it, and gradually add greater distance, until your horse is willing to tolerate temporary separation. Clicker training can be helpful.
➤ *See also barn-sour; ring-sour*

hernia A rupture of the lining of the abdomen that can cause pain and infection, strangulation of the intestine, or even potentially fatal peritonitis. Call your veterinarian if your horse develops any swelling in his abdomen.
➤ *See also umbilical hernia*

herpes virus
➤ *See equine herpes virus (EHV); rhinopneumonitis*

herring-gutted/hound-gutted Shallow in the flanks; wasp-waisted. A conformation fault. Herring-gutted horses often lack stamina.

highline A rope stretched high and taut between two trees; used for tying horses, usually while camping. The term "highline" is often used interchangeably with "picket," but it is not the same. A highline is easy, portable, safe, and reliable.

Tie ropes should be fastened so that the snap hangs about 2 feet (0.6 m) above the ground. The allows the horse to lie down but prevents grazing. It also prevents the horse from stepping over the rope and getting hung up. Multiple horses may be tied to loops in the rope; a single horse can be tied to a ring that can slide along

Hill work develops muscle tone, strength, and stamina.

the rope. Horses are generally relaxed when tied to a highline, but practice this at home in a familiar environment to be sure you can rely on it out on the trail.
➤ *See also hobbles; picketing/staking out; tying*

high school level movements
➤ *See Classical High School; dressage*

hill work Schooling horses on natural terrain, taking advantage of changes in slope. Working up, down, and across slopes is very strengthening.
➤ *See also Hangbahn training*

hindquarters The rear end of a horse, including croup, rump, and hind legs. A horse's hindquarters are his engine. A racehorse needs hindquarters that can easily propel him over moderate distances in a short amount of time; a Clydesdale needs hindquarters that can propel him forward with short strides so he can pull heavy loads over long distances without exhaustion and fatigue. A gaited horse may have shorter quarters

in relation to his back, and hind legs set farther back. If not extreme, this is not a conformation fault.
➤ *See also conformation*

hinny The offspring of a stallion and a jenny (a female donkey). Hinnies are far less common than mules for several reasons, one being that the success rate for breeding mares and jack donkeys is higher than for stallions and jennies. It can be difficult to distinguish between the two, though hinnies tend to be smaller than mules, because donkeys are generally smaller than horses and the size of the foal is limited by the size of the dam's uterus. Another difference is sometimes said to be that a mule has the body of a horse with the extremities of a donkey, while a hinny is the reverse. Hinnies do have more variability in appearance, ranging from being more horselike to more donkeylike.
➤ *See also mule*

hippotherapy
➤ *See therapeutic horsemanship*

history of the horse

Humans and horses first intermingled about 10,000 years ago, as horses migrated out of North America and humans migrated in. Horses rapidly went extinct after humans arrived in North America, due to climate change and hunting. In Eurasia people created magnificent paintings of horses in caves while hunting them nearly to extinction. By 6,000 years ago horses were greatly reduced across their former range, and humans had turned to domesticated animals for food.

But sheep and cattle were impractical in the north, as they have difficulty digging through snow and ice for food. Horses dig with their hooves, and were kept for winter meat as early as 4800 BCE, near the Caspian Sea. By 4200 BCE, people there began riding.

Riding revolutionized life on the steppe. On foot with a dog, one person can herd about 200 sheep. On horseback, human and dog can handle 500 sheep. Riding let people accumulate wealth. The idea spread, and horse populations rebounded all over Eurasia.

Around 3500 BCE, traders from Mesopotamia introduced wheeled carts pulled by oxen. Steppe people adapted the idea to horses. Now they could travel deep into the dry lands, carrying water with them to survive as they exploited new grazing areas. Vast new territories opened up for human habitation. Most people abandoned fixed settlements and took to the open steppe, living in their wagons.

Horses also brought a new level of violence. Riding made raiding more practical, and wagons made it easier to carry off property. New religions like Zoroastrianism sprang up in response to the increased violence; meanwhile, tribes began to migrate out of the most-advanced horse cultures, to overthrow and radically change established civilizations in India, China, the Middle East, and Europe. The horse tribes carried the Indo-European languages with them; these languages, which include English, Spanish, Greek, and Sanskrit, are now spoken by approximately half the world's population.

The horse changed human culture, and humans changed the horses, selectively breeding or culling to produce stronger, gentler, faster, and more beautiful animals. As horse domestication moved south, tarpan-derived horses were crossed with the Oriental subspecies to produce the Akhal-Teke and Caspian; the Caspian wasn't a particularly small horse for this period, when average horse height was 13 to 14 hands.

THE ADVENT OF CHARIOTS

By 2100 BCE, the steppe people had invented the chariot, the first wheeled vehicle built for speed. Chariots were manned by a single warrior/driver, who fired arrows while steering the horses with the reins around his hips. Chariot warfare required wealth, skill, and athleticism, not unlike today's driving sports.

Chariot warfare was rapidly exported to the empires of present-day Egypt, Iran, Turkey, and Syria. Kikkuli wrote a manual on training chariot horses for the Hittites around 1360 BCE; the oldest known horse book, it preserved in writing what had long been transmitted orally.

All empires had a strong interest in horse breeding as they transitioned to mounted warfare around 745 BCE, when the Assyrians began fighting on horseback in mountainous terrain. The first mounted archers had a horseback companion who held the reins while the archer fired. Later tack developments allowed an archer to drop the reins while firing.

Chariot warfare was made obsolete in the third century BCE by another invention from the steppes, the recurved (Cupid's) bow, which was short, powerful, and could be fired backward over the tail of a galloping horse, the famous "Parthian shot." The steppe tribes were never more dangerous than when apparently retreating; time after time, they lured enemies into pursuit, then unleashed a lethal rain of arrows.

THE PERSIANS

After the overthrow of the Assyrians by the Scythians, horse peoples formed a new empire. The Persians and Medes brought horsemanship and horse breeding to the highest level in the ancient world. Their 15-hand Nisean horses were bred to carry riders. The Persians trained them in a *haqma*—a bitless bridle with three reins, ancestor of the modern hackamore—which allowed them to achieve great collection, lightness, and maneuverability. The Greek general Xenophon, who fought in Persia in the fourth century BCE, introduced many of the Persians' horsemanship principles to the Western world in his book *Per Hippikes*.

During this time, and right through till the 1800s CE, gaited horses were popular. Transportation was on horseback, as the roads were not good enough to support wheeled vehicles at speed, and gaited horses were comfortable.

THE HORSE IN WARFARE Saddles and stirrups were invented on the steppe. The breast collar and horse collar came from China. Trade and warfare passed these innovations from culture to culture.

Europe, India, and China were invaded countless times by horse tribes out of the steppes. The steppe warriors had vast pastures and huge numbers of horses; in their armies horses outnumbered riders six to one or more. Riders could switch horses often, and always had a spare horse to eat if supplies ran low, so the army was not tied to a baggage train.

Horses were rare in settled areas, where land was used for growing crops, so horsemanship was not instinctive in the population at large. Western Europe did have a geographic advantage, however. As they left the Eurasian plain, the Asian hordes also left the grazing lands. They were less able to feed their horses, and trees and mountains interfered with many of their tactics. Though mauled at the margins, Western Europe was increasingly able to hold out against the invaders as time went on.

The Hun army traveled with hundreds of extra horses, not only as fresh mounts during battle but also to provide milk and meat.

The introduction of the metal stirrup allowed a change in military technique. Now a rider could grip a lance in a couched position, and attack with the full force of his charging horse. This led directly to the medieval knight in armor. With metal armor came a need for larger horses; horse breeders produced the Great Horse, the Friesian, and the Andalusian.

In 710 CE, the Moors invaded Spain, riding Barb horses in a style new to Europe, the jineta style. Whereas knights rode braced in the saddle, the Moorish cavalry rode in the balanced seat and emphasized speed and mobility. The style was adopted by Spanish riders for waging war and working cattle.

Nomads erupted from the steppes for the last time starting in 1210, when the Mongols under Genghis Khan invaded China and ended up conquering the world from the Pacific to the Baltic. Their horseback empire introduced many inventions, particularly from China to Europe, which bridged the gap between the medieval and modern eras. Printing, gunpowder, forged steel, a large number of new food crops, and important horse innovations changed the world forever.

While horses remained essential to warfare, elite riding academies like the Spanish Riding School in Vienna, Austria, brought the art of horsemanship to a refined level in what became known as the Classical High School.

RETURN TO NORTH AMERICA When the Ottoman Turks, also superior horsemen, choked off land trade to the Middle East, western Europe took to the seas looking for new trade routes. Their explorations, beginning with the second voyage of Christopher Columbus in 1493, ended up returning horses to America, where they had been extinct for 9,000 years. European horse breeds flowed into the Americas: Spanish jennets to the West Indies, Florida, and Mexico; English Hobbies to the British colonies; Dutch Friesians to New York; and French Bretons to Quebec. Many of these horses were of the finest stock, and their freshly mingled bloodlines produced new breeds.

Returning to the grasslands where their kind first evolved, horses multiplied rapidly. In the Southwest and Southeast, the natural horse family structure of small mare bands with one herd stallion encouraged the Spanish herds to disperse. Indian tribes stole them and began raiding their neighbors, expanding their territory and the riding idea. As on the steppes millennia before, tribes abandoned settled villages and took to raiding and roaming.

Some tribes became horse breeders; Choctaw and Chickasaw horses, and the Appaloosa of the Nez Percé are their legacy. In addition, the plains produced fine mustangs in abundance. Wild living weeded out the weak, leaving only the toughest horses of pure Spanish bloodlines—bloodlines that were bred in the Old World for trainability. In the north a different strain of mustang developed, the Cayuse, named for the Cayuse tribe of Oregon. These large, round, robust-looking horses had a mix of Breton, Canadian, and Morgan blood.

The mix of breeds in the East produced a pool of North American "hill horses," from which the modern Canadian, Morgan, Saddlebred, Walkers, Rackers, Fox Trotters, and Mountain Saddle breeds were developed. There are important differences between these horses, but it is obvious at a glance that all are related. The Narragansett Pacer was another important breed, a gaited horse developed from English bloodlines, very comfortable and tough. It contributed to most eastern breeds before becoming extinct; many Narragansetts were exported to the Caribbean, where they influenced the Paso Fino. Gaited horses were crucial for transportation, as there were even fewer roads in the New World than in Europe.

In Virginia, the Quarter Horse was developed from Hobby bloodlines, as a racehorse for short distances.

Another important influence was the Thoroughbred, the new and prestigious English horse; many important stallions were imported in the 1700s. Thoroughbreds of that time were shorter and more compact than they are today, lending plausibility to the story that the foundation Morgan, Figure, was sired by a Thoroughbred. Thoroughbreds influenced most breeds in North America.

In the Caribbean, Central America, and South America, jennet-type horses were the primary imports, brought in by the Spaniards and only rarely crossed with Thoroughbreds or Arabs. An important cross-fertilization with hobby horse lines came through the rum trade with New England. This brought great numbers of the plain-but-useful Narragansett Pacer and some Canadian horses, which influenced the Paso breeds there.

MODERN HISTORY Meanwhile in Europe, the French emperor Napoleon revolutionized horseback warfare along with everything else. Lancers mounted on ambling horses were replaced by hussars, carrying swords and pistols, mounted on Oriental-bred horses who trotted or galloped. Ambling went out of style, even in Spain. The jennet and hobby horse strains gradually disappeared; their descendants live on in the New World.

Horseback warfare continued. The British introduced horse breeding to Australia in the early 19th century. This gave the British a vast supply of warhorses for their Asian and African campaigns, allowing them to extend their empire, with political consequences the world lives with to this day.

As roads improved in North America, wheeled vehicles and trotting horses became increasingly important, for both transportation and racing. The Morgan dominated both areas until the development of the Standardbred. Draft horses increased in size and number, both on farms and in cities, where manure piled up and manure dust filled the air. Eventually the internal combustion engine put city horses out of a job and cleaned up the streets considerably; tractors replaced horses on most farms beginning in the 1930s, with some delay caused by the Great Depression. Horse populations plummeted in the industrialized world.

But in response, perhaps, to withdrawal from a connection that had existed for 6,000 years, recreational riding and driving began to rise in importance. Horse showing and horse sports continued to expand into the late 20th century, though facing a pinch from dips in the economy and an increasing dearth of open land for horse pastures and riding. Horses continue to be used in the West to work cattle, though in falling numbers. Worldwide, developing countries continue to depend on animal traction for farming and hauling, and the horse remains important.

➤ *See also evolution of the horse*

hitch, hitch horse
A group of equines harnessed together. Two horses are called a pair or team; anything larger is called a hitch. A hitch horse is leggy draft horse used in large hitches for shows. A draft horse of this type might be described as "hitchy."

hitching post/hitching rail
A hitching post is a sturdy vertical beam or round post of good diameter that is substantially anchored in the ground. A hitching rail is a horizontal pole made for tying multiple horses. Either is useful for tying horses while they are waiting to work.

hives/wheals/welts
Low bumps on the skin that might be caused by allergens that are either in the air or come into contact with the coat or skin. Hives can also be caused by the bite of an insect or the puncture of an injection. Usually, hives subside by themselves in a few hours or a day. If they are accompanied by diarrhea, fever, or respiratory problems, as sometimes happens, call a veterinarian.

hobbles A form of restraint in which two or more legs are fastened together to inhibit movement. Hobbles may be used to keep a horse near camp, while allowing him to graze. In this case the front feet are usually hobbled, using soft rope, a latigo strap with buckles, or nylon webbing. Heavy-duty hobbles may have a short length of chain between two leg cuffs. Picket hobbles are one-legged hobbles used to secure a horse to a picket line. Breeding hobbles fasten around a mare's hocks and attach to a breastplate, to prevent her from kicking the stallion or handlers.

➤ *See also restraints*

hock The tarsal bones, corresponding to the human ankle. Along with the stifle, which correlates to the human knee, the hock is one of the hardest-working joints in a horse's body, so it is vital that it be relatively large in circumference and height, and that the bones above and below it are in alignment. Stress injuries and lameness are common in horses with poorly conformed hocks.

hog back A type of jump consisting of three elements, with the middle one higher than the outside two.

➤ *See also spread*

hogging a mane

➤ *See roaching*

A FOUR-MULE HITCH

hog-tie To tie three legs of a roped calf with a narrow rope.

➤ *See also hooey*

holding a horse

➤ *See handling horses*

hollow back

➤ *See swayback*

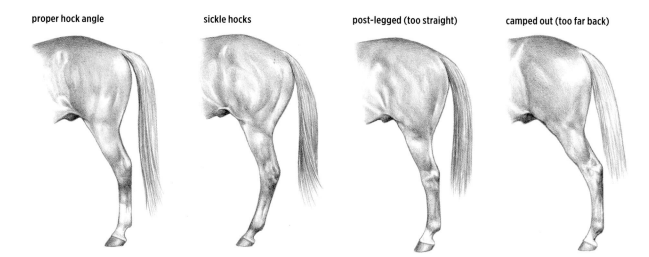

proper hock angle   sickle hocks   post-legged (too straight)   camped out (too far back)

The angle of the **hock** is key to structural strength and soundness. The hock joint should be directly under the point of the buttocks.

homeopathy Invented in 1779 by German physician Christian Freidrich Samuel Hahnemann, the idea behind this medical system is that specific substances, even poisons, can chase away in a sick person or animal the very symptoms the substance would cause in a healthy one. The short way of saying it is, "Like cures like." This approach is thought to work through the stimulation of the body's immune system. Commercial homeopathic remedies are available for horses. It is not a substitute for regular veterinary care.

hondo The eye on the end of a catch rope that forms the loop. The hondo is covered with a section of rawhide called the burner, to protect the rope from wear as it slides through.

honest horse A horse who tries to do what you ask, with no evasions.

hooey A half-hitch that is tied around the hind legs and one foreleg of a calf that has been roped and is being hog-tied.

hoof The hard external foot below the coronary band, including the hoof wall, sole, and frog. The hoof is the remnant, after eons of evolution, of the middle toenails of *Eohippus*, the primeval horse. Hooves can be dark, pale, or mixed in color. Mixed colors always run vertically on the hoof, forming stripes.

Hooves should be large but in proportion to the horse's body. Few horses have hooves that are too big, but some horses may have hooves that are too small. Small hooves will suffer extra concussion and increased wear and tear, and can lead to unsoundness later in life.

Although a horse's feet look solid and tough, they are actually full of delicate structures and are only partially protected by the hard outer wall. The sole of the foot is softer than the wall; the frog, a wedge-shaped area of soft tissue beginning at the heel and reaching two-thirds of the way toward the toe, is quite soft.

Front hooves are round, hind feet slightly elongated. Both grow outer hoof walls that extend beyond the softer portions, keeping them out of contact with most small pebbles on the ground; a large stone, however, may bruise even the artificially raised sole of a shod foot.

ANGLE The relationship between the front wall of the hoof and the ground. Hoof angle is considered correct when the hoof and pastern are in alignment, forming a line from fetlock to earth without breaking forward or back. Normal hoof angles range from 52 to 60 degrees.

GROWTH Hoof growth is essential for soundness. Growth is enhanced by exercise, proper nutrition, and proper trimming and shoeing. A hoof grows about ½ inch (1.2 cm) per month in weanlings and about ⅓ inch (0.7 cm) per month in mature horses. Hooves grow more rapidly in summer than in winter. To improve hoof growth, horses need adequate supplies of good-quality protein, along with biotin, zinc, and essential fatty acids.

SHOEING AND TRIMMING Proper shoeing can protect the hoof wall from excessive wear and damage, increase traction, correct gaits, and reduce discomfort in horses with various physical problems. Shoeing should be carried out by an experienced farrier, one who takes the time to understand your horse's condition, the work your horse does, and the terrain he will travel on.

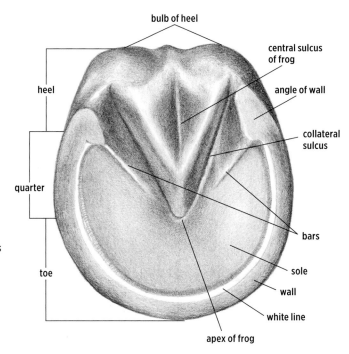

bulb of heel
central sulcus of frog
heel
angle of wall
collateral sulcus
quarter
bars
toe
sole
wall
white line
apex of frog

Most shod horses grow enough new hoof to need trimming every six to eight weeks, and sometimes in as little as five weeks during hot weather or substantially increased work. Horses who are unshod may wear down hoof naturally, but their hooves still need regular trimming.

➤ *See also abscess; barefoot trimming; blowout; bruised sole; corrective trimming; crack; farrier; founder; laminitis; navicular disease; shoes*

hoof boot

➤ *See boots (for horse)*

hoof bound
A term used for the condition that results when a contracted hoof wall presses against the internal structures of the hoof; the result of an untreated contracted heel. Without proper trimming or shoeing, the hoof wall may start to press against the coffin bone. This condition makes the horse lame and unsound.

➤ *See also contracted heel*

hoof pick
An instrument for removing dirt, stones, and debris from a horse's hooves. Picks come in several styles, but all have a sharp wedge or screwdriver-type point for digging out the material. Some have an attached brush for removing any remaining dirt, and some even include a small comb for pulling manes.

➤ *See also hoof; picking out feet*

hoof rings
Horizontal lines or ridges around the hoof wall; also called growth rings or fever rings. Hoof rings are caused by changes in diet, environment, season, or health. Very pronounced hoof rings indicate that the horse has foundered.

hoof sealer
Liquid or gel applied to the hoof wall to help maintain moisture balance by minimizing the amount of moisture the hoof absorbs. Hoof sealer should allow normal hoof respiration to be released; avoid airtight, waterproof sealers like varnish or shellac. Hoof sealer should be applied in a thin, even coat starting about ½ inch (1.2 cm) below the coronary band. Farriers and veterinarians differ on its usefulness.

hook
To fasten a harnessed horse to a vehicle, preparatory to driving. While hooking, drivers pay close attention to detail, to be sure every strap is fastened correctly. Hooking a young horse to a cart is one of the most crucial parts of training him to drive. It is very important that the first several hooks—some say the first 30—go well.

➤ *See also driving*

horn wrap
A protective webbing that wraps around the ears and horns of cattle used for roping practice, to prevent rope burns.

➤ *See also calf roping; team roping*

horse
Properly, the word "horse" refers to a full-grown male horse—gelding or stallion; a female is a mare. In everyday speech, however, "horse" is used for both males and females. The species designation is *Equus caballus* or *Equus ferus*, a large, strong mammal with four legs, solid hooves, and flowing mane and tail, capable of being domesticated and trained to perform tasks for humans.

horse agility
A competitive sport in which a person on foot guides a horse through a series of obstacles; similar to dog agility. At most levels of agility, horses wear a halter and a 10-foot (3 m) lead rope, and possibly protective boots. In freestyle agility they wear no tack. Possible obstacles include a tunnel, seesaw, jump, curtain, or podium. Horses may be asked to roll a ball, go onto a trailer, carry a load, or pick up feet.

Horse agility is on a continuum of newer trail sports that include versatility and working equitation. Agility is good for nonriding humans and may be an option for a horse that is fit but unable to be ridden. As of this printing, information is available online through the International Horse Agility Club; horse owners can download instructional material and compete in monthly online contests.

horseball Invented in the 1970s by French riding instructor Jean-Paul Depons, horseball is most aptly described as rugby on horseback, with a little basketball thrown in. As fast and furious as polo, it is a more egalitarian sport, as each rider only needs one horse per game and it can be played at different levels of riding experience. Teams of six shoot at a basketball-type goal with a soccer-sized ball with leather handles that is passed or thrown from player to player and scooped from the ground when necessary. Players must get rid of the ball within 10 seconds and may steal it from another player. Two 10-minute halves are played. At the Pony Club level, riders play bareback, using only saddle pads and a surcingle with handholds.

horseflies/tabanids A group of biting flies that attack horses. The flies may be black, brown, yellow, or gray, and they range in length from ¾ inch to 1 inch (2–2.5 cm). The female must have a blood meal to reproduce; her bite slashes the skin so that the blood flows freely and she can drink it with her proboscis. This causes an allergic reaction, and a bump, in some horses. Horseflies are prevalent where there are areas of permanently wet ground, as females lay their eggs on or near water.

Because they are such voracious feeders, often going from one horse to another, horseflies spread bloodborne diseases such as equine infectious anemia (EIA) and equine encephalitis.

horsemanship

1. A term often used to describe Western or Reining Seat equitation classes at horse shows. Horsemanship classes emphasize the ability of the horse and rider to work together. Rail work is optional in Horsemanship classes. Pattern work emphasizes control, precision, accuracy, and smoothness.

2. The body of knowledge and lore involved in working with horses. Horsemanship embraces a wide range of knowledge and skills, including horse care (nutrition, health care, hoof care, grooming, exercise needs); stable management; horse psychology; humane training; and effective riding, the mastery of which leads to one's being known as a "true horseman."

A good riding instruction program incorporates horsemanship by beginning with safety in ground handling, grooming, and tacking up, rather than starting students in the arena with the horses already prepared. After the lesson, students untack, groom, and care for their horses and equipment before leaving the barn.

horsemeat Horses were hunted for meat in prehistoric times, and people have eaten them ever since, but for many, especially in the United States, eating horsemeat is strictly taboo. Until the mid-2000s, three slaughterhouses for horses were at work in the United States. In 2005, federal inspection of these slaughterhouses was defunded. Slaughterhouses worked around the defunding by paying for their own inspection, but that was eventually determined to be illegal.

In the absence of domestic slaughterhouses, 100,000 horses a year are shipped from the United States to slaughterhouses in Canada and Mexico, where they are killed for human consumption and for zoo animal consumption. Horses shipped to slaughter include racehorses, show horses, companion horses, trail horses, and pets. Any horse going to an auction in expectation of fetching a low price is likely to meet this fate. In addition, some horses are subjected to the further stress of being live-shipped to Asia for slaughter.

U.S. horsemeat comes into question even in the countries where it is consumed. Since U.S. horses are not managed for human consumption, their bodies may contain unacceptable levels of drugs and antibiotics.

The topic of whether to reinstate domestic horse slaughter is controversial among U.S. horsemen. Some groups, notably the American Quarter Horse Association, support it as a necessary and more humane way to dispose of surplus horses. Others, notably the Thoroughbred industry, oppose it as inhumane. People who operate horse rescues tend to support it, as they face the overwhelming flood of horses without homes or jobs. In theory, domestic horse slaughter would at least spare horses the grueling trip to Canada or Mexico.

Some horsemen have responded by putting pressure on breed organizations to stop overproducing horses; the 2008 recession increased this pressure. However, those conserving what they regard as important

HORSE PROGRESS DAYS

An annual draft horse farming trade show, held Fourth of July weekend in the Midwest since 1994. The Horse Progress Days event includes field demonstrations of new equipment hitched to teams of horses and mules, vendors, clinics, and spectator events. Tens of thousands of people attend every year. Similar contests are held in Europe—this photo of a team of Clydesdales is from the British National Ploughing Championships.

bloodlines must eventually breed or lose the genetics, whether or not there is a market for the horses.

Other activists oppose all horse slaughter, without being able to point to a viable solution. And the horse industry has responded to overproduction with programs to rehome unwanted horses; success of these, as of the rescue organizations, varies according to the state of the economy.

horse sales

Horse sales may be as prestigious as the Keeneland Thoroughbred sales each spring—where young bloodstock is sold to international buyers for millions of dollars, with the prices based on the racing performance of the horses' sires and dams—or as down-home as a sale offering horses of various types and quality from the general region. Horses are also sold at agricultural sales where cattle, swine, and sheep are sold.

horseshoes

After trying other means of protecting horses' feet for a few thousand years, humans first began nailing on iron horseshoes around the fifth century CE, and have been doing so ever since. Shoes prevent excessive hoof wear; correct improper hoof shape and balance; stabilize a damaged hoof or one subject to extreme stress, such as landing after jumping; improve traction (or minimize traction, as in reining); correct gait problems; and prevent bruising of the sole.

Many ponies and horses have particularly dense hooves and do not need shoes (Arabians and Appaloosas are known for having strong feet), and horses who are not being ridden or worked are generally

TYPES OF HORSESHOES

Most horseshoes are made of low carbon steel. The vast majority are factory-made **keg shoes**, so called because they used to be shipped in kegs.

A **rim shoe** has a deep crease down the center of the entire ground surface, creating two rims for added traction.

Wide web shoes are broader, and provide a larger base of support for the foot and protect more of the sole. Racehorses wear wide web shoes made of aluminum, called **racing plates**. Innovations in design and production allow horses to train as well as race in racing plates, instead of training in steel shoes, as was formerly the practice.

A **bar shoe** has the heels joined and provides added support to the hoof and leg. **Straight bar shoes** have the bar going straight across. **Egg bar shoes** have a curved bar, making the shoe slightly oval. **Heart bar shoes** have a V-shaped bar that supports the frog. **Full support shoes** have a combination of an egg bar and a heart bar.

Sliding plates are wide-webbed shoes with a smooth surface, recessed nailheads, and extended heels. This minimizes traction, enabling a reining horse to slide to a stop on his hind feet. Reining horses frequently wear sliding plates for the whole competition season, which limits the option to take them out on a trail ride, as sliding plates are slippery.

Synthetic shoes are made of flexible rubber or plastic.

Tab glue-on shoes and **flexible cuff glue-on shoes** are glued to the hoof and are useful when the horse's hoof is too sore or in too poor a condition to nail on shoes. They can also be used to correct abnormalities in a foal's hooves.

not shod. However, most riding horses are shod with steel shoes to protect their feet from cracking and bruising. Horses who are worked on gravel or pavement should always have shoes, as should jumpers.

Shoes can correct a number of problems of the feet and legs. A good farrier can help an unbalanced horse move more evenly, can reduce "forging" (when a horse kicks his own ankles with his rear feet), and can keep a split in a hoof from leading to more serious problems.

When putting on new shoes, the farrier first trims the sole and toe, carving away the excess with a curved blade. Before being nailed on, new shoes are precisely fitted or old ones remeasured to make sure the fit is the same.

Horses often lose a shoe when turned out or while working. Sometimes the hind foot catches against the front shoe, loosening the nails; bell boots can help prevent this problem. Frequent stamping of the feet against flies is another way nails come loose. Once a shoe is loose, it needs to come off immediately and be reset by your farrier. Loose shoes that come partly off can injure the horse.

➤ *See also farrier; hoof; barefoot trimming*

horse shows

➤ *See individual show associations*

horse trial

➤ *See eventing*

hot blood
A horse of Oriental descent. These breeds have more red blood cells per unit than cold-blooded horses, for greater oxygen transportation while running. They have lighter, longer bodies for heat dissipation, with thin skin, fine hair, more efficient sweat glands, and blood vessels that stand out prominently when the horse is hot, which also facilitates cooling. The head is small; the nostrils, air passages, and lungs proportionally large. This is a horse built for heat and speed. Hot bloods tend to be livelier and more reactive than cold bloods. Breeds include Akhal-Teke, Arabian, Barb, and Thoroughbred.

➤ *See also cold blood; individual breeds; warmblood*

The Anglo-Arab is a cross of two **hot-blooded breeds**, the Thoroughbred and the Arabian.

hot fitting, hot shoeing Hot fitting is pressing a hot shoe against the bottom of the hoof; scorch spots indicate high areas that need to be rasped away for proper fit. If hot enough, the shoe will melt the hoof horn and result in a perfect fit.

Hot shoeing is a method of horseshoeing in which the shoe is heated to be shaped. It may or may not involve hot fitting.

➤ *See also cold shoeing*

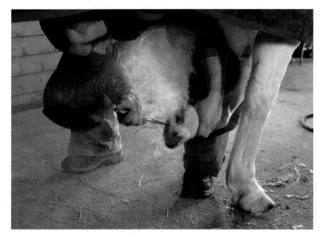

Though the horn of the hoof does not have sensation, horses need to be acclimated to the particular sounds and smells of **hot fitting**.

hot nail A horseshoe nail that is driven into the sensitive structure of the hoof. This farrier error results in temporary lameness.

hot walker, hot walking A hot walker is a mechanical device on which several arms extend out from a rotating center. A horse can be tied by its halter to each arm. When the hot walker is turned on, the horses must walk in circles until they are unhooked. This is a labor-saving device for trainers who lack the barn help to cool out hot horses by hand.

Hot walking is the process of walking horses cool; when not done with a machine, it is the job of lower-level employees.

humidity Horses cannot pant as dogs do. They cool down through air exchange in the lungs, by radiating heat away through the skin, and by the evaporation of sweat. On humid days, sweat does not evaporate well,

negating this cooling mechanism. Horses should be worked lightly when humidity is high. They should be cooled down by additional means, such as walking in a shady place—especially if there's a breeze. You may also spray or bathe a hot horse with warm to cool water (not cold), and place a fan in the stall or barn aisle.

hunter A horse of any breed that is suitable to working as a hunt horse over fences. Hunters must be graceful, have good conformation, and be able to work in a long frame with ground-covering strides. Show hunters are judged primarily on their pace, style, and manners, while classic foxhunt mounts are intended to withstand the rigors of the hunt while maintaining gracefulness and style. Today's use of hunters ranges from those shown only on the flat in Hunter Pleasure classes, to show hunters that never see an open field of fences, to horses ridden in foxhunts in the United States and England.

hunter clip

➤ *See clipping; "Common Clipping Terms," page 56*

hunter pace A competitive event, often sponsored by a hunt or a hunter/jumper association; a less exacting version may be held at horse camps and lesson barns. A trail is marked in a few miles or kilometers, and the optimal time, or pace, is determined. There may be only one trail with optional obstacles to be jumped, or there may be two trails: a flat trail and one with obstacles. Competitors, who usually ride in teams, choose the trail that best matches their abilities. A hunter pace is not ridden like a race, with teams of riders on the trail neck-and-neck. Rather, each team sets off by itself at a given time. Each team's total time is recorded, and the team that comes in closest to the optimal time wins.

➤ *See also point-to-point*

HUNGARIAN HORSE A sport horse breed originating in Hungary. Hungarian Horses are often spectacular movers, excelling at dressage, show jumping, eventing, and combined driving.

hunt seat A form of English riding that originated with foxhunting. It developed to help riders and horses handle a wide variety of terrain and natural jump obstacles. Stirrup length in hunt seat tends to be short, to assist the rider in rising into the two-point position for jumping and galloping. Working Hunter classes at shows reflect the foxhunting heritage, with a mix of formality, ease of handling, and the ability to cover ground and easily handle jumps.

hurdles, hurdle racing Light fences made of brush, which horses race over. Unlike steeplechasing, which takes place on open fields, hurdle racing takes place at racetracks.

hydrotherapy Using warm or cold water to heal injuries. Cold hosing is usually prescribed for fresh, acute injuries like sprains and bruises, and is also a palliative remedy for laminitis. Warm soaking is more likely to be prescribed for older injuries, and warm soaking with Epsom salt is helpful for abscesses.

hyperkalemic periodic paralysis (HYPP) A muscular disease that affects both horses and humans. It is caused by a hereditary genetic defect that disrupts the sodium channels in the muscles, which control muscle contraction, as well as the ability to regulate potassium levels in the blood. HYPP can result in uncontrolled muscle twitching, profound muscle weakness, and even collapse and sudden death from cardiac arrest or respiratory failure. Severity of the disease varies, with homozygous horses affected more severely than heterozygous ones.

HYPP occurs only in Quarter Horses, and is traced to a single sire, Impressive. This popular stallion has some 355,000 descendants, who dominate halter classes due to their pronounced muscle development. An estimated 4 percent of Quarter Horses are affected; the condition is not found in other breeds. The original genetic defect that causes HYPP was a natural mutation that occurred as part of the evolutionary process, not from inbreeding.

➤ *See genetic disorders, genetics*

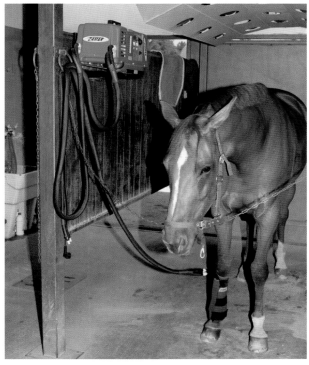

A more efficient method of **hydrotherapy** than hosing down an injured leg is this circulating system that keeps cold water moving around the affected area.

179

ICELANDIC HORSE

An ancient, five-gaited horse bred in isolation on Iceland for more than a thousand years. Though they are pony-sized, between 12.3 and 13.2 hands high, Icelandics are considered horses. Temperaments vary from fiery to placid; the U.S. Icelandic Horse Congress describes the breed as "a versatile family riding horse."

Icelandic Horses are exceptionally friendly, as they have no natural predators in Iceland. Bred in isolation, they also have little immunity to most horse diseases; once a horse leaves Iceland, it is never allowed to return.

Icelandics have five gaits: walk, trot, canter, skeið (flying pace), and tölt (a fast running walk). A rather long-built horse, they come in all colors and color patterns, including some that are rarely seen in other breeds. They are extremely popular in Europe.

➤ See also Fjord; pace; skeið; tölt

ichthammol A black, lanolin-based drawing ointment, good for treating abscesses, infected wounds, and scratches (grease heel).

idle horse A horse on forced stall rest. Idle horses require special care because the horse was not intended to be a stall-bound animal. Overfeeding must be avoided; to keep an idle horse occupied, use small-mesh hay nets or slow feeders, and enrichment such as toys. A stablemate with whom the horse has bonded can serve as a babysitter, helping to keep him calm.

impacted teeth Teeth that are trapped below and behind teeth that have already emerged. In horses, impacted teeth almost always come through on their own. Some, however, cause a tooth bump, a bony protrusion on the lower jaw, as they emerge. Tooth bumps eventually smooth out, usually disappearing by the time the horse is between five and seven years old. If there are numerous tooth bumps or if they become rapidly larger and are sensitive to the touch, the horse's dentition might not be sorting itself out. A veterinarian should X-ray the mouth and assess whether removal of any teeth is warranted.

impaction A type of colic that results when food ceases to move through a horse's intestine. This causes steady and increasing discomfort, which the horse may show by pawing or lying on his side and not moving. Although the horse may have initial bowel movements that empty the lower part of the intestine, he will soon cease to defecate.

The number one cause of impaction is dehydration. The equine gut narrows in three critical areas, and feed passing through them needs to be semiliquid. If the horse is dehydrated, the body draws water out of the gastrointestinal tract, making the contents more solid and possibly unable to pass. Monitor water intake, and take steps to warm water on cold days. Horses tend to drink less when water is cold; it may hurt the throat or stomach. Also, take measures such as flavoring the water, or carrying water from home, when you trailer your horse.

The second leading cause of impaction is parasite overload. Worms can jam the narrow parts of the gut, creating blockages.

Other possible causes include ingestion of something inedible, such as hay twine, rubber fencing, fibers from rubber tubs or old tires, and hay nets; enteroliths, or intestinal stones; bolting food without sufficiently chewing it; and tooth problems, such as the worn-down teeth of old age, which let food pass into the intestines insufficiently chewed.

If you suspect impaction, call your veterinarian immediately. Impaction is life-threatening unless the blockage is dislodged. Treatment usually involves dosing with mineral oil to lubricate and dislodge the impacted material; intravenous administration of fluids can help treat dehydration and move more water to the gut. If the impaction can't be resolved this way, surgery may be required.

➤ *See also colic; deworming; water, for horses*

imprint training of foals
Handling of newborn foals with the intention of impacting their future trainability. The concept of imprint training was handed down to us by Native American horsemen, who discovered that foals spoken to in utero and handled shortly after birth were often easier to train as mature horses. It was popularized in the 20th century by Robert Miller, DVM. Today, imprint training is used by many breeders, both professionals and amateurs. Imprinting can occur only within the first 24 to 36 hours after birth; beyond that, any changes in temperament are caused by conditioning.

The basics of imprint training involve familiarizing the foal immediately after birth, before he even stands up, with the smell, touch, and appearance of humans. The process is repeated after the foal stands, and again on his second and third days. The foal is familiarized with restraint, foot handling, grooming, and touch all over his body. Each part of the body must be gently rubbed until the foal submits; by stopping while he is still resisting, you can teach him to fear humans rather than trust them.

Imprinting can provide a tremendously positive foundation for future work with a horse, but done improperly and incompletely, it can do more harm than good. The impact depends on the education and experience of the person doing the training. Learn everything you can about imprinting before you try it on your own. Even then, on your first foal it is best to work side by side with someone who has had success with imprinting methods. Be certain to allow a first-time mother to bond with her foal before you attempt to bond with him, to keep her from rejecting him.

If you are uncertain about imprinting, or miss the delivery, rest assured that the majority of foals throughout history have been gentled by other means, and turned out just fine.

impulsion
The energy and thrust of the engaged hindquarters that drive the horse forward into collected gaits. Impulsion is pushing power from your horse's hindquarters. When a horse is moving with impulsion, his hind legs thrust more powerfully off the ground and reach more energetically forward. In the transition from walk to trot, the rider might feel the area behind the saddle rise up.

Impulsion is not the same thing as speed. A horse moving with impulsion has begun to carry more of his weight on his hind legs, to lift his back and round up under the rider, paying closer attention to the rider's aids. It requires strength and suppleness, and a mental connection with the rider.

➤ *See also collection*

inbreeding
➤ *See genetics*

This trot shows **impulsion**, an impression of forward flow. The power generated by the horse's hindquarters moves forward to the bit in an unobstructed manner.

incisors A horse's front teeth, which are used for biting off grass.
➤ *See also dental problems; teeth and age*

indirect rein A rein effect in which the rein pressure is diagonally back; the rider turns the horse to the right by rein pressure back toward the horse's left hip; this contrasts with a direct rein, which leads the horse in the direction of the turn. Indirect rein effects can be extremely subtle. Variations include indirect rein in front of the withers and indirect rein behind the withers. In Western riding, neck-reining is a form of indirect reining.
➤ *See also direct rein; neck-reining*

indoor riding arena An indoor riding arena has a roof and solid walls that allow for working horses during bad weather or after dark; typically called "an indoor." Very popular in cold climates, indoor arenas are also useful for riding in hot weather, on rainy days, or after dark. An indoor arena needs to be safely constructed, with appropriate, well-maintained footing. It must be large enough for the particular discipline; a driving arena should be larger than a riding arena, unless the facility specializes in ponies. Prefabricated buildings are available, from the size of a small dressage arena to arenas that can accommodate a line of jumps.

infertility The inability to breed or reproduce. Infertility has different causes and treatments in mares and stallions.

MARES Infertility in mares is usually caused by recent infections of the genital tract or by a systemic infection. Body condition also plays a role with mare fertility; if a mare is too fat or too thin, she may have unpredictable heat cycles or none at all. A mare with hormone problems may also fail to cycle or may cycle irregularly. High-level athletic mares may stop ovulating.

STALLIONS Infertility in stallions is typically caused by fever or inflammation. Anything that raises the temperature of the testicle for a length of time can interfere with sperm production. The decrease in viable sperm production may not be noticeable right away, as some sperm produced before the injury or illness could still be viable (it takes between 60 and 70 days to produce mature sperm). After any injury or illness, periodic semen checks will reveal whether there is a period of lower fertility or infertility, and breeding can be scheduled accordingly or postponed until sperm production is back to normal.

in front of the leg A horse who responds quickly and moves freely forward in response to the rider's leg is said to be "in front of the leg."
➤ *See also behind the leg*

infundibulum An indentation that shows up on the biting surface of the horse's incisors, usually when the horse is around six years old.

in-hand training Training done with the handler guiding the horse from the ground. In-hand training begins the day you first handle a foal. It progresses as you train him to accept a halter and lead readily; to stand while being groomed and tacked up; to side-step and back up in response to cues; to move on the longe line; and to long line. In-hand work can be very sophisticated; many dressage trainers teach upper-level movements, up to and including the airs above the ground, in hand.
➤ *See also backing up; sidepass/side step; trailering; turn on the forehand; tying*

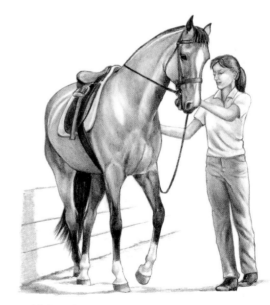

Even sophisticated movements, such as shoulder-in, can be introduced **in hand** before being worked on under saddle.

injectable supplements Vitamins, minerals, and herbs given by injection. These are frequently given to change a horse's mood or energy level at a competition; magnesium is frequently used this way. The substance in question may not be illegal, but the practice is ethically dubious and can be dangerous. Unless your veterinarian has determined that your horse needs injectable supplements for medical reasons, avoid them. You can cause serious harm or even kill the horse if the supplements upset his nutritional balance.
➤ *See also magnesium*

injection A method of administering medication into muscle, into a vein, or under the skin. The medicine is drawn into a syringe via a hypodermic needle, then injected into the horse. Injection is a highly efficient mode of administering medicine, since you can be confident the full dose was received. The primary types of injections are the following:
    Intramuscular (IM). Given in the muscle, usually in the neck, chest, or buttock.
    Intravenous (IV). Given into the vein, usually in the jugular vein of the neck.
    Subcutaneous (SQ or subcu). Given between the muscle and skin.

in-line trailer A type of trailer, no longer in production, in which two horses travel one in front of the other.
➤ *See also trailer*

ADMINISTERING VACCINATIONS

Many horsemen give their own shots, except a few, such as rabies, that are usually required to be given by a veterinarian. It is more economical for you to give common injections, such as antibiotics (some of which require multiple doses each day), than to have the veterinarian visit each time a shot is needed, especially if you have a large herd. Have your veterinarian instruct you in the proper techniques for intramuscular shots; intravenous shots, which carry greater risk, should be given only by the veterinarian.

inoculation
➤ *See vaccinations*

inside (leg or rein) The leg or rein toward the inside of the space one is working in, or toward the inside of a circle. The inside leg or rein would be seen by a person standing in the center of that space. In the open, the inside rein or leg is the one you want the horse to bend around or move away from.
➤ *See also aids; hands, rider's; legs, use of when riding; outside (leg or rein)*

instinct A horse is born with certain instincts that helped its ancestors survive in the wild over millions of years. It is important to understand and work with, not against, these instincts. Horses' instincts include the following:

- The instinct to eat, grazing for most of the day
- The instinct to live in a herd
- The instinct to reproduce
- The instinct to flee danger
- The instinct to strike out, if escape is impossible

instructor Someone who teaches riding or driving. In the United States, it is not necessary to pass any tests to become an instructor in any discipline, although various forms of certification are offered. The American Riding Instructor Association (ARIA) uses stringent tests to certify instructors at three levels in fifteen specialties. Hunt seat instructors who have achieved any level of British Horse Society certification often promote themselves based on that achievement. Dressage instructors who have studied with great masters may advertise that. Riders who were in Pony Club as children and passed some of the club's level of increasingly difficult tests may list that on their résumés.

Still, a person who is a great rider may not be a great instructor; there is a world of difference between knowing how to do something and being able to educate others. When an instructor's students have competed in important regional or national shows or they have their own valuable horses in training with the instructor, the title "trainer" or "coach" is often used. However, because

The leg nearest the center of the ring is always the **inside leg**; the outside leg faces the rail.

riding is a sport and most teachers also coach the barn's riding teams, any instructor might use the term "trainer."
➤ *See also coach; trainer*

insulin The hormone that regulates removal of glucose from the bloodstream.

insulin resistance (IR)
➤ *See Cushing's disease/Cushing's syndrome/PPID; equine metabolic syndrome (EMS)*

Intercollegiate Horse Show Association (IHSA) An organization for college students founded in 1967 at Fairleigh Dickinson University. Its purpose is to promote competition for riders of any skill level, regardless of financial status, in both English and Western equine sports. Students compete individually and as team members at both the regional and national levels. In 2015, there were 412 IHSA college teams across the United States and Canada, and 9,286 riders competing in hunt seat equitation, Western horsemanship, and/or reining. Riders compete on horses owned by the host school; horses and riders are paired by random drawing. The IHSA is a recognized member of the United States Equestrian Federation (USEF); all IHSA horse shows are judged by USEF-recognized officials.

intercoms Wireless systems that allow a trainer to communicate with students. Intercoms have a working distance of up to 900 meters (980 yards), depending on the system. Riders wear headsets in some systems, but many trainers prefer to use a lapel microphone or to rely on good old-fashioned shouting.

interference When a horse hits his foreleg with a hind leg while traveling forward. Interference can be caused by base-narrow conformation or by toed-out conformation. The problem may result in tripping and can cause injury to the horse.
➤ *See also base-narrow, base-wide; dishing; toed-in legs, toed-out legs*

International Equestrian Federation
➤ *See Fédération Equestre Internationale (FEI)*

International Society for Equitation Science (ISES)
Founded in 2004 to encourage and support research into training and horse welfare. An excellent source of cutting-edge knowledge, it encourages links between applied animal behavioral science, veterinary science, psychology, and other disciplines, and assimilation of scientific knowledge into the field of horsemanship, with a goal of improving horses' lives.

interval training
Training that incorporates a short burst of speed that increases the heart rate, followed by a brief rest period during which the heart rate is kept at a working level. For instance, canter for two minutes, do a working trot for two minutes, then canter for two minutes. Interval training improves a horse's cardiovascular fitness, and is used for endurance horses and racehorses.

intestinal obstructions
➤ *See impaction*

intussusception, as cause of colic
Telescoping of the gut; the intestine slides inside itself, much as a telescope closes, with the farthest section squeezing into the one behind it, and then both of those into the one behind it, and so on. When this happens to sections of intestine, the gut-inside-a-gut-inside-a-gut may happen enough times to completely close the space that creates a passage for digesting material and manure. In any case, the surface area for absorption of nutrients is reduced. The horse with intussusception may recover from acute colic with minor treatment but then lose weight rapidly. Surgery may be necessary.
➤ *See also colic*

IRISH DRAUGHT

The Irish Draught was the 19th-century forebear of the famous Irish Hunter. The breed, developed over centuries from Anglo-Norman and Andalusian stock, was extremely versatile, capable of pulling a plow; trotting in harness; galloping under saddle; and, in particular, jumping with courage and style.

After the Irish famine of 1847, the Irish Draught declined, and unsuccessful efforts were made to improve the stock with imported heavy breeds.

In the 20th century, the Irish Draught made a comeback. These horses now stand taller, at 16 to 17 hands high, than did their forebears, who stood no more than 15.3 hands high, but they still exhibit the breed's athleticism and amiable disposition. **Livestock Conservancy rating: Watch**

iodine

1. A useful antiseptic to have in the barn. For use on both human and equine cuts and abrasions, use only a diluted povidone-iodine solution (10%). This is also used, in mild solution (5%), as a navel dip for foals.

   Full-strength iodine can be applied to the bottom of the hooves of flat-footed horses so they don't bruise as easily; iodine toughens the tissue somewhat. Apply only to the sole of the foot; avoiding spilling it down the hoof wall (it will dry out the hoof wall) or onto tender tissues above the hoof, where it may burn skin.

2. A nutritional supplement necessary in the diet to aid growth and to regulate metabolism. Only a small amount (as little as 1 mg daily) is needed. Sufficient iodine is included in most commercial feeds. If you still think your horse lacks iodine, a little iodized salt or mineral salt (such as is afforded by an equine salt or mineral block) can supply it. Kelp products also contain iodine. But the danger is usually of supplying too much iodine rather than too little. Check with your veterinarian before adding iodine to a horse's ration.

iridocyclitis
➤ *See equine recurrent uveitis (ERU)*

iris
The pigmented area of the eye surrounding the pupil. The iris is capable of contracting or expanding to regulate the amount of light entering the eye.

Most horses have brown eyes (brown-pigmented irises). However, some have a walleye or glass eye, which is an eye with unpigmented or blue-pigmented irises; a few have partially blue irises. Some horses, like other animals, have one brown and one blue eye. The color of the iris does not affect the horse's vision.

iron
A trace mineral necessary to a horse's health. It is usually supplied sufficiently in the diet, although some horses seem to need more than the established requirement. Consult your veterinarian for more information.
➤ *See also feeding and nutrition; trace minerals*

irons
English stirrups.
➤ *See also stirrups*

itching dermatitis
➤ *See mange*

ivermectin
A drug (under many brand names) that is effective against all internal parasites except tapeworms. Ivermectin does not poison the parasites like other preparations do, but rather it paralyzes them by reacting with the gamma-aminobutyric acid (GABA) in their nervous systems. Tapeworms do not have GABA in their nervous systems.

Warning: Ivermectin has been known to cause seizures, blindness, and death in dogs, especially herding breeds. Administer ivermectin with care, sequester all tubes and spillage securely, and prevent dogs from accessing the manure of horses freshly dewormed with ivermectin.

HORSES OF ITALY

Italy was famous in the 17th century as a center of fine horse breeding. Italian horse breeds include the **Maremmanno**, the **Murghese**, and the **Italian Heavy Draft**. The Maremmanno is a rustic riding horse resembling the Barb; it is not a fancy horse, but it is strong, healthy, and athletic—it is a superb jumper as well.

The Murghese is a hardy and elegant all-purpose horse, considered one of the baroque breeds. These are honest and hardworking horses, 15 to 16 hands high and of solid colors. Both have been used for military and police purposes, as well as farmwork and hauling.

The Italian Heavy Draft is a heavy horse, with short legs, a well-muscled body, and a thick, upright neck. Generally chestnut with a flaxen mane and tail, this horse is known for its rapid pace, even when pulling a considerable load. It is currently raised for meat production.

jaw, conformation of A horse's lower jaw should be well defined, with the space between the two sides wide enough to put your closed fist into, at the throatlatch. The cheek should not be too large, as that reduces the horse's ability to flex at the poll. There should be no mismatch in length of upper and lower jaw. If the upper jaw is long, giving the horse the appearance of a parrot (parrot mouthed), or too short (monkey- or sow-mouthed), he will have difficulty eating. Because the traits are inherited, it would be best not to breed these horses.

The jaws of horses worked in bits frequently hold a great deal of tension. Some simple massage techniques can relieve this.
➤ *See also parrot mouth; teeth and age; sow mouth/ monkey mouth*

jennet A midsize, easy-gaited horse originating in Spain; extremely popular as a riding horse in the Middle Ages. Jennets were among the first horses taken to the New World by Columbus, and they formed the basis for most South American easy-gaited breeds.
➤ *See also Spanish Jennet*

jenny A female donkey.

jibbah The characteristic bulge in the forehead of an Arabian horse.

jockey A professional rider of a horse in a race; or an older term for any rider or driver of a horse.

JOCKEY CLUB The Jockey Club, founded in 1894, registers names of Thoroughbreds produced in the United States. Its mission is improving the breed and performing services for portions of the equine industry that use Thoroughbred horses, especially racing. The Jockey Club publishes *The American Stud Book*, in which the ancestry of all registered Thoroughbreds born in the United States can be found. The organization also works closely with other countries that have significant racing and Thoroughbred industries, including Canada, Mexico, the Caribbean, and some nations in South America.

jodhpurs Pants used in English riding, particularly by children. They are designed to be used with short boots called jodhpur boots, unlike breeches, which are designed for use with tall boots.

Saddle seat–style jodhpurs are relatively loose fitting in the hips and thighs to allow freedom of movement to mount and ride. They are more form-fitting around the knee to prevent chafing, but flare out at the ankle to allow a smooth fit over the top of the traditional, short jodhpur boots. Saddle seat riders often use jodhpurs for both schooling and competition; the latter are made of much finer fabric that matches or complements the coat and vest worn for showing.
➤ *See also "English Show Attire," page 103; breeches*

jog The Western term for the two-beat, diagonal gait known as a trot in English disciplines. The jog is slower and softer than the English trot, because Western riders sit the jog rather than posting.
➤ *See also trot*

"join up" The desired phase of round-pen training in natural horsemanship (NH) when the horse comes to the trainer and willingly stands near and follows him. NH trainers see this as a sign of submission, and the horse's willingness to join the trainer's "herd."
➤ *See also natural horsemanship (NH)*

JOIN UP

joint capsule The sac of lubricating synovial fluid surrounding a joint.

joint ill/navel ill An acute disease that settles in joints of foals, damaging the joints or creating permanent lameness if not caught early. The organism involved, *streptococcus*, can rapidly destroy joint cartilage and bone. There are two causes: entry of bacteria into the navel soon after birth, before it dries; and septicemia, an infection of the blood transmitted from the dam's diseased uterus.

Prevention begins with health checks and treatment of uterine infections for the mare, maintaining a clean birthing area, and making sure the foal nurses soon enough to obtain antibodies that would help him fight the bacterial invasion. But the primary prevention strategy is to treat the umbilical stump with mild iodine as soon after birth as possible.

jousting A medieval sport based on the combat techniques of knights on warhorses. Jousting persists today in two forms. The Society for Creative Anachronism (SCA) re-creates medieval jousting as part of its games at modern festivals; two riders in armor

JOUSTING

and padding try to strike each other's shields with lances; in SCA competitions, the lances have breakaway foam tips. Professional exhibition jousting, performed at theme parks, tries for a higher level of authenticity; as a result, there have been injuries and fatalities.

The other form of jousting is a regional sport, played mostly in Virginia, Maryland, and southern Pennsylvania, where riders spear rings suspended from a frame. Riders can travel the 80-yard (73 m) track at any gait, and children compete on an equal footing with adults. The rings are at the same height for all riders—6 feet 9 inches (2 m) off the ground. Despite the apparent handicap, children on ponies are perfectly capable of defeating adults. This form of jousting is the state sport of Maryland.

judging Evaluating and scoring competitions. Judges assess competitors according to a set of rules; ideally, competitors who come closest to meeting the ideals set forth in the rule book win honors in the class. However, judging is always subjective, and the judge only has one set of eyes. If a horse misbehaves or a rider makes a mistake behind his back, that can't be reflected in the final score. Also, fashion and sometimes national pride come into play. Some judges are prejudiced against certain breeds; others may have a prior relationship with a competitor. That's why the highest levels of international competition are judged by a panel, not just a single judge.

The experience level of judges varies depending on the level of the competition, from unlicensed novices with little experience in center ring to highly honored individuals who hold licenses with numerous organizations and have decades of experience officiating competitions around the world. The licensing process is not uniform throughout the industry, so each licensing organization sets its own standards. Perhaps the most prestigious and respected is the licensing system within the United States Equestrian Federation (USEF). The USEF educates and licenses judges in more than 25 divisions.

Just as the judges in the U.S. court system must know the Constitution and case law, horse show judges must know the rules of the organization hosting the competition, as well as current trends. Trends should not dictate the judge's decision; however, it's important for judges to be aware of them. The integrity of individual sports, along with the well-being of horse and human competitors, is in large part dependent on the wisdom of judges.

JUDGING JUMPING

Hunters are judged on pace, style, and manners as they travel around a course of jumps; jumpers are judged on how clean the round is—that is, how few faults (such as knocking down poles or refusing a jump) are incurred—and whether they traverse the course within the allotted time.

jumper Jumping places extra stress on a horse, so the jumper needs strong, correct leg conformation, well-built hindquarters and hocks, and a strong back. The loin area must be well developed. A short back absorbs more concentrated concussion; a long back has a weaker loin area. Choose a strongly built horse with moderate length of back. A jumper will be relatively light in the front end, wider in the hindquarters than in the front. The shoulder should be well laid back, and the neck mobile, for agility and safety in jumping.

The angles of the front legs are crucial, as all the weight is put on one front leg when landing. Pasterns should be strong and sloping, cannons flat and broad when seen from the side, and the knee wide and flat in front. Feet should be of proper size for the weight of the horse. Size and height are less crucial than build. Most jump courses are designed for tall, long-striding horses, but small horses often compensate with agility and a can-do attitude.

Above all, a jumper needs willingness and heart. The rider needs heart as well, and the ability to sit correctly without jabbing the horse in the mouth over jumps. A jump rider must be able handle a horse at speed on the flat, around tricky turns. She should be strong and fit, so she can be as helpful to her horse over the last jump as she was over the first.

jumper classes Jumping classes that are judged on time and faults. The fastest clean round wins, regardless of style or aesthetics. Rider and horse must be brave, strong, fit, agile, intelligent, experienced, and aggressive.

Jumper courses may include more complex and challenging jumps than hunter courses, including diagonal jumps (verticals with one end higher than the other); uneven oxers (one end of the front element is high; the opposite end of the back element is high); fan jumps (obstacles with a spread between oxer poles that is

There are five phases of **jumping**—the approach, the take-off, the moment of suspension, the landing, and the getaway.

TYPES OF JUMPS

Here are a few of the many types of jumps that are used in training and competition.

A **cross-rail** is simply two poles crossed in the middle; a good fence for beginners.

The **vertical**, a single set of poles or panels, looks easiest for the rider, but it is tricky for the horse's depth perception. Variations include panels that look like gates; brush boxes (narrow containers stuffed with greenery to look like a fence with a hedge); and flower boxes.

The **oxer** is usually two verticals set close together, one behind the other, with the height closely matching the depth. It's the easiest jump for the horse to see and negotiate, and should not be intimidating for new riders.

Spreads have greater width than an oxer and are often made of three elements, with the height ascending from front to back. A spread may also be created by putting two elements that have a predetermined width between two uprights. They can be tricky, especially for new riders, because the horse has to jump both height and width.

A **hog back** is a type of spread with three elements: front, middle, and back. The center part is higher than the two on the outside, which are of equal height. So that the horse doesn't miss the rear element, the rider needs to rock the horse back so he jumps bigger.

A **roll top** is solid, curved jump, a few feet in width, is often topped with a pole to raise the height. Sometimes, the jump is bare wood, painted wood, or wooden slats; more often, it is covered with artificial grass and looks like a little hillock. It is usually intimidating to horses, and maybe to riders.

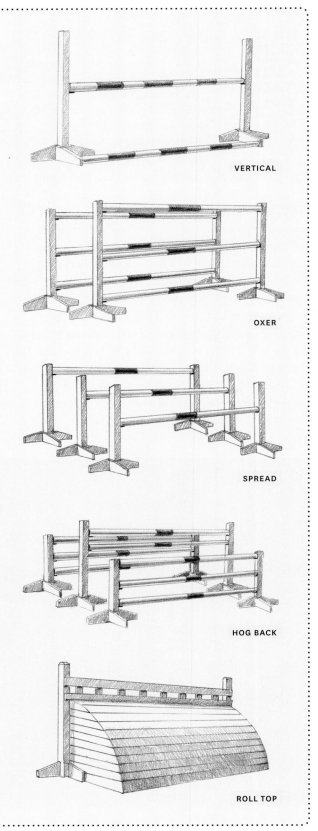

VERTICAL

OXER

SPREAD

HOG BACK

ROLL TOP

wide at one end and very narrow at the other); water jumps (verticals with a real or simulated pool of water up to 12 feet [3.6 m] across on the far side); and narrows (jumps with as little as 5 feet [1.5 m] between the uprights).

jumping

Most horses are able to jump small obstacles, and jumping can be helpful to loosening up and gymnasticizing a horse whose primary work is on the flat. It is a useful skill for any horse/rider team who do any amount of riding on trails.

Riders who want to jump need to cultivate some important skills first; a secure seat, steady hands, and an ability to control a horse at all three gaits. Once those are in place, riders learn the jumping position, a two-point seat with shortened stirrups. This can be practiced on the flat at all gaits. The mane or a neck strap can be used to steady the rider until she develops a firm position and can avoid interfering with the horse's mouth.

Jumping sports include stadium jumping, cross-country jumping, hunting, and steeplechase. Many trail and versatility classes require a small jump. It is possible to take small jumps in a Western saddle, though the horn makes it difficult to fold down over the horse's withers.

jumping grid

A straight line of carefully spaced fences, also called a "gymnastic." Jumping grids, which horses find easy, help build confidence, strength, and

HOW HIGH, HOW FAR?

The record for a high jump has been held for over 50 years by Chilean Thoroughbred Huaso, ridden by Captain Alberto Larraguibel Morales. In an official Fédération Equestre Internationale (FEI) competition, the pair cleared 8' 1¼" (2.47 m) on their third attempt.

The longest official jump, 27' 6¾" (8.4 m), was made by Something and André Ferreira at the 1975 Rand Show in Johannesburg.

flexibility. A grid must be measured accurately and the fences spaced right for them to be effective and helpful.

junior horse

1. In showing, a horse who is four or five years old or younger, depending on the breed's definition.

2. A suitable horse (of any age) for a junior rider: one that is sensible; calm; well trained for the discipline; and kind (that is, will not take advantage of an inexperienced rider).

junior rider

A rider who is 18 years old (or 17 years old by some rules) or younger.

JUTLAND

A breed of heavy horse developed in Denmark, descended from medieval warhorses. Jutlands are 15 to 16 hands high, mostly chestnut with flaxen manes and tails and feathered legs, and strongly resemble the Suffolk Punch, from which they are descended. They are the national draft horse of Denmark, and are used as beer horses by the Carlsberg Brewery in Copenhagen.

KABARDIN
(Kalmyk/Karabair/Karabakh/Karachai)

A group of ancient saddle horse breeds from Central Asia, the epicenter of world horse culture. All are small (14.1–15.1 hands high), cleanly built, adapted to harsh natural conditions, and very tough. Most are excellent mountain horses, with light, pleasant gaits. The Kalmyk and Karabakh are rare. Kabardin horses make excellent jumpers, and the Karabair is a good all-purpose horse for saddle or harness. Most are bay, dark bay, or black, but the Karabakh, more closely related to the Akhal-Teke, displays the golden sheen and lighter colors of that breed.

Kentucky wire Another name for diamond-mesh fencing material. Common in Kentucky on big Thoroughbred breeding farms, hence the name.

Kevlar The material used in bulletproof vests; it is also used in high-quality shipping boots. It will withstand bumps and knocks from a horse's hooves without the need for additional padding.
➤ *See also leg wrap; shipping boots/wraps*

keyhole race Both an exercise for your horse and a mounted game at many Western shows. A keyhole race requires horse and rider to begin at a starting line, enter a narrow lane marked with lime (ground limestone), turn around in a circle (also marked with lime) at the end of the lane, and head back to the starting line. If he puts a foot outside the boundaries, the horse is disqualified.
➤ *See also mounted games*

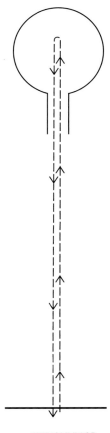

KEYHOLE RACE

KERRY BOG PONY

A rare breed of tiny pony (10–11 hands high) native to the peat bogs of southwest Ireland. Known since the 17th century, Kerry Bog Ponies have been used as pack ponies, as they are docile and extremely strong. Kerry Bog Ponies are lighter per hand of weight than most other breeds, and have a distinctive gait suitable to the soft going of a bog. They do not "track up," meaning that the hind feet don't step into the prints left by the front feet, but come just to the outside. Each foot strikes a new location, making the shallowest hole possible in marshy ground. Kerry Bog Ponies are elegant, and make fine driving ponies.

kicking When a horse strikes backward or sideways with a hind foot. Kicking is one of the horse's only natural defenses; it is an inborn survival instinct. Horses may kick reactively when startled; therefore, always speak before approaching a horse from the rear. Kicking may also occur in response to discomfort, such as girth tightening or medical treatment. Horses may kick other horses who approach too closely.

To avoid being kicked while handling a horse, approach his head first, and work back toward the hindquarters. Always work close to the horse, especially around his hindquarters. A kick will be a push or a bump if you are close; if you are a little distance away, you'll receive the full force of the blow. Watch his ears and tail, not his feet, for signs of mood. Stand on the opposite side from the leg you are working on, if possible, while applying medication or fly spray.

Be aware that dominant horses can control submissive ones by merely cocking a hind foot and threatening to kick. Some dominant horses may experiment with humans. You need to make it quite clear that you are not intimidated and will not tolerate this behavior.

Kicking is extremely dangerous. Horses can be trained not to kick while being handled or ridden. Those who continue to kick need careful handling, and their owners should think twice about taking them anywhere in public. At a show, a red ribbon tied to the tail of a horse is a sign to stay back; the horse has been known to kick another horse that gets too close.

kick wall A stall wall constructed to withstand a horse's kick. A kick is powerful enough to go through many common building materials. However it is constructed, ¾-inch (2 cm) rubber mats are excellent for lining stall walls. Besides cushioning the blow to the wall, they cushion and protect the horse's legs and feet as well.

Systems are available that will squirt a horse with water if he kicks the stall wall, in order to train him out of this behavior.

kidney colic Abdominal distress caused by kidney stones.

Kimberwicke bit/Kimblewick bit A bit designed to provide more control than a snaffle through the application of leverage; also known as the Spanish jumping bit. The Kimberwicke can have either a solid

KIKKULI THE MITTANIAN

Kikkuli was a chariot master in the Hittite empire, around 1360 BCE; he wrote the oldest surviving horse-training manual.

Transmitted on five clay tablets, it called for exercise at the pace and gallop, a rigorously controlled diet (horses were kept muzzled overnight so they wouldn't chew their mangers), and frequent swimming and washing. The horses were sometimes anointed all over with butter.

They were trained in pairs, both when hitched to the chariot and when driven from the ground. If one was killed, the other would only accept a new teammate after long retraining.

mouthpiece or a jointed one, but has two slots for rein placement as well as hooks for a curb chain. Placement of the rein in the upper slot causes the bit to work like a snaffle, with direct pressure only on the bars and tongue. Placement of the rein in the lower slot creates leverage that tightens the curb chain and adds pressure to the chin groove and poll.

Horses worked in Kimberwickes often develop the bad habit of working behind the bit since there is no true release of pressure when using the leverage slot.
➤ *See also double bridle; Pelham bit*

kinesthetic reception This is a cousin to kinesthetic intelligence, the capacity to use your whole body to express ideas and feelings (as actors, athletes, dancers, and mimes do), including the facility to use your hands

KIMBERWICKE BIT

to create or transform things (as painters, mechanics, and surgeons do). These same abilities help some people learn to ride. An instructor will notice that a student who learns through kinesthetic reception will be coordinated; will have good balance, dexterity, flexibility, muscle strength, and speed; and will have a sensitive touch.

kissing spine/dorsal spinous process impingement
A condition in which adjacent processes of the spine touch or even overlap. It can be asymptomatic, or can cause enough pain to make the horse unrideable. Kissing spine is diagnosed through x-ray, ultrasound, or thermographic imagery. Treatment consists of steroid injections, medications to decrease bone inflammation, and exercises which build core strength and encourage the back to lift, including lunging with side reins and belly lifts.

knee
The joint on the forelegs composed of carpal bones. The knee on a horse is comparable to the human wrist.

knee relief stirrups
Stirrups used to relieve rider knee pain. These include English stirrups that flex, and Western or trail stirrups that are angled, or have a thick sponge rubber foot cushion. There is also a foam shock absorber that can be fitted onto Western stirrups that relieves pressure on the rider's joints, and possibly also the horse's back. Another solution is to use a stirrup hanger placed between the Western stirrup and saddle fender, keeping the stirrup set at right angles.

knee roll
The padded front section of an English saddle, meant to cushion the rider's knee. Knee rolls may be concealed, on the underflap of the saddle, or external.

knock-kneed
Conformation fault in which the knees are closer to each other than are the upper and lower parts of the leg. This fault puts strain on tendons in the leg and on the knee itself; it often causes mobility problems. Knock-kneed horses should not be bred.
➤ *See also back at the knee; bench knees; over at the knee/buck-kneed; tied-in knees*

knots
➤ *See quick-release knot; tying*

KNABSTRUPPER

A breed of spotted horse developed in Denmark. Because of their showy markings, toughness, intelligence, and gentleness, Knabstruppers are often featured in circus performances. They are white with dark spots all over the body, sparse mane and tail, and mottled lips and muzzle.

The Knabstrupper is a riding breed that ranges in size from pony to full-sized horse. The breed has also been promoted for carriage driving. An ancient horse, the Knabstrupper traces back to Viking times, but much cross-breeding has resulted in a wide range of types, with the original type becoming nearly extinct. The spotted coloration originated in Asia and became common throughout Europe. Spotted horses were among the first that were taken to the Americas.

lactic acid A water-soluble liquid produced in muscles as a result of anaerobic glucose metabolism. Lactic acid is absorbed and used as fuel by mitochondria, with increasing efficiency in a conditioned body. In an out-of-condition body that cannot absorb it, lactic acid pools in the tissue, causing inflammation and muscle fatigue. This can also happen with insufficient warm-ups and cool-downs.

lameness Impeded locomotion due to pain. The pain may be caused by injury (a kick, for example) or infection (such as an abscess in the foot). It may also be caused by muscle soreness, or by a pulled tendon or strained ligament in the leg or even above the leg in the large muscles of the chest and hindquarters. Lameness can be caused by a bruise to the sole of the foot or by a stone caught against the sole; in the latter case, removing the stone before it can do further damage may resolve the lameness. A few of the many other causes might be arthritis, navicular disease, or inflammation of the coffin bone after a long ride over rocky ground.

To diagnose lameness, watch the horse as he walks or trots. If he has pain in a front leg, he will bob his head more than normal as he lifts his weight *off* the painful foot and places more weight on the good one. A painful hind foot or leg will create an uneven stride as he favors the problem side. This is often referred to as a hitch in the gait, a sort of stutter in motion before a leg is put on the ground.

A lame horse cannot be ridden. If you are riding a horse who suddenly exhibits signs of lameness, immediately dismount. Examine each foot for a stone, stick, or other foreign object. If you spot a nail in the foot, wait for a veterinarian or farrier to remove it so that he or she can know exactly where the puncture wound is.

A veterinarian should treat a horse who is chronically lame. Medication or special shoes, such as egg bar shoes, which are designed to take the weight off the heel, may be recommended.

Regular care from a farrier will keep your horse's feet and hooves in top condition. To minimize chances of a puncture wound, avoid riding in areas where your horse might be exposed to loose nails or sharp objects. If you observe signs of lameness without being able to discover the cause, call your veterinarian.

➤ *See also egg bar shoe; farrier; hoof; horseshoes; navicular disease*

To diagnose **lameness** and determine which leg a horse is lame on, a vet will ask to have him trotted out in hand on a hard surface, both going away and coming toward her.

laminitis An inflammation of the sensitive inner tissues of the hoof wall. The precondition of founder, laminitis is a serious and potentially fatal condition. Causes include overeating or a sudden feed change; retained placenta; high fever; severe lameness in the opposite limb; obesity; work on a hard surface; too much water after overheating; overuse of steroids; hypothyroidism; Cushing's disease; and equine metabolic syndrome (EMS).

Laminitis begins with interference to the flow of blood to the feet. This results in a lack of oxygen and swelling of the laminae, the soft and sensitive vascular plates lining the inside of the hoof wall. The feet will be hot and sore; the front feet are more likely to be affected than the hind feet. The horse may rock back on his hindquarters to relieve the pressure. If all four feet are affected, lying down may be the only way for him to relieve the pain. Fever, sweating and/or shivering, rapid pulse and breathing, and diarrhea are other symptoms.

Without treatment, the coffin bone of the foot will rotate or sink downward, which means the horse has foundered. "Founder" is the term for the structural change that occurs in the foot as a result of laminitis.

This stage is also known as chronic laminitis. Many horse people, however, use the terms "founder" and "laminitis" interchangeably.

Call your veterinarian immediately if you suspect laminitis. The sooner treatment begins, the better the prognosis.

➤ *See also carbohydrates; cooling down, after exercise; Cushing's disease/Cushing's syndrome/PPID; equine metabolic syndrome (EMS); founder; hoof*

lampas
A swelling of the hard palate just behind the horse's top front teeth. This condition may occur in a young horse who has bruised the roof of his mouth after eating hard grain or pellets for the first time. Because it is painful, it may cause the horse to stop eating temporarily. The best solution is to allow the horse to eat pasture grass or to soak the grain in water to soften it until the condition is resolved.

large strongyles
Bloodsucking parasites— bloodworms—that lodge in blood vessels and cause anemia and debility. There are some 54 varieties of strongyles (worms), both large and small, that affect horses. Three of the large strongyle species do the most damage, causing loss of appetite, anemia, emaciation, rough hair coat, sunken eyes, digestive disturbances, and a "tucked up" appearance. Often, the horse will exhibit an uncoordinated hind end. This level of damage happens with severe infestations; major infestations are most likely in horses grazed on permanent pasture where harrowing does not break up the manure piles and expose the light-sensitive eggs, interrupting the parasite's breeding cycle.

➤ *See also deworming; parasites*

lariat/lasso
A long leather or hemp rope used with a noose to catch cattle and horses from horseback or on foot; also called a reata (or riata).

latches and locks
Horseproof latches are a crucial element of a safe stable or a reliable fencing system. There are many styles of horseproof latches, some more reliable than others. Many will fail when challenged by a bored or curious horse. If you have any doubts about the security of a gate latch, add a safety chain, secured with a snap on the outside of the gate, beyond reach of a mouthy horse. In some states it is illegal to apply a lock to a horse's stall because, in the event of fire, a person needs to be able to open the stall door and let or lead the horses out.

The most popular type of stable door latch is a sliding bolt. Horses can figure these out; if you have an escape artist, try a hook with a flange that you must compress before lifting it out of the eye. The best latch on your farm should be the one on your grain bin and/or grain room door.

latent learning
Learning that has been assimilated but not yet demonstrated. Often horses given a few days or weeks off appear to have processed and absorbed lessons they did not previously seem to have mastered. Latent learning is commonly observed in horses but not well understood. It is likely a function of the horse's excellent memory and kinesthetic senses.

lateral gaits
Gaits in which front and back legs on the same side are picked up and set down in tandem. Examples include the pace, amble, stepping pace, rack, tölt, and corto.

➤ *See also gaited horse*

The true rack is a lateral gait.

HORSE CANTERING ON THE LEFT **LEAD**

lateral work Work in which the horse travels sideways, usually also moving forward. Only in the Western half-pass does the horse move sideways without forward movement. Lateral movements increase strength and flexibility.

➤ *See also half-pass; leg-yield; shoulder-in; sidepass/ side step; travers*

latigo A long leather strap attached to the cinch ring on the near (left) side of a Western saddle, used to connect and adjust the cinch. The latigo should be checked frequently for signs of wear and cleaned regularly with a wax-based leather conditioner.

➤ *See also saddle; Western tack*

lead (canter) The pair of legs on one side of the horse that strike the ground farther ahead of the legs on the other side in the canter; the leading foreleg is the *last* to strike during the canter stride. Horses naturally lead with the inside leg, which helps them stay balanced as they canter in a circle or around a corner. Leading with the inside foreleg is called cantering on the correct lead.

A horse can also pick up the incorrect lead, even when cantering in a circle. He might do this because he has a favorite lead (most horses do) or because he is stiff or sore on one side.

It is possible for a horse to be on one lead in front and another behind. This movement, called a cross-canter or disunited canter, results in a rough, jolting gait.

➤ *See also canter; counter-canter/counter-lope; cross-canter/disunited canter; gait; flying lead change; simple lead change*

CHECKING FOR THE CORRECT LEAD

When your horse is on the correct lead, his inside shoulder will be slightly farther forward than his outside shoulder, following the bend of his neck.

In a four-horse team, the two horses in front are called the leaders. The one on the left is the **near** leader, and the one on the right is the **off** leader.

leading

➤ *See handling horses*

leading rein

➤ *See direct rein; indirect rein*

lead-line class
Class in which a parent, instructor, or older friend leads a pony or horse while the young rider follows the judge's directions. Many youngsters enter their first shows in lead-line classes.

lead rope
A length of cotton or nylon rope meant to be attached to a halter and used to lead or tie a horse. A lead rope to be used with a leather or nylon web halter will have a snap at one end that attaches to the metal loop on the bottom of the halter's noseband. A lead rope to be used with a rope halter may be tied to the halter via a loop rather than attached with a snap.

➤ *See also bull snap; halter; panic snap*

LEAD-LINE CLASS

lead shank
A length of nylon or leather with a chain at one end that, in conjunction with a halter, can be adjusted over, under, or around the nose for greater control. The chain is commonly used when handling stallions or other fractious horses.

➤ *See also bull snap; halter; panic snap*

learning, by horses
Horses are superb learners; it has meant their survival in partnership with human beings. That said, they are better at being horses than at being anything else, which means they learn best things that are relevant to them. And they do have their own learning style.

For instance, horses are extremely adept at making associations. They rapidly learn that a rustling in the bushes may mean a predator could jump out, or that the brief flattening of a pasture mate's ears means they'd better get out of the way. Horses are also able to overcome some of their associative reactions through habituation, that is, repeated exposure to stimuli until they no longer react.

It is easier to teach horses to move forward than backward—they live by forward movement, and can't see directly behind themselves.

Horses learn equally well whether the stimuli are visual, auditory, or tactile, and they notice more than we do, which can lead to inadvertent cuing but also to the ability to introduce new, more subtle cues.

TRAINING SESSIONS Horses learn much better in short sessions than in longer ones. When training new behaviors, a session may be very short. One prominent trainer theorizes that new behaviors are most readily learned in three-minute sessions; this may be especially true of horses who have "learned how to learn." Clicker-trained horses who have learned to expect good things out of trying something new can often pick up a new trick with uncanny speed.

Ending the session on a successful note is an old concept in training. At the Spanish Riding School, when a stallion masters a difficult maneuver or concept, the rider often dismounts, feeds him a treat, and strips off the saddle. No further work happens that day, which helps the horse understand exactly what he did right.

Horses have excellent memories. While it takes a certain degree of repetition to confirm a lesson, drilling is rarely needed or appreciated. When the horse succeeds at a new task, don't repeat it. Quit for the day or go on to something easier. Repeat the lesson often over the course of several days, but don't drill it. If the horse understands what he did right, he will remember. If he doesn't understand, your job is to get him there.

REINFORCEMENT Horses have learned through negative reinforcement for 6,000 years. They are good at it, and can be trained to a high level with sophisticated negative reinforcement training. They are also good at learning through positive reinforcement. Some natural horsemanship trainers theorize that because the horse eats grass, which he does not have to out-wit, food rewards have no salience or teaching power. Many clicker trainers theorize the opposite: that treats have great power; it is imperative, however, to deliver them properly, at the right time, for the right reasons, in the right way, or you risk teaching lessons you never intended.

As a precocial species, horses learn easily as foals. They are genetically programmed to observe their mothers and explore their surroundings. What they can learn as foals is limited by their physical fragility, not their intelligence. As much of what they need to learn is physical, trainers need to wait for bone plates to close before they tax the young horse with demanding work like longeing. But the young horse can and should learn stable manners, and can be introduced to new stimuli.

Old horses, too, can learn new behaviors, and old-timers past the age of real work may enjoy learning tricks. The stimulation of learning can wake up an aged horse's mind.

➤ *See also clicker training; latent learning*

leasing versus buying
When riders decide they need a horse of their own, they often think immediately of buying a horse. However, beginning riders might want to consider leasing a horse instead. Buying and leasing each have pros and cons; the rider must ultimately decide which is right for her, given her particular circumstances.

THE PROS OF BUYING
- You don't have to worry about reporting to the horse's owner and riding it in the ways specified in a lease contract.

- You have an asset, if you decide you want a different sort of horse and decide to sell.

- You can bond with the animal to your heart's content.

THE CONS OF BUYING
- It is your responsibility to care for the animal for the rest of its life or sell it to a responsible owner.

- After the purchase price, you have to deal with feed costs or boarding fees, veterinary fees, and tack and equipment fees.

- You may discover that you and the horse are not suited to each other.

- If you have to sell for one reason or another, you could take a financial and/or emotional loss.

- Your horse may develop a physical problem that keeps him from being ridden or resold. You have to continue to care for him regardless.

THE PROS OF LEASING
- You can get the horse you need or want without the initial purchase expense.

- Often, the owner will include tack and pay for ordinary veterinary care, such as shots.

- In some cases, the owner will share the board fees.

- By making renewable short-term lease agreements, you can move on easily to a different horse.

- You do not have the responsibility of housing and caring for an aging horse.

THE CONS OF LEASING
- The owner may impose restrictions on your use of the horse.

- The owner may decide to withdraw the horse from leasing just when you are getting the most out of the arrangement.

- Your bonding with the horse may be limited.

- The pride of leasing is not the same as the pride of ownership.

- You may, depending on the lease, have to pay some veterinary bills you didn't expect for a horse you don't even own.

LEG MARKINGS

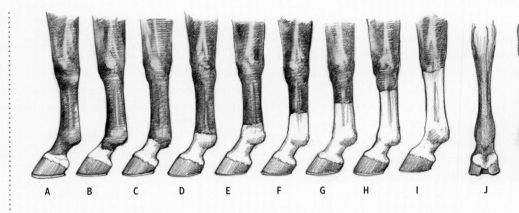

A. coronet; B. half-pastern; C. pastern; D. high pastern; E. ankle or sock; F. sock; G. half-stocking; H. three-quarter stocking; I. stocking; J. heel; K. half-heel

leg, of horse

➤ *See back at the knee; bench knees; conformation; over at the knee; spavin; speed, of horse; splint; tied-in*

legging up The practice of walking a horse on a hard surface, in hand or under saddle, for 20 or more minutes twice a week. This avoids the concussion of trotting, and is believed to tighten the lower leg tendons and strengthen the legs. Find a level stretch of pavement or packed gravel, and walk briskly, with the horse in a relaxed frame. Legging up may be done in the afternoon following a morning workout; space legging-up sessions at least two days apart.

legs, use of when riding A well-educated rider uses her legs and seat more often than her hands in directing the horse. The legs are used to drive the horse forward, elevate him, elongate his frame or stride, move him laterally, or bend him.

Legs may be used just in front of the girth, to influence the forehand; at the girth, to request more energy; or behind the girth, to influence the hindquarters. Otherwise the legs remain in continuous light contact with the horse's sides. On a well-trained horse, a leg aid is often just a brief tensing of the calf muscle or a squeeze. If a more emphatic leg aid is needed the rider may tap with her calf. If you find yourself needing to kick a horse, that's a sign that one or both of you need more training. The horse may not understand what you want,

PROPER LEG POSITION FOR BASIC SEAT

- The weight should be down in the heel.
- The inside of the calf should lie against the horse's side.
- The lower leg should stay close to the girth, except when turning or controlling the horse's hindquarters.
- The knee and toe can be turned slightly outward.
- A line drawn down from the rider's ear should pass through the hip and heel; if the horse were whisked out from under her, the rider would land balanced on her feet.

or you may be contradicting your leg aid with a rein aid. People don't understand foreign languages any better if the speaker shouts at them, and horses don't understand unfamiliar or misapplied aids any better if they are harsh.

Leg position begins at the hip and is influenced by the way the rider sits in the saddle. Sitting correctly on your seat bones will allow you to drop your leg down and back into the proper ear-hip-heel alignment.

legume hay

➤ See hay

leg up, to give

Helping a rider mount. The helper stands just ahead of the saddle and makes a stirrup with her cupped hands. The rider places her left knee in the helper's hands, and on an agreed signal the rider jumps up off her right foot, while the helper raises the left leg straight upward. When the rider is high enough, she swings her right leg over the horse's back and settles into the saddle.

GIVING A LEG UP

A variation is for the rider to bend her left leg at the knee. The helper crouches, places her right forearm under the rider's left shin, and wraps her right hand around the rider's leg just above the knee. At the agreed-on signal, the rider jumps and the helper lifts. This position allows the helper to keep her left hand free to either stabilize the rider's leg or control the horse if needed.

Getting a leg up puts the less stress on the horse's back than mounting from a two-step block or from the ground.

leg wrap

A bandage used to protect a horse's legs. One type of leg wrap is the shipping wrap, which protects the legs during travel, including when getting into or out of a trailer. Shipping wraps consist of fleece, quilted cotton, or spongy towel-shaped cloths that are the length of the horse's lower leg. They are usually held on by 9-foot (2.7 m) lengths of stretchy fabric 4 to 5 inches (10–13 cm) wide, which often come with hook-and-loop fasteners.

The same kind of wrap may be used for soreness (with or without a bracer) or to hold medication on injuries. Specialized fabrics in some bandage liners improve circulation or deliver support and compression. Cotton wraps can be used as cold bandages by soaking in cold water.

Another type is the polo wrap. These soft, somewhat stretchy lengths of fabric are 4 inches (10 cm) wide. Polo wraps lend support and protection to a horse's lower leg while he is being trained or worked; they act much as elasticized athletic bandages do for humans. Some polo wraps are made of specialized fabrics that transfer heat out to keep the horse's legs cool.

leg-yield

An introductory lateral movement in which the horse steps forward and sideways, with his body either straight or bent slightly *away* from the direction of travel. Leg-yield is commonly performed at the walk and trot.

➤ See also half-pass

leptospirosis

A bacterial disease of mammals that can cause illness and abortions. Leptospirosis is often spread by a carrier, an animal that recovers from the disease but harbors and then sheds bacteria in urine, saliva, and other secretions and excretions. Common carriers of the bacteria are rats, mice, and other rodents, as well as pigs, cattle, and dogs. Horses may be exposed through rats that live in barns and contaminate feed and water.

In horses, leptospirosis is usually not a serious disease. It may cause fever, loss of appetite, dullness, and jaundice. However, pregnant mares may abort their fetuses, and there may be problems with the kidneys, joints, and eyes in some horses. Leptospirosis has been studied as a cause of equine recurrent uveitis (moon blindness), but the connection is still not understood.

➤ See also equine recurrent uveitis (ERU)

lesson barn A barn that keeps school horses, which are used to teach riders of all levels. These barns may also have boarders at various levels, and both lesson students and horse owners may show their horses. Some lesson barns host shows; others do not. Finding the proper lesson barn for your riding goals will help you meet them safely and pleasurably.

If you want to ride well and compete in shows, either rated or local, be sure the barn will offer that opportunity when you are ready. If you want only to learn to ride and enjoy classes and trail rides, be sure the barn is willing to provide that level of teaching; some barns are "show barns" and are not interested in students who don't care to compete.

lessons, riding and driving Riding sessions guided by an instructor or trainer. Lessons may be private, semiprivate, or group. They may last a half hour (typically private) or an hour (private, semiprivate, and group). At some barns, students must arrive at least a half hour before a lesson to tack up their horses; they usually must remain at least that long afterward to cool down and groom the horse and put away tack. Adults, and even some busy junior riders, who cannot commit to a lesson each week at the same time are usually best served by scheduling private lessons individually, as time permits—but this approach is generally more expensive per lesson. Missing too many group lessons (a different number at each barn, depending on how their program is set up) usually results in forfeiting them. In any case, it will certainly mean that the student lags behind others in the class.

If you are taking group lessons and miss one once in a while, taking a private lesson can help you catch up. If you want to progress faster than the class and can leapfrog into a more advanced class, you may decide that a few private lessons will aid you. Many students also take a private lesson or two before a show so that they can get individual, targeted help with the skills and procedures they will need at the show, in addition to what has been taught in class.

Dressage and reining lessons are almost always private. Basics are learned on school horses, but the student then moves on to her own or a leased horse; the aim of both disciplines is to demonstrate the capability, suppleness, athleticism, and obedience of a horse as the rider works to improve him. Some instructors teach very effective lessons by using semiretired "school masters." A student with her own horse will usually have lessons on that horse.

Driving lessons may be group or private. The advantage with private driving lessons is that the instructor can ride along with you in the cart, observing you closely and seeing what you see; she can then step back and watch the results from the ground.

lethal genes Genes that, when received from both parents, cause death before or soon after the foal's birth.
➤ *See also genetic disorders; genetics*

levade One of the airs above the ground performed by Lipizzans of the Spanish Riding School and other high-level classically trained breeds. The levade is a test of strength and balance. Rising on his hind legs, the horse crouches at and maintains a 45-degree angle. The strongest stallions can hold this position for only 10 or 15 seconds.
➤ *See also airs above the ground; Lipizzan*

AT LIBERTY

Liberty horses perform without tack and most of the time without a rider, responding to voice aids, body language, or gestures from a whip. Liberty training used to belong almost exclusively in circuses and exhibitions; now a rising number of ordinary horsemen are training their horses at liberty, using the round-pen techniques of natural horsemanship, clicker training, or other methods. Liberty training appeals to many people who love horses and want to be around them but who have no interest in riding.

Liberty training requires excellent knowledge of horse body language, and must be done with a strong regard for personal safety. Wear a helmet. Consider carrying a whip; if the session deteriorates into play or aggression, this may save you from injury. Proceed carefully, according to a well-thought-out plan, and don't hesitate to end a session if it takes an unexpected turn. Humans are smaller and slower than horses, and have comparatively sluggish reaction times. The two species can certainly play well together, but it is incumbent on the human to keep the play safe.

It looks simple, but the **levade**, performed here by an Andalusian stallion, requires great strength and precise balance.

lice Two kinds of lice infest horses, but they cannot be transferred to humans; lice are species-specific. *Sucking lice* feed on blood; a severe infestation can cause anemia. *Biting lice* are more active, causing skin irritation and itching. Lice are found primarily under the mane or on the buttocks, rump, and tail. With close observation, you can see the lice or the eggs if you pull out a few tufts of hair where the lice have been feeding (the hair comes out easily in these spots). Lice are most problematic in winter, when the hair is long.

Affected horses are treated with insecticidal sprays and powders. Usually two treatments are necessary, because ready-to-hatch eggs won't be affected the first time. Treat brushes, blankets, saddle pads, and other equipment used on the affected horse as well, or you may reinfect him or infect other horses.

ligaments Ligaments attach bones to bones, unlike tendons, which attach muscles to bones. Ligaments help horses lock their legs to stand for long periods with little fatigue, even sleeping on their feet. They also help the horse absorb the shock of the concussion of hooves against the ground.

Injuries to ligaments are called sprains.

light horse Another term for a riding or driving horse, as opposed to a draft horse. The conformation of a light horse's back allows the saddle to fit easily and securely, and his way of going tends to be comfortable to ride or drive. Light horses include the following:

- Sport horses, such as the Selle Français, Irish Sport Horse, and Akhal-Teke

- Stock horses, such as the Quarter Horse and Appaloosa

- Hunters, such as the Irish Hunter, Thoroughbred, and Connemara

- Pleasure horses, such as the Arabian and Morgan

- Animated horses, such as the Tennessee Walker, Saddlebred, and Missouri Fox Trotter

➤ *See also conformation; way of going; individual breeds*

lightning Lightning is a danger to horses, both in the barn and out. Field-boarded horses often seek shelter among trees, unless you have a lean-to or run-in shed for them. You should install lightning rods on any outside structure; horses standing in run-in sheds without rods have been killed when the sheds were struck.

To minimize lightning risk outside the barn or run-in shed, make sure your pasture has a sheltered area where a horse can find refuge during a storm. Horses may leave exposed hilltops and seek out low ground. If your horse has a favorite spot (under a tree or by a building), check to see if puddles accumulate there after a rainfall. Such puddles can conduct electricity. You can fill this area with gravel to reduce the chance of a lightning strike.

light seat A seat that is halfway between a balanced seat (in which most of the rider's weight is on the seat bones), and a two-point seat (in which the rider's entire seat is off the saddle, with only two points—the inner thighs—in contact with the saddle). In a light seat the inner thighs support more of the rider's weight than in a full seat; in fact, the rider's seat appears to be just touching the saddle. A light seat allows the rider to change from a driving seat in full contact to a two-point seat easily while jumping a course of fences, and it allows the horse to move forward naturally as well.
➤ *See also balanced seat/deep seat; forward seat; half-seat; seat; two-point seat*

lime, use of Granulated or pelleted limestone, also called lime, is available at feed stores and farm supply stores to deodorize and help dry stalls. It is sprinkled on the floor before the stall is completely rebedded. Lime can be sprinkled on wet spots during daily cleaning as long as the horse will then be turned out, and the stall windows and doors can be left open. New bedding must be installed over the lime before the horse is readmitted to the stall. Avoid powdered lime, as it may cause respiratory problems in horses.

limit class A show class in which the horses entered may not have won more than a certain number or ribbons or cash prizes in previous competitions at the same level.
➤ *See also ribbons*

line-breeding

➤ *See genetics*

lines

Thirty-foot reins used for long lining. The term is used by some to describe driving reins.

➤ *See also harness; reins*

lineup, in a show

When a judge has finished assessing the horses in a group class, riders or drivers will be asked to line up with their numbers (on their backs) facing the judge before the winners are announced. Horses may also be asked to line up for close physical inspection, and may be asked to back while in a lineup.

lipoma

A usually benign tumor that consists of slow-growing balls of fat on thin stalks. Lipomas occur in the abdomen of older horses, especially fat ones. Unless a stalk winds around the intestine, which will cause colic and a fatal blockage if not surgically corrected, lipomas usually do not cause problems—even if an older horse has a number of them.

lipstick foam

The light foam of saliva on a horse's lips produced by gentle mouthing of the bit. Dressage riders believe that the foam shows acceptance of the bit; interestingly, lipstick foam is also produced by some horses doing dressage in a bitless bridle. The mouth movements may be related to a relaxed poll and jaw rather than the bit alone.

live-foal guarantee

Part of a breeding contract that specifies the mare must produce a live foal (commonly defined as a foal that stands and nurses) after breeding to the stallion involved.

liver chestnut

A dark red (chestnut), with the horse's mane and tail being the same color as the body.

➤ *See also chestnut coloring; color, of horse; "Red Horses," page 292*

A LIVER CHESTNUT

LIPIZZAN

A compact and powerfully built horse, the Lipizzan (or Lipizzaner) is one of the great athletes of the equine world. Originally bred in the 1500s as light warhorses, for more than 400 years Lipizzans have been synonymous with the art of classical equitation as practiced at the Spanish Riding School in Vienna, Austria.

During World War II, the Spanish Riding School was nearly destroyed by the Nazis, who removed the breeding stock from Austria. The Allied army led by General George Patton rescued the mares and foals and returned them to the breeding farm at Piber, in the mountains of southern Austria. The stallions toured the world giving performances before returning to the Spanish Riding School.

Lipizzans mature slowly and are not broken to saddle until they are five years old. They are born with dark coats that lighten as they age to become almost pure white by the time the horse is 10. Although an occasional bay adult is produced, this has become increasingly rare. Lipizzans have strong, arched necks; short, powerful legs; and sturdy barrels. Their large, dark eyes and small ears add to their appeal.

Only stallions are ridden, and it takes many years of careful and incremental training to perfect the technique of both riders and horses. As in all high-level dressage work, the rider makes no visible movements while guiding the horse through a highly controlled routine and the breathtaking leaps known as airs above the ground.

This iconic breed has a fairly small population worldwide, around 3,000; there are about 600 in North America. Because of the Lipizzan's location in a part of Europe fought over in many wars, the breed's international distribution has been essential to its survival. **Livestock Conservancy rating: Threatened**

➤ *See also airs above the ground; ballotade; capriole; courbette; croupade; levade; Spanish Riding School*

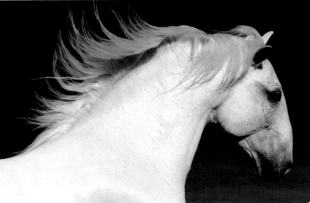

Liverpool bit The most popular style of driving bit. The Liverpool is available with a variety of mouthpieces, and with fixed or swivel cheeks. It uses a curb chain and has a variety of rein settings, making it adaptable from horse to horse, or for different levels of a horse's training.

Livestock Conservancy, The A nonprofit organization dedicating to preserving and promoting rare breeds of American livestock, including horses and donkeys. Formerly called the American Livestock Breed Conservancy (ALBC).

To be listed with The Livestock Conservancy, animals must be a true genetic breed, bred in the United States since 1925. If developed or imported more recently, the foundation stock must be endangered globally, there must be at least three breeding lines in the United States, and there must be at least five breeders in different locations.

➤ *See also "Rare Horse Breeds," below*

lockjaw
➤ *See tetanus*

locks
➤ *See latches and locks*

RARE HORSE BREEDS

In 2016, The Livestock Conservancy listed the following horse breeds as rare or endangered in the United States.

CRITICAL

(fewer than 200 annual U.S. registrations; global population under 2,000)

American Cream   Hackney Horse
Canadian   Morgan-Traditional
Caspian   Newfoundland Pony
Cleveland Bay   Shire
Dales Pony   Suffolk
Galiceño

THREATENED

(fewer than 1,000 annual U.S. registrations; global population under 5,000)

Akhal-Teke   Exmoor
Colonial-Spanish Horse   Irish Draught
   Lipizzan
Dartmoor

WATCH

(fewer than 2,500 annual U.S. Registrations; global population under 10,000)

Clydesdale   Mountain Pleasure/
Fell Pony   Rocky Mountain
Gotland   Pleasure Horse

RECOVERING

(previously listed in another category, has exceeded Watch numbers, but still needs monitoring)

Belgian

If these genetic reservoirs are to survive, it is crucial that the horses be bred—and in order to be bred, they need to be considered valuable. They must be exhibited and competed so that people see them and understand what they can do. The good news is that most breeds, even in the Critical category, have been experiencing brighter prospects. The Livestock Conservancy does excellent work in promoting the idea of rare breeds, and many people take interest in historic value and the exotic.

logging with horses
Harvesting firewood or timber with horses and mules. Equine are still used for logging, especially in ecologically sensitive areas in the American Northeast and Northwest. Compared to machinery, equines drastically reduce soil compaction and forest floor disturbance. Ground skidding can be done by a team, or a single horse if the logs are not too heavy; even ponies and miniature horses can be useful in moving appropriately sized logs.

A logging cart or arch is expensive, but safer and easier on the horses than a skid is. The logging cart suspends the front end of the log off the ground, reducing drag and allowing the team to pull heavier loads. The logger sits on the cart, so the log can't roll on him, and if the cart has brakes, he can help the team maneuver on steep terrain.

Logging is a hazardous activity. Horses need to be accustomed to the sound of chain saws and falling trees. They need to be rock-steady, and capable of starting deadweight loads without giving up. Loggers need to be strong, agile, and ever alert to hazards, including rolling logs and saplings that might snap the driver or horses in the face.

long, slow distance (LSD) training
Aerobic conditioning that builds endurance by improving cardiac capacity, muscle efficiency, and thermoregulatory ability. LSD training is used to acclimate trail horses and to bring idle horses back up to their previous level of fitness. It is a good way to condition young horses without stressing their growing bones and joints.

➤ See also competitive trail ride

long lining
Driving a horse from the ground, using 30-foot (9 m) reins called long lines. The horse wears a bridle and possibly a halter or a longeing cavesson, as well as a saddle or surcingle. The lines are run back through either the stirrup bows, rings placed higher on the saddle, or rings on the surcingle, to keep them at the proper height.

Long lining is typically the next training phase after longeing. It teaches a horse to move out, stop, and turn in response to rein pressure. It may be easiest to start long lining in a circle; this is similar to longeing and helps the horse catch on to the idea. Start at a walk; you can trot later when the horse is completely comfortable with the equipment and the process.

Long lining is especially helpful in training the driving horse. It's a good intermediate step in accustoming a horse to moving out in the world without a human babysitter beside his head. A spooky horse may benefit from lots of long lining in progressively more challenging environments where he can learn that, though his human is not beside him, he can successfully encounter new objects.

➤ *See also longe/lunge*

long trot The Western term for an extended or brisk trot.

longe/lunge Working a horse on a longe line in a circle about 60 feet (18 m) in diameter. (The term may be spelled either way—also, longeing or lungeing—but is pronounced "lunge," not "lounge.") The line is attached to the halter or bridle or to a longeing cavesson. The handler holds the line in one hand and a longe whip in the other. The horse may be worked with or without side reins.

Many young horses are trained on the longe line before learning to accept a bit and saddle. Working on the longe teaches them to balance themselves as they move on a circle and to respond primarily to vocal commands. The whip is never used to strike the horse; the movement of the lash, or sometimes popping the lash, keeps him from moving in toward the handler and encourages him forward.

Many trainers longe young horses in side reins, which are short reins with rubber or elastic inserts attached to a surcingle; this arrangement is sometimes called a bitting harness. It teaches the horse to give to the bit and carry himself in a relaxed frame. An overcheck may also be used to keep the horse from putting his head down.

Longeing is a good way to work off excess energy if a horse has not been ridden for a while or is known to act up under saddle.

Longeing lessons—in which the instructor controls the horse via the longe line while the rider is mounted—can allow the rider to concentrate on her seat and leg position without having to worry about the reins.

longeing cavesson A halter with a reinforced noseband, used for longeing. The noseband is fitted with three rings; one in the center-front, to which the longe line is snapped, and one on each side for side reins. If the horse bolts, the longeing cavesson allows for far better control than either a halter or bridle would, and the location of the center ring gives a forward impetus without pulling the headstall to one side.

LONG LINING

213

WORKING A HORSE ON A LONGE LINE

When selecting a longeing cavesson, make sure it is designed so that the longe line will not accidentally pass over the horse's eye.

Longeing converters are also available; these snap into bit rings to transform a bridle into a longeing cavesson.

longe line A long line that is attached to the horse's halter or bridle while the horse works in a circle at a set distance from the handler. Longe lines range from 25 to 50 feet (7.6–15.2 m) long and are usually made of cotton webbing. Some are easier to handle than others; the webbing can be slippery and hard to manage, a problem that can be solved by tying knots at regular intervals or by wearing gloves. Longe lines usually end with a simple swivel snap, but some have a chain shank at the end.
➤ *See also longe/lunge; longeing cavesson*

lope The Western term for canter. A lope is generally slower than an English canter.
➤ *See also canter; gait; lead (canter); trashy lope*

lying down Horses lie down to rest or roll. They lie down by buckling the knees and letting themselves down gradually. To stand, they prop themselves up on their front legs and then scramble up—the opposite of cows, who hoist the back end first.

Horses feel vulnerable while lying down. If your horse allows you to approach while he is stretched out on the ground, it is a sign of trust.

Horses may do a certain amount of groaning while lying down. It's not necessarily a sign of illness, though if you hear your recumbent horse groaning, it's worth spending a few minutes watching him.

If your horse begins to lie down more frequently than usual, make sure he's not trying to relieve the pain of colic or taking weight off a sore leg. An increase in time spent lying down may also be a sign of ulcers.
➤ *See also rolling; sleep patterns; ulcers*

Lyme disease A tick-borne disease first identified in Lyme, Connecticut, in 1976, but now found in almost every part of the United States. Carried by ticks that feed on infected white-footed mice, Lyme disease affects humans as well as horses and dogs. Symptoms in horses include persistent or recurring fever, lethargy, diminished appetite, weight loss, shifting limb lameness, muscle tremors, skin sensitivity, poor performance, behavioral change, inflammation in the eye, and laminitis. Of all these symptoms, lameness that shifts from one leg to the other may be the quickest diagnostic clue for the horse owner.

The common rash and swelling at the site of the tick bite will be hard to notice on a horse, but many horses suffering from chronic lameness, laminitis, or symptoms resembling arthritis are eventually diagnosed with the disease through a blood test.

Lyme disease is treated with oral doxycycline, oral minocycline, intravenous tetracycline, or a combination; treatment may take months to clear the infection, and is consequently rather expensive. The earlier treatment is started, the better the outcome.

There is currently no human or equine vaccine against Lyme disease. Some vets and horse owners have found the canine vaccine to be effective in horses, though its use for horses is classified as off-label. Preventive measures include use of permethrin or cypermethrin repellents, which provide protection for several hours. Clearing brush on your property is also helpful. Daily grooming and tick-checks help you remove ticks before infection. Look especially in soft-skinned areas of the body—under the mane, tail, and jaw; along the legs; and in the groin and girth area.

Lyme disease in humans, if not treated effectively, can lead to long-lasting debility, arthritis, and brain fog. Horses' response seems to vary, and most horses don't get severely ill with Lyme. But tick-borne diseases are serious, and tick control should be a focus for every horse owner.

➤ *See also parasites; pest control; ticks*

LUSITANO

The Portuguese version of the Andalusian horse. The Lusitano is based on Andalusian blood, with minor differences due to selective breeding. The Lusitano is more apt to display the convex profile of the old Andalusian, as opposed to the currently favored Oriental head. Otherwise the breeds are essentially identical. Like Andalusians, Lusitanos may be referred to as Pura Raza Española (PRE) horses.

Lusitano breeding is closely linked to bullfighting. Portuguese bullfighting requires an agile, calm, courageous horse, and also one capable of working at speed and in a high state of collection. This makes Lusitanos an obvious choice for the growing sports of doma vaquera and working equitation. Noted for their calm intelligence, Lusitanos also make excellent pleasure horses.

Maclay Equitation Finals A national championship that represents the upper levels of hunt seat equitation for junior riders (that is, riders under age 18) in the United States. Held annually since 1933, the finals, known more informally as Medal Maclay, are sponsored by the National Horse Show Association of America. Riders qualify by entering ASPCA Maclay Horsemanship classes at sanctioned shows throughout the year.

magnesium A mineral required by mammals in large amounts for energy transformation, protein synthesis, and normal function of the cells. Magnesium deficiencies can negatively affect neuromuscular tissue and the heart, as well as electrolyte balance and bone formation. Symptoms of magnesium deficiency in horses include nervousness, inability to concentrate, and problems with metabolizing carbohydrates, such as a tendency to develop abnormal fat pads and laminitis. It may be necessary to supplement magnesium, depending on soil magnesium levels in your area.

Soil magnesium levels are naturally low in many areas of the country, and are further lowered by acidic commercial fertilizers and acid rain. Supplementation is a good idea, particularly for horses or ponies with symptoms of insulin resistance (IR). If fed while horses transition to spring or fall grass, it can protect them from developing laminitis, by increasing circulation to the foot. It can also prevent tying-up.

Magnesium may be fed in formulated supplements with other minerals, or by itself. The best form is magnesium oxide, a fine white powder. Magnesium is water soluble, and it is virtually impossible to overdose orally; if you feed more than your horse needs, you will notice loose stools. The only time magnesium supplementation is dangerous is in the case of impaired kidney function. It is highly dangerous if administered by injection.
➤ *See also feeding and nutrition; pasture, horses on*

maiden class, maiden race Classes or races open to riders and horses who have not yet been winners in certain events; numbered as specified by show rules.
➤ *See also English riding; novice; Western riding*

maiden mare A mare that has never been bred.
➤ *See also broodmare*

malocclusion Abnormality of the jaw and teeth.
➤ *See also dental problems; parrot mouth; sow mouth/monkey mouth; teeth and age*

mane The long hair that grows along the top of the horse's neck, from poll to withers. The domesticated horse, *Equus caballus*, is the only equine whose mane grows long enough to fall over the neck. All others, including the extinct ancestors of the modern horse, have short manes of coarse hair that stick straight up. Humans began to breed for a long mane from earliest times, for aesthetic and practical reasons. The mane is very useful to a bareback rider, and the hair can be used for brushes and fabric. A heavy mane offers some protection from cold and insects, and helps channel water off the body, but all horse ancestors survived without it.

The length of a horse's mane is usually about the width of its neck, though this varies according to breed. Stallions grow longer manes, as do the baroque breeds. The well-cared-for mane of an Andalusian stallion may reach his knees. Mane hair regrows after being cut, and at least one breed, the American Curly, sheds its mane in the spring along with winter hair.

It is a persistent myth among horsemen that the mane hairs have no root nerves. They do have nerves, and some horses are quite sensitive to having their hair pulled while grooming. In general, however, a rider hanging onto the mane does not cause pain because she is gripping a large handful of hair.
➤ *See also pulling the mane*

Gypsy Vanners are known for their lush **manes**.

A BRAIDED MANE

mane, braiding Horses' manes may be braided in many different styles, depending on the discipline. Show hunters wear between 36 and 40 small, tight braids down the neck. Eventers wear between 16 and 21 knots. Dressage braids may be similar to event braids, or for horses with long manes, a running braid may be used. Long thick manes may be put up in an elegant diamond braid.

Carriage horses also wear braids, and draft horse manes may be put up in a mane roll, using long strips of bunting and rosettes along the top. For Western competition, the mane is often neatly banded.
➤ *See also Western banding*

mane, care of Horse owners who intend to show (Western or English) often prefer the mane to be about 4 inches (10 cm) long, though some breeds are shown with long, flowing manes. Ideally, your horse already has a neatly groomed mane that combs out easily every time you groom him. However, after a lengthy pasture turnout, especially in bad weather, you might be faced with a knotted, snarled mess of burrs or twisted dreadlocks caused by a pasture mate's teeth (bored or hungry horses sometimes chew on each other's manes).

Don't cut it all off, and don't attack it with a comb. Start by thoroughly coating the entire mane with a detangling spray or gel. Work the solution into the mane with your fingers. Wearing a pair of old leather gloves (which will build up a slick layer of detangler), begin to gently untangle the worst knots. Horsehair tends to twist together, so look for the direction of the twist and work the hairs free.

Once the biggest snarls are loosened, comb through the mane with your fingers, trying not to yank too hard. Most horses don't mind having their manes tugged, but pulling at major knots can be irritating and can also lead to loss of hair. The next step is to work with a human hairbrush, the kind with widely spaced plastic bristles. Start at the ends and brush gently as you work your way up to the crest, checking for burrs and other debris.

Don't use a comb until the brush goes the length of the mane without catching. A long mane should be treated regularly with detangler to keep it from snarling. It can be braided loosely into sections before a lengthy pasture turnout to prevent tangles and to keep burrs at bay.
➤ *See also bathing horses; grooming; pulling the mane*

mane comb A wide-toothed comb (usually plastic) used to groom the mane.

mange A condition caused by several different kinds of mites, which burrow into and bite the skin, producing intense itching. Horses will rub affected areas and may lose patches of hair and develop crusty, weeping areas and thick, wrinkled skin. Sarcoptic mange most commonly appears on the neck, where thick brown scabs form. Psoroptic mange generally is found where there is a lot of hair, such as the base of the tail and the crest of the mane, though it also appears in hairless areas, such as the udder. Chorioptic mange (or leg mange) is most active in cold weather and causes terrible itching. Horses can damage their legs by stomping in an attempt to alleviate the itching.

All itchy rashes should be seen by a veterinarian, who can determine the cause by examining a skin scraping under a microscope. There are several effective sprays and ointments to treat mange. Affected horses should be quarantined until they are well, as the condition can spread from horse to horse by direct contact, as well as through shared equipment.
➤ *See also parasites*

MANGALARGA MARCHADOR A Brazilian easy-gaited breed, averaging 15 hands high, used for ranch, endurance, and pleasure riding. The name comes from the hacienda Mangalarga, which was instrumental in promoting and marketing the breed, and from the special smooth gait, the marcha. The marcha has two forms, a broken trot called *batida,* and an amble called *picada.* In both there are moments when three legs support the body, which gives an extremely smooth ride. The Mangalarga is exceptionally comfortable to ride, but is also an active, versatile horse who excels at cattle work, jumping, and polo. Popular in Brazil, Mangalargas are increasingly being imported to the United States.

manners, of the horse

➤ *See handling horses; safety*

manty
A piece of canvas used to protect the load on a pack animal.

manure, as indicator of health
Manure from a healthy horse forms into balls that are moist and stay in a heap when passed. There are usually signs of some undigested hay and grain. Very hard and dry manure balls might indicate that your horse is not drinking enough water, which sometimes happens in winter, when horses tend to drink less. Loose manure or diarrhea can be an indication of illness, of a change of feed, or of a sudden increase in the intake of salt and, subsequently, water. Some horses have loose stools when they are nervous, upset, or in heat. Many horses also pass manure, loose or not, more frequently when nervous or upset.

If the manure is scant, check to see that the horse is passing what he eats and colic is not beginning. If you suspect sand colic, immerse some manure in water.

If sand settles out to the bottom, take the horse off sandy ground and consult your vet about dealing with the sand already in his intestines.

manure spreader A piece of equipment that is pulled behind a tractor, an all-terrain vehicle (ATV), or a team of horses. As it moves, the spreader broadcasts manure over a field.

TONS OF BENEFITS

Horse manure is valued for its high nitrogen content and ability to break down rapidly. Despite the high content and rapid breakdown, the nitrogen is released slowly, making composted manure ideal for fruit trees. Fortunately, there is plenty of it to go around. A horse can produce 50 pounds (23 kg) of manure a day—9 tons (8 metric tons) in a year.

marathon The cross-country phase of combined driving. A marathon course must be completed within a certain time frame. Competitors drive through a series of obstacles and are judged individually on time and faults. Fitness is an important component of marathon driving. The horse must return to normal temperature and heart rate within a certain amount of time.

marathon vehicle A metal, four-wheeled carriage used for upper-level marathon driving.

mare A female horse of more than four years of age.
➤ *See also breeding; broodmare; filly*

mare's milk Horses were originally domesticated for their meat and milk; mare's milk is still popular on the Asian steppes, where it is made into a mildly alcoholic drink. In the West, mare's milk is catching on as a remedy for Crohn's disease and allergies. Sweeter than cow's milk, it has 40 percent more lactose, with a protein structure closer to human milk, and more vitamin A and vitamin C.

Horse dairies tend to breed large horses, to get a larger volume of milk. In modern Western dairies, mares are milked by machine; in Asia, mares tend to be milked by hand.

markings

➤ *See face markings; "Leg Markings," page 204*

martingale
A strap that prevents the horse from tossing his head too high, called a tie-down in Western riding. There are two basic types, the standing martingale (more restrictive) and the running martingale (less restrictive). The standing martingale consists of two straps, one that circles the base of the horse's neck, and another that runs from the back of a cavesson noseband, through a slit in the neck strap, to buckle around the saddle girth. The running martingale attaches to the girth and the neck strap in the same way. Two straps with rings on the ends come up from the neck strap; the reins are run through these rings. Both types of martingale should be carefully fitted.
➤ *See also running martingale; standing martingale; tie-down*

mash
A warm bran mash is a time-honored recipe for perking up a cold or sick horse. Mashes can also be quite useful for sneaking medications into a finicky horse. It may be helpful to add applesauce to further disguise flavors. However, wheat bran is not a good food for horses, as it is high in phosphorus and contains phytase, which binds calcium and makes it unavailable.

MARWARI HORSE

The Marwari horse is the product of centuries of careful breeding in northwest India, particularly in the desert state of Rajasthan, where it was considered the ultimate warhorse. A good Marwari is between 14.2 and 15 hands high, elegant and refined, with long legs and extremely hard feet. It retains the courage and loyalty of its warhorse past.

Marwaris have curved, almost crescent-shaped ears that often touch at the tip, similar to the Kathiawari, another ancient Indian breed. Both breeds are rare, and have degenerated since the days when warhorses were prized, but efforts to save them are bearing fruit.

➤ *See also bran mash*

Luckily, any concentrate can be made into a mash, which is basically porridge. Just add enough boiling water (or water as hot as you can get it from the tap) to make the normal feed ration wet, but not dripping. Start with one part water to two parts concentrate and experiment for best results; flaked grains absorb more water than whole grains, while pellets quickly turn to mush, so the amount of water depends on what grain you're feeding.

Stir the mixture well and cover the bucket for 5 or 10 minutes to let it steam. Feed while it is still warm but not too hot for you to handle with bare hands. After use, clean the bucket and the feeder well, as wet feed spoils quickly.

➤ *See also bran; feeding and nutrition*

massage therapy

An increasingly popular form of therapy for horses, particularly for performance horses in heavy competition. A good equine massage therapist can manipulate tissue to increase circulation, relax tight spots, relieve spasms, and just generally make your horse feel better. Massage can be part of a treatment program for an injury and can actually help prevent injuries, especially in horses who are worked hard.

With a bit of study, horse owners can do massage therapy on their own horses. While you may lack the knowledge of a professional, you probably see your horse a lot more often than you can afford to have a therapist do. Learn to spot when and where your horse is holding tension, and practice working to release it. A nice rub can't do any harm, and may do a great deal of good.

mastitis

A serious infection of the udder. Although mares have two teats, there are four quarters to the udder and each teat has two openings for milk to flow through. Mastitis is an infection in one or more quarters of the udder; it is generally found on one side or the other, not both at the same time. While usually found in lactating mares, especially around weaning time when the udder is full and painful to begin with, the condition can also affect mares who are not pregnant or lactating.

Symptoms are varied, depending on the severity of the infection, but the mare will definitely show signs of discomfort as she tries to avoid bumping her sore udder with her leg. She may stop eating; run a fever; have swelling, heat, or edema in the affected area; or kick at a nursing foal.

Mastitis must be treated with antibiotics, both oral and topical. Untreated mastitis can destroy mammary tissue in one or more quarters and may make it impossible for the mare to produce milk for future foals. In rare cases, the infection can completely destroy the udder and even kill the mare.

➤ *See also udder*

maturity classes

Classes for older horses who are no longer competing at the highest levels but still have plenty to offer.

McClellan saddle

The official saddle of the U.S. Cavalry. The McClellan is still used by many long-distance riders who swear by its comfort for both them and the horse. Others find it comfortable for the horse, but not so comfortable for the rider.

➤ *See also saddle; tack*

mealy-mouthed

Lighter coloring on the muzzle and mouth that occurs on many bay or brown horses.

MCCURDY PLANTATION HORSE

A gaited horse related to the Tennessee Walker. McCurdy Plantation Horses were developed as all-purpose horses like the original Walkers, and remain closer to that ideal. Their special gait, known as the McCurdy Lick, is an exceptionally smooth singlefoot; they also perform the flat walk, running walk, rack, and stepping pace, and may also fox trot. McCurdy Horses are born naturally gaited and do not require exotic shoeing. They average 15 hands high, and are excellent trail, pleasure, and hunting horses.

MEALY-MOUTHED

measuring a horse

➤ *See hand, as unit of measurement; weight, of horse*

mecate A rein system using a rope of braided horse-hair, connected to a bosal (noseband). A mecate is usually twice as long as a normal set of reins; the extra length is tied to the saddle horn or around the horse's neck, and is used for leading.

➤ *See also bosal; hackamore*

MECATE

medicine hat color pattern A pinto color pattern in which an otherwise white horse has color only on a "bonnet" over the ears and sometimes a "shield" on the chest. Sometimes called a "war bonnet," these markings were considered by some Native American tribes to have great power and bring good fortune.

melanoma A skin tumor common among gray horses. Frequently, there is little cause for concern, though your vet should check any suspicious growth. Lumps generally appear around the genital area and under the tail and may at first be benign, but they can become cancerous and spread internally, where they might interfere with breeding, foaling, or even digestion. Internal melanomas are more dangerous. The external ones are often very slow-growing, and your veterinarian may decide to leave them alone unless they are interfering with bowel function or use of a saddle. All lumps should be checked regularly for changes in appearance and size.

Surgical removal of the tumor and freezing or burning the remaining area can be done if necessary, but there is a risk that disturbing the growth may stimulate the proliferation of cancer cells.

memory, equine It takes years to make a good horse, but only a moment to make a bad one. Their excellent memories make horses highly trainable, but it also makes them hard to handle in situations where they've previously been frightened or mistreated. A horse who suddenly becomes frightened for no apparent reason may be reacting to a stimulus he associates with a frightening event.

Because horses have good memories, it is important to train sensitively. Endless drilling is both boring and unnecessary; your horse certainly remembers his lessons. Repetition is an important part of gaining skill, but a good trainer finds ways to mix lessons up so they always seem fresh.

➤ *See also body language, of horses; handling horses; pecking order, among horses*

metabolic bone disease A general name for a group of conditions affecting bones and joints. Many of them are linked with high-glycemic feeds. When feeding growing horses, emphasize forage. If you must feed grain, add oil or fat to the feed, or choose a commercial feed with a low glycemic index.

microchipping Implanting a microchip, the size of a grain of rice, under the skin for identification purposes. Microchipping is most often done for horses who travel and compete in foreign countries, as part of their Fédération Equestre Internationale (FEI) Passport. The

MINIATURE HORSE

An extremely popular category of small pony, under 38 inches (97 cm) tall when measured at the base of the last hair of the mane on the withers. Fanciers insist that minis are horses, not ponies, but in fact the American Miniature Horse breed was founded on Shetland bloodlines, at a time when American Shetlands were becoming less popular.

Selective breeding has produced two types of minis, one refined and horselike, the other a cobby, British Shetland type. There are two height divisions: Class A, 34 inches (86 cm) or less, and Class B, 38 inches (97 cm) or less. Minis can be any solid color, and some have pinto or appaloosa coloring.

Regardless of type, a mini should look like a small pony or horse. Large heads and short legs are signs of dwarfism. Dwarf horses will probably have health problems, and a mini with any signs of dwarfism—including an underbite, a short neck, an oversized head, a strongly domed forehead, or extremely short legs—should not be bred.

Minis are popular with many people who can't handle or afford a large horse, or don't have the space. They eat one-fifth as much as a full-sized horse, can live luxuriously in a prefab garden shed and travel in the back of a minivan, and have all the beauty and personality of bigger horses. Minis are mostly kept as pets, but they are popular driving ponies, fully capable of pulling adult drivers. They are shown in hand, including in jumping classes, where the handler runs alongside. The American Miniature Horse Association notes that minis should never be ridden by anyone over 70 pounds (31.7 kg) and that parents should be cautious about allowing children to ride even a willing and gentle mount.

Draft-type minis can do a great deal of useful work around the homestead, using converted garden tractor equipment. Minis are also taking part in pulling contests; because of their low center of gravity, they can pull proportionally greater weight than draft horses, and frequently win contests judged on the proportion of its own weight the team can pull.

Minis are prone to dental abnormalities and feed-related ailments, including obesity, laminitis, hyperlipemia, and Cushing's disease. They are also far more prone to serious foaling problems, including red bag deliveries, when the foal is born still enclosed in the placenta. If you breed your mini, you *must* be there at foaling. With help, foaling usually turns out well.

➤ *See also Falabella*

microchip, a unique, permanent ID number, lasts up to 25 years. It is used to provide proof of ownership or to recover a horse stolen or lost in a natural disaster.

The microchip is injected into the nuchal ligament, halfway between the poll and withers on the left side. It is invisible, but removal causes noticeable scars, offering further protection against theft. If a microchipped horse is stolen, the microchip number should be reported to law enforcement and to the Equine Protection Registry, which will put the number on its Hot List. This can help identify the horse at a sale. Microchips do not currently have GPS capacity and can't be used to remotely locate a horse.

milking horses

➤ *See mare's milk*

milo

➤ *See sorghum grain/milo*

minerals

➤ *See feeding and nutrition; supplements; vitamins; individual minerals*

MITBAH Arabic term for throatlatch, or attachment of head and neck. The word translates literally to "the place where the throat is cut," a grim reference to butchering camels, sheep, and goats. A fine, long mitbah is much desired in an Arabian horse.

mites Tiny insects that cause dermatitis and are most active in the spring and winter. Trombidiform mites infest harvested grain (the larvae develop on small rodents, which then infiltrate the grain) and can transmit disease to animals. Affected animals will develop itchy, scaly areas around the lips and face.

Mange mites live in the hair follicles and cause chronic inflammation and intense itching, as well as secondary infections. Some mange mites burrow under the skin and can be felt as small bumps, again typically found around the face.

➤ *See also mange; parasites*

MISSOURI FOX TROTTER

An easy-gaited breed found primarily in the rural south-central states. This horse's special gait is the fox trot, a rhythmic diagonal gait with alternating three-hoof, two-hoof support. The stride in front is reaching rather than high; the hind feet slide forward, resulting in an extremely smooth, sure-footed ride. Fox Trotters make great trail and pleasure horses and are used in some western parks, where they are crossed with donkeys to produce comfortable riding mules. Fox Trotters come from the same genetic stock as Saddlebreds, Tennessee Walkers, and the Mountain Saddle breeds, and bear a resemblance to them.

➤ *See also amble; fox trot; gaited horse; "Mountain Saddle Horses," page 229*

mitt A sheepskin finishing mitt used at the end of a thorough grooming to "set" the coat and bring out a shine. It can also be used to groom the horse's face. Mitts made of microfiber may be used for washing a horse.
➤ *See also grooming*

molars
➤ *See dental problems; teeth and age*

molasses
A by-product of sugar manufacturing that provides carbohydrates and is often added to commercial grain mixes. When the molasses coats the grain and can be seen and smelled, the blend is known as sweet feed. Too much molasses will cause loose stool, so the proportion of molasses to grain should be less than 10 percent. Molasses contains about 4 percent protein and virtually no vitamins, though it is high in potassium. The sugars in molasses are very digestible and will raise blood sugar after meals. Sweet feed can lead to excessive energy, which can be remedied by replacing it with a balanced ration high in digestible fiber, and low in grain and molasses.
➤ *See also feeding and nutrition; sweet feed*

A SPOONFUL OF SUGAR

If you are training a young horse to be bridled and he doesn't want to open his mouth for the bit, smear a little molasses on it and he will get into the habit of willingly opening his mouth for it. Molasses added to a mash may help conceal medication as well.

---

mold/fungi in feed Mold microorganisms thrive in moisture and multiply rapidly in warm, damp weather. Grass hay is less likely to be moldy than legume hay, which is richer in nutrients and has a higher moisture content. Rich alfalfa hay is especially susceptible to mold and must be kept dry.

Molds to look out for are black patch disease, found on clovers and other legumes; ergot, a fungus that sometimes infects the seed heads of grasses; and the deadly *Fusarium moniliforme,* which causes moldy corn poisoning.

Feeding a horse moldy hay may poison the horse, cause colic, or cause abortion in pregnant mares. *Always* look at and smell hay before feeding it, and discard any that contains mold. Avoid feeding corn, and store all concentrates in a cool, dry place. In general horses refuse to eat moldy fodder, so if your horse leaves some of his supper, check the leavings as well as his state of health.
➤ *See also ergot; fungal infections;* Fusarium moniliforme; *hay; toxic substances*

Monday morning disease
➤ *See azoturia/Monday morning disease/tying up*

monensin/Rumensin
A drug often added to cattle feed that is fatal to horses. Just a few grams of monensin (sold under the brand name Rumensin) produce symptoms of a weak and irregular pulse, a high heart rate, abnormal lung sounds, and blue mucous membranes. The poison attacks the muscles, and the horse dies of heart failure. Buy feed from a reputable dealer, and don't give cattle feed to horses.
➤ *See also toxic substances*

monkey mouth
➤ *See sow mouth/monkey mouth*

MONGOLIAN HORSE

Genghis Khan's Mongol warriors conquered the world from China to the Baltic because of the speed and stamina of these small horses. The Mongolian horse averages 12 to 14 hands high, and exhibits the "primitive" qualities of incredible toughness and hardiness. Raised in wild-running herds, Mongolian horses are easily gentled; children ride them bareback. They graze year-round without supplemental feed, though the ground may be snow-covered and temperatures dip below −40°F (−40°C).

MORAB An American breed developed in the 1800s, of Morgan and Arabian blood. Registry rules stipulate that a registered animal may be no more than 75 percent of one of the two foundation breeds, and no less than 25 percent of the other. The cross, which has existed since the mid-1800s, was used to build and improve other breeds, including the Quarter Horse. Morabs are powerful and muscular, with a refined head and neck, good bone, and free-flowing gaits.

moon blindness

➤ *See equine recurrent uveitis (ERU)*

Morgan *(see next page)*

mounted archery

A growing sport in which riders shoot arrows at targets in timed competition. In the Korean form, riders gallop on a set course, 120 to 160 meters (394–525 feet), shooting at one to five targets. The Hungarian course is 90 meters (295 feet), and riders shoot at three central targets, faced in three directions, loosing as many arrows as possible in 16 seconds. In Turkish shooting, the target is hung on a pole 7 meters (23 feet) high, and competitors take six runs on a 90-meter (295-foot) track. In Mogu competition, one rider pulls a Mogu ball, a large ball with a wicker or bamboo framework, while one or two riders follow, shooting blunted, inked arrows at the moving target.

The Mounted Archery Association of America (MA3) sanctions competitions, including a so-called Postal Competition, in which a course pattern is distributed, competitors set it up and run it, and results are sent to the organization so riders can be scored and ranked nationally.

➤ *See also cowboy mounted shooting*

mounted games

Games and contests on horseback. Western games include barrel racing, pole bending, flag races, keyhole, and different forms of relay racing. These competitions are held at rodeos and gymkhanas, which run the gamut from local events held for fun to nationally organized professional events.

English games are frequently organized by the United States Pony Clubs, Inc. (USPC). The Games division is one of USPC's most popular. Usually played in teams of four riders, games incorporate skills like handing off, mounting and dismounting, or vaulting. A few examples include the balloon race, which involves popping balloons with a lance; egg and racket, which combines pole bending with carrying an egg on a racket; hurdle race, in which riders lead their ponies while crawling under 2-foot (61 cm) hurdles and jumping over 1-foot (30 cm) hurdles.

Fun, fast, and informal, USPC games teach confidence and balance, and often provide a second career for a small horse or pony who has been outgrown for showing. USPC competitions are for youth only, but parents have set up Games teams and competitions of their own.

➤ *See also barrel racing; cowboy mounted shooting; flag race; gymkhana; keyhole race/pole bending; Pony Club; Western riding*

MORGAN

An important American breed developed in New England in the late 1700s. Justin Morgan was a yeoman farmer who bred a fine stallion to a part-Arabian mare; the resulting foal, named Figure, was a small, sturdy, beautiful stallion. He proved himself as an incredibly hard worker, able to pull a plow all day and beat all comers in races on weekends. The horse was soon called Justin Morgan, after his owner.

The little stallion's remarkable prepotency resulted in the only breed to be named after a single founding sire. Morgans became highly prized road horses, and when imported to the West were well-regarded ranch horses. The breed dominated harness racing until the advent of the Standardbred, which was founded on Morgan and Thoroughbred blood.

When the automobile supplanted horse-drawn vehicles, the Morgan breed went into sharp decline. It was saved in the 1920s and '30s by government breeding programs, first for army remount use, and then the New England state universities. The Morgan became primarily a pleasure and show horse, with shows emphasizing a high-stepping gait.

Today's Morgan is still a small horse (14.2–15.2 hands high), but strong and well-built, with muscular hindquarters and a refined head. Most Morgans are dark with few white markings; however, in the last 20 years the breed has begun to accept so-called colored Morgans, including palominos, perlinos, and buckskins. Morgans are known for soundness, good nature, and good minds. Outside of Morgan show circles, they are primarily pleasure horses and are the predominant breed of American carriage horse.

Morgans are historically important for their influence on other American breeds. Saddlebred and Tennessee Walker foundation sires were Morgans, and Morgan blood is heavily infused in the Standardbred. Morgans were also important in the development of the Quarter Horse, the most popular breed of horse in the world.

The Morgan of traditional type has been added to the Livestock Conservancy's Critical list, though this is controversial within the Morgan community. Certainly the bloodlines that include Lippitt, Flyhawk, and old Government are not those popular in the show ring, and far fewer traditional Morgans are being bred.

MOUNTAIN SADDLE HORSES

A group of breeds that includes the Kentucky Mountain Saddle Horse and Rocky Mountain Horse. These are landrace breeds (that is, not breeds per se but uniform types that have developed in isolation within a local area) and have been unchanged in over a century. Descended from the Narragansett Pacer, and smooth-gaited Spanish horses, Mountain Saddle horses may be ancestral to Tennessee Walkers and Saddlebreds. Type varies, but these are small, attractive gaited horses (11–15.2 hands high) of great sure-footedness and stamina. They make excellent trail-riding and all-purpose family horses. **Livestock Conservancy status: Watch**

mounted police

➤ *See police horses; Royal Canadian Mounted Police*

mounting aid
A device to help solve the common difficulty of mounting a tall horse when a mounting block is not available. There are many variations. A **stirrup extension** consists of an adjustable strap and stirrups that buckle into a regular stirrup. To use it, put your right foot into the mounting aid stirrup, then quickly place your left foot into your saddle's stirrup. Kick your right foot out of the mounting aid and swing your leg over your horse's back. You can then unfasten the mounting aid and put it in a saddle bag.

A similar device, the **step-up stirrup**, attaches to a Western saddle horn, and is pulled around the back of the cantle to create an extra step. Another device lowers your stirrup 3 inches (8 cm) with the touch of a button, then locks back into place when you lift your toe.

mounting block
A stepstool that gives the rider some additional height when getting on a horse. The common mounting block is made of molded plastic with two steps and a carrying groove; three-step blocks are also available. Alternatively, you might build a set of wooden steps with a platform; just but be sure it won't

tip easily or allow your horse to get a hoof or leg caught in it.

Using a mounting block puts far less torque on the saddle and your horse's back than mounting from the ground.

mouth, hard or soft
A term to describe a horse's responsiveness to the reins. A horse is said to have a soft mouth if he responds readily to light cues from the reins. A hard-mouthed horse will ignore the rein aids, fight the bit, or even clamp it between his teeth. It is possible to retrain a hard-mouthed horse with patient and tactful handling, with great reliance on aids from the seat and leg, and very light rein contact.

The best way to avoid a hard mouth is to develop a balanced seat with good leg contact.
➤ *See also aids; hands, rider's; legs, use of when riding; seat*

mouth problems
➤ *See dental problems; teeth and age*

movement, conformation and
The way a horse moves is a result of his conformation. This is known as form-to-function. For example, a horse with a long, 45-degree sloped shoulder and long hip will move with a free-flowing stride, whereas a horse with a short, straight (55- to 65-degree) shoulder and short, steep hip will move with short, choppy strides.
➤ *See also conformation; leg, of horse; gait; gaited horses; way of going*

LEARNING FROM THE GROUND UP

A mounting block not only makes it easier for the rider to get on but also puts less strain on the girth (and, consequently, the horse) and allows the rider to settle more lightly into the saddle. If you always rely on a mounting block, however, you may be in trouble if you have to dismount on the trail and there is nothing around you can stand on to help you get back in the saddle. Therefore, you should know how to mount a horse from the ground.

moxidectin/Quest A dewormer that kills parasites in the larval stage. It concentrates in a horse's fat, and overdoses can be harmful. Weigh or tape your horse, and administer the proper amount. Moxidectin (sold under the brand name Quest) should never be given to foals.

➤ *See also deworming; parasites*

MOYLE HORSE

A strain of horse developed in Idaho from horses owned and bred by the Mormons. Moyles are notable for having "horns," small bony knobs above the eyes, like small versions of a giraffe's horns. These horses possess phenomenal endurance. A cowboy might typically work a string of up to ten horses, while a cowboy on the Moyle ranch would only have one horse, on which he could outwork anybody in the neighborhood. Moyles are long, with their forelegs far forward on their rib cages. The walking stride is exceptionally long. The liver and the spleen of a Moyle are nearly twice the size of those of other horse breeds. The population is small, and there is no breed association or registry.

mucking out stalls Cleaning manure and soiled bedding from stalls; a vital component of horse care. Stalls should be cleaned daily to prevent moisture and fumes from building up and to cut down on potential parasite problems.

Pick out manure and soiled bedding with a manure fork, and shovel up any wet spots. If possible, allow the floor to air-dry before adding fresh bedding. If the horse has to come right back in, sprinkle lime or another odor neutralizer on the wet spots and rake the remaining old bedding over them. Fresh bedding should be heaviest where the horse tends to lie down, and should be moderately banked up along the walls, to prevent him from becoming cast.

➤ *See also barns and facilities; bedding*

mud and health concerns Mud is not healthy for horses. Walking in it is hazardous, both when it's wet and sloppy (and can practically suck a shoe right off a hoof) and when it's rutted and frozen. Rolling in wet weather can coat your horse in damp, chilly mud, matting his coat and sapping his body of warmth. Standing in mud gives rise to a host of foot problems. In general, avoid muddy conditions as much as possible by spreading gravel or sand in damp areas, grooming frequently in bad weather, and making sure that outdoor turnout areas have dry places for horses to stand.

mule The sterile offspring of a male donkey (a jack) and a mare. A stallion and a female donkey (a jenny) produce a hinny, which is generally smaller than a mule. Height depends on the size of the parents; mules range from 34-inch (86 cm) mini size up to mammoths at 17.2 hands high. Mules have a reputation for being stubborn

JUMPING JACKS

Many people are unaware that mules aren't just used as pack and draft animals; they make fine riding and jumping mounts. Although not always permitted to compete in sanctioned horse shows, they can perform at high levels of show jumping and dressage.

A very different sort of competition is coon jumping, in which donkeys and mules jump without riders in a competition; it derives from raccoon hunting, when a rider would dismount and drape a coat over a wire fence. The mule would jump the fence, and the pair would reunite on the other side.

Competitive coon jumping is a timed event. The donkey or mule must stand in a box (outlined on the ground with lime) that measures 10 x 10 feet (3 x 3 m) prior to jumping the obstacle from a standstill. The jump starts at 12 inches (25 cm) and is increased 2 inches (5 cm) each round. Contestants who fail to clear the height in two attempts are disqualified. Some talented mules can coon-jump up to 6 feet (1.8 m).

SADDLE MULE

SHOW-JUMPING MULE

and mean, but mule lovers describe them as smart, curious, and sensible, with the ability to forge close relationships with people and other animals. Mules are sure-footed, agile, generally sound, and will not put up with foolish or abusive handling. Mules can do anything horses can and, according to their fans, do it all better. In addition to their well-known role as superb pack animals, they are used in harness, under saddle, for jumping, and even for dressage and hunting.

➤ *See also donkey; hinny*

mullen-mouth bits
English bits, either snaffle or Pelham, with a slightly curved, unjointed mouthpiece. Both versions are considered to be mild bits.

muscle types
All mammals have two types of muscle fiber: slow-twitch and fast-twitch. Slow-twitch fibers contract and relax relatively slowly, are more efficient, and have greater staying power. They function well in the presence of oxygen. Fast-twitch fibers, capable of quick action, perform well in the absence of oxygen. They are less efficient, more quickly accumulate lactic acid, and tire more rapidly.

Successful endurance horses have a greater proportion of slow-twitch fiber in the deep muscle of the hindquarters than less successful ones. Even their fast-twitch fibers have a higher aerobic capacity than that of unsuccessful horses. Sprinters have a very high proportion of low-aerobic fast-twitch fibers. Some Quarter Horses have nearly 100 percent fast-twitch fiber in the large muscles of their hindquarters.

Exercise can change these proportions to a degree; high-intensity training reduces the amount of slow-twitch fibers, and exercise increases the aerobic capacity of all muscle types. But there are innate breed differences. Broadly, horses who are used for long-distance or extended types of work (racing, dressage, jumping, and so on) need long, lean slow-twitch muscles. Heavily muscled horses can achieve sudden bursts of speed and quick acceleration but usually cannot sustain the effort.

➤ *See also conformation*

mustang Feral horses descended from the horses brought by the Spaniards to the New World in the early 16th century. The word "mustang" derives from the Spanish *mesteño*, meaning "stray." Horses multiplied rapidly when returned to their native habitat. Indian tribes quickly learned to ride, then to hunt and fight on horseback. For centuries on the North American continent, Indian horses and horsemanship repulsed Spanish movement north and other settlers' movement west.

The U.S. Army, recognizing the military advantage mustangs gave the tribes, slaughtered Indian horses when they could, or turned coarse draft stallions loose with Indian herds, hoping to slow down the resulting offspring. The draft horses were ill suited to living in the wild, however, and the effect was limited.

Many modern mustangs are mongrels, descended from every type of horse ever brought west. However, the environment keeps them small (13–14.2 hands high) and tough, with strong, hard feet. Spanish type predominates, as the original pool was overwhelmingly Spanish.

Mustangs come in all colors and a variety of conformations, from attractive horses with good conformation to scrubby, scrawny creatures sometimes called "broomtails." A legend of the American West, the mustang has been both romanticized and reviled, chased for sport, tamed for working cows, and slaughtered for dog food. Mustangs breed so successfully that fierce arguments about population control have raged among ranchers, wild horse advocates, and the U.S. Bureau of Land Management (BLM), the federal agency responsible for dealing with mustangs and wild burros. The U.S. Congress passed acts in 1959 and 1971 prohibiting the hunting and harassment of the animals on federal land. These acts also provided for the monitoring and management of wild horse and burro herds.

Wild horses have few natural predators, and herds can double every four years. There were approximately 40,000 mustangs ranging across 10 western states in 2014, and around 8,000 feral burros. The BLM continues to round up herds and tries to sell off horses, but as of 2014 there were over 47,000 animals that had been offered for adoption and not taken. In 2014 the BLM sold only 1,122 mustangs, a sharp drop from prerecession adoptions of approximately 6,000 to 7,000 annually.

Well-trained mustangs make excellent mounts. They are highly intelligent and very willing to form a bond with humans. Wild-caught mustangs have few negative associations with humans, and no bad habits. The Mustang Heritage Foundation, a nonprofit organization that promotes mustang adoption, runs two types of training contests annually.

Despite all the advantages mustangs can offer, and the low cost of adopting one, the backlog remains enormous. The BLM has a policy of not selling these horses to kill buyers, and faces pressure from advocacy groups to cease annual roundups. It responds that, without culling, populations will grow to an unsustainable level. As one possible solution to the problem, the BLM has been experimenting with birth control for mustangs and has had some success with this approach.

➤ *See also Spanish colonial/Spanish mustang*

mutton-withered Having poorly defined, well-padded withers. This conformation is common in ponies, and can cause the saddle to slip. A crupper strap or breastplate may be necessary for a mutton-withered horse.

➤ *See also breastplate; crupper; withers*

mutual grooming When two horses stand scratching each other; a ritualized way to solidify social relationships. Every horse living in a feral band grooms almost every other horse in that band, but spends most of his time grooming one or two friends. Horses often groom each other after an aggressive encounter.

The area most often groomed is the upper neck and withers. The rump is groomed often, the chest, throat, and front section of the barrel are groomed occasionally. When the lower neck is groomed by humans, the horse's heart rate decreases by about 11 percent in adult horses, 14 percent in foals, in under two minutes. The area in front of the withers has a direct parasympathetic connection to the vagus nerve, and grooming that area effectively lowers the horse's heart rate. The behavior probably evolved as a way to calm down from fear and stress, and restore a social bond.

Scratching and rubbing can help you form a bond with your horse. It will trigger a response; the horse's upper lip will twitch, and he may want to groom you back. But horses groom with their teeth, and that's too much for a delicate human being. You can instead encourage your horse to "groom" a post while you scratch him.

Science has not yet established what style and intensity of stroking by a human works best to calm horses. We tend to assume gentle strokes would be more soothing, but when you observe horses grooming each other (or if you trigger the grooming response when scratching your own horse) you'll discover that they rake each other vigorously with their upper teeth. Experiment to see what your horse likes best. If your horse has a heart rate monitor for conditioning purposes, it might be interesting to put it on and develop some data of your own.

Many horsemen pat or slap their open palm on a horse's neck as a sign of approval after a job well done. Science appears to indicate that horses don't actually like this, and may interpret it as aggression. A study done at the London Olympics found that two-thirds of horses accelerated when patted by their riders. A stroke or a scratch might be a better option.

muzzle

1. A horse's lips and nose. A horse's muzzle, including the hairs on it, is as much a part of his senses as his sight and hearing. Horses have extremely sensitive lips and muzzles; they can use their lips to find very small items on the ground that they can't see.

MUZZLE

2. A device that limits a horse's grazing; prevents him from biting, cribbing, or chewing wood; or prevents him from tearing at a bandage or chewing at a wound. Different types of muzzles are designed for each of these purposes.

➤ *See also grazing muzzle; whiskers*

MUTUAL GROOMING

mycotoxins Fungal toxins that can contaminate grain and other food sources. They damage the liver and kidneys and destroy red blood cells.

➤ *See also feeding and nutrition; grain; mold/fungi in feed*

mythology, the horse in The speed, power, and beauty of horses, and the way they magnify the abilities of the humans who ride and drive them, has given them a central role in myth and legend for millennia. Some of the earliest mythological horses have wings—really, just a slight exaggeration of the feeling they gave humans, for whom they were the first point of access to high-speed travel.

In mythology, horses are frequently associated with the sun; sun gods (Apollo and Surya, a Hindu deity) often drive chariots drawn by fiery horses. The Spanish bullfight is said to be an enactment of an ancient conflict between the sun, represented by horses, and the moon, represented by bulls.

Horses also have a long association with water and the sea. Poseidon, Greek god of the sea, drove a chariot pulled by white horses. Many coastal peoples sacrificed white horses by drowning them in the sea, where their spirits could serve the god. Poseidon was the father of Pegasus, the winged white horse who was the first to be ridden by a human, the hero Bellerophon. Pegasus ultimately became a constellation.

Centaurs—half-man, half-horse—were reputed to be wild, lustful, and drunken. Only Chiron had a good reputation, that of a master of many arts including medicine and archery. An immortal, he offered to die in the place of a man, and as a reward was placed in the heavens as the constellation Sagittarius.

White horses, especially stallions, have long been held sacred, which has often led to their sacrifice. This was true in ancient Persia, where love of horses was built into the first great world religion, Zoroastrianism. Ironically, Zoroastrianism sprang up partially in reaction to the increased theft and violence of a horseback world.

The patron gods of warfare are often associated with horses. Epona, the Celtic "Great Mare," was worshipped by Roman cavalrymen. She was also a goddess who protected women in labor. Romans also revered Castor, a horse tamer, and his twin, Pollux, the sons of Jupiter who were believed to protect horse soldiers in battle.

The Hindu god Vishnu has many incarnations, the final one being Kalki, a warrior on a white horse (or sometimes, the horse itself), who drives evildoers from India and saves the true believers.

Less heroic and noble are the ferocious flesh-eating mares of Diomedes, who became tame when Hercules fed their owner to them. Bringing the mares to King Eurystheus was one of Hercules's 12 labors. The kelpie was the terrifying water horse of the Scots; kelpies frequented rivers and lakes, and preyed on young women.

Ancient Scandinavians sacrificed sacred horses to the god Frey, as well as holding horse races and stallion fights in his honor. The god Odin rode an eight-legged horse named Sleipnir.

The unicorn is a mythical horse or horselike animal with a single horn. The oldest text to mention it comes from Persia in 416 BCE. There and in India the unicorn was thought to be ferocious, dangerous even to its own kind. In medieval Europe, it could only be captured by using a beautiful young woman as bait. On the other hand, it had the strange ability to purify a poisoned stream by drawing the sign of the cross on the surface of the water. It became a heraldic symbol of strength, power, and even chastity, of Christ to some and the devil to others. With rhino, narwhal, and oryx horns as evidence, it was easy to convince people of the reality of unicorns.

The crescent shape of the horseshoe has long been associated with good fortune and protection from harm, hence the arched doors and windows of many churches. Iron was also believed to have special protective qualities. Therefore, an iron horseshoe was a very protective element, often nailed up over a door. The best shoes were those found by accident, or those cast by a gray mare.

➤ *See also history of the horse*

nails, for horseshoes

Thin nails with flared heads used to secure horseshoes onto hooves. It doesn't hurt the horse to have his shoes nailed on, because the nails go into the tough outer wall, not into the sensitive sole or frog.
➤ *See also farrier; hoof; horseshoes*

NARRAGANSETT PACER

➤ An extinct breed of easy-gaited horse, once the most popular saddle horse in North America. The Narragansett, descended from the English Hobby Horse, was a small, spirited ambler, swift, sure-footed, and easy to ride. The center of breeding was Rhode Island, but Narragansett Pacers were traded widely from Canada to the Caribbean. When roads improved and people turned to driving, the breed became extinct. Narragansett blood survives in the Morgan, Canadian, Standardbred, Saddlebred, and Tennessee Walker.

nasal bone

The bone that runs along the front of the horse's face to just above the nostrils. The tip of this bone is fragile and sensitive, so care must be taken when fitting a halter and handling the face.
➤ *See also halter*

nasal strips

Adhesive strips that attach to a horse's nose above the nostrils to help the airway remain expanded and prevent lung injury and bleeding during extreme exercise. Nasal strips are used on racehorses, event horses, barrel racers, and in combined driving.

natural horsemanship (NH)

A training method based on a form of operant conditioning that works on pressure and release and negative reinforcement. Starting among Western trainers in the Pacific Northwest in reaction to rough-riding forms of training, natural horsemanship has become enormously popular in the United States since the 1980s. Training begins in a round pen, where the horse, working at liberty, is urged to circle under pressure from a swinging rope. When the horse signals submission to the trainer—NH theory regards licking the lips as a signal of submission—the trainer stops putting on pressure. The horse generally responds by coming to stand at the trainer's side, and the trainer makes that the safe place for him to be.

The trainer then teaches the horse to face and follow her, proceeds to sacking out and introducing tack, and then to a first ride. Experienced trainers can move this process along rapidly, riding a green or even a wild-caught horse within a few hours.

NH ground training emphasizes lightness, responsiveness, and respect for the trainer's personal space. Riding is done on a light or loose rein, though the heavy slobber straps typical in NH do weight the rein. Horses work off weight and leg aids.

Some clinicians—such as Monty Roberts, John Lyons, Pat Parelli, and Clinton Anderson—have become big names in the movement, holding clinics and courses; demonstrating at horse expos; and selling books, videos, and equipment. This commercial aspect disturbs some horsemen, and the clicker training community believes round penning to be training through fear, which they reject. Others, however, regard NH as a welcome revolution in Western horsemanship, which has turned away from older, more punitive and dangerous forms of horse breaking.
➤ *See also clicker training; "join up"*

NATIONAL SHOW HORSE

➤ Established as a breed in 1981, the National Show Horse (NSH) crosses the Arabian with the American Saddlebred to produce a flashy, exciting horse for the show ring. These beautiful horses are valued for their elevated movement, athletic ability, and brilliant presence. They are shown under saddle and in driving classes.
➤ *See also American Breeds, American Saddlebred; Arabian*

navel ill

➤ *See foaling; joint ill/navel ill*

navicular disease

Degeneration of the navicular bone, a tiny bone located between the coffin bone and the deep digital flexor tendon, along with damage to associated structures in the hoof. Wild horses rarely suffer from navicular disease, but it is common in domestic horses whose feet are too small in proportion to their weight, whose pastern angles are too steep, who are used for athletic activities not suitable for them, or who are kept unnaturally confined.

The main cause of navicular disease is not fully agreed upon, even by vets. Once the bone begins to break down, pain and lameness follow. Initially, the horse may seem occasionally tenderfooted in one or both front feet. As the disease progresses, he may stumble frequently and move with a short, choppy stride as he seeks to avoid putting his heels down. There is no cure for navicular disease, but early treatment can relieve symptoms and prevent further damage. Changes in exercise, special shoes, and sometimes arthritis medication can be effective. Surgery that severs nerves to the hoof is possible for advanced cases, but only as a last resort.

➤ *See also hoof; lameness; leg, of horse*

navigator (in driving)

In combined driving, the person who rides on the back of the vehicle. The navigator reminds the driver of course details, keeps track of time during the marathon and cones phases, and uses her weight to counterbalance the vehicle, keeping it from overturning. A navigator may also be called on to make emergency tack changes.

➤ *See also combined driving*

near side

The horse's left side, even when it's farther away from you. This terminology reflects the universal practice of handling horses from the left.

➤ *See also off side*

neat's-foot oil

A pale-yellow fatty oil made from the bones of cattle ("neat" is a centuries-old word for the domestic bovine). Neat's-foot oil softens stiff, new leather and helps prevent dryness and cracking. It will darken light-colored leather and can be used to stain tack to a deeper shade. Apply with clean rags until the

BUYER BEWARE WITH NAVICULAR DISEASE

A horse afflicted with navicular disease may frequently experience pain and lameness. This may motivate an owner to want to sell him, and there are ways to disguise the condition. The digital nerve can be cut, leaving the hoof without sensation and, hence, no pain. Look for two small scars, ½ to 1 inch (1.2–2.5 cm) long, above the heel bulbs of the front feet. Do not buy such a horse for hard work; the wear on the tendon, especially in the absence of pain to tell the horse when to stop, may cause the tendon to rupture.

desired shade is obtained. Check labels for petroleum additives, which will rot leather.

neck

The horse's neck is an important balancing mechanism and should be well proportioned to his body, without a pronounced crest. He should be able to flex his head easily from the poll and move his neck up and down and side to side freely. Proper neck conformation allows him to collect and extend himself as he moves. A short thick neck and heavy head are conformation faults in a saddle horse but advantageous to a draft horse, especially when he is starting to pull a heavy load.

➤ *See also conformation*

With normal or "ideal" conformation, the **neck** sits relatively high on the shoulder and the neck bones curve slightly at the bottom.

NECK-REINING

neck-reining A Western reining style in which the rider holds the reins in one hand (usually the left) and touches them to the horse's neck to signal a turn. The horse moves away from the rein, so if you want to turn left, you apply the right rein against the neck and press your right leg against the girth. Western horses are trained to respond primarily to leg and weight cues, with a very light rein.

➤ *See also aids; one-handed riding; Western riding*

neonatal isoerythrolysis (NI) A condition that arises when a foal is born with a blood type different from that of his dam. The antibodies he ingests while nursing attack his red blood cells, causing weakness, anemia, jaundice, and bloody urine. Fatal unless treated, NI appears a day or two after birth. An alternate source of colostrum must be found, and the mare should be hand-milked until her regular milk comes in. After three days the foal's intestines will no longer absorb the antibodies, so he can resume nursing from his dam.

Once a mare has given birth to a foal with NI, she should be bred only to stallions with compatible blood types.

➤ *See also foaling*

NEW FOREST PONY

A large riding and driving pony from the New Forest in southern England, where they roam in semi-wild herds. New Forest Ponies are friendly and docile, making them a favorite mount for children. Standing between 13.3 and 14.2 hands high, they are substantial, with long, sloping shoulders, deep bodies, and good legs. Action is straight, free, and active. They can be any solid color.

NEWFOUNDLAND PONY

A stocky, hardy pony descended from draft-type ponies brought to Newfoundland from the British Isles, now designated a heritage breed. Newfoundlands tend to have exceptionally docile temperaments and make good family pleasure ponies. Many reach 14.2 hands high and are strong enough to carry adult riders. They are usually black, gray, or brown, but roans are common and other colors appear. White markings are minimal and pinto coloring is not permitted in the registry. The extremely dense winter coat is often a very different color from the summer coat. In the summer, the thick mane falls to one side of the neck, but in the winter, it covers both sides. **Livestock Conservancy status: Critical**

nicking

1. Cutting the retractor muscles on the underside of the tail so that a high tail set can be achieved for the saddle seat show ring; a brutal practice, now illegal.

2. When two individuals produce an offspring superior to what would be expected by their mating; a term that has to do with genetics.

➤ *See also breeding; genetics*

nictitating membrane

➤ *See third eyelid*

night blindness
An inherited disorder predominantly affecting Appaloosas. Both parents must be carriers in order for the trait to show up, which it does fairly early on. Individuals with night blindness have difficulty seeing at night and may also have some impairment of day vision. The condition does not worsen over time, unlike moon blindness. The eyes of an affected horse look normal, and electronic tests are

necessary for diagnosis. There is no treatment for night blindness, and mares or stallions that have produced offspring with this trait should not be bred again.

➤ *See also equine recurrent uveitis (ERU); eyes*

night vision

➤ *See vision*

NORIC/NORIKER HORSE

An ancient Alpine draft breed. Norikers are agile, more lightweight than Percherons or Belgians, with small hooves and alert minds. They are used for forestry and farmwork, in parades and circuses, and also for meat production. Predominantly colored chestnut, bay, or black, about 10 percent have Appaloosa spots.

➤ *See also Haflinger*

NORTH AMERICAN SPOTTED DRAFT

A pinto draft breed first formalized in the United States in the 1990s. Horses can be of any draft blood mixture, with Percheron and Belgian being the most popular. Averaging 15 to 17 hands, they must have draft horse frame. Depth through the heart girth and flank are desirable. These horses tend to be a bit more athletic than many breeds and often used as riding horses. They are said to be "more suited for power than action." Pinto coloring is required; black and white, sorrel and white, and bay and white are the most common combinations.

Norwegian Fjord

➤ *See Fjord/Norwegian Fjord*

nosebag A bag that fits over a horse's muzzle and is fastened to his bridle or halter, in order to feed him. Nosebags are used when giving a working farm or carriage horse his lunch, or to feed horses when camping. They can also be used in group turnout settings to insure that individual horses are receiving their allotted rations, and to reduce fighting in the herd. In a situation like this, the whole herd gets nosebags put on at mealtime, the horse owner can go off and finish other chores, and then the nosebags are removed. Mesh nosebags are best for loose horses; if a horse tries to drink with one on, the water drains rapidly.

noseband The part of a halter or bridle that fits around the horse's nose, above the bit. Also called a cavesson.

➤ *See also bridle; cavesson; halter*

nose chain

➤ *See handling horses; lead shank*

nose nets Fine mesh nets that attach to a bridle or halter and fit over a horse's nose and mouth. They are intended to keep insects away, and many horsemen have found them to have a profound effect on head-shaking, which can be an almost insoluble problem that can render a horse unusable. Anecdotally, nose nets also appear to offer relief from coughing due to pollen allergies.

➤ *See also fly mask*

A NOSENET

nostrils Horses can't breathe through their mouths, as the soft palate at the roof of the mouth tends to drop, obstructing air flow. A light horse's nostrils should be wide, thin, and elastic so they expand for adequate air intake when working hard. Draft horses have small nostrils with thicker skin. They originated in cold climates, where part of nostril function was to protect the lungs from too much cold air.

Nostrils have another mechanism to warm the air, the "false pouch" (or, properly, the nasal diverticulum), a chamber just inside the nostril that protects the air aperture. The false pouch also allows the horse to snort or whistle, by blowing air through the pouch.
➤ *See also pulse and respiration; respiratory system*

novice An inexperienced rider. In most shows, the Novice division is for riders who have not competed very often. After winning several first-place ribbons or earning a certain number of points in specified shows, the rider graduates to higher levels of competition.
➤ *See also English riding; maiden class/maiden race; Western riding*

nuchal ligament The ligament that runs along the top of the horse's neck.

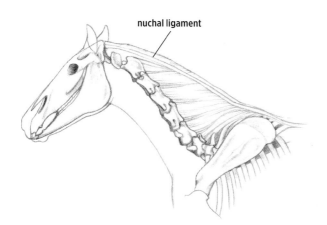

nuchal ligament

nurse mare A mare that nurses a foal not her own. Nurse mares are heavily used in Thoroughbred breeding, where artificial insemination is not allowed and where it is extremely important that the mare be rebred as early as possible. If a Thoroughbred broodmare has to travel to be bred, her valuable foal is transferred to a nurse mare. The nurse mare's own foal may go to auction, where foals are valuable for their hides and meat, or it may be sold locally to be bottle-raised.

Some rescue organizations focus on these "orphans"; they can be difficult and costly to raise and, without the social skills a mare imparts, can have behavior problems. If handled well and fed carefully, nurse mare foals can overcome their early handicaps and be successful horses.
➤ *See also orphan foal*

nursing hobbles A device applied to a nursing mare's hind legs when there is reason to believe she may kick the foal—for example, when she is being induced to take on an orphan. Hobbles are generally lined with fleece so they won't cut into the mare's legs, and they are used only until she accepts the foal she is expected to nurse. They have enough give to allow her to walk around the stall.
➤ *See also nurse mare*

nutrition
➤ *See feeding and nutrition*

oat hay, cautions Oat hay can be a suitable component of a horse's diet if it is cut before the seed heads mature. The mature straw is hard to digest and offers little nutritional value. It often causes gas colic, which can become life-threatening. Under certain growing conditions, oat hay may contain nitrates, which are harmful to horses.
➤ *See also feeding and nutrition; hay*

oats A grain that has long been staple food for horses, due to its high fiber. When fed whole, oats are less likely to form a solid mass in the gastrointestinal tract that could lead to impaction colic. Most oat varieties contain roughly 11 percent fiber and 12 percent protein.

Though long associated with horses, oats offer no particular nutritious advantage over other grains. One major disadvantage is that they raise blood sugar and can make a horse "hot" or overexcited. They are low in calcium and high in phosphorus; calcium must always be higher than phosphorus in the total ration.
➤ *See also feeding and nutrition*

obstacles, negotiating It is important for a horse to be comfortable going over, around, and through a variety of obstacles. It's important to train a horse at home so that you can safely ride on trails or in fields or compete in trail classes.

Obstacles can be constructed of poles on the ground, railroad ties forming a box or platform (covered with rubber mats), barrels, and many other objects. Gradually accustoming your horse to going through narrow spaces, through water, on and off platforms, and over poles will increase your confidence in each other. This training will also help when teaching your horse to load onto and unload from a trailer.

Work over obstacles can begin as ground work, and with horses too young to ride. It's a good way to get to know a horse, or to improve your relationship, and can have a big payoff later in the horse's career.
➤ *See also in-hand training; trail class; trail riding*

OCD
➤ *See osteochondritis dessicans (OCD)*

off Slightly lame, or behaving in an abnormally dull manner. The horse's gait may seem slightly asymmetrical, with the lameness difficult to pinpoint; or the horse

WESTERN TRAIL OBSTACLE

may be eating but displaying less-than-normal enthusiasm. A horse who is not eating is said to be "off his feed."

off billet The strap that anchors the cinch to the rigging on a Western saddle on the off (right) side; sometimes called an off-side billet. It is usually made of leather and measures 1 to 1.5 inches (2.5 – 4 cm) wide and between 18 inches and 2 feet (46 – 61 cm) long.

offset cannons
➤ *See bench knees*

off side The right side of a horse. The right side is called the off side, no matter which side is actually closer to you. Although horses are usually led and mounted from the near side, there is no reason they cannot be trained to be led and mounted from the off side as well. In some versatility competitions, mounting from the off side is one of the challenges.
➤ *See also near side*

off the bit A fully trained or "finished" Western horse is said to work "off the bit," because the rider exerts very little pressure on the mouth, relying primarily on the seat and legs as aids.

➤ *See also California-style bit; "straight up in the bridle"; vaquero; Western dressage*

off-track Thoroughbred (OTTB)

A Thoroughbred who has been retired from racing. Many OTTBs are young, sound, and athletic, with potential to go on to other careers, and they can be inexpensive. Choosing an OTTB takes care and judgment, and retraining one is not for every horseman, but in the right circumstances this can be a great option for getting an affordable, competitive horse.

oilseed meals A very concentrated protein extracted from seeds (for example, linseed, cottonseed, and soybean), which should be fed in limited amounts as a supplement to grains and hay.

➤ *See also feeding and nutrition; supplements*

older horses, care and use Older horses can provide years of enjoyment and productive use if cared for properly. A beginning rider will generally do better on an older horse with plenty of training and handling. A horse beyond middle age can still be an excellent investment, as a solid teacher or outstanding breeding animal.

Dental care becomes more important as a horse ages, as does fitness. Excess weight wears out joints; your aging horse will do better if he is kept near his ideal weight and gets regular exercise appropriate to his condition. As horses age, it becomes more difficult for them to return to fitness after a layoff, so it is best to find a way to work your older horse at least a couple of days a week, including in winter.

➤ *See also age; feeding and nutrition*

Olympic equestrian events The equestrian sports represented at the Olympic Games are Dressage, Jumping, and Eventing, which consists of three phases: dressage, show jumping, and cross-country. Medals are awarded for both individual and team performances. These are the only Olympic events in which men and women compete against each other on an equal basis. Women regularly win gold medals against male competitors. Horse sports were part of the ancient Olympic Games, and equestrian eventing has been part of the modern Olympics since the summer games in Stockholm in 1912.

➤ *See also United States Equestrian Federation (USEF); United States Equestrian Team (USET) Foundation; World Equestrian Games*

O-Mok-See

➤ *See gymkhana*

on deck The next rider to go into the ring in a competition is said to be "on deck."

one-handed riding/one-handed driving
While English riders usually keep two hands on the reins, Western riders generally ride with the reins in one hand. Also called neck-reining, one-handed riding leaves the other hand free for work. Some carriage driving techniques, such as the Achenbach system, require the driver to have reins in one hand, whip in the other. In driven dressage, the driver uses two hands most of the time but must execute some one-handed figures.

➤ *See also neck-reining*

one-on-one (penning) A Western event in which a single rider separates one cow from a small herd and pens it in a portable pen within the arena.

➤ *See also team penning*

on the bit Accepting and seeking a steady contact with the bit. A horse who is on the bit moves forward freely yet yields to the pressure of the bit with a softened neck, poll, and jaw. A horse will come on the bit when the rider's position is correct, when she is stimulating the right level of energy with her leg aids, and when she lightly receives that energy with her hands. It is a function of the entire ride, much more than just a headset.

➤ *See also above the bit; behind the bit; behind the vertical; collection; off the bit*

ON THE BIT

ABOVE THE BIT

BEHIND THE BIT

on the forehand Moving in a downhill fashion, with the horse placing disproportionate weight on his front legs as he moves. The goal of dressage, and other forms of training that emphasize maneuverability, is to teach the horse to rebalance and carry more of his weight on his hindquarters. This is a more athletic way of moving that increases a horse's strength over time and can preserve his soundness over many years of work.

➤ *See also aids; collection; turn on the forehand*

open-front blanket A blanket that has buckles or hook-and-loop fasteners across the chest.

➤ *See also blankets and blanketing; sheet*

open shows A show in which any breed can compete in the events.

➤ *See also individual show associations*

orphan foal A foal that has lost its mother during or shortly after birth; also a foal whose dam refuses to nurse it or cannot produce sufficient milk. Orphans can be fed either by a nurse mare, if one is available, or by formula, as long as the foal has gotten several feedings of colostrum. Colostrum can be obtained either from the foal's mother while she is alive or expressed from her udder after her death, or from another newly delivered mare. Otherwise, colostrum replacement must be administered if the foal is to survive.

A nurse mare is used for an orphaned foal when possible. A mare who has recently lost her own foal might be induced to accept the substitute, if the births are fairly close. If she is not inclined to nurse the orphan, applying Vicks VapoRub to her nostrils to prevent her smelling the strange foal or rubbing some of the mare's fresh afterbirth over the orphan may help her accept the foal as her own.

MILK REPLACER Foals should not be fed straight cow's milk. Although foal milk replacers are based on cow's milk, they have added nutrients to match a foal's requirements. Some also have probiotics to help digestion. Different formulations offer either more carbohydrates or more fat; foals whose guts cannot handle carbohydrates often do well with the high-fat formulations.

➤ *See foaling; nursing; nurse mare*

osteochondritis dessicans (OCD)

A developmental disorder in growing foals in which joint cartilage develops cracks and fissures. Although numerous factors come into play, OCD can be caused by overfeeding of high-protein and high-energy foods. Foals need a carefully balanced diet and plenty of exercise to develop strong bones. Too much protein can cause inflammation and interference with the normal development of cartilage into bone. A high-protein diet can also create weak spots in the legs of young horses, which can result in further inflammation, tearing, breaking, or twisting. Stress on vulnerable joints and growth plates can produce deformities, abnormal growth of the long bones, and lameness.

OTTB

➤ *See off-track thoroughbred (OTTB)*

outcrossing/outbreeding The mating of unrelated animals.

➤ *See also breeding; genetics; inbreeding*

"out in the country" leg conformation

➤ *See camped out*

outside (leg or rein) The leg or rein on the outside of the space one is working in, or toward the outside of a circle.

➤ *See also aids; hands, rider's; inside (leg or rein); legs, use of when riding*

"over and under" quirt A long, ropelike whip that is sometimes used in timed Western events. It can be held against the leg, where even a slight swing can be effective in urging a horse forward.

➤ *See also quirt*

over at the knee/buck-kneed A conformation flaw in which the knees look as though they are slightly bent forward or even buckled. Buck knees, while unattractive, are not as serious as the opposite fault, called "back at the knees."

➤ *See also back at the knee; conformation; leg, of horse*

overbite

➤ *See parrot mouth*

overcheck A check rein that fastens to the crownpiece of a driving bridle and holds the horse's head in an elevated position. It is used in racing and fine harness driving competition, rarely in carriage or draft driving.

overfacing Putting a horse at a jump or other obstacle that's too difficult for his current level of fitness or training. Overfacing can damage a horse's self-confidence and make progression in his training difficult. Increase the difficulty of obstacles very gradually. Your horse's training should be a long string of successful experiences, building in him the feeling that obstacles are easy and that he can do anything.

overmounted A term used to describe a rider on a horse who is too strong or too temperamental for that rider. If you find yourself overmounted, you owe it to yourself and to the horse to seek help from a professional trainer. Being well matched to your mount increases your chances of riding safely, enjoying yourself, and continuing to learn.

overo A pinto marking in which the white is irregular and scattered or splashy. The white usually does not cross the back of the horse between his withers and tail. At least one and often all four legs are dark; head markings are distinctive, often bald-faced, apron-faced, or bonnet-faced; the tail is usually one color.

➤ *See also American Breeds, American Paint; bald-faced; pinto; tobiano; tovero*

overreaching A fault in moving in which the hind foot catches the heel of the front foot on the same side before the forefoot leaves the ground. Also called grabbing, overreaching often results in lost shoes. Bell boots prevent lost shoes and injury to the heel.

overtracking At a walk or trot, placing the hind foot beyond the hoofprint of the same side's forefoot. Unlike overreaching, which is a fault, overtracking is a desirable motion that indicates good use of the hindquarters.

➤ *See also overreaching; tracking up*

OVERO COLORING

ovulation
➤ *See breeding; estrus*

oxer
A spread jump with a front (the take-off side of the obstacle) and a back (landing side) element that are either equal in height, or with the front element slightly lower than the back. Normally a single pole (never a plank, gate, or wall) is used for the back element. An uneven oxer is called a ramped oxer; when the two rails are even it is called a square oxer.
➤ *See also spread; "Types of Jumps," page 192*

oxibendazole
A deworming agent effective against small strongyles. It is sold under the brand name Anthelcide EQ.
➤ *See also strongyles*

Oxyuris equi
➤ *See pinworms*

pace A gait in which the front and back leg on the same side advance simultaneously; also called the hard pace. The two left feet strike the ground together and then the two right. Some horses pace as well as trot, but generally a horse does one or the other. Sometimes harness racers who are slow at the trot can be successfully switched to pacing, but changing from the pace to the trot is uncommon. The pace is generally a little faster than the trot.

Pacers were ridden in colonial times, but nowadays the gait is seen almost exclusively in horses trained for harness racing and in Icelandics (which have a "flying pace"). The pace is not considered an easy gait to ride; it is as bouncy as a trot, and the action throws the rider abruptly from side to side. Only at extreme speed does the pace smooth out and become comfortable.

➤ *See also gait; skeid; Standardbred*

pacer A Standardbred who naturally paces rather than trots.

➤ *See also pace; Standardbred*

pacing Walking incessantly along the perimeter of a pasture fence or around and around in a stall; also called fence walking or stall walking. Pacing, though often called a vice, is a stereotypy, a repetitive behavior that is usually a sign of boredom or distress.

➤ *See also stereotypy*

pack burro racing A Western sport in which runners leading burros outfitted with packsaddles and prospector's gear race on courses from 15 to 30 miles (24–48 k) long. Burros range from standard donkeys to the American Mammoth Jackstock. A competitive burro should be tough, fit, and easy to handle.

packhorse, using Equines were used as pack animals long before they were ridden and driven. Some famous breeds now used for sport—Cleveland Bays, Fell Ponies, Dales Ponies—were initially used as pack animals. Pack animals remain essential for bringing goods into mountainous locations in many countries and for some military transport. Four hooves, especially if attached to a mule, can go places no wheeled vehicle can, TV commercials notwithstanding.

Pack animals are used for recreation and hunting. They remain the best way to transport camping goods into remote locations and to transport big game out. A packhorse can carry 20 percent of his bodyweight, including the pack saddle; a mule may be able to carry

A **pacer** warms up before a race.

a bit more. Pack animals carrying food can be loaded heavily on setting out, since their load will lighten as the food is consumed.

If choosing between two horses for packing, pick the shorter one. This makes loading much easier. And don't overlook burros, ponies, and minis as pack animals. While they can't carry as much as a big animal, two or three smaller equines can share the burden. Many owners of small equines like to take them hiking. Everybody gets exercise, and the animals are of real use.

If choosing a string of animals to do serious packing, pick mules. Every mule had a mare for a mother, and they instinctively follow and stay near horses. It's common practice among outfitters to tether the horses and let the mules go free, as they will not stray far from their horse leader.

A pack horse is outfitted with a packsaddle, and there are many kinds, ranging from training or day packs, which lie directly on the animal's back; companion packs, which have a thick divided pad to keep weight off the animal's spine and breeching and breast collars; sawbuck packsaddles, which provide complete spinal relief; and saddle packs that drape over a full-size Western saddle. Owners of minis might want to check out the packsaddles used on dogs and goats to find something the right size.

Panniers (large pouches generally made out of sturdy, waterproof fabric) or pack boxes (made of bear-proof metal) are fastened to a sawbuck packsaddle. Styrofoam inserts can convert a pannier into a cooler. Securing panniers to a pack saddle the traditional way

takes knowledge of knots and ropes; the occasional packer can purchase a complete system ready to pack, with built-in side-load and top-load compartments.

The load should be balanced evenly on both sides of the horse. This prevents soreness and keeps the pack from slipping, which can cause even experienced horses to buck or bolt. As the load changes over the course of the trip, you may need to redistribute the weight or add a rock or two to the lighter pack for balance. Contents should be arranged so that nothing rattles or clunks, which could spook the packhorse.

A packhorse or mule should be trained before the trip to lead from horseback or on foot, following a few steps directly behind you. This may be essential on narrow parts of the trail. Don't hold the packhorse's lead rope in your hand while riding. Use a breakaway string attached to a D-ring on your saddle. A breakaway string is made of heavy-duty cord such as parachute cord; it is strong but will break at about 500 pounds (227 kg) of pressure, releasing a packhorse who rears back or stumbles. Using a breakaway string frees both your hands to manage your own horse, and prevents the pack horse from pulling you out of the saddle.

packing, in shoeing
Material, usually silicone caulking, used to fill the space between a full pad and the sole of the hoof. Packing prevents dirt from being trapped under the pad, and may contain antibiotics and medication. Newer hoof packing formulations use a rubberlike liquid that is applied directly to the clean, dry sole. It sets in minutes, forming a flexible pad that adheres to the foot; some of these so-called pour-on pads can be used on unshod hooves.

pad, in shoeing
Material, either leather or plastic, applied between the shoe and the hoof. Rim pads leave the sole and frog exposed and are used for shock absorption. Tube-type rim pads prevent snow buildup. Wedge pads raise the heel to bring it into balance. Full pads cover the entire sole, protect it, and keep it clean; they may provide some shock absorption. Bubble pads have a molded dome in the center on the ground side, designed to keep snow from accumulating. Note that full pads and bubble pads reduce traction. Full pads also prevent the hoof from breathing and trap moisture next to the sole, which can weaken it and allow bacteria, fungus, and yeast to grow.

PACKHORSE

A **palomino** should be "the color of a United States gold coin," according to the breed standard, but there is some variation. The horse on the left is a Palomino Appaloosa; note the patterning on the rump.

paddling A characteristic movement of horses with turned-in toes, who often swing their forelegs outward when trotting. Paddling (also called "winging out") stresses the joints and may lead to lameness. This movement, which arises from a conformation fault, is distinct from the graceful, flowing outward swing of the feet, called termino, desired in Peruvian Horses.
➤ *See also dishing; termino*

paddock A fenced area near a barn or stable that is used for exercise. Paddocks can range in size from quite small to an acre; larger areas are referred to as pastures. "Corral" is a Western term for paddock.
➤ *See also corral; pasture, horses on*

paddock boots Ankle-high boots used for riding. They have a heel and a smooth sole, and come in lace-up, zippered, and pull-on styles.
➤ *See also boots (for rider)*

paint
➤ *See American Breeds, American Paint*

palfrey Archaic term for a light riding horse, intended particularly for a lady's use.

palisade worms
➤ *See large strongyles*

palomino A bright golden color ranging from pale honey to deep copper. The mane must be at least 85 percent white or silver; white markings on legs and face are permitted. Because palomino is a color, not a breed, any breed of horse that is the correct color can be registered with the Palomino Horse Breeders of America (PHBA).
➤ *See also color, of horse*

palpation Examining or exploring by touch. Palpation can refer to either an external examination (checking legs for warmth or swelling) or an internal

RIDING IN A PARADE

Horses are many people's favorite part of a parade, and a great way for horsemen to show off their horses. Yes, they are slow, but that doesn't mean they aren't demanding. Parades are noisy and full of the unexpected. Horses may be placed in the lineup near fire engines, bagpipe or brass bands, or unfamiliar animals. A parade horse needs to be reliably quiet around these and other hazards, including sirens, darting small children, and objects being thrown. If a horse spooks, there may be no place for him to run without injuring spectators.

Parade horses, whether ridden or driven, should be bombproofed (desensitized), using some of the techniques developed for police horses. Parades are great exposure for horses, and can be good advertising for your business or your breed.

Danish **para-equestrian** and dressage champion Sinna Tange Kaastrup warms up on her New Forest Pony Labbenhus Snoevs at the 2010 World Equestrian Games in Kentucky.

examination (checking for uterine problems). Internal palpation is a risky procedure due to the danger of rectal tears, which can lead to fatal complications, even when performed by highly experienced veterinarians. Be sure to discuss the necessity of the procedure with your veterinarian, and weigh the risks against the expected benefits. Despite the popularity of rectal pregnancy exams and the new ultrasound technology, these are not always the best choice for all mares.

P&R
➤ See pulse and respiration

panic snap A clip for a cross-tie or trailer tie that can be opened with one hand in an emergency. Some panic snaps are designed to release if a horse falls or gets hung up; excessive weight or force triggers release.
➤ See also bull snap

parade class A Western show-ring class for high-stepping horses like Saddlebreds, Morgans, and Hackneys. Tack is heavily ornamented with silver. Horses are judged on manners and beauty, and are shown at an animated walk and a parade gait. Parade is a United States Equestrian Federation (USEF) discipline.

parade gait A straight, square, true, high-prancing trot that is balanced and collected, and no faster than 5 miles (8 km) per hour.

para-equestrian A discipline for people with physical disabilities, sanctioned by the United States Equestrian Federation (USEF) and the Fédération Equestre Internationale (FEI). While many people with disabilities can compete on a par with unimpaired equestrians, particularly in driving, para-equestrian opens the door to those with severe physical disabilities. Disciplines include dressage, driving, and vaulting. Competitions are leveled through a profile system that takes into account degrees of impairment. Para-equestrian has been part of the Paralympic Games since 1996.

paralytic myoglobinuria
➤ See azoturia/Monday morning disease/tying up

Parascaris equorum
➤ See ascarid

parasites Worms, flies, mites, mosquitoes, gnats, ticks, and lice. All horses are vulnerable to parasites, whose presence ranges from merely annoying to dangerous or even fatal. Common internal parasites include bloodworms (also called palisade worms or large strongyles), bot flies, lungworms, pinworms, roundworms, small strongyles, tapeworms, and warbles. Signs of intestinal parasites may include general debility or unthriftiness; a harsh, dull coat; unexplained bouts of colic; a potbelly; and loss of appetite.

All horses have some internal parasites all the time, but a conscientious deworming program and good stable hygiene can keep the infestation under control and keep your horse healthy.

As for external parasites, flying insects can drive a horse to distraction, preventing him from feeding and causing injuries from kicking and biting at the pests. Individual insect bites can be painful; hundreds of them can cause severe blood loss and open the door to skin infections. Many external pests, such a ticks, also carry diseases.

DEALING WITH PARASITES Good stable hygiene can reduce pest problems considerably. Manure management, judicious use of insecticides, pest strips and traps, and the cleaning up of damp or swampy areas are ways to cut down on the parasite population. If there are cows on the property, rotating grazing areas between cows and horses can also help, as many parasites are host-specific.

Apple cider vinegar acts as a fly repellent when added to feed or water—mix 4 to 8 ounces (118–236 mL) with the horse's daily grain, starting with a few drops to accustom the horse to the taste and determine the minimum effective amount for each horse. Flies will still land but won't bite, perhaps because the horse smells unpleasant to them. Vinegar can also be used externally on the coat to repel flies.

Many horse owners use dried garlic products as a feed additive to repel insects. This is controversial, as ingesting alliums—the onion/garlic family—can cause anemia in horses. That said, many extremely reputable companies sell dried garlic products, and thousands of horsemen use them without apparent ill effect. Some horses may be more sensitive than others, or there may be many horses out there with undetected, low-level anemia. Anecdotally, garlic appears to work better against some types of insects than others. Some

people whose horses develop sweet itch find it to be a godsend; others don't feel that the effects are worth the risk. Use of garlic is a judgment call. If you do use it, take care not to exceed recommended dosages.
➤ *See also deworming; individual parasites and medications; predator wasp*

park horse A horse ridden saddle seat. The saddle seat style derives not only from plantation riding in the American South but also from upper-class riding in city parks in Europe, hence the name.

The criteria used for evaluating park horses include outstanding refinement and elegance, suitability of horse to rider, manners, expression, willingness, quality, and gaits performed with brilliance on command. A park horse is high-stepping and handsome, a mount to draw the eye of onlookers.
➤ *See also English riding; pleasure horse*

parrot mouth A mismatch of upper and lower jaw in which the lower jaw is abnormally short and the upper teeth protrude; also called "overbite." An overbite greater than the width of half a tooth is considered an unsoundness, as it can interfere with a horse's ability to eat and keep up his energy and weight.
➤ *See also dental problems; sow mouth/monkey mouth; teeth and age*

pasitrote

1. Another name for the fox trot.

2. A term used by Peruvian Horse riders to refer to an undesirable, uneven diagonal gait with four beats.

➤ *See also fox trot; paso llano; Peruvian Horse; sobreandando*

Paso Fino *(see next page)*

paso llano A running walk performed by the Peruvian Horse. A four-beat gait, the paso llano is evenly timed and falls between a pace and a trot. There is little or no head nod; instead, the horse travels with an upward and outward rotation of the front legs from the shoulder, called termino. The footfall pattern is: RH, RF, LH, LF.
➤ *See also pasitrote; Peruvian Horse; sobreandando*

An easy-gaited breed of great beauty and style developed in the Caribbean; there are different Paso breeds in the Dominican Republic, Cuba, Puerto Rico, Colombia, and Venezuela, each called by its national name. *Note:* The Peruvian Horse (formerly Peruvian Paso) is not a Paso Fino; they are distinct breeds.

A small to medium-sized horse (14–15 hands high) that can be of any color except Appaloosa, the Paso Fino has an upright, arched neck; a well-laid-back shoulder; and fine, delicate-looking legs. The mane and tail are long and full.

The gaits are unique. The paso fino gait is slower than a walk, but the feet move rapidly, with clear, distinct footfalls. Though the paso fino is now considered a show-ring gait, Paso Finos once carried large men for hours at this gait as they rode over their plantations.

The paso corto is a relaxed, medium-speed gait about as fast as a jog; it is ideal for trail riding, though there is a show-ring version called the performance corto. The paso largo is the extended form of the gait, performed at speeds ranging from a canter to a full gallop; Pasos can also canter and gallop.

Paso Finos are common in Puerto Rico and Central America, where they are used for ranch work. In the United States they are used for trail, pleasure, and showing. Easy keepers, they have great individual personalities and bond strongly with their owners.

➤ *See also amble; gait; gaited horse; Peruvian Horse; running walk*

passage A collected trot with the hindquarters well engaged and the forehand elevated. The steps are high and the horse springs from one diagonal pair of legs to the other, appearing to be in slow motion. Passage (pronounced pa-SAHGE) is a natural gait that may be exhibited by excited horses at liberty, yet it is one of the more difficult and thrilling movements performed by high-level dressage horses.

➤ *See also airs above the ground; Classical High School; dressage*

paste dewormer A premeasured dose of deworming medication that comes in a ready-to-administer syringe.

➤ *See also deworming*

pastern The angled part of the horse's lower leg, between the hoof and the fetlock. The pasterns, which act as the primary shock absorber for the legs, should be well-proportioned and set at approximately a 45- to 55-degree angle in the front legs and a 49- to 59-degree angle in the rear. Short, upright pasterns can mean a jolting ride and eventual damage to the horse's feet and legs, while long or sloping ones are weaker and prone to strain and injury.

➤ *See also conformation; leg, of horse*

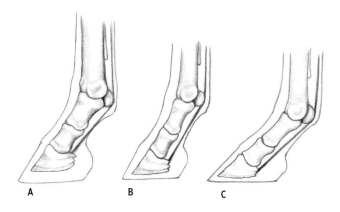

A. ideal pastern; B. upright pastern; C. sloping pastern

PASSING ETIQUETTE IN THE RING

Avoid passing on the outside (between the horse ahead of you and the rail); doing so places you and your horse in danger.

If you must pass on the outside, let the rider of the horse you are passing know you are passing by saying "Rail" loudly. (Giving a warning is a good idea even when passing on the inside; for that, simply say "Inside.")

When passing a horse who is coming toward you, remember the rule "Left shoulder to left shoulder" and stay to the right of oncoming traffic.

pasture, horses on Horses are usually happiest when turned out on grass, with a couple of equine buddies and sufficient shelter against the wind and rain. Pastured horses are less likely to suffer from respiratory or gastrointestinal ailments than those confined to stalls all day. They get more exercise and keep fitter. The owner avoids the labor of mucking out stalls and sweeping floors. Even in a harsh climate most horses can spend all winter outdoors, as long as they have access to some type of shelter and adequate food.

However, there are certain disadvantages to keeping a horse on pasture. Pastured horses must be checked at least twice daily, partly just to make sure they're still inside the fence! Injuries are more common, as horses can hurt each other while playing or establishing dominance. Too much grass can make a horse fat and lazy, and too much spring grass can cause colic or laminitis. There is also the problem of catching a horse who isn't interested in being caught.

Pastures need safe, sturdy fencing and must be free of poisonous plants and other hazards such as old farm equipment or hidden debris. Horses are very hard on grass—they're heavy, have sharp hooves, and eat all the time. Pastures must be large enough, or rested often enough, to support the number of horses kept on them. Over-grazing compacts the soil, encourages the growth of nonpalatable weeds, and can lead to erosion and long-term damage.

➤ *See also grass toxicity*

pattern A predetermined series of movements used to educate and evaluate the skills of horse, handler, or rider. A showmanship instructor may run students through patterns similar to those used in the show ring, in order to teach the skills necessary to excel in a given division. Riding instructors often combine movements like circles, figure eights, and serpentines; changes of gaits or leads; and work without stirrups into patterns that teach students how to handle their horses safely in a variety of situations. Inherent to such use of patterns is the fact that the skills tested are vital to safe handling of horses from the ground (such as stopping, walking, trotting, backing, and turning a horse in hand) and while riding.

Patterns used in competition range from those used for showmanship to the highly complex patterns used in reining competitions or dressage. Judges use patterns to separate the truly skilled handlers and riders from those trained only to have good personal form or equitation. It takes significant skill and coordination of aids to maneuver a horse, whether mounted or from the ground, through most patterns used in competition.
➤ *See also English riding; equitation; school figures; showmanship classes; Western riding*

pavement, riding on Pavement is slippery, especially for horses wearing shoes. Horses have much better traction on grass and dirt—even dry pavement is a tricky surface for your horse to negotiate. When riding along a road, stay on the shoulder when possible. If you can't avoid riding on pavement, do so at a walk. If your horse is barefoot and you frequently ride on pavement, consult your farrier. Your horse may need shoes, as pavement can wear down his hooves. Ask about ways to increase traction, such as adding borium to the shoe. You might also consider using hoof boots.
➤ *See also boots (for horse)*

pawing Horses naturally paw, digging at the ground with a front hoof when impatient, eager, and/or under restraint. It's very easy for a horse owner to confirm the habit by giving a horse what he wants, such as food or release, while he is pawing. It takes great self-discipline to outwait the pawing horse and give him what he wants only when he stops pawing. He may only pause briefly; leap on that opportunity. Clicker training can be helpful in eradicating this habit.

PAWING

Bear in mind, though, that pawing is one of the least dangerous expressions of frustration, compared, for example, to stall kicking. If you can't prevent the horse from developing the habit in the first place by giving him as much freedom as possible, and/or toys to play with, this may be one to just live with, provided the horse is not wearing down his hooves or pawing near a wire fence. Install rubber mats in areas where the horse may dig a dangerous hole, and just ignore him. Old-fashioned advice to put a chain on his leg, so that he bashes himself while pawing, seems extreme. Why risk injury for something that is not actually harmful?

Pawing can be a sign of colic or other discomfort, or imminent labor for a pregnant mare. Any unusual pawing should be watchfully evaluated.
➤ *See also stereotypy*

peanut pusher/peanut roller Terms used to describe show horses who work with their heads much lower than their withers, giving the appearance of pushing or rolling peanuts across the arena with their noses. This frame became popular in the 1980s when winners at high levels of competition worked in this manner. It was predominant in Western pleasure and horsemanship classes; however, it also was seen among some breeds in hunter classes. Throughout the 1990s, organizations that set rules for the show ring defined acceptable standards for the frame of performance horses. The most commonly accepted standard now is maintaining a frame in which the poll is carried no lower than the withers.

pecking order, among horses
The social hierarchy in a group of horses. Horses are herd animals whose social order is arranged in a hierarchy, or "pecking order," of dominant and passive animals. Horses establish dominance through behaviors ranging from laying back ears to biting and kicking. Each time animals are removed from or introduced into a herd, pecking order must be reestablished.

The top horse eats and drinks first and will drive lower-ranked individuals away, so when feeding a group of horses, spread out the hay so that all have access. Introduce newcomers slowly, preferably from an adjoining pasture at first. If the new horse accepts the current pecking order, his transition to the herd will probably be smooth. But if he challenges the leader, there could be some serious kicking and biting as they sort things out.

Most interactions are nonviolent, however. Threats constitute 80 percent of aggressive encounters between horses, and in general these are mild, such as pinning the ears or extending the neck; a wild stallion has only to lower his head to get a mare to move. Threats are frequent, averaging 1.5 per hour per horse. Once a stable hierarchy is established, the threats often become extremely subtle.

This social structure has implications for the horse owner. Horses are keenly aware of tiny details of body language, and are used to testing hierarchy to see if the power structure has changed. It's important to establish yourself as the dominant partner. This can be difficult for gentle people. Bring some awareness into your patterns of movement around your horse. Ask him to move out of your way, rather than moving out of his. Violence is not necessary, but if you feel you are in danger of being dominated, carry a whip. Many horses will instantly recover their good behavior, as the mere presence of a whip serves as a dominance threat.
➤ *See also body language, of horses; punishment*

pedigree
➤ *See breeding; genetics*

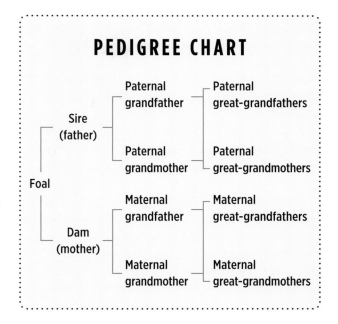

peel out A term used in cutting classes to indicate separating one or more cows from a herd.
➤ *See also cutting; team penning*

Pelham bit A combination bit requiring two sets of reins. The Pelham acts like a snaffle if the upper reins are employed. The lower reins, attached to the shanks, create leverage action. Pelhams may be jointed or bar bits, and some have small ports.
➤ *See also bit; bridle; double bridle*

PELHAM BIT

pelleted feed Pelleted feeds come in three types: grains, hay, and complete pellets that contain both hay and grain as well as vitamins and minerals. Hay pellets are ideal for horses who have trouble eating hay: those with bad teeth, many older horses, or individuals that have developed respiratory problems from eating hay. This feed is convenient to store and measure, and there is little waste. Horses on pellets don't get hay bellies and don't produce much manure, due to the concentrated nature of the feed.

The disadvantage to pellets is the lack of bulk, which the horse needs to feel satisfied and to maintain bowel regularity. Many pellet-fed horses chew wood in an effort to increase their roughage. This habit usually tapers off as the horse adjusts to the smaller portions, but you should be careful when turning a pellet-fed horse out on grass or giving supplemental hay. His stomach will have shrunk somewhat and won't be able to handle a sudden intake of unaccustomed roughage.
➤ *See also feeding and nutrition*

pen A turnout area for a horse, usually measuring no more than 50 feet (15.2 m) square, that provides a horse with outdoor living space. Because pens are small, they usually have no grass and do not allow the horse sufficient room to exercise. Pens can be surrounded by permanent fencing or created by putting together portable, metal-barred panels. In the case of the latter, extreme care should be taken when selecting the panels to ensure that horses cannot get their legs caught between the bars. The panels also need to be high enough to prevent a horse from jumping or climbing over them.
➤ *See also round pen, round penning*

penis A male horse has a retractable penis, which is housed in a sheath of skin. When urinating or mating, the male extends the penis.
➤ *See also diverticulum; sheath cleaning; smegma*

penning
➤ *See team penning*

performance class Show-ring classes in which the performance of the horse is judged, as opposed to his conformation and turnout or the performance of the rider.
➤ *See also English riding; equitation; Western riding*

PERFORMANCE CLASSES

ENGLISH PERFORMANCE

- Dressage
- Eventing (combined training)
- Hunter/jumper classes
- Saddle seat or hunter pleasure classes
- Park horse
- Show horse

WESTERN PERFORMANCE

- Cutting
- Working cow horse
- Trail
- Western pleasure
- Western riding or reining

---

periodic ophthalmia
➤ *See equine recurrent uveitis (ERU)*

perlino coloring Almost white with a rust-colored mane and tail.
➤ *See also color, of horse; genetics*

pest control Barns and stables are attractive to flying insects and rodents. Equine parasites depend on manure to complete their life cycle, so scrupulously cleaning stalls and pens and composting manure can really cut down on those pests. Flies can be controlled with sticky traps, baited water traps, or predator wasps. Pesticides can be useful if applied with caution, but they also kill beneficial insects and can harm people, horses, and other animals.

Rodents spread disease, spoil feed, create fire hazards by chewing wires, and destroy tack. Cats and traps are the best ways to handle a rodent problem. Feed bins and storage areas must be tightly sealed around lids and doors to keep mice and rats away.
➤ *See also deworming; parasites; predator wasp*

PERCHERON

A large draft horse from La Perche, a district of France. Percherons are generally black or gray, and lack the feathering characteristic of Clydesdales. Percherons are making a quiet comeback for work on small farms, for logging, and as carriage horses. With their long, wide backs, they are often used by bareback riders in the circus, where they are called Rosinbacks because of the rosin used on their backs for traction. This breed is noted for its free, elegant movement and is frequently crossed with light horses such as Thoroughbreds to make a heavy hunter or sport horse.

➤ *See also draft horse*

PERUVIAN HORSE

An easy-gaited horse from Peru, formerly known as the Peruvian Paso. Standing 14 to 15 hands high, the Peruvian Horse is deep and powerfully built, with an arched neck slightly heavier than in most light breeds. A wide range of solid colors is accepted; extensive white markings are undesirable. The Peruvian Horse's gaits are the flat walk, the paso llano, and sobreandando. The action is marked by the characteristic of termino, a swinging motion of the front leg from the shoulder. This breed offers an exceptionally comfortable ride. Peruvian Horses are brilliant and spirited yet easy to handle and ride.

➤ *See also amble; flat-footed walk; gait; gaited horse; Paso Fino; paso llano; sobreandando*

phenylbutazone (bute) A common horse medication used to reduce swelling and pain; also known by the trade name Butazolidin. Bute is relatively safe for horses and can be useful in managing injuries and lameness under veterinary supervision. It is usually obtained through a veterinarian, but many barns have extra bute on hand, and it is frequently used without veterinary consultation. Because it alleviates pain, horses are often given a dose before racing or showing; organizations have rules about how much bute can be present in a horse's bloodstream during an event. Without the feedback of pain, unsound horses on bute may overexercise and worsen the condition.

Like most nonsteroidal anti-inflammatories, bute negatively affects the digestive tract and may contribute to ulcers and colic. Young horses are most susceptible to kidney and liver damage from bute, but all horses react individually to it; therefore, it must be used with caution. Bute is available in oral syringes, tablets, or powder. Syringes are easy to use, but tablets and powder are much cheaper and can be given in a horse's feed (though the bute may need to be disguised with something like applesauce). Bute is best used as a temporary measure, as it is destructive to joints and can actually make arthritis worse in the long run.

Warning: People should never take bute as a substitute for ibuprofen or aspirin; it can cause a fatal condition called aplastic anemia.

➤ *See also "Drugs and Horses," page 95*

PHF

➤ *See Potomac horse fever (PHF)*

phosphorus The most important mineral in your horse's diet, along with calcium. Together, phosphorus and calcium build strong bones and teeth. Because phosphorus is poorly absorbed from forage sources, it is usually added to concentrates, while calcium is obtained from hay and other forage. It's important to balance the two minerals so that they are absorbed by the body and used effectively. Too much grain can impair calcium absorption and hinder proper skeletal development in growing foals. A severe calcium-phosphorus imbalance can deform the bones of even mature horses.

➤ *See also feeding and nutrition; supplements; vitamins*

photic headshaking A condition in which a horse shakes his head repeatedly for no apparent reason. Usually the headshake is vertical, but it can also be horizontal or rotary. This adult-onset condition usually appears between ages seven and nine, most often with geldings. The horse appears to have facial pain, may rub his nose on the grass as if trying to dislodge something, and may strongly prefer to remain indoors during the day. The trigeminal nerve appears to be involved. Triggers include bright light, spring/summer, and exercise; these factors can render a strongly affected horse essentially useless.

Veterinary care includes a thorough exam to rule out head, neck, and airway issues, as well as an ear exam. If no other cause emerges, there are a number of things to try, including a face mask with an ultraviolet filter, turnout at night, riding indoors, and nose nets. Nutritional supplements include melatonin, magnesium, lysine, and vitamin E. Some people have a degree of success with these approaches. Medications include cyproheptadine and carbamaze. Both act on the brain and can cause lethargy or colic. Surgery on the trigeminal nerve is an option, but it may make the horse worse, so much so as to necessitate euthanasia. This is an unpleasant and possibly painful condition for a horse to live with.

photosensitization More serious than sunburn, photosensitization occurs when a horse has eaten certain plants (including alsike clover, dried buckwheat, St. John's wort, and perennial ryegrass) that damage unpigmented skin cells, usually around the eyes and muzzle or where the horse has white markings. Liver damage can also trigger photosensitization. The damaged skin tissue reacts to ultraviolet rays by releasing histamines, which lead to swelling and itching under the skin. Outer layers of skin will peel and then begin to blister and scab over. If untreated, a horse with this condition can go into shock.

The first step to take is get the horse out of the sunlight. He can be turned out at night, but he needs to be protected during the day. Your veterinarian may prescribe antibiotics and antihistamines; corticosteroids can also help. Keep the horse away from plants that cause photosensitization, or remove those plants from the pasture.

physitis Inflammation of the physes (growth plates) of still-growing horses. The condition can lead to leg deformities, contracted tendons, or abnormal growths. It often results from overfeeding a foal or young horse in an attempt to stimulate rapid growth.

piaffe A high, collected trot in place, characterized by an extended period of suspension, seen in upper-level dressage. It is the ultimate example of collection, in which a simple release of hand allows the horse to smoothly move forward into the passage and eventually into a working trot. Piaffe helps develop back muscle and roundness, and may be performed in hand or under saddle; at the Spanish Riding School it is done in hand with the horse tethered between two pillars.

➤ *See also collection; Lipizzan; passage*

picketing/staking out Tying a horse to a rope about 25 feet (7.6 m) long attached to a picket stake, a piece of rebar 2 feet (0.6 m) long with a ring welded into the top, which is driven into the ground. The rope is attached with swivel snap so that it will swivel around the stake rather than wrap around it. Horses are tied either with a halter or with a half-hobble on a front foot.

Picketing is not as safe as using a highline. Picketed horses can get rope burns. Also, most horses can pull out a picket stake if panicked, which leaves them loose with a metal projectile attached to them. If you plan to picket your horse, teach him to accept restraint, including ropes winding around his legs.

➤ *See also highline; hobbles*

PIAFFE

picking out feet Cleaning dirt from the feet. When doing this, be sure to scrape the hoof pick away from your face so that you don't accidentally flick dirt or manure into your eye.
➤ *See also grooming; hoof*

piebald A black-and-white pinto.
➤ *See also color, of horse; pinto; skewbald*

pigeon-toed
➤ *See toed-in legs, toed-out legs*

pig-eyed A horse with small eyes. A pig-eyed horse is generally considered less attractive than a large-eyed horse and may have somewhat limited peripheral vision, making him more prone to shying.

piggin string A small rope for hog-tying calves and steers in roping events. Both hind legs and one foreleg must be tied. Riders carry the piggin string coiled in their teeth, with one end tucked into the belt, while they use the lariat. After roping the animal, they dismount and use the piggin string to tie its legs.

pinch test A way to measure a horse's hydration level. Grasp a fold of skin in the neck or shoulder area and pull it gently away from the muscle. When you release it, the fold of skin should still be visible for a couple of seconds. A marked peak after that point indicates some degree of dehydration. If the fold is still visible after 5 or 10 seconds, your horse is probably severely dehydrated and may need veterinary care.
➤ *See also dehydration*

pinto A horse with large splotches of white and another color (usually black, bay, or chestnut). The pinto colors are piebald (black and white) and skewbald (any other color and white); the pinto patterns include overo, tobiano, and tovero. The lowercase word "pinto" relates strictly to coloring. Pinto registries exist, however, and a horse of any breed can be registered as a Pinto if his coloring is correct. It is not uncommon for horses registered as American Paints to also be registered as Pintos, increasing the number of shows they can enter.
➤ *See also color, of horse; overo; American Breeds, American Paint; piebald; skewbald; tobiano; tovero*

pinworms (*Oxyuris equi*) An internal parasite that inhabits the large intestine and cause intense itching around the rectum, where the female migrates to lay her eggs. Pinworms are gray, yellow, or white and can be as long as 6 inches (15 cm). An infected horse may rub the hair off his tail trying to relieve the discomfort. A good dewormer will take care of pinworms, but stalls and pens should be carefully cleaned to get rid of eggs that may have stuck to walls, floors, and bedding. Pinworms are more common in horses kept in small areas than those pastured in roomy fields.
➤ *See also deworming; parasites*

piroplasmosis An often fatal disease carried by ticks and other bloodsuckers; it is endemic in the Caribbean, and has been found in Florida and Texas. Death results from severe anemia. If the horse recovers, he can be a carrier for a year. Symptoms include intermittent fever, depression, weakness, loss of appetite, and rapid pulse and respiration. At an advanced stage, signs of anemia and jaundice may appear, along with dark-colored urine. Treatment with medication can help, but there is no vaccine. Care must be taken to quarantine infected horses, as ticks can pass the disease from horse to horse.

pirouette A 360-degree turn with the horse's hind legs making a tiny circle as the forehand pivots around them; executed at the walk and canter. It is essential that the horse's inside hind foot not become "rooted" to the ground but continue stepping in rhythm with the gait. This differentiates it from the spin in Western riding.

placental insufficiency A common cause of abortion, especially in older mares whose uterine lining has become less efficient with age. The placenta cannot attach adequately to the uterine wall, depriving the developing embryo of oxygen and nutrients.

plater A mediocre racehorse who is entered in unimportant races.

play Play is normal among foals, who engage in mock fights, race around wildly, and apparently "practice" forming pair bonds. In the wild it drops off sharply in adulthood, but many domesticated horses continue to play as they get older. Geldings enjoy mock fights, nipping each other's halters. Some horses play with

HORSE PLAYING WITH BALL

balls, but many horse toys are more like food puzzles, and what the horse does with them is probably not pure play. Racing and bucking when released to turnout is also a form of play, and some horses appear to love racing against each other out in the pasture.

TOYS FOR HORSES Products such as balls (some scented) and rolling grain-dispensing cylinders, designed to provide exercise and entertainment for a horse. Some horses actively engage with them; others ignore them. Horses on turnout together will spontaneously play tug-of-war with objects, but by and large playing with toys is not a natural equine behavior. A bored and confined horse with nothing else to do may tip over his water bucket and pull anything he can reach into his stall, but given free choice, he'd probably prefer to eat.

PLAYING WITH HORSES Opinions differ on the advisability of playing with horses in situations where the human is on foot with a loose horse. Horseplay often involves kicking, which suggests that running or playing with large balls or other toys with loose horses is inadvisable.

Some forms of training, such as clicker training, agility, and liberty training, have a playful element, but it's wise to have a degree of protective control. It may seem to conflict with the positive reinforcement ethic, but if you are working in an enclosure with a loose horse, and doing something exciting, carry a whip. You are smaller

than a horse; the whip is a form of dominance threat that horses understand, and it establishes limits. As such, it is a form of protected contact.
➤ *See also protected contact*

pleasure class Western or English and driving competitions designed to evaluate a horse's ability to provide a pleasurable riding or driving experience. Manners, performance, quality, conformation, and presence are all important.

pleasure horse

1. A horse with a smooth, comfortable ride at all three gaits; an even, dependable temperament; and attractive, well-balanced conformation.

2. Any riding or driving horse not used for competition, but for casual fun riding.

plowing bee, plowing match A plowing bee is a noncompetitive gathering of teamsters and teams to plow a field. Plowing matches are competitive events scored for depth, straightness, and distinctness of the furrow and neatness of the ends. There may be divisions for youth and for horses and mules, as well as divisions for different types of plows and hitches.

plussed Having scored above the average of 70 points in a National Reining Horse Association routine.
➤ *See also reining*

PMU foal
➤ *See pregnant mare urine (PMU) ranching*

pneumonia A bacterial or viral disease of the respiratory system. Horses can develop two types of pneumonia. Aspiration pneumonia is often fatal, especially in foals. Food particles or medication get into the windpipe and lungs causing irritation and infection. Whenever a horse is unable to put his head down to cough (for instance, if tied in a trailer or straight stall), he is in danger of developing aspiration pneumonia.

More commonly, horses develop pneumonia from airborne pathogens, including bacteria, viruses, parasites, and fungi. If a horse is already ill or very stressed, he is more vulnerable to pneumonia. Although often a secondary infection, pneumonia can easily overwhelm a weakened system and kill the horse. Symptoms include increased respiration and a cough, listlessness, and loss of appetite. You will probably be able to hear wheezing and rattling in his lungs with a stethoscope. Prompt medical attention is required, but only a bacterial infection will respond to drugs. Viral pneumonia is much harder to treat and may not be curable. The sick horse should be kept warm and quiet, out of drafts, with light feed (moistened to reduce dust) and complete rest.

pocket The area around a pole or barrel in which you turn your horse during mounted games.

points The mane, tail, lower legs, tips of the ears, and nose.

point-to-point An amateur sport that involves jumping obstacles on a course, though originally the course went cross-country from one point to another.
➤ *See also hunter pace; steeplechasing*

poisonous plants Because they cannot vomit, horses are particularly susceptible to poisoning. They usually avoid poisonous plants but may eat them if the pasture is over-grazed. Make sure that any area where your horse is turned out is free of toxic plants, including branches hanging over fences. Your county Extension agent can tell you which plants to look out for in your area and how to get rid of them.

Horses should not be allowed to graze in yards or gardens or near ornamental plants. Many common garden plants and wildflowers are poisonous to horses, including rhubarb, buttercup, daffodil, lily of the valley, and delphinium (or larkspur). Do not let your horse graze or snatch at leaves and plants while you are out on the trail—not only is it bad manners, but it also could be fatal.
➤ *See also toxic substances*

pole bending A mounted game in which rider and horse run a course of 11 turns around 6 poles as fast as possible without touching the poles. The poles, made of plastic pipe 6 feet (1.8 m) tall, are set in a straight line 20 to 21 feet (6–6.4 m) apart. From the starting line, the horse and rider head along the line to the farthest pole, bend around it, and weave through the remaining poles

BAY WITH BLACK POINTS

(doing a flying lead change at each pole if cantering or galloping). At the last pole, horse and rider circle and bend back through the poles, then return straight along the line back to the starting point. For serious competitors, an average run takes 20 to 25 seconds.

➤ *See also gymkhana; mounted games; Western riding*

police horses

Police departments all over the world use mounted officers for crowd control, street patrols, and directing traffic. The oldest known mounted police unit is the London Bow Street Horse Patrol, which was established in 1738. Mounted police have existed in the United States since the mid-1800s. Even as cars and motorcycles became the backbone of most police departments, many urban areas kept their mounted officers. Mounted police have the advantage of height and range of vision over foot and car patrols, though they have the disadvantage of presenting a larger target.

Horses can get into narrow, twisting alleys and down sidewalks where patrol cars can't, and can move through a crowd of people—even a rioting crowd—far more easily than an officer on foot. Many police departments find that horses actually seem to defuse tension in potentially ugly situations.

Although police horses must be large and strong, they are generally chosen for their temperament rather than for their breed. A police horse must be intelligent, calm, and able to work long hours in all kinds of weather. He must be trained to handle crowds, traffic, noise, smoke, dogs, and many other distractions and hazards. Police horses must tolerate frequent trailering, lots of standing around under saddle, and hordes of strangers wanting to pet him. Large horses—often draft crosses—are best for police work, as they give their riders a better vantage point and offer greater safety if attacked by a person on the ground.

➤ *See also Royal Canadian Mounted Police (RCMP)*

poll

The spot between the ears where the skull meets the vertebrae. The poll is quite sensitive, and striking it hard can kill a horse or cause permanent brain damage—one reason to discourage a horse from rearing, especially indoors, and to protect the poll with a helmet when trailering.

POLICE HORSE

polo

A game played on horseback with long mallets to drive a ball into a goal. Having originated in ancient Persia as a training exercise for mounted warriors, polo has been played for 2,500 years. In the mid-1800s, polo was discovered in India by the British, who brought the game back to England. By the end of the 19th century, polo was very popular in the United States as well.

Played on a field measuring 160 x 300 yards (146 x 274 m), a polo match takes about an hour and a half, divided into six periods called chukkars, each of which lasts seven minutes. Each team has four players, and since they may gallop as much as 3 miles (5 km) in a single chukkar, each player needs several ponies. With such a huge playing area, the game is fluid. While players take offensive or defensive positions, those often change as play progresses.

ARENA POLO

Arena polo is played indoors, on a dirt field of 300 x 150 feet (91 x 152 m), in four chukkars of seven and a half minutes each. The ball is larger than the plastic ball used in the outdoor game. Arena polo is more affordable; only two horses are needed, which

POLO

reduces trailer size, and club fees are less without the cost of maintaining a grass field. Arena polo is played year-round, which makes progress in the sport easier and quicker. In the United States, interscholastic and intercollegiate polo are played in the arena only.

polocrosse A hybrid of polo and lacrosse, developed in the early 20th century. It was originally played indoors by teams of two, then evolved into an outdoor game with four on a side. When Australians discovered it in the 1930s, polocrosse took off as a fast-paced organized sport.

Polocrosse uses a soft, 4-inch (10 cm) rubber ball, moved down the field by a yard-long racquet with a net. A polocrosse field is 160 yards long by 60 wide (146 x 55 m), and may be grass or dirt. Chukkars are six to eight minutes. Polocrosse players only play one pony per game, for not more than 48 minutes, making polocrosse affordable for many players. It is played nationally, internationally, and in Pony Club.

polo pony A horse used to play polo. The ponies used by the British in the 19th century were only 12.2 hands high. The height limit rose steadily to the present 15 to 15.3 hands

POLO HELMETS

As of 2015, the U.S. Polo Association (USPA) did not require ASTM/SEI-certified helmets, but the subject was increasingly debated in the wake of serious injuries to upper-level players. The close-fitting polo helmet is labeled by manufacturers as an article of apparel, not a safety helmet. It lacks the high-tech innovations of helmets used in other equestrian sports.

It is certainly possible to play polo in an ASTM/SEI-certified helmet, but stigma prevents many players from doing so, though polo is one of the most rough-and-tumble of equestrian sports. The USPA does recommend using helmets certified by the National Operating Committee on Standards for Athletic Equipment (NOCSAE). These helmets are tested for ball impact, multiple impacts, and use with safety glasses, which ASTM/SEI-certified helmets are not.

high. The ideal mount combines the speed and endurance of a Thoroughbred with the quickness and maneuverability of a good cow pony. Argentina has been particularly noteworthy for the production of fine polo ponies.

pommel The upper front part of a saddle. The pommel on a Western saddle is the rounded part from which the horn rises, also called the fork.
➤ *See also saddle; slick-fork saddle; swell; tack*

pony A horse who remains small in adulthood. Ponies measure 14.2 hands high (i.e., 58 inches, or 147 cm) or less. Ponies are generally longer than they are tall, while horses tend to be equal in height and body length.

There are pony divisions for many kinds of competition, and ponies have their own shows and associations. There are many breed registries available for ponies. Most accept ponies based on ancestry; however, some register based on size alone.

Ponies have a reputation, often well-deserved, for being clever, stubborn, and cranky. However, they have carried generations of children safely through shows, lessons, and trail rides and given those children a solid base of horsemanship. Ponies can be excellent teachers for children and small adults of all levels of experience.
➤ *See also individual breeds; Miniature Horse*

Pony Club The United States Pony Club, Inc. (USPC), an offshoot of the British Pony Club. Founded in 1954 to teach English riding, the organization had, as of 2014, 492 clubs, 91 riding centers, 95 Horsemasters groups, a paid staff of fewer than 20, and nearly 3,000 volunteers serving its approximately 10,000 active members. Pony Club teaches horsemanship, including health care; nutrition; stable management; and handling and riding safely, correctly, and with confidence. It values teamwork; respect for horse, self, land, and other people; service (through its status as an almost all-volunteer organization); and education.

Pony Club disciplines include dressage, eventing, foxhunting, mounted games, polo, polocrosse, quiz, show jumping, and tetrathlon (a sport combining running, swimming, shooting, and riding). Participants can progress through as many as nine levels of proficiency, the last of which qualifies them to teach. You don't need to own a horse to belong to Pony Club, but you must have access to one when required.

With its emphasis on a thorough, practical horse education, and its carefully calibrated system to move riders along through the levels, Pony Club is considered an excellent preparation for becoming a professional. Traditionally a youth organization, Pony Club now offers an adult Horsemasters program for its volunteers.

PONY OR HORSE?

A pony is a mature horse under 14.2 hands high—but call some breeds ponies, and you may have a fight on your hands. Icelandics, Fjords, and Haflingers are good examples. The Caspian, though extremely small, has the proportions of a horse and may properly be considered as such.

The American Miniature is fiercely defended as a horse by its many fanciers, who may not realize that the distinction stems from a piece of clever advertising, meant to differentiate this strain of Shetland from others at a time when Shetland breeding had collapsed in the United States.

Many Morgans are under 14.2 hands high, and though this is a horse breed, their owners compete them in the pony divisions in open competitions.

Ride & Run is one of many contests that might be offered at a **Pony Club** gymkhana.

PONY OF THE AMERICAS (POA)

A breed developed in the 1950s by crossing Shetland Ponies with Appaloosas as well as some Quarter Horses and Arabians. The POA shows the same vivid coloring as the Appaloosa but is smaller, between 11.2 and 14.2 hands high. It is a strong, finely made pony, a good all-around pleasure mount for children and young adults.

PONYING

ponying Leading one horse while riding another. Ponying allows you to condition or exercise two horses at once, or give a young horse trail experience without a rider on his back. The lead horse needs to learn to ignore another horse crowding him and become accustomed to the feel of a rope across his croup or flank, or under his tail.

posting, as an aid Posting can be used to control a horse's speed. If you post slower, your horse should trot slower; experiment with using this to bring him down to a walk. Posting more actively should make him trot more actively.

posting trot Rising out of the saddle at every other stride of the trot. The motion was first used by postilions, who rode one of a team of coach horses and developed the technique to soften the agony of endless miles of trotting. It became common in Europe in the 1800s,

The **posting** or **rising trot** consists of two phases: rising as the outside left moves forward and sitting as it moves back.

when Thoroughbred-type horses, who used the trot as the intermediate gait, became popular as riding horses.

Posting eliminates the bumping and jouncing that accompany an active trot, allowing the rider greater comfort and control. You can also sit the trot, but it is usually easier to learn to post first.

In correct posting, the rider is on the outside diagonal, rising as the outside front leg comes forward, and sitting as the inside leg comes forward. With practice you'll be able to feel when you're on the correct diagonal, but at first you can check by glancing down at the horse's shoulders. If you're on the wrong diagonal, sit for two beats and pick up the correct one. This is also the method used to change diagonals when you change direction.

A posting trot requires sufficient impulsion from the horse's hindquarters to essentially push you out of the saddle. Beginners often try desperately to lift themselves out of the saddle, rather than allowing the horse to push them. This usually occurs because the rider is so focused on posting that she doesn't notice that the horse has lost impulsion.

➤ *See also aids; collection; diagonal; seat; sitting trot*

post-legged Having hind legs that are too straight, without a proper angle at the hock and stifle.
➤ *See also conformation; leg, of horse*

Potomac horse fever (PHF) A serious illness first diagnosed in Maryland in 1979 and now found in nearly all states. Primarily a summertime disease, it's most commonly found in horses who graze in irrigated pastures and near streams. PHF is spread by the larvae of parasitic flatworms that live in freshwater snails.

If your horse is off his feed and water, running a fever, and then develops severe diarrhea, he probably has PHF. Immediate treatment with intravenous fluids and tetracycline is usually effective, though acute cases can be fatal or can cause founder. There is a PHF vaccine; it is given in the first year, with an annual booster after that. Consult with your veterinarian about the necessity of vaccinating horses in your area.

povidone-iodine solution A dilute iodine solution. Though commonly known by the brand name Betadine, the solution is also available generically. Povidone-iodine solution is sold most often as a 10% or 5% solution, and can be diluted further in distilled water with a small amount of salt to make an effective disinfectant for wounds.

➤ *See also sugardine*

WOUND WASH

To make 1 quart:

1 quart distilled water

2 teaspoons table salt

½ teaspoon povidone-iodine solution (10%)

Quadruple all ingredients to make 1 gallon.

praziquantel (Droncit) A canine deworming product that can also be used to rid horses of tapeworms. The recommended dosage should be increased to reflect the horse's weight.

➤ *See also deworming; parasites; tapeworms*

prebiotics Feed additives that "feed" beneficial organisms in the gut; one example is yeast. If used, prebiotics should be fed daily. Soluble fiber also helps beneficial bacteria thrive. (Concentrates overfeed them, causing imbalance in the hindgut.)

predator wasp A nocturnal insect that lays its eggs in the pupae of flies that lay eggs in manure. The hatching wasps eat the fly pupae, effectively interrupting the breeding cycle of many flies that pester horses. The wasps do not bother people, horses, or other animals.

➤ *See also deworming; parasites; pest control*

pregnancy

➤ *See breeding; broodmare; estrus; foaling; gestation*

pregnant mare urine (PMU) ranching Raising foals for the purpose of collecting the mares' urine for estrogen replacement therapy. The most popular product of PMU ranching is Premarin (PREgnant MARe urINe), a conjugated estrogen tablet used to treat women with menopausal symptoms. Pregnant mares are kept in standing stalls for six months, wearing bladder bags, flexible lightweight bags that are suspended from the ceiling. The mares are turned out for foaling, and raise their foals for four months until weaning; collection takes place in winter. Since PMU ranching primarily takes place on the northern plains of the United States and Canada, where winter temperatures drop to −40°F (−40°C), this is a time when many horses would be indoors anyway.

PMU ranching has been controversial, especially as in the early days (1960s–70s) foals were mostly sold for slaughter. As the industry matured, second-generation PMU ranchers began to see the foals as an important income stream and focused on breeding quality animals, including many registered horses. The most common breed in PMU ranching is the Quarter Horse, followed, at a considerable distance, by Percherons, Belgians, Paints, Appaloosas, Standardbreds, and Thoroughbreds. The industry organization, the National Association of Equine Ranching Information Council (NAERIC), sponsors competitions and futurities for draft and ranch horses, and supports sport and 4-H programs.

PMU ranching has downsized considerably following a number of studies showing that estrogen replacement therapy could cause breast cancer. The market was briefly flooded with PMU mares and foals but has since stabilized. As of 2014, there were approximately 2,000 PMU mares in the United States and Canada, though the industry is said to be growing in China.

In North America, animal rights organizations have focused a great deal on what they believe to be cruelty in the PMU industry. Objective inspections and observations appear to support the contentions that the mares are well treated for the most part (though underexercised during their six months of confinement) and that, as they now focus on producing high-quality foals, the ranches send fewer horses to slaughter. However, actual numbers are difficult to come by, due to the controversial nature of horse slaughter. Certainly many PMU foals are sent to feed lots and then to slaughter for human consumption.

premolars The teeth used for grinding and chewing, located between the incisors and the molars.

➤ *See also dental problems; teeth and age*

prepotency The ability of a stallion to produce foals that look like him, no matter what the mare's breeding is.

➤ *See also breeding; genetics; pedigree*

ASK BEFORE YOU BUY

When you have found a horse you might want to buy, find some time to discuss the horse with the veterinarian when the seller isn't around. Ask:

- Is this horse the age he's claimed to be?
- Are there any obvious problems that I should be aware of?
- Is his vision okay?
- Do you think he's physically capable of performing as I want him to?
- Does he seem suited to my needs and experience?
- How do the X-rays, if any, look?
- Is it possible the horse has been drugged?
- What other tests would you recommend?

prepurchase exam

Before buying a horse, have him checked out by a veterinarian. If he passes this exam, he is said to have "vetted out." The vet should examine the eyes, heart, lungs, legs, and hooves. She may draw blood for a Coggins test, drug screening, or genetic tests. You will also want the vet to confirm the age of the horse (it should be within a year of what you've been told). You may want to have X-rays taken to rule out navicular disease.

Ethical vets will not perform prepurchase exams on horses being sold by their clients. No vet can tell you for sure that a horse is or will remain problem-free, but the prepurchase exam can reassure you that you know what you're buying.

pressure and release/reward

Horses are said to be "into pressure" animals; that means that the instinctive response of an untrained horse to pressure is to push back against it. If you push against an untrained horse to get him to move over in his stall, he will lean back against your hand rather than moving

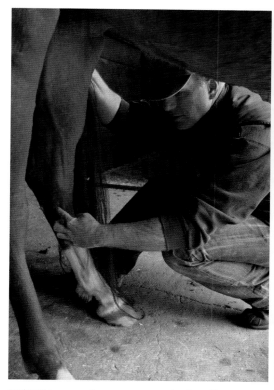

During the **prepurchase exam**, a veterinarian will pay close attention to leg and hoof structure, and also look for signs of lameness. Compressing a joint for a minute or so, then asking the horse to immediately trot out, can expose hidden soreness.

over. A tied horse who pulls back and feels pressure on his poll will pull back even harder. A horse who feels strong bit pressure will respond by pressing even more strongly on the bit.

This is counterintuitive to many people, who think that the proper response to pressure is to yield to it. Horses can learn to respond that way, but only if you teach them.

This is why the release of pressure is such an important part of training. Ask an untrained horse to move over by applying light pressure, and release the pressure the instant you sense him thinking about moving away from it. He learns from, and responds to, the release, which functions as a reward as well. You can cement the idea of moving away from pressure very quickly, and develop a horse who can generalize the response, by using clicker training or natural horsemanship techniques.

MENTAL/SPATIAL The combination of pressure and release is the foundation of natural horsemanship (NH) and round penning. The pressure is mental and spatial. The trainer invades the horse's personal space with a swinging rope or her own body language, and starts him circling. When she sees signs that he'd like to submit, she releases the pressure and allows the horse to stop circling. Ideally he'll come to her in a process called "joining up." NH trainers focus a lot on their own body language, and many believe it is the key to their success. However, experiments have demonstrated the same results using a radio-controlled car. It appears that sophisticated NH training doesn't rely on your ability to mimic a predator or a lead mare. It does, however, require understanding of pressure and release.
➤ See also aids; natural horsemanship; round pen, round penning

prizes Trophies or cash given to winners. Most trophies become the property of the winner, but some remain the property of the show, with the winner receiving a replica. Challenge trophies are donated by an individual or business and are returned by the winner after a year. Prizes may also include blankets, coolers, halters, saddles, and other useful items.

Cash prizes are usually based on the amount of the entry fees for a given class, plus an added purse. Cash prizes can be substantial in Western sports—cutting, reining, barrel racing—where top riders can win thousands of dollars or generous college scholarships.
➤ See also ribbons

probiotics An inoculant of bacterial cells designed to increase the population of desirable bacteria in the gut. Probiotics don't need to be fed every day; they should be needed only occasionally, following deworming, for instance, if drugs such as antibiotics are being given orally, or if the horse overheats.

produce (of dam) A class in which a mare's progeny are judged together for type and uniformity.
➤ See also get (of sire)

Professional Association of Therapeutic Horsemanship (PATH) International

Formed in 1969 as the North American Riding for the Handicapped Association (NARHA), PATH International is the leading organization in the field of equine-assisted activities and therapies (EAAT). The nonprofit organization is centered in the United States but has a worldwide reach. As of 2015, PATH International had 866 Member Centers; 4,600 certified instructors and equine specialists; more than 7,600 members; and more than 62,000 clients, including nearly 4,000 military veterans. The mission of PATH International is to promote safety and optimal outcomes in EAAT for individuals with special needs. Therapeutic modalities include hippotherapy, equine-facilitated mental health, driving, interactive vaulting, competition, ground work, and stable management. The organization also sets standards, offers accreditation for centers, certifies instructors, and offers a wealth of continuing education programs for its members.
➤ See also para-equestrian; therapeutic horsemanship

professional horseman The term is defined differently by various associations, but if you're over 18, you're generally considered a professional if you are paid to ride, drive, or show at halter; train or board other people's horses; give lessons, seminars, or clinics;

or endorse products. The term also sometimes applies if you accept prize money in competitions.

profiling a class

When a judge looks at the side view of a group of horses in a halter class. Profiling allows the judge to make comparisons between individual horses.

➤ *See also judging*

progesterone

A hormone that stops a pregnant mare's heat cycles and maintains the pregnancy. Insufficient levels of progesterone can cause an abortion. A mare who habitually aborts early in her pregnancy can be treated with supplemental progesterone to help sustain future pregnancies.

progression of the aids

Also known as an "increasing of aids." For example, if a horse does not respond to light leg pressure, increased pressure might be followed by a light tap of with the crop. The aids progress in severity until the horse responds. Riders must consistently ask first with the mildest aid, and instantly reward even the beginning of response.

➤ *See also aids; pressure and reward; seat*

proprioception

A sense that uses cues from your inner ear and from receptors in your muscles, tendons, and joints to convey to your brain how your body is moving and where it is located in space. In riding, you rely on proprioception to adjust your legs, seat, and hands while you look ahead to see where you're going. Horses use proprioception, too, and many training techniques are designed to develop it. The best way to develop proprioception in the young horse is to turn him out on varied terrain, where he will learn to handle himself in real-world conditions far better than a human can teach him to do.

protected contact

A clicker training term for working with a horse from outside his enclosure. The idea of protected contact originated with dangerous zoo animals, who can be clicker trained to stand for medical treatment. It's a good way to start working with a horse who has dangerous habits or who is completely unknown to you. Targeting, impulse control (not biting or mugging for treats), and even foot handling can be taught from the other side of a safe fence. When you are on foot among horses, a whip can be a form of protected contact.

➤ *See also clicker training; sacking out*

PROFILING A CLASS

protein The main structural component of the body, consisting of chains of amino acids. The 22 amino acids compose all protein. The liver can synthesize 12 of them; the remainder are called essential amino acids and must be supplied in the diet. The match between the needs of the animal and the amino acids provided by a feed determine protein quality. Protein quality is not often assessed for horse feeds; if you suspect your protein quality is inadequate, feed a commercial amino acid supplement. High urine output with a strong smell of ammonia is a reliable indicator that the diet is low in essential amino acids.

Insufficient protein can lead to poor growth, poor performance, insufficient muscle development, and a lack of appetite. Mares need extra protein during the last trimester to ensure proper development of the fetus and healthy nursing. If a horse is slow to shed out his winter coat, a little extra protein can help the new hair grow in more quickly.

On the other hand, too much protein can be dangerous. It can lead to kidney damage and eventually toxic levels of the by-products of protein digestion. If too much protein is fed to young horses, their growth rate may lead to contracted tendons, bone malformation, and inflammation of the cartilage and bone. Too much protein can make a horse "hot," or overly energetic and hard to handle.

All common feeds provide some protein. Soybeans and legume hay provide the highest concentration; they should be fed only to horses with high-level needs for protein.

➤ *See also feeding and nutrition; hay*

proud flesh Puffy flesh protruding from a wound that won't heal; scar tissue. Cuts below the knee or hock are susceptible to proud flesh, which can result in ugly scarring. Prevent proud flesh by looking your horse over daily. If you spot a lesion that needs suturing, call a veterinarian. (Suturing needs to be done promptly, or it will be unsuccessful.) If the injury does not need sutures, clean it thoroughly and apply a topical anti-bacterial. Avoid any member of the furadantin family (e.g., nitrofurazone); these products, usually yellow, can retard healing and sustain bacterial growth.

If your horse does develop proud flesh, the area may need to be treated with a caustic ointment provided by a veterinarian or, in severe cases, surgery.

provided horse A horse provided by the organization hosting a show. For example, at an Intercollegiate Horse Show Association (IHSA) show, competitors ride horses provided by the host college, rather than ones they are familiar with.

PRZEWALSKI'S HORSE

Przewalski's horse

A stocky, primitive-looking horse native to Mongolia, the only truly wild horse in existence. Przewalski's horse has never been domesticated. These horses can survive great extremes of temperature. Their narrow nostrils limit the amount of freezing air they take in per breath, and their large nasal passages warm the air before it reaches the lungs. Their shaggy coats are always dun-colored with a dorsal stripe, and their manes are upright.

The Przewalski's horse was once thought to be an ancestor of the modern horse. Genetic analysis shows this to be untrue. The Przewalski's horse shares a common ancestor with other horses, but diverged sometime between 160,000 and 38,000 years ago.

In the late 20th century the Przewalski's horse became extinct on the steppe, though a small population survived in zoos. A successful Dutch breeding program increased the numbers and allowed a herd of these horses to be released on a Mongolian horse refuge, where they continue to thrive.

➤ See also evolution of the horse; history of the horse

psoroptic mange

➤ See mange

puissance

A jumping contest focused on height. Competitors jump in rounds; the jumps decrease in number but increase in height, from a starting minimum of 4′ 6″ (1.3 m).

pulley rein

A rein effect used when a horse is running and out of control. This is a very strong check on the bit, in which you shorten your reins, brace one hand against the horse's neck and pull up and back on the other rein.

➤ See also aids; progression of the aids

pulling back (vice)

Resistance to being tied in which the horse pulls back hard on the lead rope or cross-ties; it is a hazard to him and to everyone around him. All horses should be trained to stand patiently while tied. It does not come naturally to them, as they instinctively push (or pull) into pressure.

pulling contest

contest in which teams of draft horses or ponies pull progressively heavier loads, sometimes on a sled called a stone boat, other times pulling against a machine called a dynamometer. The pull is a measured distance that varies regionally. Divisions are based on the weight of the team, though all sizes of horse may compete in a free-for-all contest.

In divisions judged by percentage of the team's bodyweight it can pull, Miniature Horses frequently win, as their lower center of gravity is an advantage. There is also a mini pulling circuit, which is a good chance for children to participate in the sport. Pulling contests are a frequent feature of country fairs.

A PULLING CONTEST

PULLING THE MANE

pulling the mane To thin and shorten the mane by pulling longer hairs out a few at a time. Does it hurt? Accounts differ; certainly many horses act as if it does. One study showed that horses' heart rates rise during mane pulling, whether they had a visible reaction or not. Measures often taken to reduce the stress, and presumably the pain, of mane pulling include working from withers to poll, pulling the mane after a workout so the pores are open, and using a topical numbing agent on the neck. For sensitive horses, consider using a pair of thinning scissors or a specialized comb to accomplish the same look.

➤ *See also mane; mane, care of; roaching*

pull-off A long-handled tool designed to grip nails and pull them from hooves. Also used to pull shoes.

➤ *See also horseshoes*

pulse and respiration A horse's normal pulse is between 30 and 42 beats per minute, and his normal respiration is 12 to 20 breaths per minute. These are averages; you should establish what your own horse's normal pulse and respiration are so you know what might indicate illness. Check for pulse and respiration when your horse is at rest and has not been exercising.

- To count respiration, just watch the horse's nostrils or flanks as he breathes. Count either exhalations or inhalations, but not both.

- To get the horse's pulse, use a stethoscope to count the heartbeat, or put your fingers on the large artery that runs across the lower jaw (under the bone). The pulse can also be felt at the fetlock joint.

➤ *See also temperature (horse); vital signs*

punishment Often confused with negative reinforcement, punishment is an aversive stimulus that *follows* a behavior. For example, your horse bites you and you smack him on the chest. It is essentially a form of retaliation and has a limited place when dealing with horses.

Check a horse's **pulse** by pressing your fingers against an artery and counting the heartbeat with your eyes on your watch. The pulse is felt most easily in the large artery that runs under the jaw, on the underside of the tailbone, or at the digital artery, near the fetlock joint.

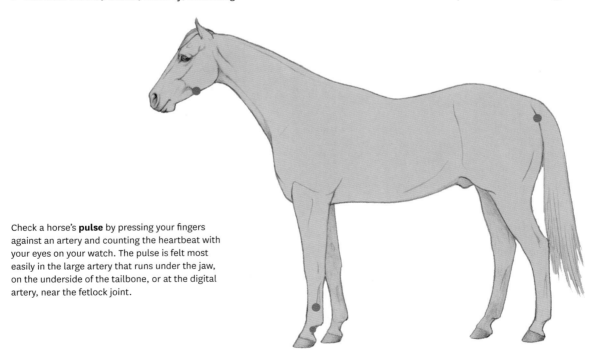

Horses frequently mete out **punishment** to one another without actually making physical contact.

Yes, horses use punishment with each other. If a horse transgresses against a horse higher in the herd hierarchy, he will be bitten or kicked, and may learn to fear and avoid the other horse. But humans are not horses, and fare poorly in rough-and-tumble interactions with them. Also, it is rarely useful to teach a horse to fear you. Good horse handling minimizes the chance for misbehavior to occur; for instance, a horse known to bite can be groomed and tacked up on cross-ties. Punishment is not a teaching tool. Hitting your horse will never teach him to enter a trailer or set himself up for a jump.

That said, when a horse bites, kicks, or otherwise threatens bodily harm, many people instinctively strike, using whatever they have in their hands. This is using punishment in its second role, which is to interrupt behavior. That is a legitimate goal, and usually works temporarily. However, it doesn't give the horse specific information about what you actually do want him to do. He may learn not to bite, or he may learn that next time he bites he'd better duck away quickly. A horse punished for refusing a jump may only learn that it is unpleasant to be near jumps. Punishment is no substitute for patiently and thoroughly training the horse to do what you actually want him to do.

➤ *See also body language, of horses; pecking order, among horses*

puppy paws When a rider holds the reins with hands turned down from wrists like a begging dog. Some instructors will call attention to a rider's "puppy paws."

➤ *See also aids; hands, rider's*

purebred A horse (or other animal) with proven lineage of the same breed. A purebred should not be confused with a Thoroughbred, which is a specific breed. Each breed registry establishes requirements for the number of generations of proven ancestry. You can have a purebred Thoroughbred but "thoroughbred Quarter Horse" is a meaningless term.

putting down a horse
➤ *See euthanasia*

pyrantel tartrate (Strongid C) An effective
drug against ascarids (roundworms) that can be given in feed daily to reduce infestation.

➤ *See also ascarid; deworming; parasites*

quagga An extinct relative of the horse. The quagga was a subspecies of the plains zebra that ranged throughout South Africa but was wiped out by Boer settlers in the 1880s. It was yellowish brown, with stripes on its head, neck, and shoulders only.

quality A term that describes a horse's overall conformation, action, and refinement. Quality in horses is determined by the ideals of the breed and gender you are evaluating. One breed may consider refinement of bone and joints and smoothness of skin and coat to be indicators of high quality. Another breed may consider these same points to be signs of poor quality.

quarter, of hoof The part of the hoof wall just forward of the heel.
➤ *See also hoof*

quarter crack A crack that develops in the quarter of the hoof. Cracks usually occur when a horse is barefoot and the hoof wall becomes too long or the hoof is brittle. There are several ways to heal a crack, but time is the main factor. As with a broken fingernail, the hoof just has to grow until the crack is completely trimmed off. In the meantime, your farrier might trim the area surrounding the crack slightly shorter than the rest of the hoof to relieve pressure on the crack. He might also rasp a small notch at the top of the crack, which spreads out the pressure when weight is put on the foot. In some cases, special clips are used to hold the crack together while it grows out.
➤ *See also hoof*

POPULARITY CONTEST The Quarter Horse is the most popular breed in the United States, followed by the American Paint and the Thoroughbred. The next tier, considerably smaller in numbers, comprises Arabians, Appaloosas, and Morgans, in roughly that order. Worldwide the three most popular breeds are the Quarter Horse, the Arabian, and the Paint.

Quarter Horse *(see next page)*

quarter line The imaginary line halfway between the centerline and the rail in an arena.
➤ *See also arena work; "Arena Dimensions," page 10; centerline; school figures*

quarter marks Decorative patterns combed into the hair over a horse's rump; seen on dressage horses and in some hunter classes. Where glitz is permissible, some riders use glitter gel in their quarter marks.

quarter method A showmanship method during the inspection phase of a Halter class, in which the handler moves to the opposite quarter from the one the judge is evaluating. *Note:* Some organizations have adopted rules requiring that handlers *not* use the quarter method, so make sure you understand the show regulations.

QUARTER CRACK

QUARTER MARKS

QUARTER HORSE

The most popular horse breed in the world, with over 5 million registered as of 2014. The Quarter Horse originated in colonial Virginia as a racehorse. The Chickasaw Horse was the foundation stock; these horses, of Spanish origin, came to Virginia via Florida. Virginia had no tracks or even long stretches of straight road, so races were staged over a quarter mile (0.4 k)—at a time when the English Thoroughbred was racing in multiple 4-mile (6.4 k) heats.

When a Rhode Island stallion of Spanish blood, Old Snipe, defeated their racehorses, Virginians imported some of his get, and the Quarter Horse was born. Then called "short horses," or "Quarter-Pathers," they were faster than Thoroughbreds in the Virginia races. Quarter-Pathers remained in favor until distance racing became popular in America around 1850.

At that point, the breed went west with settlers as an all-purpose horse. Crossed with other horses, such as mustangs and Morgans, Quarter Horses became robust ranch horses with great cow sense.

The Quarter Horse was well established before significant Thoroughbred imports began. Only Janus, imported in 1752, had any impact on the early breed. Thoroughbreds have been repeatedly crossed into the breed over the centuries since, and the American Quarter Horse Association (AQHA) has not completely closed the stud book.

Today, Quarter Horses outnumber most other North American breeds by a factor of 10 to 1. Cowboys still ride them on the range, and they make wonderful pleasure and competition horses. There is also an active Quarter Horse race scene.

Quarter Horses come in distinct types: halter horse, Western pleasure, racing, and cutter/reiner. Halter horses are large, with heavy muscling of the hindquarters. Though this looks strong, it makes them less desirable for active sports. Halter horses may also have small, "tidy" feet, which can lead to lameness.

Pleasure horses and racehorses are longer-bodied, taller, and lankier, and translate well to English disciplines like hunt seat. Cutters and reiners are small, square-built, very athletic horses. Quarter Horses can be any color, with limited white markings. Sorrel is the most common color, comprising one third of registered horses. Along with their many good qualities comes a disadvantage: a genetic tendency toward navicular disease and the slight possibility of developing hyperkalemic periodic paralysis (HYPP), a genetic disorder that is found only in this breed.

➤ *See also genetic disorders; hyperkalemic periodic paralysis (HYPP); "Thoroughbred Progenitors," page 357*

QUARTER HORSE

QUARTER PONY

A small stock-type horse, 11.2 to 14.2 hands high. Quarter Ponies are quick and agile, with a calm disposition. Heavily muscled, they have short, broad heads and slightly arched necks. Quarter Ponies are excellent youth horses for Western sports. There are several registries with slightly differing rules, but these have begun to consolidate.

quarter-turn A 90-degree turn in either direction.

quicked hoof An injury caused by a farrier who has either trimmed the hoof too deeply and exposed sensitive sole or driven a nail into the sensitive laminae. In either case, a quicked hoof is prone to serious infection; permanent damage may be done to the coffin bone if not treated properly. The first situation is usually best treated by placing pads and shoes on the hoof, possibly with an iodine-based hoof packing material intended to toughen the sole. The second should be treated like any other puncture wound in the hoof: Clean it well, soak it in warm water and Epsom salt, and have it seen within a day by a veterinarian.

➤ *See also farrier; hoof*

quick-release knot Any knot that is easy to untie even if a horse is pulling against it; these knots don't get tighter if the horse pulls. Use only a quick-release knot when tying a horse—it is essential to be able to free your horse in a hurry if he is panicking or if an emergency arises. If the horse cannot break free from an object when panicked, he might take both the lead rope and the object with him, doing irreparable damage to himself in the process. Most people already know a slipknot, which is used by many horsemen.

If your horse learns to release himself by pulling the free end of the rope, run that end through the loop; this is referred to as a "safety" knot. He won't be able to untie himself, but be aware that you won't really have a quick-release knot anymore.

➤ *See also tying*

TWO QUICK-RELEASE KNOTS

(1) Pass a loop of the rope through the ring. (2) Twist the loop several times, leaving an "eye" at the end. (3) Take the free end of the rope, make a fold (bight), and slide the bight through the eye. (4) Slide your hand up the rope to tighten the knot.

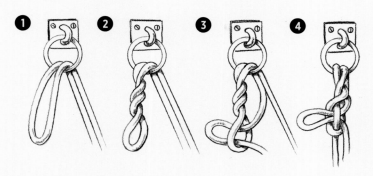

(1) Run a couple of feet of the rope through the ring and hold both pieces in one hand. (2) Make a fold (bight) in the tail end of the rope, cross it over the two pieces in your hand and through the resulting loop. (3) Pull the bight through the loop until it is about 6 inches (15 cm) long and the knot is secure, then slide the knot up to the ring.

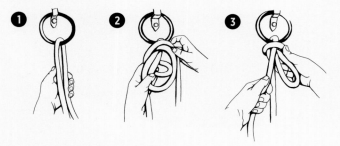

Note: When tying a quick-release knot, keep your fingers out of loops. If your horse pulls back suddenly and your fingers are in the loops, the result could be amputation of one or more fingers. Learn the knot without a horse attached. It is safest to attach the tie rope first, then snap that into your horse's halter and unsnap the lead rope.

quidding Partially chewing hay and then spitting out pieces of it. You will notice these small "quids" on the floor around his feed rack. Quidding usually indicates a tooth problem.

quirt A Western-style crop with a short handle and rawhide lash. In a closed or California-type rein, the romal connects the side reins and provides a built-in quirt.

➤ *See also crop; romal; whip*

quitting
➤ *See refusal, run-out*

quittor A chronic inflammation in the lateral cartilage of the hoof, leading to abscess. It usually requires surgery. Quittor is distinguished from the more common hoof abscess by the location of the breakthrough discharge. Quittor discharges above the coronary band, abscesses at the coronary band. The condition is more common among draft horses than saddle horses.

ROMAN NOSE

rabicano A horse with white hairs in the base of the tail, and along the body between the front and hind legs. The rabicano gene is little understood, but is distinct from the roaning gene.

rabies A fatal virus that affects the central nervous system; all mammals are susceptible. Rabies is carried in the saliva of infected animals, who transmit it by biting or by licking wounds or lesions on the skin of another animal. Rabies can have a long incubation period, because the virus travels through nerve cells rather than the bloodstream. Once it reaches the brain it is always fatal. People can be treated successfully after exposure, but there is controversy over whether this will ever work for animals.

Symptoms vary widely and can be mistaken for many other illnesses, but some common signs in horses are drooling, difficulty swallowing, aggression, lethargy, and weakness in the hindquarters.

If rabies is common in your area, ask your veterinarian about vaccinating your horse. If he is exposed to a rabid animal, a booster will be necessary and he should be quarantined for 90 days. An unvaccinated horse who is exposed may have to be put down or put into strict quarantine for six to nine months, with as little human contact as possible.

racehorse
➤ *See flat racing; harness racing; Thoroughbred*

racing
➤ *See flat racing; gaits; harness racing; pace; "Racing Terms," page 126; speed, of horse; Standardbred; steeplechasing; Thoroughbred; Triple Crown*

rack A four-beat gait in which each foot meets the ground at equal, separate intervals. The rack is smooth and highly animated, performed with great action and speed. A racking horse needs to elevate his head and lower his back in a slightly hollow carriage. For this reason, racking for a long time can lead to back problems. Horses that rack must also be ridden at the walk and trot to allow them to stretch their backs.

Footfall at the rack

RACKING HORSE ➤

An American gaited breed related to the Saddlebred and Tennessee Walker, popular in the southern United States. Racking Horses are midsize (15.2 hands high on average) and well built, known for having good bone and sound legs. They have a naturally smooth, fast rack. The emphasis is on speed and correctness of gait rather than on exaggerated elevation of knees and hocks. The Racking Horse is used for pleasure riding, trail riding, bird-dog field trials, and showing.

➤ *See also amble; American Breeds, American Saddlebred; field trials; Missouri Fox Trotter; pace; rack; Rocky Mountain Horse; Tennessee Walker*

The rack is a gait of great animation. The rider feels the horse's shoulders roll and climb and his hindquarters bob up and down, yet the saddle remains still and level, and the horse's head does not nod or swing.

Gaits in the rack family include the fino fino of the Paso Fino horse (the slowest) as well as the paso corto, paso largo, saddle rack, singlefoot, tölt, and true rack. The saddle rack is performed at 8 to 10 miles (13–16 k) per hour, and the true rack can reach over 25 miles (40 k) per hour. Fast racking is energy intensive, but slower versions like the paso corto can be used for trail riding.

rail The fence line of an arena or ring.

rail class Term for a flat class without jumps or obstacles.

rail work

1. Work that takes place primarily on the outer edge of an arena or ring. Rail work forms the basis for most basic riding education of horse and rider because the rail provides a form of security.

2. The portion of a competitive class that's judged "on the rail"; the horse is worked through all gaits, often combined with separate performance of a pattern with or without obstacles. An example of such a class would be Hunter Hack, in which horses are judged equally on rail work and their performance over two fences.

rain, horses and Rain doesn't seem to bother most horses. They are well protected against the average summer precipitation, and it doesn't hurt them to get wet. However, they should always have shelter in case of a thunderstorm or if it's cold and windy as well as rainy. Keep in mind, too, that some horses feel itchy when wet and may try to rub themselves against a handler. In areas where it rains a lot, be aware of rain rot, a skin disease caused by a funguslike organism that thrives in dirty, wet conditions.
➤ *See also rain rot/rain scald*

rain, riding in Rain can make surfaces slippery, can damage leather tack, and can make horses itchy and irritable. Trail riders and anyone who need to get a horse fit in damp climates often ride in the rain anyway.

Raincoats especially designed for riding will drape over your saddle to protect it. Accustom your horse to

This trail rider is prepared to keep going despite the **rain**, with a good raincoat that covers her upper legs and most of the saddle. The one rule everyone should always follow is to avoid riding in thunderstorms.

being ridden in rain gear before it rains. Ponchos can flap or rustle, and the rain pattering on them may disturb some horses. Use a rainproof helmet, or wear a plastic helmet cover. An extended visor may be useful if you wear glasses.

rain rot/rain scald

RAIN ROT

A skin condition caused by a funguslike organism (*Dermatophilus congolensis*) that horses pick up when they roll in the dirt. When the dusty hair gets wet, the organism can multiply and cause the skin to form scabs; the hair mats into clumps and falls out. Before rain rot becomes visible, it can be felt as bumps under the skin that may be sensitive when groomed.

Rain rot is self-limiting; if you leave it alone, it will go away. But that takes time, and the condition is uncomfortable and can become quite widespread. Treatment typically involves soaking the scabs in a warm, iodine-based shampoo or other anti-fungal product. This makes it easier to remove the scabs, and also kills the causative organism. There are a number of effective topical preparations that can be used between baths. Once the scabs are gone, continue with the shampoo for a few days until the scabbed areas heal. Severe cases may require a systemic antibiotic or fungicide.

To avoid spreading rain rot among horses, do not share grooming tools, tack, saddle pads, or other equipment. Thoroughly clean any items that can be washed or disinfected.

ranch riding

A Western pleasure class in which a horse and rider complete a pattern that includes the extended lope, as well as three maneuvers that may include a sidepass, a 360-degree turn, and simple or flying lead changes. The class is judged on execution, not timing. The horse is expected to be more forward moving than in a standard Western pleasure class.

ranch sorting

A sport related to team penning. In ranch sorting, two riders work together against the clock to move 11 calves, one at a time, from one pen to another.

➤ *See also team penning*

rare horse breeds

➤ *See Livestock Conservancy, The*

rasp

The file used by farriers. Riders' rasps are also available. Either straight or V-shaped, they fit easily in a saddle bag. When using a farrier's rasp, be careful not to rasp your own knuckles. Gloves are a good idea until you become adept.

ratcatcher

A collarless shirt worn with formal hunt or show attire. To complete the look, the rider wears either a choker collar of the same fabric as the shirt or a white stock tie, which wraps around the throat like a scarf.

➤ *See also choker; "English Show Attire," page 103; stock tie*

rating a cow

In Western sports like penning or roping, keeping a cow under control without crowding it or backing off too far. Each cow has its own control zone (similar to a human's "personal space"), and horse and rider need to gauge the optimal distance for maneuvering an individual cow most effectively.

The ability to **rate a cow** is an important skill for a ranch horse.

Rearing on cue is one thing, but a horse that routinely rears, either under saddle or on the ground, is dangerous and needs to be retrained.

rating a horse

1. Controlling and regulating a horse's speed. Rating is an essential skill for eventing, combined driving, and trail riding, where the horse must finish within a certain time frame, and with good vital signs. It is also important for riders on equestrian drill teams, who must match their speed to others to make the choreography work.

2. In jumping, positioning a horse and adjusting his stride before a jump so that he takes off in the correct spot. This requires an advanced understanding of a horse's gaits and striding, as well as a high level of coordination of aids. Improper rating can lead to unsafe and dangerous jumping.

rearing
When a horse raises his forelegs and stands on his hind legs. Rearing while being handled or ridden is a defensive response that, if left unchecked, can develop into a seriously dangerous habit. Horses who rear and flip over have killed many riders. A horse who rears habitually should be handled by a professional trainer.

If your horse rears while being led, don't pull back against him. He may resist the pressure and flip over backward. Turn him to one side and get him moving forward.

If a horse rears while you are riding, *do not* pull on the reins. Lean forward, put your arms around his neck, and hang on. If he feels like he may go over backward, kick your feet free of the stirrups and prepare to bail.

reata
➤ *See lariat/lasso*

recessive gene
➤ *See genetics*

rectal palpation
➤ *See palpation*

recurrent airway obstruction (RAO)
➤ *See heaves*

REARING REMINDER

Jessica Jahiel, lecturer, clinician, and author, uses the following rhyme as a reminder of how to deal with a rearing horse: "When in danger or in doubt, run in circles, scream and shout." A loud scream or yell can distract a horse about to rear. Circling him and moving him forward prevents him from going up on his hind legs.

According to Jahiel, "Have a plan so that you can act without hesitation at the very moment that the idea of rearing comes into the horse's mind. And you must be sensitive to what the horse is doing and thinking . . . so that you will sense that tiny hesitation and send him forward into a turn before the rear actually happens."

---

red dun coloring
A light red-and-tan body color, with reddish, white, flaxen, or mixed mane and tail. Like any dun, a red dun has a dorsal stripe and often has striping on the legs and withers.
➤ *See also color, of horse; dun coloring; "Red Horses," next page*

red mange
➤ *See mange; parasites*

red roan coloring
Coat color with an equal mix of auburn and white hairs.
➤ *See also color, of horse; "Red Horses," next page; roan coloring; blue roan coloring*

RED DUN COLORING

RED HORSES

Red horses often have red points, and some have distinct red "corn spots" that resemble kernels of corn. Red coat colors include the following:

BLOOD BAY. A clear, even red; the most common shade of bay. Bay is base-black, so the mane and tail are always black.

CHESTNUT. Medium red with red or flaxen mane and tail.

LIVER CHESTNUT. Very dark red with somewhat lighter mane and tail.

RABICANO. Red with white speckling on the sides and belly.

RED DUN. Very light red, usually with darker mane and tail.

RED ROAN. Red and white hairs evenly mixed.

SORREL. Light, clear red, lighter than chestnut, often with a light mane and tail; or for draft horses, three or more shades of red, with light points.

STRAWBERRY ROAN. Light red evenly mixed with white, often with red points.

red worms

➤ *See deworming; large strongyles; parasites; small strongyles*

refusal, run-out

A refusal is when a horse stops in front of a jump; it is penalized in jumping classes, and three refusals can result in elimination. Refusals can also result in a fall for the rider. Horses refuse for many reasons, including lack of impulsion, poor placement going into the jump, poor rider position, or being asked to jump fences they aren't ready for.

A run-out is when a horse goes to the right or left of a jump instead of over it. These are mostly caused by rider error in positioning for the jump, or the rider being unbalanced in the saddle.

rein-back

A Western term for backing up a horse.
➤ *See also backing up*

reined cow horse

A Western competition in which each contestant runs a reining pattern, works cattle in a herd, and then works a single cow.

reinforcement, in training

Anything that, occurring in conjunction with a behavior, increases the probability that the behavior will be repeated. Positive reinforcement (+R) is something the animal wants—food, play, a scratch, freedom. Negative reinforcement (−R) is something the animal wants to avoid—rein pressure, leg pressure, an unpleasant sound.

REFUSAL

REIN-BACK

REINFORCE THE AID

In conventional training parlance, the phrase "reinforce the leg aid" means to follow a nonresponse to the leg by using the whip, or possibly spurs. The horse is given the chance to respond to the milder aid first, and usually learns to do so.

The sliding stop is a crowd-pleasing component of **reining** competition.

reining A Western competition in which the horse works at speed, performing changes of pace and direction, large and small circles, spins, and the showy sliding stop, halting with his hindquarters set deep underneath him and his hind feet sliding. The stop should be solid and square, without a great shift of the rider's balance, which tends to cause the horse to hollow his back and brace his front end. In the old days the horse might throw his head up while stopping, but current fashion is for him to stop with his head low.

A good reining horse listens to his rider without anticipating the pattern and responds immediately to the aids. He performs calmly but has quick reflexes and moves fast while staying controlled. Reining requires speed and strength from a horse and, from the rider, an ability to control the horse with seat, weight, and leg aids. Despite its name, reining doesn't actually involve the reins very much, except in the early, training phase. Good reining horses work on a loose rein.
➤ See also aids; Western riding; Western dressage

reins The straps that attach to the bit or hackamore, by which the rider controls the horse.

In English riding, the reins are connected in a single loop from one side of the bit to the other, and are usually made of braided or laced leather, cotton webbing, or pebbled rubber. Smooth reins usually have hand stops, small leather straps crossing the rein. These options enhance grip, which is important for English riders who often ride on contact. Multicolored training reins offer a visual cue for correcting rein length; riders can glance down to check if both hands are on the same-colored rein sections, and an instructor can tell a student to move to a different color band to loosen or tighten the reins. English reins attach to the bit using a buckle or a hook stud.

In Western riding, the reins are most often open or split, and may be flat, round-braided, or woven leather; rope (nylon or polypropylene); or horsehair. Trail riders often like poly or nylon rope reins that can get wet without becoming slippery, and that can be used for tying a horse during rest stops.

Western reins may lace to the bit or be attached with trigger snaps or buckles. Many attach using leather water loops, also called slobber straps. These keep expensive reins from dipping into the water when a horse drinks. Slobber straps are designed to be easily replaced. With a light pair of reins, slobber straps also weight the rein and pre-signal the horse. This results in greater lightness of the aids.
➤ See also bridle; English tack; lines; Western tack

reinsmanship class, in driving A class in carriage pleasure driving in which the driver's skills are judged.

remuda A group of trained stock horses used on a ranch to work cattle.

renvers Also referred to as haunches out; a suppling exercise in which the horse carries his hindquarters toward the outside of the circle being ridden. The maneuver can be executed along the rail or in a schooling figure, such as a circle or a figure eight.
➤ *See also counter-flexion; half-pass; shoulder-in; travers*

reproduction

➤ *See breeding; estrus; foaling; gestation; pregnancy*

reserve champion

➤ *See prizes; ribbons*

respiration

➤ *See pulse and respiration*

AVOIDING RESPIRATORY PROBLEMS

If your horse has breathing problems, feed him with his head down, to let mucus drain out rather than into his lungs. Feed dry, good-quality hay to eliminate fungal spores. Keep a clean barn to avoid ammonia fumes from manure and urine, or keep the horse turned out. Keep up to date on vaccinations, especially if there will be contact with off-farm horses.

restraints A restraint prevents, restricts, or controls a horse's movement. Bits and bridles are a form of restraint, in that they allow a rider or driver to control the horse.

Some form of restraint is usually required for veterinary care or situations that might trigger the horse's defensive responses. The type of restraint used depends on the situation and the personality and experience of the horse and handler(s).

The most common forms of physical restraint are the following:

HALTER AND LEAD SHANK WITH CHAIN. The chain can be run either over or under the horse's nose; the latter adds a higher degree of control. This is used to hold a horse still or keep him from overpowering a handler while being led.

TYING. Obviously, a tied horse can't go anywhere, but he can do a lot of sidling and, if overstressed, may pull back. Don't rely on tying for extremely stressful care or procedures.

HOBBLING. Hobbles tie or cuff two legs together, limiting movement. Or you can hobble only one leg by attaching one end of a hobble to the pastern, then lifting the foot and buckling the other end around the horse's forearm. This means the horse must stand three-legged. Breeding hobbles can be useful for doing a pelvic or rectal exam.

TWITCHING. A twitch can be a wooden stick with a loop of chain or rope on the end, or a clamp that looks like tongs. The twitch is placed on the horse's upper lip and tightened. It was once thought to create pain; however, it is now believed that it stimulates mechanoreceptors in the skin that activate a release of endorphins in the brain similar to those released during acupuncture. In an emergency you can try a shoulder twitch: Grasp a fold of skin in the shoulder area and roll your hand forward.

BLINDFOLD. A blindfold inhibits movement and can calm a fearful animal.

STOCKS. Stocks restrict the movement of the horse by enclosing him on all sides. Most stocks are built out of tubular pipe and are commonly used when shoeing draft horses, because of the sheer weight of their hooves and their power should they decide to resist.

CHEMICAL RESTRAINT. Many sedatives are used for horses. Only a veterinarian should administer chemical restraints.

➤ *See also cross-tying, cross-ties; handling horses; picking up feet; twitch; tying*

retained caps

➤ *See cap; dental problems; teeth and age*

return-in-season
A clause in a breeding contract that entitles the owner of a mare to rebreed her to the stallion if she fails to become pregnant or to produce a live foal in the contracted season.

➤ *See also live foal guarantee*

rhinopneumonitis

➤ *See equine herpes virus (EHV)*

Rhizoctonia leguminicola
A toxic fungus that causes black patch disease on clovers and other legumes. If a horse eats infected plants, he can get "slobbers," or irritated salivary glands. More serious effects are fetal malformation or abortion, digestive upset and weight loss, or even death if the fungus is eaten in sufficient quantities. But a case of slobbers is usually a minor, aesthetic problem. The only time to worry about slobbers is if the saliva becomes thick, if the horse runs a fever, or if he has difficulty swallowing.

➤ *See also poisonous plants*

rhythm beads
A training tool in which a string of beads with bells or rattles is attached to the horse, either on a breastplate or in his mane. The noise helps the rider hear whether the horse is moving evenly and in good cadence. Some horses appear to find this relaxing, and may even move in a way that influences the sound. On the trail, rhythm beads alert wildlife and other riders that a horse is approaching.

Horses are aware of rhythm and tend to move in sync with it, which is why some riding teachers like to incorporate music into a lesson. Adding rhythm beads to a musical lesson can help riders hear if they are working with the beat.

riata

➤ *See lariat/lasso*

ribbons
Ribbons are given to the top riders in each class at a horse show, to signify placement: blue for first place, red for second, and so on. The champion is the competitor within a show division who has won the most points overall; reserve champion is the one with the second-most points. Championship ribbons are rosettes with streamers in the first, second, and third place colors. Reserve championship ribbons combine second, third, and fourth place colors.

A championship is generally awarded within a division. A grand championship is awarded in a larger division. At a breed show a horse might be English Pleasure Champion based on placings in Pleasure classes, and Grand Champion Mare based on points in other classes, such as halter classes.

➤ *See also prizes; "U.S. Ribbon Colors," next page*

Ride-a-Buck/Sit-a-Buck

➤ *See dollar bill class*

A CHAMPION RIBBON

U.S. RIBBON COLORS

Rank	Color
First place	Blue
Second place	Red
Third place	Yellow
Fourth place	White
Fifth place	Pink
Sixth place	Green
Seventh place	Purple
Eighth place	Brown
Ninth place	Dark gray
Tenth place	Light blue
Grand	Blue, red, yellow, and white; or solid purple
Reserve grand	Red, yellow, white, and pink; or purple and white
Champion	Blue, red, and yellow; or solid purple
Reserve champion	Red, yellow, and white; or purple and white

Note: In Canada, red is first and blue is second.

Ride and Tie A competition that combines endurance riding with long-distance running. Each team consists of two people who switch off between riding a single horse and running on foot. All teams start out on horseback at the same time, and the runners follow. After the first rider has covered as much distance as she thinks the runner can handle, she dismounts, ties the horse, and takes off on foot. The first runner finds the horse, climbs on, and goes after her partner. During the race, the people must switch off a minimum number of times, and the horse must go through vet checks.

Most Ride and Tie events cover 10 to 20 miles (16–32 k), but can be as short as 6 miles (9.6 k) or as long as the World Championship contest at 40 miles (64 k). Teams can be any age or gender. A "century" team has two humans and a horse whose ages add up to 100 or more. In addition to human partners who can run long distances under rugged conditions, the sport requires a horse who is able to handle the stop-and-start activity, not to mention standing tied as he is left behind by his rider and then passed by other horses.

rider up At a show, the term "rider up" signals that the rider is mounted and ready for her class.

ridgeling
➤ *See cryptorchid*

riding fence Riding along the fence line on large ranches and farms to check for breaks, holes, or sags. Riding fence is an important maintenance chore; all pastures and fenced areas should be checked regularly.

riding ring
➤ *See "Arena Dimensions," page 10; arena events; arena work*

rigging The straps that hold the cinch and the saddle tree together on a Western saddle.
➤ *See also Western tack*

rigging dee The D-ring that holds the tie strap or latigo of a Western saddle. The latigo runs through a ring on the cinch and loops several times between the rigging dee and the cinch ring to hold the cinch in place.
➤ *See also Western tack*

rim pad Pad inserted between a hoof and a horseshoe that rims the hoof and does not cover the sole or frog.

rim shoe Horseshoe with a deep crease or groove in the surface, running from heel to heel; used for mild traction.

ringbone A form of osteoarthritis (bony arthritis) that is most often found on the pastern but that can also affect the coffin bone within the hoof. Ringbone is classified as *high* when it affects the proximal phalange (pastern bone closest to the fetlock joint), and *low* when it affects the medial phalange (pastern bone just above hoof) or distal phalange (coffin bone); and *articular* or *nonarticular* depending on whether the interphalangeal joints are involved. It's most common in older horses with straight pasterns, but can also be caused by kicks and wire cuts. The main symptom is swelling around the fetlock, and a noticeable bony enlargement above the coronary band. Lameness may or may not be present.

Many cases of ringbone go virtually unnoticed, but the condition can cause severe lameness if there is bony growth within the joint. Ringbone that affects the pastern joint or coffin joint does not have a good prognosis for treatment. It is believed that ringbone is a heritable trait, so horses with ringbone should not be bred.

Treatment is unnecessary if there is no lameness. In high articular ringbone, the pastern joint can be surgically fused and the horse can return to full use. Low articular ringbone is untreatable; fortunately, it is the least common type.

ring etiquette Ring etiquette helps prevent dangerous situations. The following are basic rules of ring etiquette:

- Enter the arena only when the gate is clear and move quickly to the center to avoid getting in the way of riders on the rail.

- Keep your horse at least 8 feet (2.4 m)—one horse length—away from other horses.

- If your horse is crowding the horse in front of you, make a small circle or cut across the ring without getting in the way of other riders.

- Pass on the inside whenever possible, and call out to the rider ahead in a clear voice, "Passing," before you do so.

- Give quiet voice cues to avoid agitating other horses.

➤ *See also "Passing Etiquette in the Ring," page 257*

ring of muscles Muscles along a horse's top and bottom line.

When a horse is using his **ring of muscles** correctly, he stretches his back and neck, and contracts his belly muscles, pushing vigorously with his hind legs.

ring-sour Reluctant to perform in the arena. A horse who has been worked too hard or too repetitively may become ring sour. He'll look for ways to leave the ring or evade your commands, and will generally exhibit a negative attitude. Variety and change of pace while training and exercising keep both horse and rider fresh and interested. Many ring-sour horses work hard at careers more interesting to them, such as trail riding.
➤ *See also barn-sour; herd-bound*

ringworm A fungal infection of the skin that causes hair to fall out in distinct round spots. Lesions form a week to a month after exposure. Ringworm spreads between horses who share tack and grooming tools. Some families or breeds seem to be more susceptible than others. Young horses, older horses, and ones with compromised immune systems are more vulnerable.

Ringworm should be treated promptly by isolating the infected horse and bathing him with an iodine-based shampoo. Allow the shampoo to remain on the skin for 20 to 30 minutes before rinsing thoroughly. Repeat daily for four or five days, and then twice a week until all infected areas are healed. The horse should be on turnout if possible, with plenty of fresh air and sunshine. All grooming tools and other equipment must be disinfected. Make sure your horse has enough vitamin A, zinc, and selenium in his diet, as a deficiency of these can encourage the development of ringworm.

Ringworm is one infection you can catch from your horse, and share with household pets. Be meticulous about washing and disinfecting your hands and arms after handling and treating a horse with ringworm.
➤ *See also parasites*

rising An age descriptor. When a horse is described as "rising three" it means he is almost three years old.

rising trot
➤ *See posting trot*

roaching To cut or shave a mane or tail quite short. This practice, also called "hogging," is common in cutting and other fast-action sports to prevent the reins from tangling in the mane. Roaching is traditional in some breeds, such as the Fjord.

Roaching shows off the unique striped mane of the Norwegian Fjord.

road founder Laminitis caused by working a horse on a hard surface, like pavement. It can also happen if a horse is worked hard and fast after a radical change in shoeing. For example, a horse who has been barefoot but is newly shod and worked hard can develop road founder.
➤ *See also laminitis*

roads, riding on
➤ *See pavement, riding on*

roadster classes Horse show classes in which horses—chiefly Standardbreds, Morgans, Saddlebreds, Arabians, Hackney Ponies, and Shetlands—are shown in fine harness or under saddle with an emphasis on speed. In some harness classes horses pull a light four-wheeled wagon, in others a racing sulky, sometimes called a "bike." They are shown first at a jog, going clockwise (in other classes, entries perform first going counterclockwise).

After the judge has looked them over, they reverse direction and are asked for a road gait, a fast, brilliant, well-balanced trot. The horse should be responsive and easy to rate. When told, "Drive on," horses should reach their top trotting speed, which should remain balanced and correctly cadenced. They must show speed and quality of gaits. The horses are then lined up without headers; they are expected to stand quietly in line.

The same gaits are asked for in Roadster Under Saddle. In both Harness and Saddle Roadster classes, handlers wear stable silks. Roadster is a national discipline recognized by the United States Equestrian Federation (USEF).

roan coloring
Roan is a mix of dark and light hairs, giving the overall coat a mottled or speckled appearance. A mix of black and white hair is called blue roan, while brown or auburn and white is called red or strawberry roan.

➤ *See also blue roan coloring; color, of horse; red roan coloring*

roarer
A horse who makes a loud, roaring sound when breathing heavily. This unsoundness can interfere with breathing and can thus limit use of the horse. The condition can sometimes be fixed with surgery. Tie-back surgery sutures the loose cartilage, but it can lead to aspiration or chronic cough. A new technique fuses a joint in the cartilage. Nerve supply surgery is less successful.

rocker toe, rolled toe
A rocker toe is a horseshoe that has been bent upward toward the hoof at the toe. A rolled toe is rounded or beveled on the outer edge of the ground surface at the toe. Both are used to ease and direct break over.

➤ *See also barefoot trim; breakover; horseshoes*

Rocky Mountain Horse *(see next page)*

rodents
➤ *See pest control*

A RED ROAN

ROCKY MOUNTAIN HORSE

One of the Mountain Saddle breeds from eastern Kentucky. Rocky Mountain Horses are midsize (14.2–16 hands high) with wide chests, well-sloped shoulders, and handsome heads. A landrace breed, they exhibit variable type, some being more Spanish in appearance, others more similar to modern breeds. The natural gait is a singlefoot. Rockies do not trot. They can canter, but most riders don't ask them to, as the singlefoot gait is both comfortable and fast.

Rockies often exhibit unusual colors. The body is always a solid color, preferably chocolate (a form of liver chestnut), but any solid color is accepted. Excessive white markings are not acceptable. The long manes and tails are often cream or dark blonde. **Livestock Conservancy status: Watch**

➤ *See also Mountain Saddle Horses*

rodeo A demonstration of Western riding skills that originated in the mid-1800s on large Texas cattle ranches where groups of cowboys would gather to socialize and show off their roping and riding skills. The first recorded rodeo involved teams from different ranches and took place in Colorado in 1869. Before becoming regulated contests with arenas, loading chutes, and grandstands, rodeos were held in town squares or on main streets.

Modern rodeo events include bareback riding, saddle bronc riding, bull riding, bulldogging (steer wrestling), calf roping, and barrel racing and other speed contests. There are both adult and youth divisions. Rodeo riding is physically grueling, but many contestants are drawn by the thrill, and the high purses winners can take home. Rodeos are controversial, with some people believing that riding bucking horses, in particular, is abusive.

Others point out the long lives of bucking horses and their light workload.

BRONC RIDING is the quintessential rodeo sport. In bareback riding, the horse wears a halter and a single rope, a wide strap around his girth with a sturdy handle attached just behind the withers, and a bucking strap or cinch that is pulled tight around his loins. The rider mounts in a chute and grips the handle. The horse is then released into the ring. The rider must stay on for eight seconds, his free hand clear of the horse's body, raking the horse on the shoulders with his spurs. If he's still on board after the whistle sounds, pickup men gallop alongside to pull him clear of the bucking horse.

Staying on a frantically bucking horse might seem easier with a saddle but it can, in fact, be more complicated. For one thing, while the stirrups in the saddle bronc event offer added balance, if the rider drops one during the 10-second ride, he's disqualified, and if his foot slips through and he's thrown, he could be dragged and badly hurt. The reins give little control since they are attached to a halter, not a bridle and bit. Some riders opt to remove the saddle horn, as grabbing it ("pulling leather") will also disqualify them, and it could hurt them if the horse decides to drop and roll.

In both bareback and saddle bronc riding, points are given to both horse and rider by two judges. A maximum of 100 points is theoretically possible, but scores in the 70s are considered remarkable, while many very good riders are happy with a score in the 60s.

CALF ROPING AND BULLDOGGING involve teamwork between rider and horse. In calf roping, the rider ropes a galloping calf and immediately leaps off his horse,

running to the calf to flip it over and tie three of its legs together. The horse must keep the rope tight enough to prevent the calf from escaping, but not so tight that it pulls over the calf before the rider can get to it. The tie must hold for five seconds to count. A good run takes just 12 or 13 seconds.

In bulldogging, or steer wrestling, two riders gallop alongside a steer. One of them acts as the hazer, keeping the steer from veering away. The other rider must leap off his horse, grab the 700- or 800-pound steer, and yank its horns around to bring it to the ground. The slightest miscalculation will leave the bulldogger sitting in the dust looking foolish while the steer careens around the arena. Experienced bulldoggers with well-trained horses can bring down a steer in about five seconds.

➤ *See also Western riding; individual classes*

BULLDOGING

rollback

1. A reining maneuver in which the horse performs a sliding stop, then rolls back over his hocks (180 degrees) to go in the opposite direction. He brings his front feet down into his original tracks at a lope on the opposite lead.

2. In a jumper class, a turn immediately after a jump toward a jump in a different direction.

rolling Horses roll to scratch itches, stretch weary muscles after a workout, and coat themselves in dust or mud to block insects. Some horses can roll completely over from one side to another; others have to roll on one side, get up, and then roll on the other. After rolling, your horse will usually give himself a big shake and wander off looking for something to eat.

Rolling or getting up and down more frequently than usual can be a sign of colic, so be aware of your horse's normal behavior. A horse who rolls because of colic can twist a gut; he should be kept moving, preferably by hand-walking.

➤ See also colic

rollkur A controversial form of dressage training in which the horse is worked with a hyperflexed neck, also called working "low, deep, and round." It has been used in dressage since the 1980s by many successful Dutch and German competitors. Its defenders believe that it teaches the horse to round his back up

A horse worked in **rollkur** often has its chin tucked tightly to its chest.

and creates more brilliant action in front. Detractors consider it contrary to the classical ideals of dressage, as the position is achieved by force and works from front to back, rather than back to front. The Fédération Equestre Internationale (FEI) took action to limit the use of rollkur in 2010, but it is still seen, particularly in the warm-up ring at upper-level events, and has been the subject of petitions and boycotts. There have been no well-conducted studies on the effect of rollkur on horse health.

roll top A solid, curved jump with a rail at the top.
➤ See also "Types of Jumps," page 192

romal A piece of leather that connects the ends of Western closed reins and forms a Y. The tail of the Y hangs down the horse's neck and can be used as a quirt.

Roman nose A facial shape that is somewhat convex from just above the eyes down through the nose. Also called "ram's head," for its resemblance to the shape of a sheep's face.
➤ See also conformation; dished face

rope halter A halter made of knotted rope. Rope halters are stronger than leather halters, and the narrow rope gives more effective control with some horses. However, the throatlatch knot can be hard for an inexperienced handler to fasten and, because the lead rope is often fastened with a knot, it can be hard to remove quickly.

All horse owners know that horses, especially gray ones, particularly like to **roll** after being bathed.

Rope halters provide for easier fit than leather or nylon halters do, and the knots apply more emphatic pressure to the horse's cheeks and nose. Natural horsemanship clinicians often sell their own designs of rope halters, which are said to operate on specific pressure points. Some rope halters have a lead rope incorporated

ROPE HALTER

in the design; others are used with attachable leads. So-called bronc nosebands are broad, decorative nosebands that attach to a rope halter. Other rope halters have stiffened rawhide nosebands, similar to a bosal.

Rope halters are used in natural horsemanship because of the increase in sensitivity of the horse to the handler's signals. Positive reinforcement trainers consider rope halters aversive, because the knots and thin rope may cause pain. They prefer flat web or leather halters.

➤ *See also halter*

roping

➤ *See calf roping; cattle roping; rodeo; team roping; Western riding*

roping wrap A piece of inner-tube rubber wrapped around the saddle horn to prevent the rope from slipping.

round bone When the tendon and the bone below the knee are too close together.

➤ *See cannon bone; flat bone*

round pen, round penning A round pen is an enclosure made of pipe, wood, or metal panels, usually measuring 66 feet (20 m) in diameter. The pen serves as a safe place to turn out young horses and provides a smaller space to work a horse from the ground as well as in the saddle.

"Round penning" is shorthand for the natural horsemanship technique of working with pressure and release to control a horse's movements without physical contact, and get him to choose to "join up" with the trainer.

➤ *See also "join up"; natural horsemanship; pressure and release/reward*

ROUND PENNING

roundworms

➤ *See ascarid; deworming; parasites*

rowel A small pointed wheel on the shank of the spur. Most rowels rotate freely, which makes the spur much milder than it would be otherwise.

➤ *See also spurs*

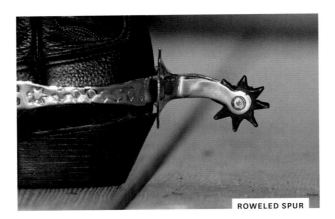

ROWELED SPUR

Royal Canadian Mounted Police (RCMP)
Established as the Northwest Mounted Police in 1873, the RCMP has evolved into one of the world's most visible law enforcement agencies. The word "Royal" was added by King Edward VII in 1904, and in 1920 the unit was officially declared the national police force. Today, the RCMP deploys more than 20,000 officers (not all on horseback) in a variety of duties, from municipal policing to international peacekeeping. Until 1966, all recruits went through equestrian training, but now officers must apply to become part of that unit.

The famous red tunics and broad-brimmed hats have been part of the uniform from the beginning, and the vivid image of the Mountie "always getting his man" has inspired hundreds of stories, novels, and films. The famous musical rides evolved from riding drills in the 1870s that were open to the public and have since become popular internationally.

The RCMP established a breeding facility in 1939 (the current farm is located in Packenham, Ontario) to produce the large, elegant, athletic black horses that are as famous as their colorful riders. A cross of primarily Thoroughbred and Hanoverian bloodlines, with Trakehner and Anglo-Arab, RMCP horses are 16 to 17 hands high and 1,200 to 1,400 pounds (544–635 kg), with strong, clean legs and a pleasant disposition. They must be able to jump and do dressage movements, as well as tolerate miles of travel and hours of performing (more than 125 shows a year). About half of the approximately 20 foals born each year make it to the intensive training program, which begins when they turn three.

➤ *See also mounted police; police horses*

> **REASONS FOR RUBBING**
>
> When a horse rubs his head against you, it may seem like an endearing gesture of affection, but it is actually a dominance behavior that can easily get out of hand. Discourage your horse from rubbing his head against you, and try showing your affection for him by patting or scratching his neck and withers instead of his nose and forehead.
>
> ➤ *See also body language, of horses*

rug A heavy horse blanket.

Rumensin

➤ *See monensin/Rumensin*

run

1. A turnout area designed for exercise rather than grazing. An enclosure measuring 20 x 100 feet (6 x 30 m) is sufficient for your horse to trot, but if you want to encourage him to gallop, the run should be at least 200 feet (61 m) long, with enough room at the ends for him to turn around safely while moving fast.

2. The gallop. This term is used in Western riding.

➤ *See also gait; gallop*

run-in shed A three-sided shelter. Although horses can live perfectly well outdoors without man-made shelter, they do need some place to get out of the wind and rain. If there isn't a natural windbreak in your pasture, a simple three-sided shed provides relief from the elements. Flies prefer hot, sunny areas, so having a shady spot can make a big difference in your horse's comfort level.

A run-in shed must be large enough to comfortably hold all the horses in the pasture; allow 142 square feet (13 m²) for each horse, with one side completely open to avoid injury if all the animals should decide to enter or leave the shed at once. The shed should be built on the highest ground available and face away from the prevailing winds (usually coming from the north). The walls need to be sturdy, with no sharp protrusions or gaps, and the roof should pitch slightly away from the front of the structure to keep moisture from accumulating.

running away

➤ *See aids; bolting; pulley rein*

running martingale
A piece of tack designed to aid in the control of a horse that carries its head too high. A loop of leather goes around the horse's neck, with a strap that attaches to the girth/cinch and divides into two straps that end in rings. The reins run through the rings and the straps provide a point of leverage.

➤ *See also martingale; standing martingale;*

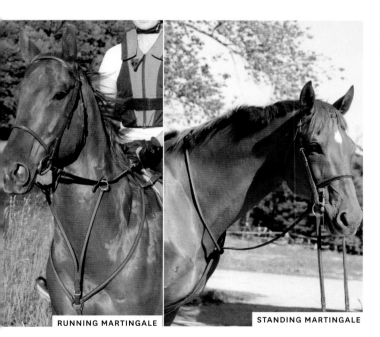

RUNNING MARTINGALE   STANDING MARTINGALE

running up stirrup leathers
On an English saddle, sliding the iron to the top of the back stirrup leather (the one closest to the saddle) and pulling the whole loop forward through the iron. This keeps the irons from flying around and striking the horse, and makes it easier to put the saddle on and take it off.

With a Western saddle, the stirrups hang free. When you tack up, loop the off-side stirrup over the saddle horn to get it out of the way.

➤ *See also saddle; stirrups; tack*

RUNNING UP STIRRUP LEATHERS

running walk
A smooth, fast gait natural to Tennessee Walking Horses and some other breeds. It has the same cadence as an ordinary walk. The head nods, but the back remains level and steady.

➤ *See also gait; gaited horse; Tennessee Walker*

rushing fences
In jumping, coming up to a fence too fast. This usually means the horse jumps flat or inverted rather than rounding his back and popping his hocks over the obstacle. This isn't a problem in steeplechasing, where speed is of the essence and the jumps (usually hedges) are forgiving, but in most kinds of jumping, you don't want your horse to drag his feet. Taking a shorter approach to the jump gives your horse less time to get up speed.

rust
A type of fungus that infects grain and grass; rusts appear as reddish brown patches. Ingesting rust-contaminated feed can cause colic, while breathing in rusts can create respiratory problems.

SABLE ISLAND HORSE

A breed of feral horses on Sable Island, off the east coast of Nova Scotia. They are stocky, thick-bodied, shaggy horses of French, Spanish, and possibly English blood, 13 to 14 hands high, usually bay or brown. They run free without management and without natural predators. Sable Island Horses are one of the few gene pools of early breeds not "improved" by selective breeding. They could be a valuable source of genetic material in the future.

sacking out Desensitizing a young or nervous horse to potentially frightening or startling stimuli. The term comes from the practice of taking an empty feed sack and flapping it near a tied horse, laying it across his back, sliding it across his legs, having him step on it, and so forth, until he stops reacting.

Sacking out as practiced by old-fashioned trainers and cowboys was a frightening experience in which the horse was snubbed tight and subjected to the stimulus until he submitted in a form of learned helplessness. As practiced by modern trainers, it is more often a calm, methodical introduction to different objects and materials until the horse sees each as no big deal.

saddle The job of a saddle is to distribute the pressure of the rider's weight away from the horse's spine and onto his ribs. It also provides a more secure seat for the rider than the horse's bare back does.

HISTORY For the first 2,000 years of domestication, horses were ridden bareback or with a saddle cloth, possibly fastened on with a strap. Weight placed directly on horses' spines caused damage and unsoundness over time. Riders suffered as well, as their dangling feet and legs swelled and ulcerated. Despite this, the saddle was not invented until roughly 2,400 years ago, by the Scythians, a nomadic steppe tribe.

The Scythian saddle consisted of two pillows of hide, stuffed with deer hair or grass, girthed with a leather band. It was stabilized by a breast band and crupper. Later saddles had wooden arches or forks at front and back, fastened to rigid bars that lay on either side of the spine. A saddle like this rested on a pad. The seat might be built directly on the tree, or might be a hammock of tough leather suspended between the arches. In medieval saddles the bars began to have elongated tabs to grip the horse's shoulders and loins; the front tabs can still be seen on the underside of an English saddle.

MODERN TYPES Today, there are two basic types of saddles: English and Western, with the Australian stock saddle and southern plantation saddle being hybrids of

the two. English saddles are flat, that is, without a horn; some, like the park saddle and racing saddle, may actually have quite a flat seat, but dressage, all-purpose, and jumping saddles will have a deeper, curved seat.

Having the right saddle is essential for any specialized discipline. You can't ride saddle seat in a jumping saddle, for example, and jumping is a lot more difficult in a park saddle. An all-purpose English saddle is adequate for the lower levels of dressage and jumping, but a specialized saddle can make a big difference by putting the rider in the correct position.

DIFFERENT TYPES OF SADDLES

Dressage saddles have deep seats; long, straight flaps; and stirrups that are set far back.

Jumping saddles have a more forward seat and flaps with deep knee pads for a secure grip.

To be as light as possible, **racing saddles** are tiny and flat; and because jockeys spend most of their ride crouched above the horse's back, they have very short stirrups.

Western saddles offer a secure seat with the traditional horn and a high cantle.

An **endurance saddle** may look like a modified Western saddle, with a high pommel and cantle, but it has no horn and the seat is designed for comfort and safety.

Western saddles differ according to usage as well. Trail and pleasure saddles are lightweight, often with a padded seat. Ranch saddles have a strong horn, reinforced rigging, and a flatter seat; an old-fashioned ranch saddle puts you in a chair position, resting back on the cantle with your feet forward. A barrel racing saddle has a high cantle and horn and a deep pocket seat, to hold you in on those tight turns, while cutting and reining saddles have a lower horn and flatter seat to allow hip movement. A roping saddle is extremely strong, with reinforced rigging and a sturdy horn.

Endurance saddles are lightweight, with no horn. They have attachment points for a breast collar, horn bags, and saddle bags, and are designed for comfort for horse and rider. Plantation saddles are similar to endurance saddles but may be more cut-back at the pommel to accommodate the high head carriage of a gaited horse.

➤ *See also English tack; sidesaddle, riding; tack; Western tack*

saddlebags
Bags designed to hang across the back of a saddle or on the horn to carry supplies. They are usually made of leather, polyurethane, or nylon; thermal bags are available to keep food or drink cold. Cantle bags are long, narrow, curved bags that buckle behind the cantle. There are saddlebags for English riders as well. Pommel bags snap into D-rings at the front, and cantle bags at the rear. English cantle bags come with a pocket that slips over the cantle to secure them to the saddle.

saddle blankets, saddle pads
Blankets or pads placed under the saddle. They protect the horse's back by absorbing sweat and cushioning pressure created by the weight of rider and saddle. It is more important to choose a pad or blanket that will do its job effectively than one that looks good. Be careful to buy a pad or blanket that fits your saddle and horse well. Excessive padding can lead to dangerous slippage of saddles.

Pads are designed to fit different styles of English saddles (dressage, all-purpose, park) and come in a wide variety of fabrics and thicknesses, from thin and quilted to thick and fluffy. Emphasis is placed on air circulation, cushioning, and nonslip qualities. Pads are usually contoured to fit the shape of the horse's back.

Many Western riders use heavy wool pads under their saddles. Wool absorbs moisture and helps release heat, keeping the horse's back cooler. High-tech pads incorporate a gel bladder to absorb energy. Western pads may or may not be contoured. Many are highly colorful. Blankets are also used under Western saddles; they are usually rectangular, folded in half, and brightly colored. A decorative saddle blanket may be used over a utilitarian pad.

SPECIAL PADS Shims and riser pads may be used to fine-tune saddle fit. Seat risers and wedge pads can lift a saddle in the front or back, to correct the slope of a saddle. Contour pads relieve pressure on the withers.

Some English saddle pads come with foam inserts that fit in pockets on the pad for incremental correction to saddle fit. If you have your saddle's fit analyzed and find that it could use adjustment, this can be a low-cost alternative to having your saddle restuffed or buying a new saddle. It can also be used to adjust to changes in the horses back as he matures, builds muscle, or ages.

saddlebred
➤ *See American Breeds, American Saddlebred*

saddle covers, saddle carry bags
Saddle covers protect your saddle from dust and mold-causing moisture in the tack room. Saddle carry bags are heavier and designed to make it easy to carry a saddle when traveling to a competition.

saddle fitting
A saddle must fit both horse and rider properly. Poorly fitting saddles can cause problems ranging from saddle sores to training difficulties. English saddle trees come in wide, medium, and narrow. Western saddles are designated full quarter horse bars (FQHB, or wide) or semiquarter horse bars (SQHB, or medium). Seat size is measured in inches, with the 16 to 18-inch range suiting most adults.

In a well-fitting saddle, the deepest part of the seat should be level with the ground. The cantle should be slightly higher than the pommel; the degree depends on the style of saddle. The saddle must contour to the horse's body, with adequate clearance above the withers; you should be able to slide your hand underneath the saddle along the shoulders beneath the withers. Under the pommel or fork, there should be 3 to 3½ inches (8–9 cm) of clearance on a new Western saddle, 2 to 2½ inches (5–6 cm) on a broken-in one. On an

English saddle, clearance is closer to 1½ to 2½ inches (4–6 cm).

With a rider in the saddle, there should still be an open channel over the withers that extends all along the horse's spine. The weight-bearing parts should not extend beyond the last rib. The spine can't bear weight beyond this point.

A girthed saddle should remain stable in every direction; gripping it at the horn or pommel and cantle and trying to rock it back and forth and side to side is the best way to observe how the saddle will behave under a rider's weight.

Sweat marks on the saddle pad indicate where the saddle makes contact with the horse. Dry patches on a pad after riding indicate points where the pressure against the horse's back is so intense that he can't sweat, or where the pad isn't in full contact with his back. A horse who actively resists being saddled, or has sore or puffy spots, is likely a victim of poor saddle fit. Telltale signs of poor fit include saddle galls.

Faulty saddle fit can be remedied by restuffing the saddle (for English saddles) or by adding shims or other special pads. Western saddles can't be restuffed but can often be fitted with special pads as well.

➤ *See also bars; English tack; twist (of a saddle); Western tack*

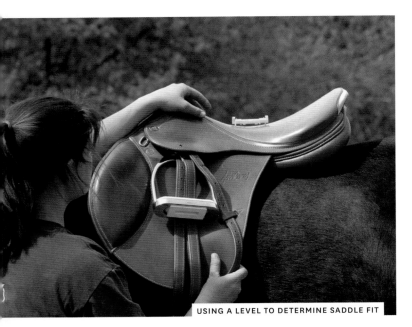

USING A LEVEL TO DETERMINE SADDLE FIT

saddle galls Spots of white hair in the saddle area, where the skin has been rubbed raw by improperly fitting tack; often seen on the withers.

➤ *See also saddle fitting*

saddle rack

1. A structure upon which a saddle is hung. The rack must give good support to the saddle tree and provide sufficient ventilation to dry the underside of the saddle. It's best for each saddle to have a separate rack. Collapsible versions are handy in aisles or grooming areas to hold tack while getting ready to ride. Saddles should not be stored on the floor.

2. In gaited riding, "saddle rack" is a term for the second-most-common easy gait; also called singlefoot, corto, or slow tölt. The saddle rack has an even footfall set-down timing and a 1-2-3-4 beat, like the walk. In speed it ranges from the slow fino fino gait of the Paso Fino, done almost in place, to about 8 miles (1.6 k) an hour. It is a comfortable gait to ride, despite the very active movement of the croup and shoulders.

➤ *See also tack room*

saddle seat A form of riding designed to show off the gaits of high-stepping horses like Saddlebreds, Morgans, Hackneys, and Arabians. The rider uses a park saddle, also called a Lane Fox or cut-back saddle. These saddles are quite flat, and are cut back at the withers to accommodate the high head carriage of the horse. The rider sits farther back on the horse than in other forms of riding, which encourages some of the lateral gaits. Stirrup leathers are quite long, but the rider should remain balanced over her feet and post gracefully; she rides very upright, and carries her hands high to maintain a line with the high-headed horse's mouth.

Saddle seat riding looks radically different from hunt seat or dressage riding, and is easily misunderstood by riders unfamiliar with it. It requires as much skill as any other kind of riding, and while the horses are much more animated, their excitement should not be misinterpreted as fear. Be aware that saddle seat riding develops a different set of muscles in the horse, and reschooling will be necessary to build the muscling for other kinds of riding, should you set out to retrain a saddle seat horse.

➤ *See also English riding; equitation; park horse*

SADDLE SEAT

saddle seat showmanship
Showmanship in saddle seat attire, sometimes with a full bridle rather than a halter.

➤ *See also showmanship classes*

safety
Horse-related injuries account for over 100,000 emergency room visits annually in the United States; most of the injuries result from falls while riding. Head and neck trauma is most common, followed by arm and leg injuries. Approximately 11,000 people a year experience traumatic brain injuries from horse-related accidents—far more than football. Less than 5 percent of reported horse-related injuries are from bites.

To reduce the possibility of injury:

- Wear a helmet while riding—every single time you ride. Eighty percent of riding-related deaths are the result of head injuries.

- Wear safe footwear: boots that are at or above the ankle, have hard soles, and have a heel at least ½-inch (1.2 cm) high. This helps prevent life-threatening injuries that can occur when a rider's foot slips through the stirrup during a fall.

- Avoid loose clothing. During a fall, loose garments can catch on the saddle and cause a rider to be dragged.

- Consider wearing a safety vest that can protect your neck and ribs.

- Wear full-seat breeches or chaps with suede to increase grip in the saddle.

- Develop your seat, and stay in good physical shape.

- Stay mentally alert while riding.

- Avoid overfacing your horse. Ride him where you feel comfortable, and expand your horizons gradually.

- Learn and practice an emergency stop.

- Learn and practice a "calm down" cue, such as head-lowering.

- Be sure all equipment is strong and in good condition.

- Don't ride alone, if possible. If you must ride alone, tell someone where you're going and stick to that plan.

Above all, safety around horses is a state of mind. Maintain awareness, be deliberate in your actions, and develop the habit of asking yourself, "If I do that, what's going to happen?" If you can imagine an accident scenario, you can manage your horse and the circumstances in order to prevent it.

➤ *See also body language, of horses; handling horses; "Passing Etiquette in the Ring," page 257; pulley rein*

THE "CALM DOWN" CUE

A calm horse is a safe horse, so many trainers teach horses a "calm down" cue. It's unreasonable to demand that a horse never become excited. Excitement happens, either from external stimuli like encountering stray dogs or being trucked to a show, or within a training session when the horse is asked to work at speed. Trainers don't teach the horse to *stay* calm; they teach him to *calm down*.

Fortunately, horses do reliably calm down if they lower their heads, and they can be taught to do this in hand and under saddle, in response to a rein or verbal cue. The behavior is first practiced in comfortable settings and expanded to more exciting or frightening situations, and provides a useful fallback that can help riders take control without using force.

salmonellosis A disease caused by a common bacterium that makes many animals, including humans, quite ill. Salmonella may be present in a horse's gut without causing problems, but it can flare up if the horse is ill or otherwise stressed. Infected individuals may have a high fever, watery diarrhea, and excessive thirst. Pulse and respiration are rapid. Because the disease develops so quickly, some horses die within a few days of extreme dehydration; others may linger for weeks before dying. Recovery is possible but may be slow; the horse may have chronic diarrhea for months. Salmonellosis is most severe in newborn foals.

Treatment consists of giving fluids and electrolytes, both orally and intravenously. Some veterinarians give antibiotics, but there is concern about strains of the bacteria that have developed resistance to certain drugs. Ill horses must be completely quarantined, to the extent that your boots and clothing should be changed before you work with healthy horses. The bacteria spread through manure, so all tools and equipment used around the sick horse should be kept separate and disinfected regularly. There is no effective vaccine at this time.

salt (sodium chloride) A mineral needed by all animals to maintain body fluids, transmit nerve signals, and maintain cell membranes. Horses need 0.1 percent sodium in the diet, increased to 0.3 percent if pregnant or working. They have a ready appetite for salt and will eat what they need. Salt is usually offered in blocks that can be left in stalls and pastures. However, some horses don't lick enough salt and may need to have it offered loose. Feed companies make horse-formulated loose salt mixtures; ask the feed store manager what is available.

salt block Salt is an important part of a balanced ration. Situate salt blocks in places that have good drainage, to minimize waste; in rainy areas, the salt block should be in a covered area. You can offer a plain and a mineral salt block together so horses can choose.

Horses usually do well with salt blocks, but as they have soft tongues, rather than raspy tongues like cows, some horses don't enjoy licking a salt block; they may bite or scrape it with their teeth. You can buy a loose salt mixture, or bash the salt block up and put it in a pan or corner feeder.

Himalayan salt—pinkish due to mineral content—comes in bricks, granules, and hanging salt licks. It is said to have a good balance of natural minerals but is more expensive than other types of salt.

sand colic

➤ *See colic*

SALT BLOCK

Sarcocystis neurona

➤ *See equine protozoal myeloencephalitis (EPM)*

sarcoid tumors

External tumors. Like warts, some sarcoid tumors are caused by a virus and may appear for no apparent reason. Other sarcoids develop after an injury; in fact, wounds that are not properly cleaned or that are subject to continued irritation (on the joint, for example) are most susceptible to sarcoids. Initially, the tumor looks like proud flesh (excessive granulation tissue that sometimes protrudes from a healing wound), but it will not respond to medications used to heal wounds.

While sarcoid tumors will not spread through the bloodstream, they do spread and grow locally. Regrowth is often stimulated by removal, but sometimes surgery is successful, as is burning or freezing the tumor. An effective technique has been to create a vaccine from the tumors to stimulate the horse's own immune system, essentially by feeding the tissue to the horse after removal.

Other treatments include heating or freezing the tumor, cisplatin chemotherapy, acyclovir (a topical antiviral), topical immiquimod (a bloodroot preparation), or fluoride preparations, including fluoride toothpaste. An herbal preparation called Sarcoid Salve, used in conjunction with immune-support herbs, has been reported to be successful, and mushrooms for immune support can also work. Sarcoids are individual, and treatment can temporarily create ugly, open wounds. Consider carefully whether treatment is necessary, and be prepared to try different methods.

sarcoptic mange

➤ *See mange*

sawbuck

A traditional pack saddle formed by pairs of wooden supports onto which you tie your load.

schaukel

An advanced dressage exercise that requires the horse to move from a rein-back directly into a forward gait. It increases strength in the horse's hip flexors, biceps, and quads. It should be done in brief intervals, with rest periods in between.
➤ *See also rein-back*

school figures

Standard patterns used in schooling and in tests such as dressage and reining. They include such maneuvers as volte (a small circle), figure eights, changes of direction, half-turns, cross-the-school, cross-the-diagonal, up-the-centerline, and serpentine. School figures provide a common language that can be used by student and instructor. They allow the student to develop coordination of aids, and they develop the horse's strength, flexibility, and responsiveness. Test figures are of prescribed dimensions; accuracy in producing them is revealing of a rider or driver's degree of control, and of a horse's athleticism.
➤ *See also arena work; centerline; pattern; quarter line; serpentine; suppling*

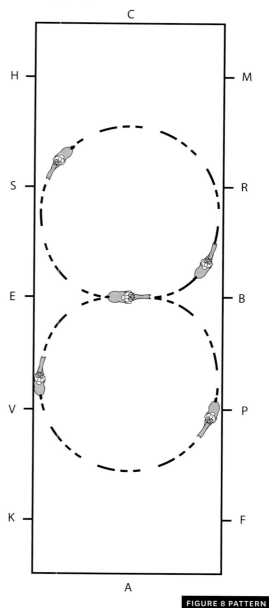

FIGURE 8 PATTERN

school horses Horses who are ridden in lesson programs. Many school horses spend their lives being ridden by inexperienced riders. On the one hand, they may become difficult to motivate or may find ways to take advantage of a rider's lack of knowledge. On the other hand, a good "schoolie" can be a great teacher and confidence builder. Ideally, a lesson program will have a variety of school horses; riding a wide range of horses helps beginners become competent riders.
➤ *See also lessons, riding and driving*

schooling Riding or driving sessions that start at a lower level of training and work systematically and sympathetically toward a higher level. Schooling a horse differs from exercising in that the schooling rider or driver pays careful attention to the development of a specific skill or set of skills in the horse.

schooling shows Shows that are designed as practice shows for both novice and experienced riders. They are a good way to gain experience for both rider and horse. Some schooling shows are just for fun, with innovative classes, games on horseback, and no formal dress code. Others resemble regular competition and offer the opportunity for participants to receive feedback from the judge.
➤ *See also showmanship classes*

score
1. In Western riding, to break quickly from the gate to overtake cattle in a Working Cow class.
2. Points received in a competition.

scotch In reining, a horse who appears to have half-halted while in the midst of a rundown prior to the sliding stop is said to have scotched. It appears most often when a rider misreads a pattern or is unaware of the exact location of the marker. It does not result in a penalty but does lower the score for the maneuver.

scotch bottom shoes A shoe used in draft horse showing. Scotch bottom shoes are weighted and flared to enhance the apparent size of the hoof and the flashiness of the gait. They encourage a flared, overgrown foot that can lead to lameness.

scratch To withdraw an entry from a class or race before the competition begins.

scratches A fungal (sometimes bacterial) skin problem picked up when horses walk through wet areas. Scratches, also called grease heel or greasy heel, affects the lower legs, possibly entering through a cut or scrape and causing the area to become crusty, scabby, and swollen. Light-colored pasterns and rear pasterns seem to be more susceptible to the disease, which can be prevented by keeping the horse out of wet areas and treating small lesions promptly, before the infection spreads.

Treatment is to clean the area thoroughly and apply a mix of one part nitrofurazone ointment (an antibiotic), one part dewormer paste (a paste containing a benzimidazole), and one part dimethyl sulfoxide (DMSO). A lanolin-based ointment such as ichthammol or Corona is also effective, as it is thick and stays on longer. Ichthammol softens the scabs, doing away with the painful necessity of picking them off. Do not apply bandages; you want the area to stay open to the air to promote healing.

Many horsemen have their own "infallible" remedies for scratches. It's worth listening to others' ideas, but it's most important to keep a close eye on your horse's pasterns and treat scratches early. The lesions may be very small; the first sign you see may be swelling of the legs.

scribe Person who assists the judge by recording scores during events that require detailed scoring. This allows the judge to remain focused on the horse's performance while recording scores. The use of scribes is required in many events because effective judging is virtually impossible without them. This is an opportunity for a volunteer to learn the sport from an expert, while playing an essential role in putting on a competition.

search and rescue, horses in Horses can be useful in searching for missing persons, and mounted search-and-rescue units are organized to provide backup for police and forest rangers. It may take a mounted unit some time to deploy, as horses typically have to be trailered in from a distance. Once they are on the scene, however, they offer advantages. A rider is higher than a person on foot and has a better view. The horse provides a second, better pair of eyes and ears, and a sense of smell that is comparable to a dog's. Horses can be trained to air-scent and alert on a quarry, just like tracking hounds, but even an untrained horse can provide information to a sensitive rider. Finally, when the missing person is located, a horse may be able to provide transport.

Search-and-rescue horses need to be well-trained trail horses in excellent condition so that they can continue the search until the person is found. They need to be desensitized to rescue vehicles and equipment, possibly including helicopters. Being part of a search-and-rescue team can be a rewarding way to give back to the community.

seat The rider's position in the saddle. The most common and versatile style of seat is called either "basic" or "balanced" seat, which can be adapted easily as a rider progresses to different disciplines.
➤ *See also aids; balanced seat; half-seat; posting trot; sitting trot; two-point seat; weight, as an aid*

seat of corn (of hoof) A part of the sole of the foot, located near the heel in the angle between the bars and the hoof wall.
➤ *See also hoof*

seat saver A cover that fits over a saddle to save both the saddle's seat and the rider's seat from wear. Seat savers may be made of fleece, foam, or gel.

seat shrinker A seat cover that can adjust the seat of a Western saddle to fit smaller riders; ideal for growing children or people of different sizes who share saddles.

seedy toe In a hoof, a stretching or separation of the white line (the junction of the sensitive and insensitive laminae). In seedy toe the white line looks fibrous and is open to invasion by dirt, moisture, and harmful organisms.
➤ *See also white line disease*

selenium A mineral needed in trace amounts. Selenium is vital for proper muscle development and to maintain immune function. Mild deficiency may result

The balanced rider adjusts her **seat** depending on the horse's gait.

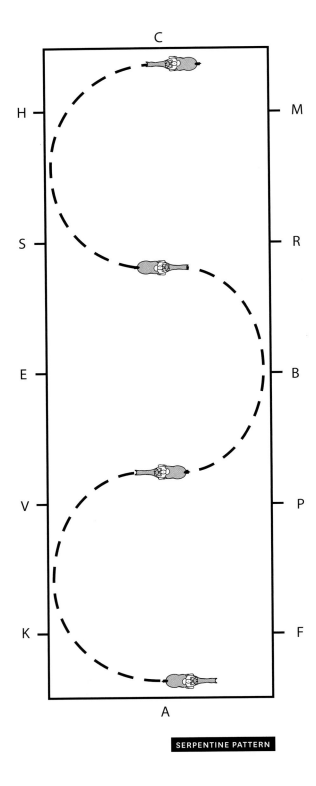

SERPENTINE PATTERN

in a compromised immune system; extreme deficiency may result in wasting and death. Consult your vet if you think supplementation is needed. Note, however, that selenium is toxic if eaten in large quantities—certain plants such as locoweed, most vetches, and some varieties of aster store high levels from the soil.
➤ *See also azoturia/Monday morning disease/tying up; poisonous plants*

self-carriage Balanced and independent carriage by the horse of his own body, without leaning on the reins for support.

serpentine A series of half circles performed in an S-like pattern; used to teach or test riders and horses; excellent for developing coordination of aids in riders and suppleness in horses. Riders can be asked to ride a serpentine at any gait, showing changes of diagonal or lead. Serpentines can be shallow or deeply rounded. Each version has a different gymnasticizing effect.
➤ *See also gymnasticizing; school figures*

serum hepatitis/Theiler's disease
➤ *See hepatitis*

set

1. To hold the hands steady in one position and keep even pressure on the bit without pulling back on the reins.

2. A group of competitors in cutting or team penning who use the same bunch of cattle. After the cattle have been used a certain number of times, a new bunch is brought in for the next set.

settle

1. To gather a bunch of cattle into a calm, compact herd.

2. When a mare becomes pregnant, it is said that she has "settled."

3. Some patterns require that a horse be "settled"—that is, calm and standing quietly for a specific time period—before proceeding with the next maneuver.

shafts Two parallel poles between which a single horse is attached to vehicle or implement. The shafts are connected to the harness with traces and sometimes bellybands and tugs.
➤ *See also driving; harness*

SHACKLEFORD BANKER PONY

A population of Spanish-bred ponies living wild on the Shackleford Banks of coastal North Carolina; frequently called Bankers. They are protected by federal law. Owners round them up and remove a few periodically when numbers become too large. Bankers are hardy and well adapted to life on the island, where they live on salt grass and dig to find fresh water.

SHAGYA ARABIAN

A strain of cross-bred Arabian horses developed in central Europe since the 1500s, Shagya Arabians have bigger frames and bones than purebred Arabians. They excel at jumping, dressage, endurance, eventing, and driving; are very friendly with people; and make excellent family horses. The predominant color is gray.

➤ *See also Arabian*

shaker foal syndrome
The result of botulism poisoning, which is nearly always fatal. Affected foals quiver and get very weak before collapsing.
➤ *See also botulism*

shank
1. A lead shank is a lead rope or strap with a chain. To "shank" a horse means to jerk on the lead attached to the chain that runs either over his nose or under his chin.
2. The shank of a curb bit is the part that extends below the mouth. Reins are attached to slots in the shank. The longer the shank, the more pressure it exerts on the bars and chin groove if a rider pulls back on the reins. Rules limit the length of a shank in competition.

➤ *See also bit; handling horses; lead rope; lead shank*

CURB BIT WITH SHANK

shear mouth
A condition in which a horse's lower jaw is abnormally narrow. The top molars can eventually wear the bottom ones down at such an angle that the teeth begin to slide past one another. If the abnormality is noted in time, proper dental care can keep the grinding surfaces normal and prevent a serious problem.
➤ *See also dental problems*

sheath
The pocket of skin that protects the penis of a male horse.
➤ *See also bean; diverticulum/blind pouch; penis; smegma*

sheath cleaning
It is conventional wisdom that male horses should have their sheaths cleaned periodically to remove smegma, a waxy, odorous combination of dirt, dead skin cells, and fatty secretions that build up in the folds of the sheath. Long considered an unpleasant but necessary part of conscientious horsekeeping, sheath cleaning has recently come under question. Some studies appear to show that sheath cleaning actually increases levels of bacteria in the sheath. Smegma may in fact be protective; certainly wild horses do not have their sheaths cleaned.

However, some horses produce more smegma than others, and some do seem to develop problems if cleaning is neglected. Thus, when to clean the sheath is an individual determination; it could be once a month or even just once a year. Most horses will become used to having their penises handled if it's done regularly, and many will let the penis down completely, which makes the job easier. Have a veterinarian teach you how to do this procedure safely.
➤ *See also penis; smegma*

shedding blade
A curved metal blade with serrated teeth for pulling off loose hair. The serrated edge of a shedding blade can be used after the rubber currycomb to remove loose hair. Lay it against the horse's coat and sweep in the direction of the hair. The smooth edge can be used to scrape off water after a bath.

shedding in spring
➤ *See Cushing's disease/Cushing's syndrome/PPID; grooming; hair*

sheet
A lightweight covering used to protect against flies, to keep a newly washed horse clean, to reduce sweating on very hot days, to cool out a sweaty horse on a cold day, or to keep rain and dirt off a horse at pasture. Some sheets are designed for turnout, while others are only appropriate for use in stalls or while the horse is tied or being walked.
➤ *See also blankets and blanketing*

TYPES OF SHEETS

Sheet	Description
Anti-sweat sheet	Made of mesh fabric, often cotton, to wick away sweat and keep the horse cool. For use indoors in very hot weather. Some also work as fly sheets.
Cooler	Designed to wick moisture from wet hair; often used after a bath or hard workout on a cool day. Allows the horse to cool off slowly without becoming chilled. Made of wool, wool blend, or polyester fleece, a cooler covers the horse loosely from poll or shoulders to tail.
Fly sheet	Usually made of a synthetic mesh that keeps flies from landing on the horse. Some models have leg straps and can be used for turnout. A good alternative to fly spray during heavy fly seasons. Fly hoods are also available to protect the head.
Rain sheet	A waterproof sheet to keep horse and tack dry.
Quarter sheet	A sheet used while riding in cold weather. It fastens under the saddle or over the rider's legs, and covers the horse's loins and haunches.
Scrim sheet	A light mesh sheet to keep a tacked-up horse clean while waiting ringside.
Stable sheet	A light sheet designed to protect the coat from dirt and dust. Used in stall after a bath or before a show to keep the horse clean.
Turnout sheet	Heavier than other sheets and designed for wear in pasture or paddock. It offers some protection against wind and rain.

SHETLAND PONY

A sturdy work pony originating in the Shetland Islands of northern Scotland. Shetlands have been the beloved playmate and first mount for generations of children. The original Shetland Pony was a miniature draft horse, capable of carrying heavy loads (even adult riders), pulling small plows, and working long hours in the mines hauling coal cars. He had a shaggy coat and thick mane for protection against the severe weather of his homeland.

After Shetland Ponies were imported to the United States, breeders developed a slimmer, sleeker version, more like a Hackney Pony, standing between 10.3 and 11.2 hands high. These show Shetlands are lively and flashy, while the fuzzy, rotund, old-fashioned Shetland (a maximum of 10.2 hands high) tends to be gentler. Well-known for their ability to work bolts and latches with their lips, Shetlands are smart, curious animals who might outsmart inexperienced or absentminded riders.

➤ *see also "Shetland Steeplechasing," page 339*

shelly hoof A hoof with a weak wall that tends to split and flake away.

shipping boots/ wraps Boots or wraps designed to protect a horse's legs when traveling in a trailer. Shipping boots come in many different styles, but generally have self-fastening straps and a durable outer layer of heavy nylon or even Kevlar (the same material used in bullet-proof vests). Shipping

SHIPPING BOOTS

wraps are similar to other leg wraps but use taller, thicker quilts and wider bandages. They are intended to protect the coronary band and the bulb of the heel.

As part of training your horse to load and unload from a trailer, accustom him to the sensation of the boots or wraps on his legs. Right before a show isn't the time to discover that he won't load because the shipping boots make him crazy.

There are times when shipping wraps don't make sense. If they don't fit or if you don't know how to put them on properly, they can entangle a horse and cause injury. In hot weather, they can cause his tendons to overheat. Seasoned travelers going short distances may not need wraps; inexperienced or fussy travelers should have that protection, but not until they have been trained to accept them.

➤ *See also leg wrap; trailering*

shortening the mane
➤ *See mane, care of; pulling the mane; roaching*

short shoeing Applying shoes that are too small. A shoe should extend beyond the heel, below the midline of the cannon bone, so that the leg is adequately supported. Since horses often step on the exposed heels of their front shoes and tear them off, many farriers use shorter shoes to save themselves a return trip. One or two cycles of short shoeing may do no harm, but

SHIRE

A large draft breed, the average Shire stands 17 hands high and weighs over 1 ton (907 kg). Generally black, brown, or gray, Shires have long, thick hair on their lower legs. They were developed in England from the heavy warhorses of the Middle Ages, and were used for hauling freight. In spite of their size and great strength, they are gentle and good-natured. Populations declined following the 1930s, as with all draft breeds, but the Shire is currently more numerous, both in the United States and globally, than in many decades. **Livestock Conservancy status: Critical**

long term it could cost your horse his soundness. This is one of the most common and harmful shoeing errors. Make sure your horse is wearing the right size shoes.

short-stirrup classes
Jumping classes for children under 12. The fences are 2' 3" (69 cm) or less, and include verticals, small walls, and spreads. Judges look for a smooth, correct round, with the horse on the proper lead at all times, and also consider riding style.

shotgun start
When all competitors in a race leave the starting line at the same time (often at the signal of a starter pistol) rather than in staggered heats.

shoulder, conformation of
Horses with long, well-sloped shoulders generally have good withers and proper pastern angles, giving them flexibility and good length of stride. A straight or upright shoulder usually accompanies more upright pasterns and a choppier, shorter stride.

shoulder, popping
An evasion in which the horse, when asked to turn, resists by bending his head toward where you want to go but continues to move his front legs and shoulders in the original direction.
➤ *See also aids*

shoulder-in, shoulder-fore

Lateral movements that many horsemen believe are among the most important suppling exercises. In shoulder-fore, the horse is bent slightly to the inside and his inside shoulder is aligned with his inside hip. In shoulder-in, the horse's forehand comes off the rail about 30 degrees, which puts the horse's forehand and hindquarters on separate but parallel tracks. Shoulder-in strengthens the hindquarters and helps develop straightness. Like all gymnastic exercises, it is tiring and should not be overschooled.

➤ *See also half pass; renvers; travers*

Show jumping: Beezie Madden rides Breitling at Spruce Meadows, Calgary, in 2015.

show jumping

Jumping competition that takes place in a ring as opposed to a cross-country course. It is one of the phases of eventing.

➤ *See also eventing; jumper classes; jumping; Olympic equestrian events; steeplechasing; "Types of Jumps," page 192*

showmanship classes

Show-ring classes in which handlers are judged on their mastery of the skills required to show a horse in hand. The horse's quality and conformation are not considered, except as a reflection of the handler's ability to show the horse to its best advantage. Judges of higher-level classes expect handlers to be aware of their horse's shortcomings so they can condition, groom, and present him in a manner that accentuates his strengths while minimizing his weaknesses.

shying

A fear reaction, when a horse leaps suddenly away from an object that startles him. Some calm, well-schooled horses rarely shy, while others will startle at any unusual sight, including things they have seen before. A previously calm horse who starts shying may be developing a vision problem, or could be receiving too much grain in his daily ration. Some horses do dramatically better on low-glycemic diets, or with the use of a calming supplement such as magnesium.

The horse is hardwired for fear, with the largest amygdala (the part of the brain responsible for fear and flight) of any domestic animal. Given that horse behavior causes 61 percent of horse-related accidents, and that one serious accident takes place for every 350 hours of horse-related activity, shying is a significant problem that the equestrian needs to work hard to prevent.

You can increase a horse's impulse control and make him less prone to shy by working him through obstacle courses, in hand and under saddle. This can be done in the ring at home and will pay dividends in the outside world. A horse who is used to playing with and working around unusual objects will come to accept many new objects. Wind, bright sun, and biting flies may still bother him, but a piece of flapping plastic will lose much of its power to disturb him.

Shying is a genuine fear response, but it may not indicate that the horse is actually afraid of the stimulus that precipitated the shy. Some trainers think of shying in terms of stimulus stacking—the accumulation of stimuli that the horse finds upsetting, until the last straw overcomes his self-control. For instance, a windy day creates unusual sounds and unexpected movement; a workman is using a loud tool in the area; it's feeding time, and other horses are running around excitedly; and the rider asks him to do something difficult. The stable cat running across his path may simply be more than he can take. When your horse is overwhelmed, instinctive reactions kick in, and they are not the horseman's friend.

Riders can anticipate and often prevent shying by being aware of the horse's stress level and, in stressful situations, presenting him with "kindergarten" behaviors that he can succeed at. When leading a horse past something scary, skilled handlers walk between the object and the horse. If he leaps away from it, he won't leap on top of the person leading him. In hand or riding, focusing the gaze beyond what's frightening the horse is also helpful, as is greeting the object as if it were a person. Keep in mind that things look physically different to his eyes than they do to yours, and his senses may be flooded by smells and sounds you can't even perceive.

If the horse does shy, yelling at him only confirms his opinion that there's danger present. Speaking calmly, restraining him as lightly as possible, and turning him in a circle are better strategies. Many highly acclaimed trainers do not hesitate to dismount if a horse is dangerously frightened.

➤ *See also fear (in horses)*

sickle-hocked
A conformation fault of the hind legs, also known as "too much set to the hocks." Sickle hocks can be seen from the side if you draw an imaginary line to the ground from the point of the buttock. An ideal set of leg allows such a line to touch the hock and travel down the back of the cannon bone and through the heel. On a sickle-hocked horse, the hock has too much angle, which pushes the cannon bone forward and places the heel well ahead of the line that's drawn to the ground. This fault places enormous stress on the hock joint and can lead to serious lameness and problems with curbs.

➤ *See also leg, of horse*

sidebone
A hard, bony growth found at the hoof head or coronary band and back toward the heels.

A HORSE SHYING

Sidebone is most often found in draft horses or horses with short pasterns. Lameness is uncommon except during the initial inflammation stage that indicates the beginning of a process that leads to ossification of the lateral cartilages.

sidedness
In humans, left-handedness or right-handedness. Many horses display a similar tendency to be more flexible on one side of the body than the other. A trainer should take great care to work the horse equally to both sides to prevent this from becoming accentuated. Sidedness in horses may be innate, or it may reflect handedness and habit on the part of their handlers.

sidepass/side step
A Western maneuver in which the horse moves straight sideways. Since there is no forward movement, the sidepass is not used in dressage.

sidepull
A bitless bridle in which the action of the reins is simple pressure backward or sideways on the cavesson, without leverage action on the headstall.

➤ *See also bitless riding; bridle; hackamore*

side reins Training equipment used to help the horse improve flexion and develop a strong "ring" of muscle throughout his body. Side reins are most often made of leather with a rubber ring that allows some elasticity and give during a longe-line workout. They attach to the bit and either a surcingle or a saddle ring.

It is vital that side reins be adjusted properly and readjusted as the horse develops in its training program. These are somewhat advanced tools that should only be used by educated horsemen.

➤ *See also longe/lunge; ring of muscles*

sidesaddle, riding Riding in a specially designed saddle with both legs on the left side of the horse. Historically, sidesaddle was the "proper" way for women wearing long skirts to ride. Sidesaddle riding, or riding "aside," is no longer mainstream, but it does enjoy waves of popularity among people interested in history and costume.

Riding aside is not as difficult as most people imagine and is an excellent exercise for all riders to learn balance. The sidesaddle rider must be balanced, forward, and centered around her right thigh. Theories about the position of the right foot differ, with some experts believing that the heel should be down, while others prefer that the right foot be relaxed and pointing toe-downward or pressed against the horse's shoulder. The double horn makes the seat quite secure; remember that Victorian women went hunting sidesaddle, jumping large obstacles in the field.

Sidesaddle classes take place at many large shows. A Mexican exhibition quadrille, Escaramuza Charra, features teams of 6 to 12 riders on high-spirited horses, wearing colorful lacy dresses and riding sidesaddle.

➤ *See also saddle*

sight
➤ *See vision*

A MEXICAN QUADRILLE EXHIBITION WITH SIDESADDLE RIDERS

signs of illness

➤ *See body language, of horses; colic; pulse and respiration; temperature (horse); veterinarian; vital signs*

silage/haylage

Grass or other forage preserved by anaerobic fermentation. Silage is not widely used for horses in North America. In Europe, however, grass silage often replaces hay as horse feed. It is easier to make than hay in rainy areas, and can be very useful for horses with heaves or hay allergies. Horses can also eat well-made corn silage, though this is less common.

In the United States, haying conditions are generally more favorable, and horsemen have not developed expertise with feeding silage to horses.

➤ *See also feeding and nutrition; hay*

silent heat

When a mare in heat fails to display obvious signs. Mares with regular silent heats may need more social stimulation (that is, the presence of a stallion) to show signs of estrus. Occasionally, silent heats indicate some problem with the reproductive tract, although a mare with silent heats may at other times have normal, more obvious heats as well.

➤ *See breeding; estrus*

simple lead change

Changing leads in the canter or lope by slowing to a trot or walk or halting before picking up the new lead.

➤ *See also flying lead change*

singlefoot

➤ *See saddle rack (2nd)*

SINGLEFOOTING HORSE

An easy-gaited breed developed in the American South for trail, endurance, and ranch work. Singlefooting Horses are meant to be working horses, not show-ring horses. They work cattle and compete in Western sports, while delivering a smooth ride. The registry maintains an open book, meaning that it accepts horses of any breed with a demonstrated singlefoot gait, but a type is beginning to emerge similar to the old-type Morgan. All colors are acceptable in the registry.

single horse, singles In driving, one horse put to a vehicle. Competitions for single horses are often abbreviated to "singles."

singletree A bar to which the harness traces attach so that a single horse can pull a vehicle or farm implement. Also called a swingletree.
➤ *See also doubletree; whiffletree/whippletree*

sire A horse's male parent; a stallion.

sitting trot In English disciplines, riding the trot without posting. The sitting trot can be difficult for novices or for anyone riding a horse with a large, bouncy stride. It is extensively used in upper-level dressage. Western riders do not post in the jog, except in certain movements of Western dressage.
➤ *See also posting trot*

six-up Three pairs of driving horses hitched one in front of the other.

skeið A term for the rapid pacing gait of the Icelandic horse; also called the flying pace.
➤ *See also Icelandic horse; tölt*

skewbald A coat color that has large patches of brown, or any other color besides black, on a white background.
➤ *See also color, of horse; pinto; piebald*

skid boots Boots that protect the rear fetlock/ergot area from getting kicked or rubbed raw in the dirt when a horse stops hard and suddenly, as when reining, cutting, or roping.

skijoring A sport in which a person on skis is towed by a horse. Skijoring is an organized sport in both Europe and North America, but it differs in form in each area. In Europe one person drives the horse while skiing behind him; the event is a simple race on a track. In North America, one person rides the horse and a second skis or snowboards behind him over a course that involves moguls, jumps, and sometimes ring spearing.

AMERICAN-STYLE SKIJORING

skin problems

➤ *See mange; rain rot/rain scald; ringworm; sarcoid tumors; scratches; warts*

sleeping sickness

➤ *See equine encephalitis*

sleep patterns

Horses are neither nocturnal (active at night) nor diurnal (active by day) but are what biologists call cathemeral; they alternate periods of foraging and periods of rest around the clock. Their habits are highly adaptable, with stabled horses doing most of their sleeping at night, when they are confined without human disturbance. In hot weather horses tend to spend much of the day dozing in the shade.

Horses sleep between five and seven hours a day, in one of three positions: standing on their feet; resting on the midline of the belly with legs folded under (sternal recumbent); or stretched on their sides (lateral recumbent). For truly deep sleep horses must lie down, as REM sleep occurs only while lateral recumbent. Horses require much less REM sleep than humans do, and as they are very hard to rouse from it, they stretch out only if they feel secure.

Much of horses' sleep time is spent on their feet. They are able to lock their limbs so that they can doze off without falling, though a truly sleep-deprived horse, or one with narcolepsy, may go into REM sleep standing up and partially collapse. Horses sleep in small increments, taking 20 to 50 tiny naps a day. Foals in their first few weeks sleep much longer and lie down more often than older horses do.

Horses lie down more frequently in the open than in stalls. Though we may think of the stall as a safe place, many horses apparently experience it as a place of confinement and possible danger. Horses tend to sleep facing an escape route, allowing them to flee without intervention of the thought process. In group situations, one horse will typically remain standing.

STANDING

STERNAL RECUMBENT

LATERAL RECUMBENT

A team of Haflingers pulls a **sleigh**, which is designed for several passengers. A cutter is a sleigh built for two people.

sleigh, sleigh rallies A vehicle on runners, pulled behind a horse or pair over snow. Sleigh rallies are winter driving competitions on snow.

slicker-broke A horse who will not shy, buck, or bolt when his rider puts on a slicker or does other unusual activities in the saddle.
➤ *See also sacking out; shying*

slick-fork saddle A Western saddle that does not swell out below the horn. A slick-fork saddle allows the rider more comfort and freedom of movement than a swell-fork saddle does. For added security, especially when working youngsters, some riders add bucking rolls (also called bronc rolls) to a slick-fork saddle.
➤ *See also bucking rolls/bronc rolls; swell*

sliding plate
➤ *See horseshoes*

slobber bar A metal bar connecting the two shanks of a leverage bit; a slobber bar stabilizes and improves the performance of certain bits. It does collect quite a lot of slobber as well.

slobbers
➤ *See Rhizoctonia leguminicola*

slobber straps
➤ *See reins*

slow amble/slow gait One of the gaits demonstrated by five-gaited horses. At full speed, this gait is called the rack. It is a four-beat gait that resembles the pace, except that each foot hits the ground individually.
➤ *See also amble; American Breeds, American Saddlebred; five-gaited horse; gait; gaited horse; pace; rack; three-gaited horse*

slow feeders Hay and grain feeders designed to make the horse eat more slowly.
➤ *See also hay bags/nets/feeders*

small strongyles Like large strongyles, these worms are bloodsuckers. They inhabit the intestine and cause anemia and debility, as well as ulcers that can lead to fatal hemorrhaging. All horses are infested with small strongyles to some degree, and a rigorous deworming program is essential in controlling them. Because the worms emerge seasonally from the intestinal wall, deworming must take place at certain times to be effective. In northern climates, this is in late winter and early spring, and in southern climates in fall and winter.

Ivermectin is effective, but many types of small strongyles are resistant to frequently used drugs. Work with your vet to find a deworming program that meets your needs.
➤ *See also deworming; parasites*

smegma A buildup of dirt, dead skin cells, and fatty secretions that accumulates in the sheath or around the udder. In a male horse, enough smegma may accumulate in the diverticulum to form a "bean," a hard ball that may need to be removed manually.

➤ *See also diverticulum; penis; sheath; sheath cleaning*

smut A fungus that appears as black powdery clumps on the seed heads of grasses. Grain contaminated with smut is toxic and can cause convulsions, paralysis, and rapid death if eaten. Smut can also cause colic and bring on respiratory problems if inhaled.

➤ *See also rust*

snaffle bit A bit that acts on the corners of the mouth, the bars, and the lips. The snaffle is one of the most widely used bits because it is one of the gentlest. Most trainers use a snaffle on green horses, and most instructors put snaffles in the mouths of their lesson horses.

Most snaffles have jointed mouthpieces. Many horsemen believe this is what differentiates a snaffle from a curb, but some snaffles have a straight, unjointed mouthpiece. The differentiating factor is the direct pressure on the corners of the mouth, the bars, and the lips, as opposed to the leverage action of a curb bit.

Snaffles come in a variety of styles, from the smooth, round-ring snaffle to the full-cheek Dr. Bristol snaffle. They also include a wide array of Western types, often hybrids with curb-style shanks like the popular Tom Thumb bit. Some of these are designed to be used in transition to a curb bit; as they use leverage, they really should not be described as snaffles.

The vast majority of snaffles have a single- or double-jointed mouth piece that lies across the horse's tongue. Double joints, like the French link or the dog bone of Western snaffles, allow the bit to work more softly on horses with thick tongues or low palates. Some Western snaffles are linked in the center by a so-called life-saver, an O-shaped ring that helps keep the bit from pinching the tongue.

Though the snaffle is regarded as a mild bit, not all snaffles are mild. The thicker the mouthpiece, the milder its action. Thin mouthpieces can literally slice a horse's tongue. Twisted wire or chain mouthpieces transform a snaffle into something that must be used with great care. Shanks on a snaffle can produce a nutcracker action on the mouth unless they are three-jointed.

➤ *See also bit; bridle; tack*

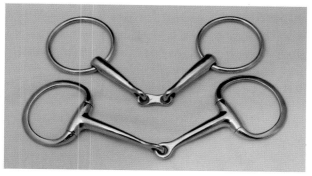

The French (top) and eggbutt snaffle are just two of numerous types of snaffle bits.

snatch To grab abruptly at the bit or reins. Snatching, on the part of either the rider or the horse, is a habit to be discouraged.

sneakers, riding Sneakers with a heel, specifically designed for riding. These are the only kind of sneakers you should wear while on a horse. Regular sneakers aren't a good choice because a shoe without a heel can slide through a stirrup and get caught; if you fall, you could be dragged. Even if you're not riding, regular sneakers offer little protection against sharp hooves.

➤ *See also boots (for rider)*

snip A patch of white hair between and below the nostrils, above the upper lip. A snip may be quite broad or just a few hairs.

➤ *See also face markings*

snowballing Buildup of snow on the bottom of the hoof. Snowballing happens more often with shod than with barefoot horses, and can cause slipping and injury. The best prevention for a shod horse is to put on tube-type rim pads, which flex and dislodge the snow.

SNOW FOR WATER While horses will eat snow in winter if they are thirsty, they use a lot of energy and body heat melting it and warming it. Always make sure your horse has access to unfrozen water in winter, and keep an eye on his intake, as most horses drink less in cold weather.

soaking feet For many types of leg and foot injuries, your veterinarian will recommend that you soak the affected area in warm water, perhaps with Epsom salt added. The best choice is a soaking boot designed for horses (there are various styles available), but a rubber bucket or a plastic feed supplement tub will work also. Avoid using a metal bucket; it may clang if the horse bangs against it and is not as giving as rubber or plastic.

Get your horse used to putting his foot in the boot, tub, or bucket before adding any water. Once he'll stand quietly, add water that is slightly warmer than his body temperature. As he accepts the water, you can add Epsom salt and then gradually add hotter water (as hot as he'll tolerate, but not hot enough to burn).

It's easier to soak with two people—one to make sure the leg stays in the soaking device and one to handle the water supply. Soaking for 20 to 30 minutes a day for three or four days clears up most infections. Usually, the veterinarian will recommend covering the wound between soakings to keep out dirt and wetness. There are also special boots to protect injured hooves.
➤ *See also boots (for horse); hoof*

SOAKING A HOOF

sobreandando A Peruvian Horse lateral gait that is generally faster than the paso llano, with a longer stride and more overreach.
➤ *See also paso llano; pasitrote; Peruvian Horse*

socks White markings on the leg that extend above the fetlock but not above the knee or hock.
➤ *See also leg markings*

social grooming
➤ *See mutual grooming*

sodium chloride
➤ *See salt (sodium chloride)*

soft in the face A term used to describe a horse who responds to the aids without stiffness or resistance in his head and neck. Guiding a horse with light reins and gentle but consistent contact produces a horse who is soft in the face. A soft horse responds willingly and quickly to subtle aids; he is aware of his rider at all times.
➤ *See also mouth, hard or soft*

soft mouth
➤ *See mouth, hard or soft*

sole bruise
➤ *See stone bruise*

sole of hoof The bottom of the hoof, in front of the frog. A healthy sole is slightly concave to absorb pressure from the weight it bears. It should be thick and hard to protect against bruises.
➤ *See also hoof*

sorghum grain/milo A good horse feed, though not available everywhere. Sorghum grain, also called milo, should be rolled or crushed before feeding and mixed with a bulkier food such as oats. It is about 80 percent digestible nutrients with 8.5 percent protein, but only 2.3 percent crude fiber.
➤ *See also feeding and nutrition; grains*

sorghum grass/Johnson grass/Sudan grass (*Sorghum* spp.) Common in pastures in the southwestern and southeastern United States, this grass

SORREL COLORING

can be quite toxic after a drought or hard frost, when it produces cyanide.

soring An inhumane practice, common in the 1950s and 1960s, used to accentuate a saddle seat horse's gait and high-stepping action by irritating the forelegs with chemical or mechanical means. A sored horse quickly lifts its front legs to relieve the pain, resulting in more "brilliant" action in the show ring. The Horse Protection Act of 1970 and its amendment in 1976 seek to ensure that responsible horse owners and trainers will not suffer unfair competition from those who sore their horses and that horses will not be subjected to the cruelty of soring. The practice is widely prohibited and is no longer a problem for most breeds, but the rule is not well enforced on the "Big Lick" Tennessee Walker show circuit.

sorrel A type of chestnut coloring; reddish brown or reddish-gold coat color, often with a lighter mane and tail. The term is usually applied to Western horses.
➤ *See also color, of horse*

sound Free from any fault, injury, or illness that inhibits the horse's ability to perform its designated purpose. The old phrase is "sound in wind and limb," meaning that there is not a problem with lungs or legs.

Horses can be serviceably sound despite a minor unsoundness that only partly inhibits functioning. For instance, a horse with a fused bone spavin might have an uneven gait yet be pain-free; such a horse could be considered serviceably sound as a trail horse or as an equitation mount or showmanship horse, but would not be sound for pleasure or dressage competition. This same horse might be sound for breeding, though a detailed assessment of conformation should be conducted to be certain the lameness is not due to an inheritable conformation fault.
➤ *See also conformation; heaves; respiratory system; roarer*

sow mouth/monkey mouth A term used to describe an underbite. Sow mouth is less common than its opposite, parrot mouth. If the upper molars are not kept trimmed, they will form hooks that can puncture the lower gum.
➤ *See also dental problems; parrot mouth; teeth and age*

spade bit A Western curb bit with a high port and a "spade," a spoon-shaped piece of metal that presses against the roof of the horse's mouth. Spade bits can appear quite cruel to the uneducated eye. In practice, they are introduced only at the end of an exacting process of training. By the time a horse is carrying a spade bit, he is usually working "straight up in the bridle." The balance of the bit influences how he carries his head; if he raises his head, the spade presses against his palate, but if he lowers it, the bit returns to a neutral position, without any action by the rider.

The spade is considered a signal bit. Its construction allows the horse to sense when the rider picks up or moves the rein. The trained horse responds to the signal rather than to contact. The horse works with a draped rein, responding mostly to weight and leg aids, and light neck-reining.

➤ *See also bosal; bridle horse; neck-rein; vaquero*

SPADE BIT

Spanish Jennet A breed created to provide a registry and association for colored Paso Finos or Peruvian Horses in North America. Spanish Jennets may be all pinto colors, and leopard-complex (Appaloosa) coloring is also allowed. Accepted foundation horses were chosen based on show records, conformation, and quality of gaits as well as color. The Spanish Jennet stands between 13.3 and 15.2 hands high. It is an aristocratic, rounded, muscular horse with a refined yet sturdy appearance. This is a new breed with a small population as yet.

➤ *See also Paso Fino; Peruvian Horse*

Spanish Riding School The most prestigious school of riding in the world. The Spanish Riding School in Vienna, Austria, is world-famous for the performances of the Lipizzan stallions. Though an Austrian institution, the school is called Spanish because the original bloodlines of the Lipizzan horse were Spanish.

➤ *See also airs above the ground; Classical High School; individual maneuvers; Lipizzan*

SPANISH BARB

A hot-blooded horse with Spanish and Moroccan Barb blood, bred by the Spanish in North America in the 16th and 17th centuries. The breed was near extinction when conservation efforts began in the 1970s. The Spanish Barb Breeders Association evaluates and registers horses that meet its exacting criteria.

The Spanish Barb has a distinctively Spanish head, a heavy crested neck, and a long sloping shoulder. It is smoothly muscled, with a short back, rounded croup, and excellent feet and legs. Averaging 14.2 hands high and weighing between 850 and 1,000 pounds (386–454 kg), the Spanish Barb comes in all colors. The temperament is described as "fire and feather," high-spirited yet gentle. Spanish Barbs have excellent cow sense.

➤ *See also Barb*

Any of a group of strains descending from the Spanish horses that arrived in the New World in the 16th century. In comparison with the mustang, which is heavily mixed with the blood of other European breeds, Spanish Mustangs and Spanish Colonial Horses have been identified through DNA testing as being of predominantly Spanish descent.

The Spanish Mustang is wiry and solidly built, with long muscles and strong legs and feet. He has a Roman nose and an arched neck, with a flowing mane and tail. Ranging from 13.2 to 14.2 hands high, he weighs 1,000 pounds (454 kg) or less, and is known for his alert, even temperament as well as stamina and energy. He comes in a variety of colors, both solid and spotted.

Spanish Mustang Strains

Several strains of mustang have been found living isolated in the mountains, where they maintain unmixed Spanish bloodlines. They include the following:

CERBAT. Cerbat Mountains near Kingman, Arizona. One of the purest groups of feral Spanish horses. Small (13.2–14.2 hands high), sure-footed, tough, and extremely easy to handle and train. Some are gaited.

NOKOTA. Developed from a herd confiscated from the Sioux chief Sitting Bull in 1881. They are rangier and larger than southern mustangs. Their ears often hook slightly at the tips.

KIGER. Kiger Mountains of eastern Oregon. Closely linked to the horses brought to America by the Spaniards, with almost no mixture of other blood. All are dun; small horses, between 14 and 15 hands high, with a classic Spanish head; quick, agile, naturals at working cattle.

PRYOR MOUNTAIN. Pryor Mountains of Montana. Attractive, proud, fiery, and exceptionally easy to train if handled gently. Sure-footed and athletic, with high action and a smooth amble, they sometimes exhibit termino.

SULPHUR HORSE. Sulphur Springs area of Utah. Usually dun, with strong Spanish characteristics; narrow-built but deep, with short backs, good necks, and long cannons. They must pass a physical inspection before being admitted to the registry.

WILBER-CRUCE MISSION HORSE. Descended from horses brought to southern Arizona by Father Eusebio Kino in the late 1600s. They have good conformation and extremely hard feet, and make good ranch and trail horses.

➤ See also mustang

Spanish traits A group of traits that identify a horse as of predominantly Spanish blood. As traditional breeds worldwide are modernized and "improved" with Arabian and Thoroughbred blood, some horsemen have become concerned to conserve the Spanish traits as valuable in themselves and as a source of genetic diversity.

Spanish traits include a small size; a heavy-boned head, sometimes long and often convex in profile; a heavy neck; heavy shoulders and hindquarters; heavy, dense bone; large hooves, with high heels and soles; an angled croup and low tail set; and smooth gaits with little animation. Spanish-bred horses are typically gentle and trainable, with excellent cow sense.

Spanish walk An artificial gait in which the horse stretches the forelegs high and well forward at the walk. The Spanish gait is used as a training exercise in classical dressage, for improving concentration and coordination, as shoulder gymnastics, and in exhibitions. It is taught in hand first, and then under saddle.

spares kit In driving, a repair kit required in many competitions—and a good idea whenever you are driving. A spares kit should include a leather punch, a vise grip, a hammer, a screwdriver, a strip of rawhide for lacing, a rein splice, a trace splice, a hoof pick, and the appropriately sized wheel wrench for your vehicle. A spare bit, a spare halter, and a spare lead are also a good idea.
➤ *See also driving*

spasmodic colic
➤ *See colic*

spavin Either of two types of blemishes affecting the hock joint: bone spavin and bog spavin.

Bone spavin, also known as Jack spavin, is the name given to a bony enlargement on the inside, lower part of the hock. Veterinarians do not fully agree on the cause; however, horses with weaknesses in their legs or hocks are more prone. Predisposing factors include, but are not limited to, hocks that are not "square" or tend to taper from top to bottom when viewed from the front; small hocks; tied-in hocks; sickle hocks; and cow hocks. Horses ridden before their hocks are fully developed are also at risk. A horse with a bone spavin may be lame until the bone fuses, and he may thereafter have an asymmetrical gait.

Bog spavin is the name given to a spongy swelling of the lower inside of the hock joint. The most common cause is actually a predisposing factor—upright hocks, or hocks that lack angularity between the bones above and below the joint (tibia and metatarsal). It is most common in young horses that are placed in training before their hocks are fully developed and in breeding stallions. Symptoms other than the obvious swelling are rare, except when the spavin initially develops.
➤ *See also leg, of horse; sickle-hocked*

SPANISH WALK

speed, of horse With the exception of cheetahs, some antelopes, and the brown hare, no other animal is faster than a horse, and none can outrun a horse over distance. Horses can reach a top speed of about 43 miles (69 km) per hour, compared to a cheetah's 65 miles (105 km) per hour. A racing greyhound runs at about 42 miles (67 km) per hour. Because the horse's stride is mechanically and metabolically efficient, he can sustain speed for much longer than other species. This has been key to the horse's survival as both a wild and a domestic species.
➤ *See also gait; flat racing; harness racing*

speedy cutting A form of interference in which the inside of diagonal hind and forefeet brush; most often seen in trotting racehorses.

spin A reining maneuver in which the horse pivots 360 degrees on his inside hind foot. A spin differs from a pirouette in that the pivot foot is anchored to the ground and does not continually step in proper gait sequence.
➤ *See also pirouette; reining*

splay-footed Having hooves that turn outward from the fetlock joint. A splay-footed horse often causes himself harm, sometimes serious enough to result in unsoundness. He can't walk straight and true because his hooves are not centered under his legs, so his feet tend to "wing" inward and often hit the opposite leg. This interference of gait can cause serious damage, resulting in lameness.
➤ *See also leg, of horse*

splint bones, splints The vestigial second and fourth metacarpal (front leg) and metatarsal (rear leg) bones. In the modern horse these stabilize the bones of knee and hock. These small bones can be fractured or tear loose from the cannon bone due to exercise; areas of inflammation or fractures involving a splint bone are informally referred to as "splints."

Symptoms of splints are a lump on the interior of the leg, usually a front leg; heat; tenderness; and possible lameness. A fractured splint bone must be removed surgically. A "popped" splint bone will resolve with ice, pressure bandages, and anti-inflammatory drugs. In either case, the horse almost always returns to full use, though the enlargement may remain.

SPIN

splint boots
➤ *See boots (for horse)*

spontaneous combustion, of hay Freshly cut hay generates a startling amount of heat through bacterial activity, especially if high in clover or alfalfa content. Check stored hay frequently to make sure the internal temperature of the stack or bale is no higher than 150°F (65.5°C). At 175°F (79.4°C), the hay will begin to smolder from the center until reaching oxygen at the edge of the stack, whereupon it will burst into flames. If it gets to 185°F (85°C), call the fire department to supervise removal of the hay from the barn.

All hay should be stored in a building separate from the barn, if possible. If in the barn, have a buffer zone of at least 100 feet (30 m) between the hay storage area and the stable and tack room. Make sure all hay is well cured before storing it.

spook, spooky To spook is to startle easily. A horse given to shying is often called spooky.
➤ *See also shying*

spooned-heel shoe A horseshoe that has had the tips of the heels forged thin and bent up to fit closely to the heels of the hoof. Spoon heels are used to prevent the horse from tearing off his front shoes by stepping on them with his rear hooves.

sport boots

➤ See boots (for horse)

sport horse Any horse, purebred or not, that is suitable for dressage, jumping, eventing, driving, or endurance riding. The term is generally applied to warmbloods, and may be used within other breeds, such as the Morgan, to describe a horse best used for sport rather than the show ring.

spread A jump consisting of two to four fences set close together. Spreads can be from 2½ to 6½ feet (0.8–2 m) wide.

spur An artificial aid used to reinforce and refine the natural leg aid. A properly used spur can deliver a precise signal, most useful in lateral work. Spurs should be worn only by riders who have been educated in their use. Riders must have full control of their lower legs and be able to ride with an independent seat before advancing to wearing spurs. Riders who lack such skills may jab their horse's sides with the spurs.

There are many types of spurs, ranging from bumper spurs—loops of metal with no point—to short blunt spurs commonly worn by dressage and hunt riders, to roweled spurs of various sizes. Heavy, blunt-tipped rowels are milder than rowels with multiple sharp points, as the pressure is spread across a broader area. The rolling action of the rowel also makes the spur milder than it would be if it were fixed.

Like whips, spurs have a bad reputation. They can be used to cause pain, which is abusive. However, used by an educated rider on a trained horse who accepts and understands them, spurs can be a refined tool of communication.

➤ See also aids; reinforcement, in training; rowel

ENGLISH SPUR

squamous cell carcinoma Cancerous growths that appear around the eyes of horses with little skin pigmentation; the growths may also appear around the vulva or sheath on light-colored horses. Horses with unpigmented eyelids should not spend a lot of time in the sun. Keeping them stabled on bright days, using a fly mask, or applying a human sunscreen can help prevent carcinomas. Any bump or sore around your horse's eyes that doesn't heal or go away should be examined by a veterinarian.

Carcinomas can be removed by radiation, freezing, or chemical burning, or by using immunotherapy (injecting a vaccine that stimulates anticancer cells). The location of the growth will determine the safest course of treatment. In some cases, removal of the eye is necessary.

➤ See also sunburn

stable flies A biting fly (*Stomoxys calcitrans*) similar in appearance to common houseflies. They populate stables, breeding in manure. Stable flies feed on blood, and inflict painful bites on the lower legs, belly, flanks, under the jaw, and the chest. Some horses can be driven to a frenzy by the bites. Others spend the day stomping their legs, which can damage their hooves and joints, loosen shoes, and cause weight loss.

Stable flies are controlled by removing manure and spreading it thinly to dry it out, or by composting it. Fly predators and various kinds of fly traps are also helpful in reducing the numbers.
➤ *See also predator wasp; parasites*

stableizer A restraint device modeled on the war bridle but more effective and humane. It fits over the horse's head like a halter with a covered cord that goes under the upper lip. The application of pressure behind the ears releases endorphins, which block pain and relax the horse, while the pressure on the gums inhibits the release of adrenaline, keeping the horse even calmer.
➤ *See also handling horses; twitch; war bridle*

STABLEIZER

stable wrap
➤ *See standing bandage/stable wrap*

stadium jumping
➤ *See show jumping*

stake out
➤ *See picketing/staking out*

stall
➤ *See barns and facilities*

stall chewing
➤ *See cribbing*

stallion An intact male horse with at least one testicle descended. Usually a male horse is referred to as a colt until it is mature, which ranges from three to five years, depending on the breed. Stallions require specialized care in nearly all areas, from feeding and exercise to handling and training. It is a job best left for experienced horsemen.

stall walking
➤ *See pacing; weaving*

Standardbred *(see next page)*

standing at stud When a stallion is available for breeding to mares owned by persons other than the stallion's owner.
➤ *See also breeding; stallion*

standing bandage/stable wrap A piece of quilting held in place with a stretchy roll bandage, often used with liniment on a lower leg to reduce swelling and fluid accumulation. Although it can stay on overnight (without liniment, which could burn the skin), a standing bandage should be removed for at least 1 hour out of every 12- to 16-hour period. It doesn't matter which direction you wrap the bandage, but it is important to use even tension without pulling on the flexor or extensor tendons. Make sure the quilt stays smooth, with no wrinkles or lumps.

STANDARDBRED

An American breed developed for harness racing, on a foundation of Narragansett Pacer, Morgan, and Thoroughbred blood. Originally, as of 1871, Standardbreds had to meet a timed standard of trotting 1 mile (1.6 k) in 2 minutes and 30 seconds before being allowed in the registry, hence the name. (Today's Standardbred trotters are faster, however.) Standardbreds either trot or pace at great speed without breaking stride; some do both, but most have a preference. Most Standardbreds trace back to a foundation stallion named Hambletonian, whose foals were natural trotters.

Standardbreds make fine sport horses, though off-track Standardbreds may have some things to learn about cantering. Because retired racing Standardbreds are used to the commotion of the track, they are safe mounts and are often retrained for use by police departments.

Measuring around 15 to 16 hands, these horses are generally dark in color and less finely built than Thoroughbreds, with plainer heads, heavier bodies, and stockier legs. They are valued for their toughness and stamina as well as their pleasant, calm personalities.

➤ *See also harness racing; pace; trot*

standing martingale A strap attached from noseband to girth, designed to prevent the horse from tossing his head or holding it too high; similar to the Western tie-down.

➤ *See also bridle; martingale; running martingale; tie-down*

star A white spot on a horse's forehead. A star may cover most of the upper part of the horse's forehead above and between the eyes, or it may be just a few white hairs.

➤ *See also face markings*

stargazer A horse, often ewe-necked, who carries his head too high.

staring/standing hair A horse's coat is said to be "staring" when it is rough and harsh-looking and stands away from the skin. This can happen after a shampoo, but it can also be a sign of poor nutrition or another ailment.

steeplechasing

Racing over jumps. Steeplechasing originated in England, where the most famous race is the Grand National, but has become a popular form of racing in the United States as well. In American point-to-point races, amateur riders race over not-very-high fences, sometimes across hunting country. Brush races are between 1½ and 2¹³/₁₆ miles (2.4–4.5 k), over a steel frame 52 inches (132 cm) high stuffed with plastic "brush" to simulate old-fashioned hurdles. They take place on a track.

But the sport is best known for its beautiful and picturesque cross-country races. These are held over timber fences—natural wood fences made of boards, logs, or post and rail. In major races like the Maryland Hunt Cup and the Virginia Gold Cup, fences are around 5 feet (1.5 m) high and the distance is 4 miles (8 km). Spectators arrive early for picnics and socializing, then sit on the grass close to the fences or the finish line to watch.

Steeplechase horses are mostly ex-flat racers. They must be 3 years old to race over hurdles, 4 years old to race over timber. They typically have a longer racing life than flat racers, competing until around age 13 in the bigger races, then at lower-level and amateur races before being retired to eventing, show jumping, or foxhunting.

Steeplechase jockeys can be taller and heavier than flat jockeys; the maximum weight in a steeplechase is around 140 pounds (64 kg). Amateurs and juniors compete on an equal basis with professionals; junior riders can apply for a license at age 16.

Non-Thoroughbreds can compete in Field Master Chases, 1-mile (1.6 k) races over 2' 6" (76 cm) fences. Riders follow a field master, who sets the pace, and are penalized for passing him. The field master leads over the fences, then riders race to the finish.

SHETLAND STEEPLECHASING

Shetland Ponies are often terrific jumpers, and Shetland steeplechasing is gaining popularity. It began in Great Britain and has been recently imported to the United States, where it is featured at large shows like Devon. Ponies race in an arena, over appropriately sized jumps. The cute factor is outsized.

➤ *See also Shetland Pony*

STEEPLECHASING

stereotypy An abnormal repetitive behavior, such as pacing, pawing, or weaving. Traditionally described as "vices," stereotypies in horses are usually the result of stress and confinement.

➤ *See also pacing; pawing; weaving*

steward The official at equestrian competitions who is responsible for interpreting the rules of the regulating organization. The United States Equestrian Federation (USEF) has the largest educational and licensing program for stewards in the United States and Canada. USEF stewards are highly educated professionals who serve to protect the integrity of the sport. They assist judges in making sure there is a level playing field for all competitors by enforcing the rules. Stewards actually have a slightly higher level of influence than judges, as they can report inappropriate or illegal conduct by judges to the regulating organization.

stifle The large joint between the thigh and the gaskin, just behind the flank, with a kneecap similar to that of a human. The stifle should be positioned well forward, in a line with the hip bone above it. It should be wide and well muscled, with the same degree of angulation as the hock joint. The stifle and the hock are the two most important joints in propelling the horse forward. The locking mechanism of the stifle, along with locking the elbow and the support of the strong nuchal ligament at the top of the neck, allows the horse to sleep standing up.

➤ *See also leg, of horse*

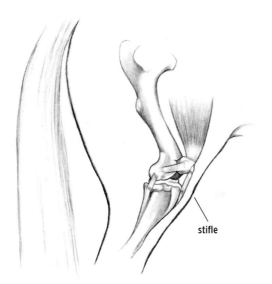

stifle

stirrups Stirrups afford the rider greater stability and control of leg position (though it is a good idea to ride without stirrups periodically to develop an independent seat). English stirrups are made of steel, aluminum, lightweight polymer, or nylon; they attach to the saddle with narrow leather straps (leathers), with holes and buckles to adjust the length. Western stirrups are thicker and wider, and may be made of leather, metal, or wood.

Stirrups must fit properly. With your foot in the stirrup, there should be room to slip a pencil between your boot and the side of the stirrup, on both sides. Rubber stirrup pads can improve traction. They are commonly used on English stirrups, but wraparound versions are also available for Western saddles. Don't use rubber pads if you're wearing rubber-soled shoes with treads; they may stick.

Safety stirrups are designed to release the foot if a rider falls, to prevent her from being dragged. The Peacock safety stirrup has a rubber band on the outside of the stirrup, which pops off if the rider falls. For adults it's best to use a stirrup with a curve in the outside branch, such as the Australian or Icelandic safety stirrup, or the MCD Intelligent Stirrup, which combines flexing branches with an adjustable offset eye.

SPECIALIZED STIRRUPS Another stirrup innovation is the OnTyte system, in which a special magnetized stirrup is used with a boot that has a metal strip inserted in the sole. Developed to help a rider who was recovering from an accident, it has proved to have other applications and is FEI-approved.

There are several styles of stirrups designed to make riding easier on the hips, knees, and ankles, such as an offset eye (the part of the stirrup bow through which the leathers loop) for English stirrups. This lets the leathers lie flatter against the saddle. Jointed branches assist the rider in lowering her heels without strain. Shock-absorbent pads can also help. Western riders also have the option of angled stirrups, or of using a hanger between the stirrup and fender that sets the stirrup at a right angle to the horse; this takes strain off the knee. Shock-absorbing pads or cushions, or specially designed trail stirrups, are also available.

Of all riders, jumpers rely most on their stirrups, and there are many innovations in this area, focusing on creating a lightweight stirrup with a large, grated footbed for maximum grip.

For most types of English riding, your stirrup leathers should be roughly the same length as your arm. To measure, place your fingertips at the top of the leather and stretch it out along your arm. The bottom of the stirrup should fit into your armpit. Jumping requires a somewhat shorter stirrup, while dressage riders use a longer one. Western stirrups are also longer, to allow for many hours in the saddle.

➤ *See also running up stirrup leathers; saddle; tack*

stock horse Traditionally, a horse used to work livestock; today, a horse used for Western sports. Modern stock horses are more specialized, and less versatile and durable, than the old-time ranch horse. Stock horses need to be fast, agile, and powerful, and should have good cow sense.

➤ *See also Western riding*

HISTORY OF THE STIRRUP

Before stirrups, riders let their legs dangle. After many miles their legs swelled painfully. Mounting was also a problem. Riders vaulted onto the horse, or carried rope ladders and braced them in one hand at the horse's withers. Soldiers put a short peg on their spear-shafts, jabbed the spear into the ground, and mounted that way, but many a swordsman impaled himself while trying to mount, including the Persian king Cambysis in 553 BCE.

The first approach to stirrups were the loops of rope or leather used in India. The rider stuck a couple of toes through the loops. By the 300s CE, the Chinese had the stirrup—first a single stirrup, used for mounting, rapidly followed by the paired stirrups we use today. It's impossible to know whether the Chinese invented the stirrup or borrowed it from the Huns, but the idea spread rapidly. The Huns brought stirrups to Rome in 451 CE, and soon everyone was using them.

➤ *See also history of the horse; saddle*

stockings White leg markings that go above the knee and/or hock.

➤ *See also "Leg Markings," page 204*

stocks

➤ *See restraints*

stock saddle

➤ *See Western tack*

stock seat The basic seat used for Western riding. "Stock seat" and "Western" are used interchangeably.

➤ *See also seat*

stock tie A narrow white scarf that wraps around the throat, rather like an ascot, and is often fastened with a small pin; part of formal hunt or show attire. Stock ties were originally worn by hunters as a convenient way of carrying an extra bandage in case of injury.

➤ *See also "English Show Attire," page 103; ratcatcher*

stock up A condition in which the legs become swollen due to decreased circulation, often as the result of inactivity. Horses who are not used to being confined may stock up overnight in a stall. The edema goes away as soon as they are able to exercise. A horse's legs might also stock up if he stands for a long time on a hard surface, if he kicks violently at something, or if he otherwise strains the legs. A horse with scratches may stock up without the lesions on the pastern being easily apparent.

➤ *See also scratches*

stomach

➤ *See colic; digestive system; feeding and nutrition*

stomach tube A plastic tube 8 to 10 feet (2.4–3 m) long that is fed through the nostril to the back of the throat and down the esophagus to the stomach. It may be used to feed a foal who is not nursing, give fluids to a dehydrated horse, or to administer mineral oil to a colicky horse.

➤ *See also colic; foaling*

stone boat A sled used for hauling rocks on the farm or in pulling contests.

stone bruise Injury to the underlying layer of the sole; usually due to stepping on stones or frozen ground. A bruise is not usually a serious injury, though it may require rest or use of a hoof boot for a while. However, an infection in a bruise can spread to the laminae or a bone or joint, so a stone bruise should be carefully monitored.
➤ *See also hoof*

straight bit/bar bit A bit with no joint or curves. It is vital to fit a straight bit correctly because it is rather unforgiving. The horse's tongue size, palate depth, and bar width must be taken into consideration.
➤ *See also bit; bridle; tack*

straight-pull trailer/tagalong trailer
➤ *See trailer*

straight stall/tie stall A narrow stall with side walls and a manger. Horses are tied while in straight stalls and cannot turn around or lie down. Straight stalls are best used temporarily, for horses who have plenty of turnout and other opportunities to lie down.
➤ *See also barns and facilities*

"straight up in the bridle" A bridle horse is said to be working "straight up in the bridle" when he consistently carries his head vertically, with the rein draped. This is the goal of bridle horse training.
➤ *See also bridle horse; spade bit*

strangles/shipping fever An acute, extremely contagious upper respiratory disease caused by the bacterium *Streptococcus equi*. Strangles spreads when the horse inhales or ingests the bacteria, through nose-to-nose contact or shared drinking water. The most obvious signs of the disease are fever, abscess formation around lymph glands (most commonly under the jaw), and raspy breathing. Horses may appear dull or lethargic, lose their appetite, and have profuse nasal discharge before swellings appear.

Penicillin should be used early in the disease, before the lymph nodes abscess. After the abscess antibiotics can prolong the disease. Since it may be difficult to detect mild swelling, it is probably best not to treat, but let the disease run its course. The infected horse should be isolated, and strict hygiene should be observed. There is a vaccine available for prevention, but it is one of the least effective. Prevention of strangles is mostly a matter of hygiene and careful quarantining of new arrivals.

straw bedding A traditional, comfortable, and readily available bedding for horses. Straw, however, has some drawbacks. Oat straw becomes slimy when wet, and is often eaten by horses, causing hay belly. Barley straw is less palatable, but if horses do eat it, it can cause colic. Also, it has barbed awns that can irritate eyes and gums. Wheat straw is the best straw bedding, but is expensive. Straw bedding makes for a bulky manure pile; on the other hand, if there are mushroom farmers in your area, you may be able to sell them your manure pile if the horses are bedded on straw.
➤ *See also bedding; mucking out stalls; barns and facilities*

strawberry roan
➤ *See red roan coloring*

Streptococcus equi
➤ *See strangles*

stress, effects on horses Stress depresses the immune system, leaving a horse open to infection and illness. Horses are particularly susceptible to respiratory ailments when stressed. Vaccinations should not be given during times of stress, such as weaning, training, or transporting, because the horse will not build up peak immunity.

Sound management and handling of horses requires that humans expand their awareness of the effects of stress on horses. This requires an understanding of how individuals vary. Conditions that stress one horse may keep a different horse engaged and interested in his surroundings. Just like people, some horses relish a life filled with complex demands, while others need simpler, more relaxed lives to thrive.

STRESS REDUCERS

Horses can be stressed by many different factors, including sudden changes in their routine or surroundings, inadequate nutrition, lack of water, strange noises, pain, fear, toxic or allergic reactions, hard work, and exhaustion.

Stress reducers include scratching the neck and withers, using a gentle voice, playing music in the barn, and asking the horse to do some easy task. Lowering the head is both a sign of reduced stress and a way to reduce stress. Teach the horse a cue for putting his head down. Then remember to ask him for this behavior in moments of stress. It seems to calm horses down. Practice using it in distracting situations, and you'll build yourself a "calm down" cue that can be useful in an emergency.

stride versus step A **stride** is a complete sequence of steps within a gait. All gait sequences start with the set-down of a hind foot. A half stride occurs with the set-down of the opposite hind foot, a full stride with the set-down of the original hind foot.

A **step** is the distance between the set-down of one front hoof and the other, or one hind foot and the other. In walking or marching steps, each hoof of the transverse pair is flat on the ground for a split second as weight is transferred. In running steps, one hoof of the transverse pair is lifting as the other sets down. In leaped steps, both hooves are off the ground for a split second.
➤ *See also track*

strike A pawing motion in which the horse brings a foreleg up and out, intending to make contact. Both sexes may do this upon meeting a new horse who seems to present a challenge; a strike is often accompanied by a squeal. Horses may also strike reflexively in response to fear or pain, but some horses do it maliciously. A horse who strikes habitually needs to be handled by a professional trainer.

stripe A straight or slightly wavy line of white hairs running all or partway from forehead to muzzle; narrower than a blaze. Some horses have a star, a stripe, and a snip; when joined, they often look like a lightning bolt.
➤ *See also face markings*

Strongid C
➤ *See pyrantel tartrate/Strongid C*

strongyles
➤ *See deworming; large strongyles; parasites; small strongyles*

strung out A term used to describe a horse moving with his back hollow and his hind legs not engaged. A horse who is strung out seems to be barely stepping his hind feet under his body, whereas a horse working "in frame" steps well up under his body.
➤ *See also collection; impulsion*

stud (for traction)
➤ *See calk*

stud (horse) A stallion used for breeding purposes.
➤ *See also breeding; stallion; standing at stud*

stud book The registry of a breed, which records vital information on each horse registered by that organization.
➤ *See also breed association/breed registry; pedigree*

stud colt An intact (unneutered) male horse less than four years old.

stud farm/stallion station A facility with one or more stallions standing at stud to which mares are sent to be bred. A mare can either stay at the farm until the birth of the foal or return to her own barn for the pregnancy and birth.
➤ *See also breeding*

stud fee/breeding fee The charge for breeding a mare to a particular stallion. An owner may charge a lower stud fee for a young stallion or even offer free breedings to get some foals on the ground. As the stallion's reputation becomes established, the fee generally goes up. Stud fees generally contain some provision for repeat breedings if the mare fails to settle on the first attempt, and may also contain a live foal guarantee.

sucking wind

1. In some parts of the United States, "sucking wind" refers to the instance of air being sucked into a mare's vaginal tract when she moves, due to a defect of the vulva. Such mares are sometimes known as "windsuckers."

2. In other parts of the country, the term refers to cribbing, also sometimes called windsucking.

➤ *See also cribbing*

suckling An unweaned foal.

sugardine An antiseptic paste made from two parts ordinary white table sugar and one part povidone-iodine solution (10%) and used to treat wounds, burns, hoof abscesses, and thrush. It can also be used to toughen the soles of a horse's hooves. Although this is a home remedy, your veterinarian may recommend it in certain situations and can guide you in its use. Sugardine has the advantage of being extremely inexpensive and easy to use. It reduces swelling and speeds healing.

➤ *See abscess; povidone-iodine solution; thrush*

sulky A light, two-wheeled cart pulled by a single horse.

➤ *See also driving; harness*

summer sores/habronemiasis Sores caused by the larvae of a stomach worm deposited by horseflies and stable flies that are feeding on skin wounds (often found on the lower legs) or moist areas, such as the corner of the eye or the sheath. The flies become infected by feeding on manure containing the

SUFFOLK PUNCH

An English draft breed developed from Jutland Horses brought to England by the Vikings. Bred to work heavy clay soil, Suffolks have smaller feet than most draft horses and no feathering. They are short-legged, well-rounded horses of moderate size (16.1–17 hands high). Suffolks are always chestnut, ranging from dark liver chestnut to golden. Prized as easy keepers and easy to work with, they are an ideal breed for horse-powered farming and logging.

There are over 600 registered Suffolks in the United States and only about 200 in England, but this undercounts the population, as many horses are never registered and geldings are usually sold without papers. There may be as many as 1,500 Suffolks in the United States, and perhaps another 1,800 worldwide. Numbers continue to increase; the moderate size and quiet temperament of the Suffolk is an asset, especially for younger, inexperienced farmers. **Livestock Conservancy status: Critical**

stomach worm larvae, which create constant sores by trying to develop on the skin rather than the stomach.

Summer sores are marked by a refusal to heal; instead the lesion often grows bigger as time passes. Wounds, which look circular after a few weeks, will usually ooze fluid and be very itchy. If untreated, the wound may heal when cold weather arrives, but the larvae can live for up to two years in the skin and sores will reappear in the spring. Deworm with ivermectin in two doses, three to six weeks apart, to kill most of the larvae. Wounds should be kept clean and protected from flies to prevent summer sores.

sunburn Although most horses are protected against the sun by their coats, light-colored horses or horses with white facial markings, especially around the mouth and eyes, are susceptible to burning in strong sunlight. Keeping the horse indoors on bright days, using a fly mask, or applying a human sunscreen lotion or thick ointment (like zinc oxide) around the eyes and muzzle can help prevent burning.

➤ *See also melanoma; photosensitization; skin problems; squamous cell carcinoma*

supplements Vitamins, minerals, herbs, and other nutraceuticals that are added to a horse's normal rations.

Supplement types include the following:

- Calmers, usually herbal or magnesium-based

- Weight supplements, usually fat-based

- Digestive tract supplements to improve gut health and prevent ulcers and colic, often containing probiotics, enzymes, and mineral buffers

- Joint supplements, often containing glucosamine, chondroitin, hyaluronic acid, herbs, or a combination

- Hoof supplements, usually mineral-based

- Senior supplements

- Anti-inflammatories such as methylsulfonymethane (MSM)

- Electrolytes

- Supplements to address specific health problems like anhidrosis, cough, or metabolic disorders

In fact, most horses don't need supplements unless working extremely hard; health problems, pregnancy, or lack of sufficient nutrients from hay or pasture are other reasons to consider a supplement.

Some supplements are toxic in large quantities, so read dosages carefully. Others are fattening, and fat horses are prone to performance and soundness problems. Overfeeding supplements to foals can create permanent skeletal malformation. Determine the need for supplements on an individual basis. Ask your veterinarian for advice if you're unsure. If you are competing, make sure your supplements do not contain any banned substance.

➤ *See also feeding and nutrition*

suppling Improving flexibility, the foundation for balance. A stiff horse is usually resistant and unable to perform in a relaxed, soft frame—a frame that is as important to casual trail riding as it is to high-level competition. Suppling exercises help a horse gain flexibility. They range from carrot stretches that supple the neck and back muscles and spinal joints to circles, serpentines, and lateral work under saddle.

➤ *See also carrot stretches; school figures*

surcingle

1. A strap of leather or nylon buckled around a horse's barrel to keep a blanket in place.

2. A piece of training equipment similar to a harness girth, used for ground driving. Rings on the surcingle can be used for attaching an overcheck and crupper. Some trainers use a saddle instead of a surcingle, running side reins to the girth, and driving lines through the stirrups.

3. A strap of leather or nylon with a padded metal loop at the top to prevent a horse from rolling all the way over and thus getting cast in his stall; known as an anti-cast surcingle.

4. A piece of equipment used in equestrian vaulting, fitted with two strong handles and two or more loops to aid vaulters in the various gymnastic movements.

surgical colic A colic, such as a torsion, that cannot be cured without surgery.

A MOMENT OF **SUSPENSION** AT THE TROT

suspension The moment in the trot or canter when all four hooves are off the ground. In certain gaits the suspension may be elevated or the moment of suspension may be prolonged.

suspensory ligament The ligament that connects the bones of the knee to the bones of the fetlock in the front leg, and the bones of the hock to the bones of the fetlock in the hind leg. Damage to this ligament can cause a lifetime of lameness problems.
➤ *See also leg, of horse; conformation*

LIGAMENTS VERSUS TENDONS

Ligaments connect bone to bone. Tendons connect muscle to bone. Both are tough and fibrous; injury to either causes lameness that may be difficult to heal, with tendons healing somewhat more easily than ligaments.

swamp fever
➤ *See equine infectious anemia (EIA)*

swayback A marked dip in the back between the withers and point of hip; also called a hollow back. Swayback results from either a congenital conformation fault; too little calcium in a growing horse's diet; old age; hard work; or carrying many foals. A swayback tends to be weak and is a detriment to speed. A swaybacked horse may tire easily or become sore.

Reflexive hollowing of the back in response to grooming or while riding indicates soreness or resistance within the horse's body. It is felt by sensitive riders as stiffness; less experienced riders will often just feel as if their horse is uncomfortable to ride. It has numerous possible causes including, but not limited to, an injury to the horse, poorly developed riding skills, mismatched horse/rider combination (for example, a rider who is too large for the horse), or an ill-fitting saddle.

Though it can have several other causes, a **swayback** is often a sign of old age.

sweating Sweat is a crucial part of a horse's thermoregulatory system, removing about 70 percent of his excess heat. Sweat is mostly water, so sweating robs the body of fluid in and between cells. This causes skin texture to change, gut sounds to quiet, and blood to thicken as a horse dehydrates.

Horses sweat during exercise or on a very hot day, just as humans do. The physical characteristics of a horse's sweat can be an indicator of his fitness. Compared with a fit horse, an out-of-shape horse loses more electrolytes and protein through his sweat, causing sticky sweat that smells and works into a lather. Horses in good condition have watery, clear sweat with less odor. A horse in improving condition will begin to sweat earlier in a workout, and sweat more.

Sweating can cause dehydration and deplete electrolytes. Do everything you can to keep your horse's hydration up. Hosing him with cool water at the end of a workout takes over the function of sweat without your horse having to pump more fluid out of his own body.

Sweating while at rest in cool weather can be a sign of illness. A lack of sweat after exertion or in hot weather (anhidrosis) is a serious concern.

➤ *See also anhidrosis*

sweat scraper A plastic, rubber, or metal implement used to flick sweat or water from a horse's body. The smooth side of a shedding blade can be used as a sweat scraper.

sweepstakes A class or race that offers prize money to a certain number of winners, based on a previously determined scale. The money comes from entry fees as well as an additional "purse," which is sometimes donated by an individual or corporate sponsor.

sweet feed A mixture of grains and pellets held together with molasses, which cuts down on dust. Horses love sweet feed because of the molasses, but it spoils quickly if not kept in a cool, dry place. Dry molasses still cuts dust but is less perishable. Molasses is high in potassium and is easily digestible, but it raises blood sugar after meals. Many behavioral problems with horses can be helped by replacing sweet feed with a well-balanced feed high in fiber and low in grain and molasses.

➤ *See also feeding and nutrition; supplements*

swell The front part of a Western saddle, under the horn, which on a swell-fork saddle swells out; also called the fork. A swell adds to rider security.

➤ *See also slick-fork saddle*

synthetic tack Tack made of manmade materials, not leather. Synthetic tack can be comfortable and well constructed, though leather tends to be more durable. Synthetics are easy to care for (no saddle soap needed!), are lightweight, and can get wet without damage. Trail riders were early adopters of synthetic bridles, and synthetic harnesses can be significantly lighter than leather ones, making the job of harnessing a large draft horse much easier.

Different synthetic materials have their drawbacks. When riding in a synthetic saddle, make sure to check the girth after mounting, as some types compress with a rider on board. The tree of a synthetic saddle will have a shorter life than that of a good leather saddle, which with care can last a lifetime. Some synthetics become slippery when wet. Biothane reins should have a section of nylon or leather where you hold them.

➤ *See also saddle; tack*

tack The gear that people put on horses to control them—from halters to harnesses. If a horse wears it on his body in the course of any type of work, it's tack.
➤ *See also bit; bridle; cinch; English tack; hackamore; halter; harness; martingale; saddle; saddle blankets, saddle pads; synthetic tack; Western tack*

tacking up The process of saddling and bridling a horse.

tack room A separate room within a barn for storing tack. A tack room should be insulated, well ventilated, dry, rodent proof, and well organized. Tack trunks take up a lot of space, so when building or renovating a barn, make the tack room as large as you can. A room 10 x 22 feet (3 x 7 m) will take up the space of two box stalls, and is a useful size.

The tack room is best located near the grooming and saddling area. In an unheated barn, a tack room can be independently heated or have a freezeproof cabinet for storing medications. Sun can be destructive to leather, so any windows should have shades. A tack room should have plenty of hooks and saddle racks. Shelves and cubbyholes help with organization. A washer and dryer, sink, and hot-water heater are nice amenities. A whiteboard or clipboard should hold an up-to-date list of important contact numbers: veterinarian, farrier, feed store, and fire department.

tagalong trailer
➤ *See "Towing Hitches," page 366; trailer*

tail A horse's tail consists of a short length of bone, the final vertebrae of the spine, covered with long, flowing hair. The tail channels water off the body, brushes away flies, and communicates a horse's emotions.

Horses raise their tails when excited, an action called "flagging"; the degree of lift depends on the breed and level of excitement. They slash their tails as a warning to other horses and to people; the tail-slash is part of the vocabulary of bluff, and one worth paying attention to, as a bite or kick may follow.

A horse wrings his tail (swishing it in circles or moving it rapidly up and down), when annoyed or stressed. When mounted, keep your horse away from the heels of a tail wringer or you could be inviting trouble. In some classes in the show ring, tail wringing can mean points off your total score. More important, it signals that something, either tack or your aids, is bothering your horse, and you need to get to the bottom of it. However, not every swish of the tail is a sign of stress. Horses working hard at difficult maneuvers like canter half-pass or tempi changes often swish the tail as part of balance changes.

What humans do to a horse's tail, in the name of style or practicality, can affect the tail's natural functions. Docking the tail, for example, takes away the horse's ability to swish flies. Another unethical practice is blocking, an attempt to prevent tail wringing by using an injection to partially paralyze the nerves of the tail. The effect lasts for several weeks, and although the practice has been banned by all major show associations, it still happens. Repeated nerve blocking can create permanent damage; it can even interfere with normal defecation and urination. When purchasing horse, make sure his tail hangs and moves normally; if you have any questions, ask your veterinarian to examine the tail during the prepurchase exam.

Another practice banned by some show organizations is nicking, in which muscles on the underside are cut to allow for use of a device called a tail set to make a high arch. This used to be common on the Saddlebred circuit, but it is becoming less popular. Although artificial, the tail set doesn't permanently damage the tail in the way that blocking can. But if the tail isn't kept in the set most of the time, it will flop over. Another common practice is to use a bustle, a large cushion strapped under the tail to hold it up and influence the muscles. The elevation created by using a bustle is temporary.
➤ *See also banging a tail; bustle; docking; nicking; tail, care of; tail rubbing; tail wrapping*

SMOOTHING UNRULY HAIRS

If your horse's tail head tends to get fuzzy and messy-looking, you can train the top hairs to lie smooth and stay neatly braided at a show. Resist the temptation to snip hairs that stick out of the braid. Instead, dampen the tail head with water or a tiny bit of conditioner, comb the hair smooth, and make a French braid for about 8 inches (20 cm). Leave it this way for one or two days, if it is not braided too tightly, and then take it out and dampen and smooth the hairs again.

BRAIDED TAIL

tail, braiding
For competition purposes, horse and rider must present a certain appearance, depending on the class. For some classes the mane and forelock are braided while the tail is left loose, but for many hunter competitions the tail must also be braided. Never braid the tail without also braiding the mane and forelock.

tail, care of
To keep a horse's tail looking good, brush it when clean and dry. Like manes, tails can be conditioned after a bath, or misted with detangler before brushing, to minimize breakage. Brush starting from the bottom, a few inches of tail at a time, using a sturdy hairbrush with wide-set bristles. Combs tend to grab and pull out hair.

Trimming a tail helps to keep it thick. Horses can step on too-long tails, pulling out hairs. A straight, blunt cut, called a banged tail, is tidy and looks good. Tails may also be trimmed in a tapered cut.

Some horse owners keep their horses' tails in braids during the winter. The tail is braided in a single braid, which is then doubled and tied up with a strip of gauze. This can be done in late fall after the flies have disappeared.

Good nutrition promotes a good-looking mane and tail. In particular, hoof supplements can improve the growth rate of the hair.

tailing
Dismounting and holding on to the horse's tail when climbing steep hills. Don't pull; just let the horse tow you. A horse needs to be trained to tolerate tailing. If you plan to do a lot of tailing, use long reins that clip onto the bit. That way you can unclip one end and hold the other, to keep control of the horse.

tail rope
A rope that is tied to a mare's tail and brought forward to a neck strap. A tail rope is sometimes used during breeding to keep the tail out of the stallion's way, but more often the mare's tail is just bandaged.

tail rubbing
Horses can't reach the top of their tails with their teeth, so if they're itchy, they will rub against a fence, a stall wall, a tree, or even another horse to get relief. An itchy tail head can be caused by soap residue, dirt, lice, ticks, or pinworms. Horses may rub their tails when their udders or sheaths are itchy, since that's the closest they can get to the problem. Shedding also makes horses feel itchy. Once a horse develops the habit of rubbing his tail, he may just keep doing it.

Rubbing breaks off hairs and creates bald patches. Rinse your horse thoroughly after a bath, check frequently for skin problems and external parasites, and deworm regularly to discourage tail rubbing.

tail wrapping
Temporarily covering the dock and part of the tail with a length of material. When a mare is being bred or is about to foal, her tail is wrapped to keep it clean and out of the way. Sometimes a tail is wrapped to train the top hairs to lie flat. Most often, tails are wrapped to protect them during trailering.

You can use a self-closing type of tail wrap with a rubberized interior that grips the hairs, or you can wrap the tail with a stretchy bandage. In both cases, be careful to use light, even pressure when fastening the wrap. A tight bandage cuts off circulation and can damage the dock, causing hair to fall out. Tail wraps should be left on for only an hour or so at a time.

tandem In driving, two horses hitched one in front of the other.

tapadero A leather hood that attaches to the front of a Western stirrup and protects the foot against brush and thorns. Similar hoods, lined with fleece, are sometimes used on English stirrups for cold-weather riding.
➤ *See also stirrups; Western tack*

TAPADERO

THE TARPAN AND THE KONIK

A wild primitive horse that roamed through eastern Europe and the Ukraine until the late 1800s, the tarpan influenced the bloodlines of many light horse breeds. In the 20th century breeders worked to reconstruct the tarpan, and now a semiwild herd lives in Poland.

The Konik is a small Polish breed, once thought to be a direct descendant of the wild tarpan. This has been proven to be untrue, but the Konik, a strong and good-natured large pony, has been selectively bred for uniformity of color (grulla) and a wild-looking type. Many live semiwild, and play a role in keeping marshy wildlife reserves hospitable for a large range of species.

KONIK MARE AND FOAL

TEAM ROPING

tapeworms A parasite that can inhabit the intestines and rob horses of nutrients. Tapeworms are more common in cats and dogs, but horses can pick up the mites by grazing. Tapeworms can cause colic if present in sufficient numbers to create a blockage in the cecum. They are more prevalent in warmer climates, where their life cycle depends on orbatid mites, which take on the immature tapeworms that hatch in manure.

Tapeworms are resistant to many dewormers. Pyrantel pamoate given at high doses will kill them, as will the canine dewormer praziquantel (Droncit).
➤ *See also deworming; parasites*

tartar buildup Horses on pasture rarely develop tartar, as the roughage cleans the teeth and gums. Finely ground foods like pellets and mashes are more likely to create problems, most commonly on the canine teeth. Tartar removal is part of regular equine dental care.
➤ *See also dental problems; teeth and age*

team penning A Western competition in which teams of three riders must separate a designated trio of cows (marked with large numbers) from a herd of 30, and move them from one end of the arena to a pen at the other end. An experienced team can pen their cattle in about 30 seconds.

A penning horse needs to have good cow sense, quick reflexes, speed, and endurance. Riders must be alert to each other's whereabouts and need to communicate well. Team penning is a casual, family-friendly sport that has become popular all over North America.
➤ *See also ranch sorting; Western riding*

team roping A popular Western competition in which two riders (a header and a heeler), work together to rope a steer. The steer is released from a chute and gets a head start of between 10 and 25 feet (3–7.6 m). The riders start out simultaneously, but the header throws his rope first and pulls the steer around so that the heeler can rope the back legs. Once the heeler makes his catch, he "dallies," or wraps his rope around the saddle horn, and takes up the slack. In the meantime, the header turns his horse to face the steer, whereupon the timing flag is dropped.

Headers and heelers practice long hours on their technique to get it right every time on a moving target. A good horse can help the rider by getting into the right position, rating the steer properly, and knowing when to back off or speed up to keep the rope taut.
➤ *See also Western riding*

tears, in the eyes Tears in a horse's eyes can indicate conjunctivitis or a blocked tear duct, or they can be a symptom of a more serious problem. If the condition persists, call your veterinarian.
➤ *See also eye problems; vision*

teaser A gentle stallion kept for the sole purpose of teasing mares. He can be of any breed.

teasing A process used on breeding farms to detect when mares are ready to breed. Mares are introduced to a stallion over a fencelike structure or teasing chute; this allows handlers to remain safe, since striking, biting, and kicking are common reactions of both stallion and mare during this process. A mare in heat will show interest in the stallion; if not in heat, she will usually react aggressively. With mares who do not "show," the stallion's reactions may be enough to tell the breeder if she is in heat.

Some mares need to be teased at the time of breeding in order to make them more receptive. This is done in the same manner as teasing used for heat detection. Each mare responds differently to teasing and being bred, so it's important to be flexible in the approach used to both processes.
➤ *See also breeding; estrus*

teasing wall A solid wall about 4 feet (1.2 m) high that separates a mare and stallion before mating. It allows the horses to indicate their level of interest without injuring one another.

teeth and age Equine teeth are made of three different materials that vary in hardness. The teeth wear away at varying rates over the years; to compensate for the constant grinding that occurs with grazing, the permanent teeth continue to erupt over the horse's lifetime. The amount and the type of wear allow an experienced horseman to tell, within a year or so, the age of a particular horse.

While aging by the teeth is a complicated and inexact science, there are some basic facts and general guidelines that all horse owners should be familiar with. An adult horse has 36 teeth: 12 each of incisors, premolars, and molars. He may also have up to 4 wolf teeth, which

WHAT A HORSE'S TEETH TELL

You often can tell a horse's age by his teeth. Look for wear, angle of teeth, and the appearance of Galvayne's groove. By 2½ years the permanent central incisors appear, but no wear is visible. By 5 years all permanent teeth are in, and the central incisors show wear. In male horses the canine teeth have appeared.

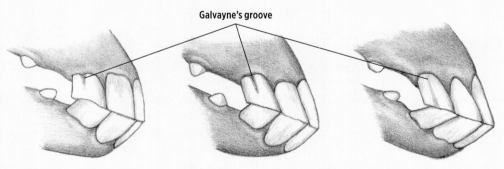

Galvayne's groove

By 10 to 12 years of age, Galvayne's groove appears on the top corner incisors, and the teeth are increasingly slanted. The wearing surfaces of the incisors becomes less oval and more round.

By 15 years, the teeth become longer and more slanted. Galvayne's groove has extended halfway down the tooth. From the front, the lower incisors appear shorter than the uppers, and the middle incisors are becoming rounder.

By 20 to 22 years of age, Galvayne's groove has extended the length of the corner incisor; it will disappear by age 30. The teeth slant even more, and have space between them, and, in some cases, the lowers may be worn almost to the gum line. The surface of the incisors appears triangular.

Remember, however, that horses are individuals and their environment and genetics may affect the appearance of their teeth.

generally erupt just in front of the premolars at about five or six months of age. The wolf teeth sometimes interfere with the bit, and many horse owners have them removed. Premolars are permanent teeth located in front of the molars. Between the premolars and the incisors is a section of gum called the interdental space or bars. Male horses (and some mares) grow a set of four canine teeth in this space.

By nine months, a foal has all his deciduous, or baby, teeth (12 incisors and 12 premolars), and over the next three months will grow his first set of permanent molars. It takes four to five years for all the deciduous teeth to be replaced by the much larger permanent ones.

By age 10, an indentation known as Galvayne's groove becomes noticeable in the incisors. As the horse ages this groove lengthens, and, eventually, as the teeth continue to erupt, reaches the lower edge of the tooth and is worn away. A very old horse may have only little stubs of teeth, which he could end up losing completely.

The upper jaw is approximately 30 percent wider than the lower jaw. Horses grind their food with a sideways motion, so the teeth wear unevenly, and eventually sharp ridges form on the outer edges of the upper molars and the inner edges of the lower molars. These ridges cut the inside of the mouth and make eating quite painful, so regular dental checks are important.
➤ *See also age; deciduous teeth; dental problems; float; Galvayne's groove; impaction; parrot mouth; shear mouth; sow mouth/monkey mouth; wolf teeth*

teeth clapping, in foals
A submissive behavior of foals and young horses, who will clap their teeth together with lips drawn back in response to an older horse. This appears to be a ritualized version of social grooming, and always dampens aggression from the older horse.

temperament
The horse's basic set of reactions and attitudes. Some horses are highly reactive to external stimuli; others are phlegmatic. Some are bold, while others prefer to hang back and see what happens to the more forward, curious herd members.

Temperament has been key to the horse's survival into modern times. If he had not been tamable and easily trainable, he would now be extinct. That trainability and ability to get along with humans is important to breeders as well as to people who handle horses.

Broadly speaking, horses with excellent temperaments are calm in novel situations, friendly toward people, curious, and intelligent; they avoid injuring themselves or others. Some of these traits are fairly obvious when you first meet a horse, and others you learn over time. To assess a horse's temperament, it can help to have some knowledge of the pedigree. Certain personality traits are handed down through generations; if the granddam was girthy, the horse you are looking at may also be girthy, or he may have inherited another progenitor's calm nature.

Temperament is often something you discover after you've acquired a horse, something you learn to live with. Only experience will tell you if your horse reacts to a justified smack on the neck by putting his ears forward and stopping his unruly behavior, or retaliates with a bite or kick.
➤ *See also body language, of horses; handling horses*

temperature (horse)
A healthy horse has a normal temperature of 99.5 to 101.5ºF (37.5–38.6ºC), tending to be slightly lower in the morning and slightly higher in the afternoon or after exertion. You may see seasonal differences as well, with lower temperatures normal in the winter and higher ones in the summer. To learn what's normal for your horse, take his temperature (along with pulse and respiration) twice a day for three days, and average the readings. Choose a time when he is at rest, not just after work or when he's excited.

Use an animal thermometer with an eye in one end that allows for a string to be attached, making it easier to retrieve if necessary. Lubricate the tip with a small amount of room-temperature petroleum jelly or vaginal lubricant. Mercury thermometers must be shaken down until the thermometer registers less than 96ºF (35.5ºC) and should be left in place for two minutes before reading. Electronic digital thermometers are much faster than glass thermometers, and some have a memory capacity.
➤ *See also pulse and respiration; vital signs*

tempi changes
Flying changes of lead performed after each stride or every two or three strides. The sequence and frequency of the flying lead changes is determined by the dressage test or by the choreographer to keep time with the music in a kür, or dressage musical freestyle.
➤ *See also dressage; flying lead change*

TENNESSEE WALKER/TENNESSEE WALKING HORSE

An easy-gaited breed developed in Tennessee in the 19th century. Tennessee Walkers perform three gaits, the flat-footed walk, the running walk, and the canter. Most do not trot; the running walk is apt to be their fastest gait; at some 12 miles (19 km) per hour, it is as fast a trot. The Tennessee Walking Horse, like the American Saddlebred, is descended from the Narragansett Pacer, Canadian, Morgan, and gaited Spanish horses.

In so-called Big Lick show classes, horses wearing built-up pads under heavy shoes carry the running walk to an extreme, with giant strides and great overreach of the hind feet. Because the shoeing extremes often cause unsoundness, a former Big Lick show horse is not a good bet as a pleasure horse. But the old-fashioned Walker is an excellent family, children's, and trail horse, with comfortable gaits and a quiet temperament. Some breeders emphasizing these older traits produce purebred Tennessee Walkers they call Heritage Walkers, with good bone, a natural running walk, and the kind disposition the breed was always known for.

termino A swinging motion of the horse's front leg from the shoulder that is characteristic of the Peruvian Horse's gaits: fast walk, paso llano, and sobreandando.

tetanus/lockjaw A fatal disease particularly dangerous to horses. The bacterium that causes tetanus, *Clostridium tetani*, is a normal inhabitant of the horse's gut, so is always present in manure. Wounds, especially punctures, provide an entry for the bacteria, and it spreads to the central nervous system after incubating for one to three weeks or even longer. The disease is caused by a toxin released as the bacteria grows.

The term "lockjaw" comes from the paralysis that results, which makes it difficult for the horse to move his mouth and, eventually, to breathe. Symptoms begin with muscle stiffness and spasms; as the nerves are affected, the slightest stimulation can send the horse into a frenzied overreaction. Treatment is usually difficult and expensive; mortality rate is between 30 and 80 percent.

To prevent tetanus, horses should receive an initial vaccination series, and annual boosters. Everybody who works around horses should also have regular tetanus boosters.

➤ *See also botulism*

Theiler's disease

➤ *See hepatitis*

therapeutic horsemanship Equestrian programs organized to provide therapy for people with special needs. Therapeutic horsemanship—also referred to as equine-assisted activities and therapies (EAAT)—includes riding, driving, vaulting, and various types of unmounted work with equines. EAAT programs offer children and adults with special needs the chance to exercise, socialize, and gain strength and confidence.

In a **therapeutic horsemanship** class, students are often led by walkers until they gain enough strength and skill to control the horse independently.

As defined by the Professional Association of Therapeutic Horsemanship (PATH) International, therapeutic riding is any mounted activity intended to improve the cognitive, physical, and/or emotional well-being of the rider. In contrast, hippotherapy (physical, occupational, or speech therapy that uses equine movement) is conducted by a licensed medical professional. Recognized by many insurance companies, hippotherapy (which comes from the Greek word *hippos*, for "horse") is primarily a medical treatment versus a recreational sport. Both therapeutic riding and hippotherapy can benefit people with autism, cerebral palsy, developmental delays, epilepsy, multiple sclerosis, muscular dystrophy, visual or auditory impairment, and a host of other conditions. Rhythmic motion is beneficial for many health disorders. Riding moves the body in ways similar to the human gait, improving riders' flexibility, balance, and muscle strength. Beyond physical benefits, riding can boost confidence, independence, cognitive skills, and emotional well-being.

Therapeutic riding clients are frequently children, but numerous programs serve a military veteran clientele, providing support to veterans who have lost limbs or who have been diagnosed with post-traumatic stress disorder (PTSD).

Therapeutic driving is a great activity for those who cannot ride or for riders who wish to broaden their experience. The client handles the reins, which are attached to a special halter fitted over the driving bridle. The instructor has reins that attach to the bit, and can take control if needed.

Therapeutic or interactive vaulting is a modified form of traditional equestrian vaulting, which involves gymnastic movements performed on horseback, often set to music. Vaulting provides numerous mental and physical benefits, including self-esteem and confidence building.

Equine-facilitated psychotherapy and equine-facilitated learning are interactive processes led by licensed mental health professionals in conjunction with equine professionals. The sessions generally involve unmounted work with equines, and clients set goals related to mental health.

Many therapeutic horsemanship programs accept volunteers, who perform a multitude of tasks, from grooming horses to leading and sidewalking in lessons. Reputable programs provide training to volunteers

THOROUGHBRED PROGENITORS

Thoroughbreds have improved the horse population worldwide, contributing size, stamina, speed, excellent conformation, and "heart" to hundreds of other breeds. The origins of the three founding sires of the breed are still being debated and researched, but they are commonly held to be the Byerly Turk, descended from a Turcoman/Arabian cross called Place's White Turk; the Darley Arabian, who was probably also a Turcoman cross, and who brought great beauty to the Thoroughbred; and the Godolphin Arabian, another Turcoman/Arabian cross who contributed his deep, sloping shoulders and middle-distance speed.

Discussion of Thoroughbred origins usually focuses on these stallions, but the foundation mares, Irish Hobbies and Running Horses, were equally important.

The Irish Hobby was a small, refined ambling horse and sprinter, known in Ireland from around 1000 BCE. A quarter-mile racer and comfortable riding horse, it was extensively exported to England, where it formed the basis of the Thoroughbred, and to America, where it was a key progenitor of the Quarter Horse, Mountain Pleasure breeds, and other American breeds.

Running Horses were the sprinting racehorses of England in the 17th and 18th centuries, a mixture of Hobby and Galloway blood. (The Galloway was a small wiry horse from the Yorkshire area.) Bred to middle-distance Turcoman-cross horses like the Godolphin Arabian, they produced the Thoroughbred. It would be a mistake to think of Hobbies and Running Horses as stodgy cold bloods who needed enlivening. They were quick, nervous, and extremely fast horses for short distances.

➤ *See also Arabian; flat racing; Mountain Pleasure Horses; Quarter Horse; Thoroughbred/English Thoroughbred*

---

both in horsemanship skills and in working with clients. Volunteers often report that their work carries a therapeutic benefit for themselves even as their focus is on helping others.
➤ *See also Professional Association for Therapeutic Horsemanship (PATH) International*

therapeutic shoeing
Shoeing to protect and support a damaged hoof or leg, or to influence movement to facilitate healing.
➤ *See also hoof; horseshoes*

third eyelid
The nictitating inner membrane of the eye, which extends from the corner of the eye to cover the eyeball. It is usually visible only if there is infection or injury.

Thoroughbred (see next page)

thoroughpin
A distension of the synovial membrane that protects the tarsal sheath. This swelling, just above and in front of the point of the hock, can be "pushed through" from the outside to the inside of the hock, and vice versa. Most horses with thoroughpin are only briefly lame, and treatment is usually not needed.
➤ *See also lameness; leg, of horse; unsound*

threadworms (*Strongyloides westeri*)
A type of worm that is chiefly damaging to foals. Horses develop immunity to threadworms several weeks after birth, but newborn foals are vulnerable. The dam should be dewormed right after giving birth, as the larvae lie dormant in the mammary tissues until the foal begins nursing, whereupon they migrate into the milk. Threadworms can affect a foal's lungs and liver and cause diarrhea.

In addition to deworming the dam regularly, keep her udder clean and pick up manure daily to prevent the foal from nibbling at it. Foals that develop heavy parasitic infestations may never reach their full health potential.
➤ *See also deworming; parasites*

three-day eventing
➤ *See eventing*

THOROUGHBRED/ENGLISH THOROUGHBRED

The world's premier racing breed, developed in England in the 17th century from Irish Hobby and English Running Horse strains, crossed with hot-blooded Barbs, Arabians, and a Turcoman-Arabian cross exemplified by the Godolphin Arabian, one of the breed's three foundation sires. The Hobby contributed sprinting speed, and the hot bloods, particularly the Turcomans, contributed middle-distance speed, defined as elite racing capacity over several miles.

The English had been passionate about racing for centuries, but the sport was never regularized. King Charles II systematized it with a set of written rules, and numerous racetracks around the country, all built to the same basic specifications. Charles promoted heat racing, or "King's Plate racing"; horses needed to complete at least two, and possibly as many as four, 4-mile (6.4 k) courses in a single day, while carrying some 160 pounds (73 kg). Breeders didn't care what bloodlines the horses came from, as long as they could win. The horse produced by this rigorous performance testing was strong and sound, with great stamina and heart.

Horses who could win at King's Plate racing became valuable as breeding stallions. It became important to know a horse's exact ancestry, and the term "Thoroughbred" was coined around 1750 to describe a racehorse whose pedigree was completely known and of proven race stock.

The Thoroughbred registry traces all of its members to 3 founding sires and 43 mares; no new blood has been added since the 18th century. Today's Thoroughbred competes over much shorter distances than did its ancestors, but it remains the world's fastest horse at distances of ½ mile to 10 miles (0.8–16 k). Warmbloods and most sport horses carry some Thoroughbred blood. Thoroughbreds make fine hunters, polo ponies, and pleasure horses, although retired racehorses need special training to make the transition to "civilian" life.

Perhaps because of this, Thoroughbreds are currently out of vogue in the elite jumping sports, where it is more fashionable to have a European warmblood. But thousands of healthy young Thoroughbreds retire from racing every year, and the discerning horseman and student of bloodlines can acquire a fine athletic mount at a reasonable price if she is prepared to put in the time to train and condition him. Many in the West have long sworn by the Thoroughbred as a ranch horse, believing that there is no finer or tougher horse.

Lean and athletic, Thoroughbreds stand anywhere from 15 to 17 hands high. They have refined heads, prominent withers, and deep chests. They can be black, bay, chestnut, or gray. Roans and palominos, and, very rarely, paints occur. Thoroughbreds can be high-strung and nervous, but much depends on how they are handled. A Thoroughbred cross often makes a wonderful mount for the less advanced rider.

The Thoroughbred has had a great impact on many breeds worldwide. Most European sport horse breeds were developed by crossing the Thoroughbred on native carriage horse stock. The Quarter Horse has been heavily influenced by Thoroughbred bloodlines, both at the beginning of the breed and by continual infusions of new blood. The American Saddlebred, Morgan, Peruvian Horse, Selle Français, American Standardbred, Trakehner, and even the Welsh Mountain Pony have Thoroughbred breeding in their backgrounds. One of the great values of the Cleveland Bay is that it has *not* been developed with Thoroughbred influence.

➤ *See also flat racing; speed, of horse; "Thoroughbred Progenitors," previous page*

three-gaited horse A Saddlebred that performs at the walk, trot, and canter only.
➤ *See also amble; American Breeds; five-gaited horse; gait; gaited horse; rack; slow amble/slow gait*

three-point seat A term used most commonly to differentiate a rider's position from the two-point seat, in which a rider has lifted her seat out of the saddle, thus having contact with the horse with only two points, her legs. Three-point contact is described by some as a base of support in which the seat bones and pubic bone form a triangle in the saddle, with the rider's weight evenly distributed over the two seat bones. Other people describe the three points as the two feet in the stirrups, and the seat in the saddle. If an instructor tells you to adopt three-point contact, ask what she means.
➤ *See also two-point seat*

three-track
➤ *See shoulder-in*

throatlatch

1. The strap on a bridle or halter that runs under the throat and prevents the tack from being pulled off over the head.

2. The area of a horse's neck just behind the jaw.

➤ *See also bridle*

THROATLATCH

thromboembolic colic Colic caused by a blocked blood vessel in the abdomen or rear legs.
➤ *See also colic*

thrush An infection of the frog of the hoof, caused by anaerobic bacteria or fungi that thrive in wet, dirty conditions. Horses whose hooves are rarely cleaned and who stand in mud and manure are susceptible. The condition starts as black spots on the sole or a grimy layer on the frog, accompanied by a foul odor. If caught at this stage, the infection can be treated with iodine or bleach (every day until it clears up). But if it progresses, the frog can begin to decay. A nasty, black secretion indicates the necessity for a visit from the veterinarian, who will trim off the infected tissue and recommend a special disinfectant treatment. Sugardine, a home remedy, can be effective against thrush. If untreated, thrush can cause lameness.

It is easier to prevent thrush than to cure it. Clean your horse's hooves daily and make sure he is not standing on boggy or muddy ground for long periods of time. Winter and early spring are times to be particularly vigilant. Once thrush occurs, it can be hard to get rid of, especially if the underlying conditions persist.
➤ *See also sugardine*

ticks Bloodsucking arachnids that attach themselves to warm-blooded animals to feed. Commonly found in brushy pastures and tall grass, ticks carry a number of diseases dangerous to humans and horses, notably Lyme disease (from tiny deer ticks) and Rocky Mountain spotted fever (from what are often called dog ticks), so be careful when removing and destroying them. Veterinarians recommend spraying attached ticks with a synthetic pyrethrin insecticide, waiting five minutes, and then spraying again. This should cause the tick to drop off without you needing to handle it. Wash the attachment point with a mild antiseptic.

If possible, keep horses away from tick-infested areas. Mow brush in pastures and lanes. It's possible to spray heavy infestations with an insecticide that is safe for horses, but you do a lot of damage to beneficial insects at the same time. Protect horses by spraying with a synthetic pyrethrin like cypermethrin. You can also use natural pyrethrin, but will need higher concentrations. Permethrins are also a good tick repellant. Deworming with ivermectin will kill any attached ticks, but it does nothing about the ones that bite the next day.
➤ *See also Lyme disease; parasites; pest control; piroplasmosis*

tied-in knees Legs with reduced cannon diameter and decreased tendon area just below and in back of the knee. The circumference is smaller here than the measurement just above the fetlock joint. This usually means that the tendons are too small and lacking in strength, compromising the strength of the joint. The horse may be prone to unsoundness.

➤ *See also leg, of horse*

TIED IN AT THE KNEE

tie-down A strap that connects from the noseband to the cinch, in Western riding; it keeps the horse from raising his head too high. It also helps him keep his head in position through tight turns and gives him something to brace against when holding a roped steer. Similar to a standing martingale in English riding.

➤ *See also martingale; standing martingale*

tie stall

➤ *See barns and facilities; straight stall/tie stall*

TIGER HORSE

An American breed established in an attempt to re-create the old-type Appaloosa, with its Spanish-type conformation and easy four-beat gait known as the "Indian shuffle." Two breed associations with slightly differing goals were established in the 1990s.

The Tiger Horse has leopard-complex coat patterns, an intermediate four-beat gait, and at least some Spanish conformation characteristics. Horses from several breeds are accepted in the registries, including Appaloosa, Spanish Mustang, any of the Paso breeds, and some of the lesser-known Spanish breeds such as Florida Cracker. The name comes from the Spanish *tigre*, which refers to the patterned coat.

➤ *See also Appaloosa*

timothy A kind of grass, good for grazing or hay.

➤ *See also hay*

A TIE-DOWN IN USE

TOBIANO

tobiano A pinto coloration. According to the American Paint Horse Association, a horse who meets the following specifications is considered tobiano:

- The horse is white, with white crossing the back or rump.

- The dark color usually covers one or both flanks.

- Generally, all four legs are white, at least below the hocks and knees.

- Generally, the spots are regular and distinct as ovals or round patterns that extend down over the neck and chest, giving the appearance of a shield.

- Head markings are like those of a solid-colored horse—solid or with a blaze, strip, star, or snip.

- The tail is often two colors.
➤ *See also overo; pinto; tovero*

toed-in legs, toed-out legs Having hooves that turn in toward each other (pigeon-toed) or turn out (splay-footed). Both conditions predispose a horse to problems because the joints are more subject to strain.
➤ *See also legs, of horse; splay-footed*

tölt A smooth, fast, four-beat amble performed by Icelandic horses. The horse always has one or two feet on the ground, and can tölt as fast as a fully extended trot or a canter.
➤ *See also Icelandic horse; gait; gaited horse; skeið*

Tom Thumb bit

A jointed Western bit with short shanks.
➤ *See also bit; bridle; Pelham bit*

TOM THUMB BIT

tongue injuries

Although an infrequent occurrence, horses do bite their tongues—in a fall, for example. A severe bit improperly used can damage the tongue, and if the reins are dropped and the horse steps on them and jerks his head up, he can hurt himself quite badly. Most of these wounds, although they bleed profusely, will heal on their own. But if a horse with a tongue injury is having trouble eating or accepting the bit, call your veterinarian.

tongue tying Tying a horse's tongue down so that he can't get it over the bit. This is usually not legal in the show ring, but is occasionally done with racehorses. A horse can be injured if his tongue is tied too tightly.

topline A horse's back, from the withers to the dock. A well-proportioned horse has a shorter topline than underline. Each breed has its own ideal topline. For example, the Arabian halter rules describe the ideal topline as "relatively level," whereas the Thoroughbred ideal prefers a slightly sloped croup.
➤ *See also conformation; underline*

torpedo grass (*Panicum repens*)
➤ *See grass toxicity*

torsion
➤ *See colic; digestive tract; surgical colic*

tovero A pinto coloration, a mixture of tobiano and overo, which may be produced by breeding one to the other. It was once rare, and the genetics are less well understood than other pinto color patterns. According to the American Paint Horse Association, a horse must meet the following specifications to be considered tovero:

- Dark pigmentation around the ears may expand to cover the forehead and/or eyes.

- One or both eyes are blue.

- Dark pigmentation around the mouth may extend up the sides of the face and form spots.

- Chest spot(s) vary in size and may extend up the neck.

- Flank spot(s) range in size and may be accompanied by smaller spots that extend forward across the barrel and up over the loin.

- Spots, varying in size, are located at the base of the tail.
➤ *See also overo; pinto; tobiano*

towing a trailer
➤ *See "Towing Hitches," page 366; trailering*

toxic substances In addition to poisonous plants, mold, and fungi, substances harmful to horses include antifreeze, pesticides, fungicides, lead paint, and overdoses of medicine. Horses should also not eat any feed meant for cattle or other livestock unless it has been approved for use by a horse veterinarian.
➤ *See also blister beetle poisoning; mold/fungi in feed; monensin/Rumensin; silage/haylage*

TPR (temperature, pulse, respiration)
➤ *See vital signs*

trace clip
➤ *See clipping; "Common Clipping Terms," page 56*

trace minerals Minerals needed in very small amounts; also called microminerals. These include chromium, cobalt, copper, fluorine, iodine, iron, molybdenum, selenium, sulfur, and zinc. The easiest way to supply these is with a trace-mineralized salt. More effective, and more expensive, is to feed complexed or chelated minerals; the extra cost may be worth it during growth, lactation, weaning, and old age.
➤ *See also calcium; feeding and nutrition; phosphorus; salt (sodium chloride)*

traces Heavy leather straps that connect a harness to a vehicle or farm implement. Traces start at the collar and attach to a singletree.
➤ *See also harness*

track

1. A racing venue.

2. The line of travel followed by a moving horse. For example, a horse is said to be "tracking left" if he is moving counterclockwise around the ring (that is, with his left side facing toward the center) or if he is two-tracking during a half-pass. The track of a gait is the impression left by hooves in the dirt as the horse moves forward. It includes overstride, understride, and tracking up. The track may be used as part of the definition of a gait, or as an assessment of how well the horse is moving.

tracking up When, at a walk or trot, the horse's hind feet step into the tracks made by his front feet; sometimes called capping. As it shows good use of the hindquarters, tracking up is desirable. Even more desirable is overtracking, when the horse's hind feet overstep the prints made by the front feet.

➤ *See also overtracking*

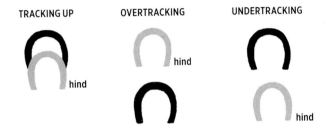

TRACKING UP   OVERTRACKING   UNDERTRACKING

hind   hind   hind

trail class An arena competition that involves riding a course with obstacles similar to ones you might find on a trail ride, such as crossing a bridge, opening a gate, sidepassing and backing in complex patterns, stepping into a small square area and making a complete circle without touching the outlines of the space, and cantering over a series of poles. Classes are judged one obstacle at a time; the rider is responsible for memorizing the course and completing it in the correct order.

In Indian Trail classes, horses are encouraged to look at and consider each obstacle before going through it. In Pack String classes, a handler guides a saddle horse and two to five fully loaded pack animals through an obstacle course, physically controlling only her mount and the first animal in the pack string. The rest must follow the leader or respond to voice commands. In In-hand Trail classes, young, miniature, or geriatric horses are led through obstacles. In driving, Gambler's Choice classes are timed obstacle courses.

➤ *See also slicker-broke; turn on the forehand; turn on the haunches; versatility trail competitions*

trail riding For many riders, trail riding is the most fun you can have on horseback. It's a chance to use all the skills you've acquired in the ring, while meeting the challenge of going over uneven terrain with constantly changing surroundings. Before going out on the trail, you should be able to negotiate small obstacles in a half-seat (practice over cavalletti); maintain a deep, balanced seat if your horse shies; and be able to handle a horse who might not want to go across a shallow stream or through a scary-looking gap in the trees.

Ideally, you shouldn't trail ride alone. Horses draw courage from one another and are apt to be quietest in a group. But in real life many people do ride alone,

TRAIL CLASS

TRAIL TIPS

- Respect "No Trespassing" signs.
- Cede the right of way to bikers and hikers.
- Don't let branches snap behind you into the next rider's face.
- When going uphill, lean slightly forward (your horse may want to canter, as it's easier for him).
- When going downhill, lean slightly back and be prepared for a rush at the bottom as your horse seeks level ground.
- Return to the barn at a flat walk, making your horse travel in a zig-zag line if necessary to distract him and keep him from picking up speed.
- Stay alert yet relaxed.

A well-trained trail horse takes all obstacles in stride, which includes going through or over water as required.

for the most part safely. Tell someone where you're going and how long you expect to be gone. Carry a cell phone, a water bottle, a whistle, and a knife on your person, not strapped to the saddle, which could conceivably take off without you.

For group rides, keep a consistent pace and a safe distance between horses. Be aware of potential kickers in the group, and stay well away from them. Don't rush past other riders; you might spook their horses. Either alone or in a group, don't let your horse snatch at branches and grass. Avoid muddy ground; don't contribute to erosion problems that may result in the trail being made off limits to riders. Aim to leave the landscape exactly as you found it.

➤ See also safety; shying; trail class

trail trial A casual trail riding competition over 6 to 8 miles (9.6–12.8 k) with at least six judged natural obstacles. Riders start at three- to five-minute intervals and ride at a comfortable walk. The ride is not timed,

but obstacles are. Each should be completed within 30 to 60 seconds, and each competitor has three chances to complete the obstacle. Obstacles may include crossing bridges, backing in a figure eight, picking up a hat while mounted, going through a cowboy curtain (long strips of heavy fabric or nylon hung from an overhead rail), negotiating a gully, and standing still while an unusual sound goes off nearby.

Horse and rider are scored separately, and then scores are combined. Horses are judged on forward, calm competence; riders on balance, lightness, and subtlety. Trail trials are popular in California, Texas, Nevada, and Oregon, and the sport is growing. Trail trials, which are open to riders of all ages, make an excellent family sport.

➤ See also competitive trail riding; endurance riding; trail class; versatility trail competitions

trailer The box towed behind a vehicle for transporting horses. The vast majority of trailers are designed to carry two horses, but there are larger ones that can carry multiple horses and/or quantities of equipment and feed.

A STOCK TRAILER consists of a large open space with slatted sides. A hinged center divider can separate the front from the back, or be fastened back against the wall. A single horse, or horses who know each other well, such as a mare and foal, can be transported loose in a stock trailer, which allows them to find their balance and move around. Because of the airy, open design, stock trailers are more comfortable for some horses, and typically easier to load into. The horse can also be turned around inside and unloaded walking forward. The open sides can be drafty, but some models can be closed with Plexiglas inserts.

STRAIGHT-LOAD TRAILERS are the common two-horse trailers in which the horses ride side by side, separated by a divider. The horses load from the back and ride facing forward. These are usually the lowest-priced, and are easy to drive as they are the same width as the towing vehicle. The horse must back out to be unloaded, and with a manger in front, the horse is unable to lower his head to clear his respiratory tract.

A SLANT-LOAD TRAILER enables the horses to load and ride diagonally, which is convenient, but may not be comfortable for horses traveling over longer distances. They come in two-horse and larger versions. They have an open, inviting interior. The horse can be tied with a long lead, allowing him to lower his head, and in many models he can turn around to unload going forward. Slant-load trailers can also be useful for hauling hay and equipment.

REVERSE-LOAD TRAILERS have both a front and back door. Horses load in one door and out the other without having to be turned or backed. Horses can ride facing forward or rearward.

Trailers are entered either by a step-up or using a ramp. Step-ups are simplest and least expensive, but can be difficult for lame or older horses to negotiate, or for people loading equipment. Ramps may be full (the entire width of the trailer) or individual (the width of one stall.)

Trailers may be made of steel, fiberglass, or aluminum. Whatever the material, they should be strongly constructed and well-maintained, with particular attention paid to brakes, suspension, and flooring. The trailer needs to fit the horse it will be hauling; for a 16-hand horse that means a stall that is 34 inches (86 cm) wide and 80 to 84 inches (203–213 cm) tall. White is the best color for a trailer, inside and out, as it stays cooler in sunny conditions and is more inviting to walk into. It also allows rust damage to be more easily spotted.

TOWING HITCHES

There are three types of hitches used to attach a trailer to a towing vehicle: fifth-wheel, gooseneck, and straight-pull.

A FIFTH-WHEEL is a small version of the hitch used on semitrucks. The trailer attaches to an angled disk mounted on the truck bed. It is the safest hitch available for hauling heavy trailers.

A GOOSENECK hitch is a ball mounted in a pickup bed, a design that distributes weight more evenly between both axles of the towing vehicle. A gooseneck is considered the safest type of trailer hitch for small and midsized trailers.

A STRAIGHT-PULL OR TAGALONG hitch is a ball mount attached to the towing vehicle; it is the only type of hitch available for cars and vans. *Warning:* A straight-pull trailer should never be attached to the bumper of a truck or SUV, even if such trailers are referred to by the manufacturer as "bumper-pull" trailers. Though a good choice for two-horse trailers, straight-pulls can be hard to maneuver and hook up.

trailering Transporting horses in a trailer or van. Horses need to be trained to enter and exit a trailer willingly and safely. A lack of trailering skills makes a horse less usable and salable, and it adds stress and time to any situation that involves transporting him.

STOCK TRAILER

STRAIGHT-LOAD TRAILER

SLANT-LOAD TRAILER

trailer cams Video cameras that can be installed in the trailer to allow you to monitor the horses while on the road.

trainer A professional who trains horses. A trainer may or may not work with you and your horse together. Many trainers have their own facilities; the horse is brought to them for training, and the owner may be able to come observe how things are going.

In turning your horse over to someone else, you are taking a risk. Professional trainers have every incentive to paint themselves as experts in their field, and many are highly ethical. However, there are many stories of horses coming home from a trainer with behavioral problems they didn't have when they left. It is your responsibility to investigate any trainer thoroughly before committing your horse to her. Ask for references. Ask successful riders with happy horses who trained *their* horses. Ask to watch a few training sessions.

Any trainer should be comfortable with you coming to her facility to check on your horse. Don't abuse the privilege, but drop in often enough to be sure you understand what is happening with your horse. And if you feel your horse is not being handled well, don't hesitate to take him home.

➤ *See also coach; instructor*

training competitions
Competitions in which trainers are given an unstarted, untouched horse, and have a fixed amount of time to get him ready for a ridden competition. Extreme Mustang Makeover is one that happens over a few months; the Road to the Horse, which uses young Quarter Horses, takes place over a few days.

training scale
A conceptual hierarchy intended to provide humane building blocks for a horse's athletic development. The training scale comes from ideas promulgated in classical French and German riding. The scale is still evolving and is not always linear. But in rough order, the principles are as follows:

- **RHYTHM.** There is regularity and cadence of the gaits.

- **LOOSENESS (OR SUPPLENESS).** The horse is physically relaxed so that he works freely through his back while being mentally alert. (Some training scales place looseness before rhythm, or on the same tier, as they are both interrelated and fundamental.)

- **CONTACT.** The rider has a straight line of contact, bit to hand to elbow, and the connection is steady, soft, and elastic.

- **IMPULSION.** The horse starts to use his full body to move, shifting his center of gravity toward his center rather than traveling on his forehand.

- **STRAIGHTNESS.** The horse tracks with his forehand in line with the hindquarters on both straight and bending lines at all three gaits.

- **COLLECTION.** The horse moves his center of gravity farther back, and his hind legs step farther forward, showing more elastic movement in hip, stifle, and hock.

When working with the training scale, don't expect to be moving along it in a straight line. All six concepts interrelate, and you may move back and forth frequently between rungs on the ladder as your training progresses.

TRAKEHNER

A German warmblood breed, developed in the 18th century in the East Prussian town of Trakehnen as a cavalry horse. Since the 1920s, Trakehners have won numerous Olympic medals, excelling at dressage and jumping. They also won many steeplechase races. Standing 16 to 17 hands high, the Trakehner is muscular and elegant, with a noble bearing. Trakehners are usually bay, brown, black, or gray, but piebalds of good conformation are allowed.

The Trakehner Trek
In World War II, as the Soviets closed in around Trakehnen, the Germans evacuated the stud farm; most of the horses fell into Soviet hands. Meanwhile private breeders hitched their Trakehners to wagons and fled in midwinter, covering 600 miles (966 km) in two and a half months. Of 80,000 Trakehners in East Prussia before the war, only about 800 made it to West Germany by war's end. These formed the nucleus of the West German breeding program. Meanwhile the Soviets kept up the breed as well, and used it to improve their own horses.

AN ALTERNATIVE TRAINING SCALE Australian trainer and scientist Andrew McLean has proposed an alternative training scale, which he uses at the Australian Equine Behavior Center (AEBC). Greatly simplified, it is as follows:

- **BASIC ATTEMPT.** Reward the smallest try.

- **OBEDIENCE.** There is an immediate correct response from the horse.

- **RHYTHM.** The horse sustains speed and gait from a single cue.

- **STRAIGHTNESS.** The horse sustains the line he is put on.

- **CONTACT.** The horse maintains a consistent outline, on light contact.

- **PROOF.** The horse will do all of the above in any environment.

tranquilizers

It is sometimes necessary to use tranquilizers to calm a horse who isn't responding to other forms of restraint, such as a twitch or stableizer. Tranquilizers can be useful for horses who become unmanageable during medical procedures (suturing a wound, floating teeth, and so forth), when being clipped, while traveling, or in other stressful situations. Tranquilizers should be used only under the supervision of a veterinarian, because different horses react differently to these medications.

Mules require more tranquilizer, and recover more rapidly, than horses; mule owners must make sure the veterinarian understands that, or a dangerous situation could develop. Tranquilizers should not be used to load a horse into a trailer, as they may compromise his sense of balance, leading to injury. They are no substitute for good training.
➤ *See also acepromazine/acetylpromazine maleate; restaints; stableizer; twitch; xylazine*

transition

A change from one gait to another, or a change of speed within a gait. An upward transition is to a faster gait or pace, while a downward transition is to a slower one. Transitions should be smooth, with subtle aids from the rider and prompt responses from the horse.
➤ *See also aids; gait*

trappy

1. A term used to describe a short, choppy stride.

2. A term used to describe a jump course with many sharp turns.

trashy lope

A lope that is too slow and slips into a four-beat gait. A trashy loper will look as though he's loping in front while trotting behind. A correct lope is a slow, collected, three-beat gait.

travers

A lateral movement in which the horse moves forward with his shoulder at the rail and his haunches slightly inside the perimeter, so that he is moving on two tracks; also called haunches-in. In dressage, the rider expects a real curve to the horse's body, rather than just having the front and back legs moving on different tracks.
➤ *See also half-pass; renvers; shoulder-in*

travois

A primitive sled consisting of a platform or netting supported by two long poles that are crossed over a horse's shoulders. The ends of the poles drag behind on the ground. A version of the travois was invented by all peoples as they began using animal traction, including most recently the Plains Indians.

treats, feeding to horses

Many horses love carrots, apples, and other sweets. However, conventional wisdom discourages hand-feeding. If done improperly, it can encourage nipping and biting. As an interim step, you can give treats in your horse's feed bucket or drop them on the ground.

TREADMILLS FOR HORSES

While not a replacement for being ridden, treadmills can supplement a horse's exercise program if care is taken to keep the program short enough to prevent injury or sourness. Because a workout on a treadmill takes approximately half the time needed for other types of exercise, it can be useful on days when time is short.

Horse treadmills can also be used to power farm equipment.

Horse can be trained to observe proper treat etiquette. Clicker training, which involves the use of treats, offers many protocols for refining treat giving and preventing mugging. At the least, horses should learn that frisking or nipping humans will never result in a treat. Reward them for standing near you facing forward, *not* mugging you.

When hand-feeding a horse, place the treat on the palm of your hand, with fingers flat and together, so the horse can take the treat without catching any part of the body.

Warning: Never offer any horse a treat from between your teeth. You could be badly hurt.

➤ *See also clicker training*

treeless saddle

A saddle, usually made of synthetic materials, that lacks a rigid tree. They are usually lightweight and comfortable to ride in, and appeal to people who dislike whips, bits, horseshoes, and so on around horses. Many people think treeless saddles are more humane.

But saddle trees were invented, after millennia of experience with treeless riding, for a very good reason. The tree distributes a rider's weight and spares a horse's back from injury. Also, without the stabilizing framework of a tree, treeless saddles may be prone to shift. This causes some riders to overtighten the girth.

If you do decide to go treeless, make sure that your weight does not press on the horse's spine. And watch for back pain in your horse. The saddle may seem comfortable initially, but over time the lack of support can cause problems.

trick training

Non-utilitarian horse behaviors designed to entertain and amaze audiences. Common horse tricks include "laughing" (the flehmen response), "counting," picking up items from the ground, kneeling, and lying down. Teaching tricks can be a fun activity when riding isn't an option, and science shows that each new behavior your horse learns increases his ability to learn still more.

Figuring out how to train a trick is creative, challenging work. Use a positive approach, like clicker training, and don't teach a horse to do something annoying or potentially dangerous. With all tricks, it's important to put them on cue; this means that in the absence of the cue, the horse does not offer the behavior. With the growing popularity of ground work among horsemen who are not interested in riding, trick training is gaining fans.

trip

One circuit of a course over fences. Announcers at a show commonly say, "There are two trips remaining," when two competitors are still waiting to ride.

Trick training is a fun alternative to riding that can develop the relationship between horse and human.

triple bar A type of jump with three bars at ascending heights. The standards can be placed farther away from one another to give more spread.

➤ See also "Types of Jumps," page 192; spread; show jumping

Triple Crown A famous trio of American races consisting of the Kentucky Derby (established in 1875 and run at Churchill Downs in Louisville, Kentucky); the Preakness (first run in Baltimore, Maryland, in 1873); and the Belmont Stakes (established in 1867 in Elmont, New York). The challenge is steep, as there are only two weeks between the Derby and Preakness, and three between the Preakness and Belmont, which is also a longer race.

In 1973, Secretariat won the Triple Crown, breaking a 25-year drought and setting records for all three races that remain unbroken. Two more horses, Seattle Slew and Affirmed, won in the 1970s.

It was another 37 years before American Pharoah won in 2015, becoming only the 12th horse to win the Triple Crown in 140 years. Great racehorses who did *not* win the Triple Crown include Man O' War, Seabiscuit, and Kelso.

WINNERS OF THE TRIPLE CROWN

1919 Sir Barton

1930 Gallant Fox

1935 Omaha (sired by Gallant Fox)

1937 War Admiral

1941 Whirlaway

1943 Count Fleet

1946 Assault

1948 Citation

1973 Secretariat

1977 Seattle Slew

1978 Affirmed

2015 American Pharoah

trombidiform mites

➤ See mites

trophies

➤ See prizes; ribbons

trot A two-beat gait in which the horse's diagonal pairs of legs move together. The trot is an intermediate gait, faster than a walk, slower than a canter.

➤ See also gait; posting trot; sitting trot

TROTTINGBRED PONY ➤ An American breed of pony harness racers, developed by crossing Standardbreds with Welsh, Hackney, and Shetland Ponies. Measuring under 51½ inches (131 cm) shod, these ponies race over ½-mile (0.8 k) distances. They can also be ridden and used for pleasure driving.

TSAGAAN SAR A Mongolian horse race and national celebration dating back to the time of Genghis Khan. The race is 15 miles (24 k), and the jockeys are boys and girls ages 5 to 12. On the day of the race, horses are ridden 15 miles (24 k) to the starting point, then galloped back to the finish line, which is in the middle of the festival.

turnback men The two assistants in a cutting class who keep the chosen cow facing the competitor. Meanwhile, two herd holders keep the rest of the herd settled.

➤ See also cutting; Western riding

turn on the forehand A maneuver in which the horse pivots his hindquarters around his inside front foot. It is performed from a halt, with the horse standing squarely on all four legs; his forefeet remain virtually in the same spot while his hindquarters move in a semicircle of 180 degrees so that he faces the opposite direction. The turn on the forehand is a basic exercise taught in the initial stages of training in nearly every discipline. It helps teach the horse how to move away from leg pressure, encourages him to use his hindquarters, and is the beginning of teaching lateral work.

➤ See also hindquarters; legs, use of when riding

turn on the haunches A maneuver in which the horse turns his forequarters around his inside hind foot, while maintaining a regular four-beat walk rhythm; it appears in lower-level dressage tests. The horse makes a small circle with his hind legs and a larger circle with his forelegs. He is bent in the direction of travel.

In Western riding, horses are taught to turn on the haunches by pivoting on the inside hind foot, which remains planted.

turnout

1. The appearance of a rider and horse in a competition (correctness of attire and tack, cleanliness and neatness, appropriate braiding of mane and tail, and so on).

2. The time a horse spends out of his stall in a pasture or paddock, where he can roam at will. Horses should have some time every day (the more the better) in a safe, open area that includes shelter from bad weather. A turnout area can range from a small corral to acres of pasture, but fresh air, exercise, and interaction with other horses are important to maintain a healthy horse.

turnout blanket/turnout sheet
➤ *See blankets and blanketing; sheet*

twin foals While mares often produce multiple eggs, they rarely sustain a twin pregnancy. To develop normally, the fetus must have contact with the entire placenta, and twins do not have enough room for this contact. The mare will often absorb one of the embryos on her own. If she doesn't do so within the first several weeks, she is likely abort one or both fetuses later on. However, a mare who does deliver twins should be able to raise them, if given adequate nutrition.
➤ *See also foaling*

twist (of a saddle) The narrowest part of the seat. Women, especially those with round thighs, tend to be most comfortable in a saddle with a narrow twist; those with a wider pelvis will be more comfortable in a wider saddle.

twisted intestine
➤ *See colic*

twitch A restraint in which the horse's upper lip is pinched and held in order to make him stand still. This can be done by hand or with a piece of equipment designed for this purpose. A chain twitch is a loop of chain or rope attached to a wooden handle. A so-called humane twitch, usually made of aluminum, looks like a pair of pliers; a rope attached to the handles can be wrapped around them, and a clip on the end of the rope can be attached to the halter for hands-free use.

Twitching triggers the release of endorphins that calm the horse and increase his ability to handle pain. Not all horses will react calmly to being twitched, however, and you should only try it with a mature horse who is used to being handled. If you use the twitch gently and massage his nose afterward, he should accept the procedure.

In the absence of a twitch, you can try hand-twitching the horse, by firmly grasping the upper lip. Another way to twitch a horse is to grab a fold of skin on the shoulder and roll it over your fingers. This method also releases endorphins that help the horse relax.

Always have two people around when twitching a horse, one to control the twitch and the other to do whatever it is the horse doesn't want done to him.
➤ *See also restraints*

PUTTING ON A CHAIN TWITCH

two-handed riding English riders almost always ride with one rein in each hand, but Western riders usually hold both reins in one hand. For some events, such as barrel racing or Western dressage, or for training purposes, a Western rider will ride two-handed; more rarely, some English riders will ride with one hand on the reins to develop coordination of seat and body signals.

➤ *See also one-handed riding; neck-reining*

two-point seat A seat in which the rider sinks her weight into her heels, lifts her seat slightly out of the saddle, and allows her upper body to come forward, more or less mimicking the angle of the horse's neck. The two points of contact with the horse are the rider's legs. This position, also called a jumping position, allows the rider to absorb the motion of the trot or canter without bouncing on the horse's back.

➤ *See also half-seat; light seat; three-point seat*

two-track

➤ *See half-pass; lateral work; leg-yield; travers*

TWO-POINT SEAT

TYING DOS AND DON'TS

- Do use a halter and a strong rope.
- Don't tie your horse by the bridle.
- Do use a quick-release knot or panic snaps.
- Do tie your horse at about eye level (his) and at arm's length (yours).
- Don't tie him too long (could get a leg over the rope) or too short (very uncomfortable for him).
- Do train your horse to stand patiently for a reasonable period of time without fidgeting and fussing.

"two wraps and a hooey" In calf roping, the rider not only ropes the calf but also immobilizes it by tying three of its legs together. Using a short leather piggin string, she wraps it around the legs twice and fastens it with a hooey, or half-hitch knot.

➤ *See also calf roping; hooey; piggin string*

tying Standing tied is a skill that all horses should have—but not all horses do. Tying is a form of restraint, which horses instinctively resist until trained otherwise. A horse who won't stand tied is inconvenient to work with, and can be a danger to himself and others. Make sure he'll tie before you buy. If you have a horse who does not stand tied, work with a good trainer to teach him that skill. This training needs to be done in a safe manner to avoid injuring the horse.

➤ *See also bull snap; cross-tying, cross-ties; ground-tie; panic snap; quick-release knot; safety*

tying up

➤ *See azoturia/Monday morning disease/tying up*

tympanic colic Colic caused by gas.

➤ *See also colic*

typey A term used to describe the degree to which a horse exemplifies breed standards. A typey horse bears a strong resemblance to breed ideals.

udder A mare's udder has two halves, with each half containing two quarters, just like a cow's. However, where a cow has four teats, the two quarters on each side of the horse's udder feed into a single teat with two openings.

It is important for horse owners to become familiar with the normal feel of their nonpregnant mare's udder so they are aware of changes that occur during pregnancy or as a result of injury or illness. Handling the udder helps prepare the mare to accept her foal's nursing, or medication in case of mastitis.

UDDER PROBLEMS Most mares never experience problems with their udders. One issue, sometimes indicated by tail rubbing, is irritation to the udder resulting from a buildup of smegma, a combination of dirt, sweat, and dead skin cells that accumulates between the teats. It is usually a problem only in mares who are worked to the point of sweating on a regular basis. This irritation can easily be avoided by rinsing the udder after workouts.

Any injury or major change to the udder, such as increased heat, lumps, or growths, requires veterinary attention.

The most serious udder problem is mastitis, a relatively common bacterial infection.

➤ *See also foaling; mastitis*

A mare's **udder** is much smaller and less visible than a cow's or a goat's, but foals find it just fine. They typically nurse from four to six months before being weaned.

ulcer A lesion in the digestive tract, caused by stress, unnatural feeding schedules, intense training, nonsteroidal anti-inflammatory drugs (NSAIDs), or possibly viruses. Horses are prone to ulcers in modern domestic settings. In the wild their stomachs always contain a small amount of high-fiber feed, which keeps acid levels low. Horses fed large, infrequent, grain-based meals have empty stomachs for hours at a time, then too-full stomachs for a short time, allowing acids access to unprotected areas of the stomach lining. Also, intense exercise compresses the stomach, forcing acids into the less-protected area of the stomach.

Symptoms include grinding the teeth, slobbering, and lying in odd positions to alleviate discomfort. These signs of gut pain will ease after feeding. Some ulcers are "silent," showing no outward signs until the ulcer perforates the stomach wall, usually causing death.

To prevent ulcers, feed a high-fiber diet, including as much forage as possible. Spread hay intake throughout the day, with frequent feedings or slow feeders. Give a few pounds of alfalfa hay before sending horses out for exercise to buffer the stomach acid. Feed additives based on calcium carbonate or other antacids can also help. Ulcers can be treated with drugs like omeprazole, which inhibit gastric acid secretion and reduce pain.

umbilical hernia A soft swelling at the navel caused by an imperfect closure of the muscles. The opening allows a portion of the omentum, the protective tissue of the gut, or possibly even a part of the gut itself, to get caught between the abdominal wall and the skin. Most hernias resolve by themselves or with minor assistance by pushing the swelling back into the abdominal cavity. However, if you sense any increase in heat or the size of the swelling, call a veterinarian, as this could indicate that the gut itself is involved and an impaction or infection might be developing.

➤ *See also hernia*

underline The underside of the horse's body from the point of the elbow to the stifle joint. The underline should be longer than a line from the last cervical vertebra to the point of the hip. This allows the horse sufficient room for proper striding. Horses with underlines equal to, or shorter than, their toplines are prone to injuries from forging and overreaching.

➤ *See also conformation; topline*

underrun heels/underslung heels

An often irreversible condition in which the angle of the hoof wall at the heel is lower than the toe angle by 5 degrees or more. The heel must be trimmed short, and corrective shoeing will be needed, possibly wedge shoes or pads with extended or egg bar heels.

UNDERWEAR FOR RIDING

If you are not wearing comfortable underwear when you get to the barn, it's only going to get more uncomfortable once you're in the saddle. Companies that sell riding apparel usually sell underwear specially designed for riders. Pantyhose can be helpful (for both sexes) under breeches or jeans, or you can try wearing padded biking shorts.

A sports bra is probably a good idea as well, particularly for large-breasted women. Choose one designed for riders. One manufacturer advertises its bra as "Inspired by the sitting trot." That's a company that understands a woman's needs!

uneven wear of teeth

➤ *See dental problems; teeth and age*

ungulate

1. As a noun, the group of hoofed, herbivorous, quadruped mammals that includes horses, camels, elephants, hippopotamuses, hyraxes, rhinoceroses, ruminants, swine, and tapirs.

2. As an adjective, a word meaning "having hooves."

unhorse

To unseat a rider from a horse.

United States Dressage Federation (USDF)

A national nonprofit organization with dozens of chapters around the United States that provides information on dressage competition. The USDF administers numerous educational and licensing programs for instructors, as well as competitors in the sport of dressage. It also provides incentive awards for riders to be recognized at various levels of competition, essentially year-end and career high-point awards.

The rhinoceros is an unlikely looking relative of the horse, but both are classified as **ungulates**.

United States Equestrian Federation (USEF)
The governing body for national and international equestrian sports, including the Olympic Games. Founded in 1917 as the Association for American Horse Shows, the organization evolved over the years and took its present form in 2003, when it signed an agreement with the United States Equestrian Team to create a uniform organization out of many parts.

USEF rules govern competitions in dressage, driving, endurance riding, eventing (combined training), hunt seat equitation, hunter/jumper, para-equestrian, reining, roadster, saddle seat, vaulting, and Western riding. The organization also governs various breed shows. USEF-sanctioned horse shows are each given a rating of AA, A, B, or C, with AA-rated shows being the most prestigious and C-rated shows geared to local riders.

The USEF oversees selection of the Olympic-level United States Equestrian team. Riders and horses are chosen annually from among applicants who have qualified by accumulating enough points in competition or by winning in selected shows. Riders may be professionals but do not need to own their own horse and in many cases will ride a horse owned by someone else. However, the best combinations tend to be a pair who have worked together for a long time in many different circumstances.
➤ *See also Fédération Equestre Internationale (FEI); Olympic equestrian events; World Equestrian Games*

United States Equestrian Team (USET)
In partnership with the United States Equestrian Federation, the USET Foundation "supports the competition, training, coaching, travel and educational needs of America's elite and developing International High Performance horses and athletes."
➤ *See also United States Equestrian Federation*

United States Eventing Association (USEA)
A nonprofit educational organization that organizes, promotes, and adjudicates eventing competitions in the United States.

United States Pony Club
➤ *See Pony Club*

unsound A horse who is unable to do the work expected of him, whether through lameness, a sore back, or a respiratory ailment. Unsoundness can be temporary or permanent.
➤ *See also lameness; respiratory system; sound*

unthrifty Unable to extract nutritional benefit from food. An unthrifty horse is thin, with a harsh, dull coat. Parasites are a frequent cause of unthriftiness because they rob the horse of much-needed nutrients.
➤ *See also deworming; parasites*

upward transition
➤ *See transition*

urinary stones Mineral salts that crystallize in the urine. Horses, especially males, sometimes suffer from this condition. A urinary stone can block the urethra, causing painful urination and colic. If the stone is in the urethra, it can often be removed by catheter. Surgery may be required if the stone is in the bladder.

urine Normal horse urine is yellow, cloudy, and has a strong odor. Brown urine can occur during an episode of azoturia (tying up) and also is a symptom of some forms of poisoning. It is a sign that the muscles are breaking down and being excreted, and it warrants an emergency veterinary call.
➤ *See also azoturia/Monday morning disease/tying up; poisonous plants*

urticaria An allergic reaction that causes small bumps or hives on the surface of the skin.

uveitis Inflammation of the uveal tract of the eye (the iris and related structures). It can be caused by trauma to the eye, bacterial infection, or tumors. Symptoms include redness, swelling, tearing, sensitivity to light, and a cloudy or bluish haze in the eye. Veterinary consultation is important, as treatment varies depending on the cause. Uveitis caused by trauma or infection should clear up with treatment. If it recurs, it is labeled equine recurrent uveitis (ERU).
➤ *See also equine recurrent uveitis (ERU)*

vaccinations Injections that stimulate antibodies in the blood to fight off the harmful effects of bacterial or viral infection. Once an animal is exposed to a mild form of a disease through a vaccination, he can better resist infection caused by the disease pathogens.

Horses are more capable of building immunities if they receive vaccinations at a time when they are already healthy and in good condition. An ill, stressed, or undernourished animal may not have the reserves to effectively produce antibodies and therefore may not be sufficiently protected if exposed to a contagious disease via vaccination.

Vaccination protocol is highly regional, responding to local conditions. Some diseases are rare or absent in certain areas of the country, so vaccination for them is unnecessary unless a horse will be traveling. Veterinarians develop vaccination protocols for their localities, and should also be able to provide guidance when a horse is to be shipped out of state or out of the country.

vacuum, for grooming A vacuum cleaner especially designed for grooming horses. Vacuums are helpful in spring and fall, when horses are shedding and it may be too cool for baths. Vacuuming removes loose hair, scurf, and dirt, keeping clothing, saddle pads, and blankets cleaner. Horses must be trained to accept the noise and feeling of vacuuming, but most adapt to it and even seem to enjoy it.

Vacuums vent air out the back as they work, which can send dust or hair back into the air. Built-in models vent the exhaust outside the building. They also lack the hazard of an electric cord underfoot.

Warning: Vacuums should never be used to suck up water or vacuum a wet horse. You could seriously shock yourself or the horse. Some vacuums do come with a blower feature for drying wet horses, but the nozzle should not come in contact with the horse.

van, horse A single truck-and-box unit designed to transport horses. Horse vans can carry up to nine horses and are the most comfortable option for long-distance hauling. They have better suspension and more effective insulation, and they give the horses a quieter and smoother ride than truck-and-trailer combinations do. They are, however, more expensive than trailers and, as single-purpose vehicles, less utilitarian than trucks.
➤ *See also trailer*

vaquero A Mexican cowboy. Vaqueros herded cattle throughout the Southwest during the 18th and 19th centuries, where the word evolved into "buckaroo," to describe a cowboy. There has been a marked increase in interest in the vaquero style of horsemanship in recent years. At its best, it brings horse training and riding to a high art.
➤ *See also bridle horse; California-style bit; "straight up in the bridle"; Western dressage*

vaulting An internationally recognized equine sport involving gymnastics performed on the back of a trotting or cantering horse, along with the movements used to mount and dismount the horse. Individual and team competitions are held at all levels, from preschool to Pony Club to the World Equestrian Games (WEG). Some therapeutic horsemanship programs also offer interactive vaulting activities.

Vaulting can increase rider safety: Because vaulters are continually shifting their positions on a moving horse, they develop superb balance, flexibility, and confidence,

VAULTING

along with a great sense of rhythm. For people who can't afford a horse, vaulting may be an ideal sport; several team members share one horse, which keeps costs low.

Vaulting horses wear a vaulting surcingle and a thick pad. The handler controls the horse via a longe line and a specialized cavesson. A vaulting horse spends his working life trotting or cantering in a circle, often carrying multiple riders, and therefore needs to be steady and sound. A broad back is also an asset.

➤ *See also therapeutic horsemanship*

Venezuelan equine encephalitis (VEE)

➤ *See equine encephalitis*

versatility trail competitions A trail horse competition aimed at the versatile working horse. Extreme trail challenges may take place indoors or out.

VERSATILITY COMPETITION, LOG DRAG

They are judged on time and points, and any breed may participate. They emphasize horsemanship, smoothness, calmness, finesse, forward movement, control, attitude, and quickness. Challenges may include opening gates; dragging items; loading into a trailer; carrying things; jumping; riding over natural terrain; dismounting and remounting; and handling loud noises, smoke, and water in various forms.

➤ *See also "Extreme Cowboy Race," page 115; doma vaquera; working equitation/doma trabajo*

vertical A simple jump consisting of standards and poles.

➤ *See also "Types of Jumps," page 192*

vesicular stomatitis (VS) A highly contagious virus most commonly found in South and Central America and Mexico, but that can spread into the United States. With symptoms similar to foot-and-mouth disease, VS isn't normally fatal, but health officials are careful to limit its spread.

The virus is carried by insects and in the saliva of infected animals. It is also carried in the fluid of the blisters that are a symptom of the disease. The blisters form around the feet, teats, nostrils, mouth, tongue, and lips. As they swell and break, lesions form that make eating and drinking so painful that the horse may actually die of dehydration or starvation.

There is no specific treatment for VS; the disease is self-limiting and usually resolves within two weeks. Care includes using a mild antiseptic mouthwash or ointment on the blisters to relieve pain and to guard against secondary infection of the sores left by broken blisters. Thoroughly clean and disinfect any area used by an ill horse (including trailers), and wash and change your clothes and shoes before handling a healthy horse.

VESICULAR STOMATITIS WARNING An outbreak of VS must be reported to local authorities, and all affected horses must be quarantined. A farm with a case of VS is not considered safe until 30 days after the lesions have healed.

vest, protective

PROTECTIVE VEST

Sleeveless apparel designed to protect a rider or driver from injury in case of a fall. Some protective vests are made of high-density foam. Others incorporate air-bag technology; if the rider falls, a lanyard attached to the saddle deploys the airbag, protecting the neck, torso, hips, and spine. Some stables require safety vests for jumping students. They are mandatory in many cross-country and combined driving competitions, and a good idea for rough rodeo riding. Some horsemen even wear them when working with unruly horses on the ground, to lessen risk of injury from being struck or trampled.

➤ *See also helmet, safety; safety*

veterinarian

veterinarian A doctor of animal medicine. Many veterinarians specialize in either small animals (pets) or large animals (livestock, including horses). The best way to find a good vet is to ask local horse people with high standards for their recommendations.

WHEN TO CALL THE VET

It's time to call the vet when a horse is exhibiting any of the following behaviors:

- Not eating, showing radically changed tastes, or not drinking
- Having trouble chewing, slobbering, dropping food
- Coughing
- Acting depressed or lethargic, acting anxious or uneasy
- Shivering or sweating inappropriately
- Lying down frequently, pawing excessively, rolling a lot
- Showing a change in stool: diarrhea; hard, dry manure; not passing manure at all
- Having difficulty urinating
- Standing in an odd or uncomfortable position
- Having a runny nose or discharge from eyes

It's best to call the veterinarian early on rather than waiting to see what happens and risking further complications. Unless your horse is in a life-threatening situation, take note of the following before calling so that the veterinarian has the best information possible:

- General health and vital signs (temperature, pulse, respiration)
- Capillary refill time
- Gut sounds, if you suspect colic
- Degree of lameness, if this is the problem

The more information you can provide to your veterinarian via telephone, the better she can instruct you in how to manage the situation until she arrives. This information will also help her assess the critical level of your horse's needs. A veterinarian may receive multiple calls for help within the same time frame. It is vital that she be able to care for the most critical first. (It also can save you money if the vet doesn't have to consider your visit an emergency. Many vets add a premium charge for emergency calls.)

When it *is* an emergency (see "Emergency Calls," next page), you'll get better service if your vet trusts you to be fully informed.

➤ *See also capillary refill time; colic; lameness; parasites; prepurchase exam; pulse and respiration; temperature (horse); vital signs*

FINDING A VET ON THE ROAD

If you need a vet while you're traveling with your horse, call **1-800-GET-A-DVM**. This service, run by the Equine Connection, lists the names of local veterinarians who are members of the American Association of Equine Practitioners. Online, check **aaep.org/info/getadvm**.

vetting out

➤ *See prepurchase exam*

vice

➤ *See stereotypy*

vision A horse has the largest eyes of any land mammal and the largest retinas. That alone ensures that the horse sees differently than we do. One major difference is that images are magnified 50 percent greater by the equine eye than by the human eye; when your horse shies at a candy wrapper blowing in the wind, he's seeing something the size of a magazine. The horse's vision has great impact on our interactions, and it's worthwhile to understand the ways in which what he sees differs from what we see.

Feral horses spend 50 to 60 percent of their time grazing with their heads lowered and eyes near the ground. Thus, ground-level visual stimuli are particularly salient for them. They watch the distant horizon for predators, so they have evolved to have a broad visual field, and eyes prominently located on the sides of the skull. The location of the eyes, the size and curvature of the cornea, the size and horizontal shape of the pupil, and the angular extent of the retina all give the horse monocular vision in a wide field. The horse can see slightly greater than 200 degrees in the horizontal plane; the human eye, with its circular pupil, can achieve only 150 degrees.

The horse's peripheral vision approaches 360 degrees. Through the lateral part of this range he sees a different image with each eye. However, contrary to common belief, horses do possess interocular transfer; that is, stimuli seen by one eye are recognized by other.

The horse has only a small field of binocular vision in which he can clearly see an object with both eyes. This area is located some distance in front of his forehead. He must position his head properly in order to focus and to bring his binocular vision into play. Horses will raise and lower their heads, and arch their necks, to find the exact position where an object comes into focus.

BLIND SPOTS Because his eyes are placed toward the sides of his head, the horse has blind spots, areas where he cannot see things unless he turns his head or moves his body. Blind spots include the area directly behind his tail and immediately in front of his forehead. Horses tend to react violently to any sudden activity in their blind spots, perhaps because in general nothing takes them by surprise. For your own protection, alert the horse to your presence whenever you approach his blind spots, by speaking calmly. Countless injuries happen because a horse is startled by a handler.

Despite their lateral eye placement, horses are good judges of depth and distance, as befits an animal that relies on speed. To use binocular vision to judge depth, as when jumping, the horse must be allowed to raise his head. For unknown reasons, male horses have better ability to judge distance at speed than females. However, horses in general are probably better at this than humans.

Like many wild mammals, horses see distant objects most clearly. Arabians are noted for recognizing their owners from afar. However, horses have difficulty focusing on an object less than a meter away.

A horse has nearly 360-degree peripheral vision, but he has **blind spots** directly in front of his face, behind his tail, and under his head.

LIGHT AND DARK Horses evolved to do much of their feeding at dawn and dusk, and to be on guard against nighttime predation, so they need to see well at low light levels. In fact, horses see better on an overcast day than on a sunny day. The typical brown iris has beneficial adaptations to low light levels. Thus, while their visual acuity is poor in daylight compared to that of humans, it is better than that of humans at night.

Horses' eyes have light-collecting power similar to those of owls, dogs, and gray squirrels; worse than those of cats, rabbits, and rats; and much better than those of humans. They have fewer cones than we do; they also have a reflecting structure, the tapetum lucidum, which reflects light back through the photoreceptor layer.

This adaptation comes with a downside. Horses are easily blinded by exposure to sudden bright light or abrupt changes in light level. Human eyes adjust from bright sunlight to darkness in about 25 minutes. Horses' eyes need 45 minutes—important to remember when out riding through field and forest, or just leading a horse into a darkened stall or trailer. On the plains where they evolved, light levels changed gradually, primarily at sunrise and sunset. When moving

from fields to woods and back again, trail riders need to remember that for many minutes after making the transition, the horse is essentially flying blind. This also has strong implications for working and competition in indoor arenas. Horses are often warmed up outdoors in bright light, then brought into a darker arena to jump fences they can barely see. High-end competitions often use intense lights, but smaller competitions may not. Competitors can help horses adjust by warming up in the shade, and giving them the longest possible time in the indoor arena before starting to jump.

Conversely, horses tolerate bright light better than we do, due to bodies called corpora nigra, or iris bodies, cloud-shaped, pigmented structures that hang over the iris, partially shading light from entering the pupil. The pupil's narrow, horizontal shape decreases the amount of light entering the eye from above and below, and the long, downward-angled eyelashes also act as a sunscreen or visor. Given that they evolved on the largely treeless grasslands, it makes sense that they are sun-adapted.

Horses can see color in a narrow range, similar to that of colorblind humans. They basically see variations of two main hues. They frequently confuse red and green, see blue poorly and yellow well, and overall probably rely less on color than on textural differences to distinguish objects from their environment. However, without strong color cues they have greater difficulty perceiving objects than do humans, particularly distant objects. A rider may see someone in a distant field; the horse may only see that person when she moves. And given that the horse has 20/30 vision, compared to the rider's 20/20, the horse needs to be 50 percent closer to see the same details. Thus the horse may shy at something the rider has been watching for several minutes—and the unprepared rider often calls that horse an idiot!

Visual cues are highly important in recognition of other horses, and help stallions know when mares are in heat. Small movements are more noticeable to horses than they are to humans. It is easy to give an inadvertent cue to a horse; maybe you twitch a finger as you are about to ask him to back. To him, that is the cue, and if he does back he is not anticipating, he is obeying. On the positive side, the horse's ability to notice small movements makes it easy to give a performing horse a cue that will be invisible to the audience.

Finally, while horses have some variability in their reactions to color, it has been proven that they load more readily into trailers with green mats rather than with the more common black mats.

A HORSE'S-EYE VIEW

Your horse sees things differently than you do. To avoid being surprised or upset by his seemingly irrational reactions, remember this:

- Things look 50 percent larger to him.
- He sees a far wider range than you do, but in a rather unfocused way. He keeps half an eye on everything.
- He is easily blinded by changes in light level and stays that way for a much longer time.
- He may be frightened by people or objects in his blind spots.
- Yellow really pops for him; blue and red are harder to see.
- He can easily detect small motions you may not notice.
- He needs to raise his head to judge distance, as when approaching a jump.
- To focus on a strange object, he prefers to look sideways at it rather than straight on.

PERCEPTION Horses are not good at categorical perception. Their visual perceptions are hyper-specific, meaning that to a horse a hose stretched on the ground is a completely different object from a neatly coiled hose and a sloppily coiled hose is yet another object. Horses are also noncategorical in their other senses. If exposed to a chaotic, jumbled daily environment, they can become accustomed to that, but their awareness of change is not diminished. They need to be trained to trust the environment and their handlers, and when stressed, that training can break down.

Interesting new research appears to show that horses recognize human facial expressions. When shown photographs of humans with either angry or smiling faces, the horses in the experiment shifted their heads to view an angry expression with the left eye. Many animals make this shift when viewing threats; images seen in the left eye are routed through the right side of the brain, which handles fearful emotions.

➤ *See also eye problems; pig-eyed; shying*

vital signs Temperature, pulse, and respiration (TPR). Here are the normal vital signs for a resting horse who weighs 1,000 pounds (454 kg):

- Temperature (rectal); 99.5–101.5°F (37.5–38.6°C)
- Pulse: 30–42 beats per minute
- Respiration: 12–20 breaths per minute

Horses may deviate slightly from these norms yet be perfectly healthy. Establish what's normal for your horse so you will know when he is unwell.

vitamins A horse on good pasture or high-quality hay has no need of supplementary vitamins. If you determine that your horse requires additional vitamins because of poor feed or his current condition, consult with your veterinarian about appropriately supplementing the diet.

➤ *See also feeding and nutrition; supplements*

vocalizing, of horse

Though highly social, horses do not communicate much by means of voice. They evolved on open grassland where they were rarely out of sight of each other, and most of their communication is through body language. They do use sound in certain situations, however, and can certainly learn to discriminate among vocal cues.

A horse will give a low nicker at the approach of a familiar person (especially one with food) or when greeting an equine friend. A nicker is a soft sound formed with the mouth shut.

A squeal is louder, and expresses aggression. Whinnying is a very loud sound, varying in pitch; separating two horses who have bonded can produce endless, noisy whinnying as they pine to be together again. A truly furious horse will produce a sound often described as a scream, and fighting stallions make loud roaring noises as they struggle with each other.

A horse may snort with alarm at a new sight or smell, and some horses seem to snort playfully. A blow, a rapid pulse of air through the nose, can be heard from several hundred feet away, and is used to express alarm.

➤ *See also body language, of horses*

voice, as an aid

In riding the voice is considered a secondary aid, like a whip or spurs, used when the horse is not responding to the primary aids (weight, legs, hands). It can be helpful in reassuring young horses, or in waking up a horse who is tuning you out. The horse learns verbal cues for the gaits on the longe line, and these can be carried over to riding as well. In driving the voice is one of only three aids and takes on added importance. Use of the voice is not permitted in dressage competitions and is discouraged in other types of competition as well, so it's a good idea to fade verbal cues if you aspire to show.

Voice aids should be carefully thought out. If they sound too similar to one another, they may confuse the horse. People who acquire horses from the Amish often wonder what verbal cues their horses know. The Amish use English cues to facilitate the sale of horses. But if your horse understands a language you don't speak, it's not the end of the world. Horses are quite capable of learning several cues for the same behavior.

➤ *See also aids; handling horses*

COMMON VOICE COMMANDS

Command	Response
Get up	Move ahead
Whoa	Stop immediately
Easy	Slow down
Gee	Move to the left
Haw	Move to the right
Back	Step backward
Over	Move to the side

volte

A dressage term meaning a small circle, perhaps 20 feet (6 m) in diameter, made by the horse.

volvulus

A twist in the intestinal tract.

➤ *See also colic*

vomiting

The horse has inadequate reverse peristalsis—the vomiting mechanics of humans, dogs, and cats—and therefore cannot vomit to cleanse his digestive tract of spoiled or toxic foods. Food can return upward from the stomach, but structures in the back of a horse's throat keep it from exiting through the mouth and force it through the nostrils or, worse still, back down into the lungs, causing pneumonia. Vomiting is so difficult for horses that the stomach may actually rupture in the process. This is one reason colic is so dangerous for the horse.

➤ *See also colic; digestive system; stomach*

VS

➤ *See vesicular stomatitis (VS)*

wagon train treks A type of historic reenactment/slow-moving trail ride popular in the West. A typical event includes 15 to 20 wagons and as many as 150 people, as well as a support crew ferrying in supplies in pickups. Wagon train treks are great ways for families, even nonriders, to enjoy horses and the outdoors together. Many retrace the routes of early settlers, and some are open to riders as well.

PONY EXPRESS REENACTMENTS

Every year the National Pony Express Association (NPEA) holds a 10-day reenactment of the Pony Express ride. Five hundred horses and riders cover 1,996 miles (3,212 km) between California and Missouri. Volunteer riders gather from all over the United States to participate.

WALER ▶

A light, mixed-breed saddle horse developed in New South Wales, Australia, exported to British military forces in India during the 19th century. The present-day Australian Stock Horse is the descendant of the Waler.

walk A slow four-beat gait in which each foot strikes the ground separately.
➤ *See also gait; running walk*

walking a horse down

1. A phrase used interchangeably with "cooling out a horse," after a workout, to help his pulse, respiration, and temperature return to normal.

2. A method of catching a horse in a pasture by simply walking after him, quietly and persistently, until he allows himself to be caught.

➤ *See also cooling down, after exercise; handling horses*

walk-trot classes Classes held at competitions of many breeds and disciplines, where the only gaits called for are the walk and trot. In dressage, the first tests at the introductory level call for walk-trot movements only. At any type of competition, a rider who ordinarily shows at a higher level may exhibit a green horse at the walk-trot level to introduce him to showing.
➤ *See also English riding; green horse; Western riding*

wall of hoof The hard outer covering of the hoof, from the coronary band to the ground. The wall should be relatively smooth and free from cracks and rings. **Rings** on the hoof wall are ridges that run parallel to the coronary band; deep rings may indicate previous founder. **Grass rings** are much shallower rings that may indicate stress in the animal's life, such as a change in diet or environment.
➤ *See also hoof*

warbles The larvae of the cattle grub, best known for burrowing into the backs of cattle and horses, forming cysts. This can create terrible sores that become infected if not treated carefully. Ivermectin is the best treatment. Cattle pastured near horses should also be treated.
➤ *See also parasites*

war bridle A type of restraint created by running a rope over the horse's poll and under his upper lip or around his nose. Other variations include a simple slip knot fastened around the jaw, which was widely used by Native Americans, and a variant on the rope halter, which loops around the poll and jaw or nose. War bridles can be quite harsh and should be resorted to only when it is absolutely necessary to control a horse against his will.
➤ *See also restraints; stableizer; twitch*

warmblood A type of horse developed in Europe from "cold-blooded" draft horses and "hot-blooded" Thoroughbreds and Arabs. Warmbloods are more accurately described as a type than as a breed. Control and consistency are determined by the way individuals are approved for registry and breeding. Stallions must be approved by licensed authorities from the breed organizations at a "keuring," a rigorous examination and judging process. Mares are also evaluated. Keurings evaluate horses on conformation, temperament, movement, and athletic ability.

There are numerous warmblood registries, many named after a country or region of origin (e.g., Dutch Warmblood, Hanoverian, Holsteiner, Selle Français, and Trakehner), but these are not breeds in the strictest sense. Warmblood stallions may be eligible for breeding in several warmblood stud books.

Warmbloods are large horses, with lengthy strides, uphill movement that facilitates lightness of the forehand, and great athleticism. They excel at jumping, eventing, and combined driving. These large horses need more time to mature than lighter breeds do. In Europe, they often aren't started under saddle until they are five or six years old. If fed too much protein as foals and ridden too early, warmbloods can develop hock and other joint problems. Some warmbloods are hard to handle, as they can be stubborn and prone to fits of temper, especially when young.

➤ *See also breed; cold blood; hot blood*

warm-up exercises Exercises designed to loosen a horse's muscles and increase blood flow. This increases oxygen delivery to the horse's muscles, which prevents early buildup of lactic acid during the workout. Lactic-acid buildup causes fatigue and prevents the horse from benefiting from the workout.

A proper warm-up has two stages. Walking for 5 to 10 minutes on a long rein allows the joints to regain mobility, gets the fluids moving, brings up the horse's respiration rate, and gives his muscles time to limber up. It also helps him adjust mentally. Older horses may need a longer amount of time.

After loosening up, the intensity of the exercise should gradually increase: trotting and cantering at simple figures, using a posting trot or light seat. This stimulates blood flow, makes the muscles more pliable, and warms up the horse's tendons and ligaments.

SOME WARMBLOOD BREEDS

Canadian Sport Horse

A warmblood developed in Canada starting in 1926 from Canadian draft mares crossed on Thoroughbreds. Currently Canadian Sport Horses, Thoroughbreds, and warmbloods of other breeds are being used in the breeding program. Stallions undergo a rigorous inspection and performance test before being accepted for breeding.

Danish Warmblood

A modern riding-horse breed developed in Denmark, particularly well suited to dressage.

Dutch Warmblood

A sport horse developed by breeders in the Netherlands after World War II. Dutch Warmbloods can be high-spirited but are generally good-natured and willing. Standing 16 to 17 hands high, these long-bodied horses are sometimes plain but always have good action and strength. They excel at jumping and dressage. They are bay, brown, or chestnut, with some white markings allowed.

Hanoverian

A German warmblood breed founded in 1735 by England's King George II (a German who was also Elector of Hanover) with the intention to create good horses for the army and agriculture. George used Holsteiner stallions, crossing them with English Thoroughbreds. The breed was later improved with Cleveland Bay and other coach horses to create two strains of horse, one for pulling coaches and artillery, and one for riding. The horses were also used on the farm, and were required to be able to pull a plow.

After World War II, breeders shifted focus to producing riding and sport horses. Today, the large, powerful Hanoverian excels at both show jumping and dressage. Hanoverians stand about 16.2 hands high, and are all solid colors.

Holsteiner

A German warmblood dating to the 13th century. The Holsteiner originated as a cavalry horse; was developed as an elegant, although heavy, coach horse in the 17th century; and is currently used as a sport horse. In recent years, the breed has been refined with the introduction of some Thoroughbred blood. Exceptionally strong and good-tempered, today's Holsteiner excels at show jumping and dressage. A large horse, he stands between 16 and 17 hands high. He is intelligent and comes in all solid colors.

Oldenburg

Originally bred as a powerful and elegant carriage horse, this German warmblood has been cross-bred with Thoroughbreds and other lighter horses to produce an all-around sport horse with light, springy action and good jumping ability. Oldenburgs are big, muscular horses, standing 16.2 to 17.2 hands high. They are generally dark in color, with chestnuts becoming more common. They are known for their energetic yet equitable temperament.

Selle Français

The Selle Français (French Saddle Horse) is a warmblood with outstanding jumping ability and a notably pleasant temperament. An individual of this breed stands between 16 and 17 hands high and resembles a Thoroughbred, but with more bone and muscle.

Swedish Warmblood

Known for brilliant performance in the dressage ring, the Swedish Warmblood also shines in jumping, driving, and other competition. This tall, elegant horse with excellent gaits and willingness to learn has won medals in nearly every Olympic equestrian competition since 1912.

Westfalen/Westphalian

A German warmblood breed, developed from a farm horse breed. Somewhat heavier than the Hanoverian, which it closely resembles, it is one of the world's most popular competition breeds, known for spectacular movement and trainability. The body is deep and muscular, with powerful sloping shoulders and very strong hindquarters.

Dutch rider Hans Peter Minderhoud on Escapado, an Oldenburg

Swedish rider Helena Persson on Bonzai, a Swedish Warmblood

After 5 or 10 minutes, more demanding work like small circles, serpentines, leg-yields, and other lateral work can begin, as the warm-up blends into the main work of the day. Warming up and stretching, both before mounting and in the saddle, are also helpful for riders.

➤ *See also cooling down, after exercise*

warts Skin growths caused by a virus. They are common in young horses who haven't built up immunity to the virus, but they usually disappear on their own after some time (several months to a year). They can spread from infected horses through small lesions and cuts in the skin where the virus can enter, as well as through shared grooming tools.

Warts generally appear around the muzzle and nostrils but sometimes are found in the ears or other parts of the body. They are not a serious problem for horses unless they grow thickly enough to interfere with breathing. Have your veterinarian examine larger warts and decide whether to deal with them surgically.

washing horses

➤ *See bathing horses*

water, crossing When trail riding, always cross a brook or stream at a shallow place where you can see the bottom. Deep, rushing water can be very dangerous. Footing in a brook can be treacherous, so go slowly and let your horse feel his way. It might make sense to dismount and lead your horse.

Let your horse stop for a drink if he wants, but be aware that some horses will lie down in water. Pawing might be a sign of imminent rolling, so get him moving! If your horse is nervous about crossing water, let a more experienced companion lead the way. A lot of horses are just like cats when it comes to getting their feet wet and may need plenty of encouragement before stepping into water. However, trust your horse's instincts if he's usually confident but becomes wary of crossing.

Be very careful when riding in a boggy area or swamp. A muddy path that would support your weight might give way under your horse and bog him down. Struggling to get out of a hole could cause your horse to panic and injure himself.

➤ *See also trail riding*

A well-trained horse will **cross water** confidently, without rushing, but proceeding carefully with senses alert. A rider who trusts her horse will sit still and give him his head.

CHEAP AND EASY WATER HAULING

If you need to lug water to your horse, use a cat litter jug (emptied and cleaned out, of course). These large plastic bottles have wide, comfortable handles and screw-on tops. Even if you lose the top, the neck of the bottle is small enough that you won't slop water.

Some horses can be fussy about their drinking **water**, but others enjoy playing around in the trough or will even drink directly from a hose.

water, for horses

Paying meticulous attention to your horse's access to water is one of the most critical things you can do to ensure his health and well-being. Water is the most essential nutrient and should be available to horses at all times. At rest on a cool day, a horse needs about 1 gallon (3.8 L) per 220 pounds (100 kg) of bodyweight. Requirements increase with temperature and work. A horse working in hot weather can require up to 20 gallons (76 L) a day. Horses can lose several gallons through normal sweating and urination.

Clean water should be offered free-choice. However, if the water is of poor quality, or is too warm or too cold, horses may not voluntarily drink enough. Water requirements also increase with the amount of dry matter in the feed. Horses eating hay and grain need more water than horses grazing fresh pasture.

Check your horse's water source daily. Ponds can become stagnant, and even running brooks may freeze. Automatic waterers can malfunction, so check daily to make sure yours is working.

Keep buckets and waterers clean. Leaves or vegetation can leach tannins into the water, making it taste bitter. Empty, scrub, and refill water troughs every couple of weeks. If you find algae, rinse with a solution of 5 teaspoons (25 mL) of bleach to 25 gallons (95 L) of water. If you have continuous flow of water through the trough, you can put goldfish or small catfish in to eat the algae.

Horses tend to drink less water when it is very cold. Heated water tubs are more than just a convenience to keep you from having to chop ice; they can entice your horse to drink a normal amount and thereby prevent an impaction colic.

Horses often refuse to drink unfamiliar water, which is a problem if you are hauling them long distances. You can haul some home water along with them. Another idea is to start flavoring the water at home with something like apple juice or powdered drink mix; once the horses are used to that, they should accept strange water with the added flavor.

To encourage drinking, keep free-choice salt available.

After strenuous exercise, limit your horse's water intake to a few sips until he is completely cooled down; too much water too soon after exertion can lead to founder. A very warm horse can be sponged or hosed with tepid water to cool him off and wash the sweat from his coat. Cold water not only is uncomfortable for him but also can cause his back muscles to stiffen.

way of going

The overall look of a horse as he moves, including his manners, natural impulsion, and presence.

weaning foals The proper time for weaning varies according to the size and health of the foal, but it is generally done between two and six months of age. Keeping a foal with his dam longer than this is difficult for the mare if she is pregnant again, and can lead to a spoiled, badly behaved yearling.

Traditionally, foals and mares were abruptly parted and put into separate pens where they could neither see nor hear each other. This is extremely stressful for the foal, who is still emotionally dependent on his mother. A foal who is removed abruptly may not eat for several days and could injure himself by trying to climb the fence to find his dam.

A more humane way to accomplish weaning is to put mare and foal in adjacent pens with sturdy, high wire fencing between them (no gaps for the foal to get his head through). The foal can't nurse but will be reassured by the sight and smell of his mother. It also helps for him to have other weanlings or companions in the pen with him.

It will take a couple of weeks for the mare's milk to dry up. She should be on restricted food at this time, and unless it's very hot, you can limit her water as well, to speed up the drying process. Hand-milking to relieve the pressure in her udder will only encourage further milk production.

➤ *See also breeding; foaling*

weanling A foal who is not yet a year old but is no longer nursing. Weanlings need lots of exercise, the company of other horses (preferably their own age), and a diet with adequate protein and energy for good growth. Forage is best: pasture and grass hay, with some alfalfa and grain for protein.

A common mistake is feeding young horses too much protein, which causes rapid growth and can lead to a variety of skeletal problems. On the other hand, this stage of life is a time of rapid growth, and the weanling foal needs the nourishment to support this. A weanling who will mature around 1,100 pounds (499 kg) should be gaining 1½ to 2 pounds (0.7–0.9 kg) a day at the age of six months. He should not be overly fat or overly thin. Use a weight tape to monitor weight gain, and be prepared to adjust his feed accordingly. Consult your veterinarian with any concerns, as either underfeeding or overfeeding can negatively impact your weanling's future.

For socializing and exercise, the best solution is to keep weanlings on pasture in a group. Feed them separately from mature horses to ensure that the youngsters are getting enough to eat. Fillies and colts should be separated fairly early on, as puberty can come early.

Contact with humans is important, too. It's never too early to start teaching ground manners. Be aware, however, that work on the longe line is too stressful for young ligaments and should be avoided or limited until age two or older.

➤ *See also feeding and nutrition; foaling; gelding; protein; sacking out; weaning foals*

weaving Swaying side to side on the forehand, moving the head and neck continuously. Weaving usually takes place in a stall, especially near a door or window where the horse can see out. This almost hypnotic behavior is a sign of anxiety, restlessness, or boredom. Providing some toys for the stall and arranging for more exercise or turnout time will probably alleviate the problem.

➤ *See also pacing; stereotypy*

web halter A halter made of strong nylon weave. Web halters are the most commonly used of all halters because they are inexpensive and come in a variety of colors. If the hardware is well made, a web halter is nearly unbreakable, which could be dangerous if the horse gets caught on something. If you must leave a web halter on during turnout, use one with a breakaway leather crownpiece or fuse.

➤ *See also halter; rope halter*

weighing feed A horse's ration should be determined by weight, not volume. Each crop of hay or grain may differ in weight, due in part to variances in moisture and mineral content, so it is vital to your horse's well-being that you weigh your standard measure each time you receive a new load of feed. Weigh a bale of hay, then divide that weight by the number of flakes/slabs of hay in that bale to determine the number of flakes your horse needs at each feeding. Weigh a full grain scoop so you know how many scoops your horse needs of the new feed to equal the weight he received of your previous feed. You need to do this even if you don't change rations. A corn/oat mix can differ by as much as 25 percent depending on the moisture content and quality of the grains.

That said, experienced horsemen judge this by feel, and by the way the horse looks. You can use a scale to teach yourself how to estimate the right amount, but weight alone is not enough. You will need to judge hay quality, and fine-tune feeding to your horse's changing seasonal needs. Bottom line: There's no substitute for the human brain at feeding time.

➤ *See also feeding and nutrition; hay; pelleted feed*

weight, as an aid One of the primary aids, along with your legs and hands. This is especially true in Western riding, but it is also a major component of all high-level training and riding. Beginning with a deep, balanced seat, you can cue your horse to turn by shifting your weight slightly in the direction you want to go. For example, putting more weight on your outside stirrup can keep your horse from falling in to the center as he canters in a circle. In general, the horse shifts to step *under* your weight. This is counterintuitive to many riders, who tend to lean *toward* an outside leg as they administer the aid, in a desperate attempt to gain leverage; often the leg aid isn't working because it is counteracted by the weight aid.

Learning to control how you weight your seat bones can make an immense difference to your riding. It requires subtle control of your core muscles, and can be helped by a thorough study of riding biomechanics. The reward is an apparently effortless, beautiful ride with invisible aids, and a real sense of oneness with your horse.

➤ *See also aids; seat*

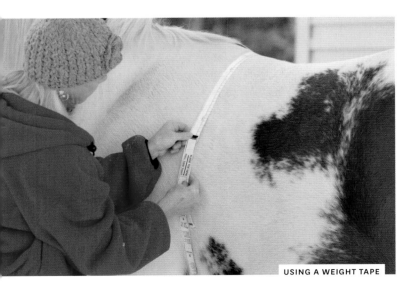

USING A WEIGHT TAPE

AVERAGE WEIGHT OF HORSES

Type of Animal	Weight
Draft horse	1,500 lbs (680 kg)
Saddle horse	1,250 lbs (567 kg)
Pony	500 lbs (227 kg)

weight, of horse You need to know your horse's weight in order to estimate the correct dosage for deworming and other medications. The most accurate way is to use an actual livestock or truck scale. At a trucking weigh station, you can weigh your truck and trailer empty and then load the horse and weigh it again.

A simpler, and more common, method is to use a weight tape, which measures the girth just behind the front legs. The tape should be wrapped snugly around the body. This method, however, gives only a rough estimate of weight.

A more accurate calculation is to measure the heart girth with a nonstretching measuring tape (a piece of nonstretching string will do as well; it can then be measured on a carpenter's tape or yardstick, if that's what you've got). Then measure the horse's body length from shoulder to haunch. To calculate total weight, multiply the heart girth measurement by itself, then by the body length, and then divide that total by 330. The equation is Heart girth × Heart girth × Body length ÷ 330 = Total bodyweight

Example: Heart girth = 72"; Body length = 61"

72 × 72 × 61 = 316,224

316,224 ÷ 330 = 958

A mobile phone app is available that can do these calculations rapidly.

weight tape A specially calibrated tape that is used to roughly calculate a horse's weight.

WELARA PONY

A pony breed created by crossing Arabians and Welsh Ponies. Welaras are beautiful, sound, and athletic. They are best known as hunter ponies but are also well suited to jumping, trail, and driving. They must measure between 11.2 and 15 hands high, and are considered a sport pony. The true Welara must be a combination of Welsh and Arabian blood, no less than one-eighth and no more than seven-eighths Welsh or Arabian.

➤ *See also Arabian; Welsh Pony*

WELSH PONY

A sturdy, elegant British pony that has lived in Wales since before Roman times. There are four sizes, ranging from the Welsh Mountain Pony, under 12 hands high, to the Welsh Cob, 13.2 hands high and up, with no upper limit; some Welsh Cobs reach 15 or 16 hands high. Welsh Ponies have a deep body, energetic gaits, and great hardiness and agility.

All solid colors are accepted; gray, brown, and chestnut are the most common. Welsh Ponies are popular children's mounts, and cobs easily carry adults. Welsh Ponies are seen in all kinds of show rings, including jumping and driving classes.

well-sprung ribs

Ribs that curve out from the backbone and project back and down, forming a wide rib cage; the opposite of slab-sided. Horses with well-sprung ribs have a shorter back and loin, and greater lung capacity.

Western banding

A Western show grooming process in which the mane is divided into 30 or 40 tiny ponytails with small rubber bands. It is vital to practice banding until it is perfected. A sloppy banding job can distract from an otherwise excellent turnout.

At its highest level, banding can be used to disguise conformation weaknesses. A horse with a short, thick neck can be made to appear as if his neck is longer and slimmer by increasing the number of bands used; the more bands, the longer the neck appears. A neck that is too slim can be made to appear thicker by reducing the number of bands used.

WESTERN BANDING

Western dressage

A combination of traditional dressage and Western riding. A relatively new form of competition, Western dressage has become popular in many different breed organizations. Many Western trainers have long employed dressage principles in their training. Western dressage allows them to focus their training by riding tests. While regular dressage rewards large horses with extravagant motion, smaller horses of stock and pleasure types can excel at Western dressage.

Western dressage is a progressive training system with six levels of tests. Introductory tests take place at the walk and jog only. Later tests include lengthened and collected work at all three gaits, as well as shoulder-in, leg-yield, and half-pass. The desired end product is a handy, willing, safe, and calm horse with light, pure gaits.

Competition takes place in an arena 20 x 40 meters (66 x 131 feet) or 20 x 60 meters (66 x 197 feet). A Western dressage horse should not be shown with a draped rein. Instead, there should be light rein tone between horse and rider, with the horse's neck arching and stretching forward. Gaits parallel those of traditional dressage, though stride length is not expected to be as extravagant. However, slow-moving or dull gaits are not rewarded. Gaited horses can compete at Western dressage.

Western dressage is ridden in working Western tack and attire. Modern stock-type or all-purpose saddles are suitable. Close-contact saddles with stirrups set to allow the rider's heel to fall under her hip are generally best. Helmets are permitted. Riders may use a bosal, snaffle, or curb bit and one or two hands, but are not allowed to change from one hand to two hands during the test. Unlike classical dressage, Western dressage permits use of the voice as an aid.

Cowboy Dressage Dressage is a related discipline, inspired by the work of Eitan and Debbie Beth-Halachmy and their Morgan horses. While Western dressage grew out of modern competitive dressage, Cowboy Dressage, a trademarked term, has an ethos more closely related to vaquero horsemanship. Western dressage is ridden with a lightly stretched rein, cowboy dressage with a draped rein. Western dressage is recognized by USEF/USDF horse shows; Cowboy Dressage is not. Cowboy Dressage includes a "Challenge Course" that incorporates trail elements, as well as in-hand, vaquero, and gaited tests.

➤ *See also dressage*

western equine encephalitis (WEE)

➤ *See equine encephalitis*

Western horse

➤ *See stock horse*

Western riding

A riding style developed in the United States, Canada, and Australia from the work done by Mexican vaqueros on cattle ranches, and more recently by the American cowboy. Western horses are almost always ridden on a loose, looped, or draped rein, rather than working on contact as do English horses.

The bridle, whether bitted or bitless, acts as a signal, in conjunction with weight aids. Neck-reining is frequently used; when the rein is touched against the neck, the horse moves away from the touch. The cues of a good Western rider, like a good dressage rider, are often invisible.

Western riding encourages a long leg and a relaxed, balanced seat; the original Western riders spent all day in the saddle, hard at work, and the style reflects that. While there are many styles of Western saddle, with different points of balance, the basic saddle should allow the rider to stand in the stirrups without contortion and to ride with the weight over the balls of the feet.

Because of their desire for a steady, even-tempered animal, Western trainers and riders spend a lot of time enhancing a horse's ability to do tasks in a relaxed way, with a long and low frame. An exception to this rule is the vaquero style of horsemanship, in which the horse may work in a collected frame. Even here, the emphasis is on versatility and the ability to come down from an explosive gallop to a flat-footed walk. The ideal Western horse is one you can imagine getting work done on, without spending a lot of time negotiating with him.

The proportions of rider and horse in Western riding are different from those in English. English riders tend to be about one-fifth or less of the size of their horses (but not too small, to avoid the rider's getting "lost" in the saddle). Western riding uses a ratio of about one-fourth, so the rider appears larger on an appropriate horse.

DISCIPLINES

Western show ring disciplines include Equitation, Showmanship, Pleasure, and Trail. Performance disciplines are legion, ranging from ranch-based competitions like cutting, team penning, roping, bronc riding, and various ranch horse contests to reining and high speed games such as pole bending and barrel racing. The new sports of Western Dressage and Cowboy Dressage appeal to many riders, as do the continually evolving types of ranch and trail versatility sports. Doma vaquera is a Western sport, and Working Equitation competitors often use Western tack as well. Cowboy Mounted Shooting offers the appeal of dressing up in period costume as well as fast-paced target practice.

Out in the real world, many pleasure and trail riders prefer the comfort and security of a Western saddle as well. Parade horses are almost always ridden Western, in tack sporting a dazzling amount of bling. Unlike with

English riding, the various disciplines don't demand large variations in the basic seat or in tack. Specialists will want specialized saddles, but the difference between these saddles is not enormous, unlike the differences among a park saddle, a dressage saddle, and a racing saddle.

PREFERRED HORSE BREEDS

The quintessential Western breed is the Quarter Horse, and they dominate Western sports. Paints, Appaloosas, mustangs, Arabians, and certain gaited breeds like the Missouri Fox Trotter are also popular. However, most saddle horse breeds can be competitive in Western sports, and comfortably ridden in Western tack. Baroque breeds like the Morgan and Andalusian are particularly suitable for vaquero-style riding.

SHOWS

Western showing is dominated by massive breed organizations and sport and rodeo associations. Most breed associations sponsor competition in a wide array of disciplines, and the sport associations offer open competitions. Many Western sports offer prize money or academic scholarships, making them quite lucrative for top competitors.

➤ *See also arena events; cutting; half-seat; mounted games; neck-reining; one-handed riding; reining; rodeo; roping; stock horse; stock seat; versatility trail competitions; weight, as an aid; Western Dressage; team penning; Western dressage; Western tack*

WESTERN COMPETITIVE CLASSES

CONFORMATION. Overall body structure of horse is judged, as well as action at the walk and jog.

SHOWMANSHIP. Skill of handler and turnout of horse are judged, according to the rules of the specific show.

WESTERN HORSEMANSHIP. Skill of rider is judged. Also called Stock Seat Equitation.

WESTERN PERFORMANCE. Horse's abilities are judged, according to guidelines of the specific show. Includes events such as cutting, reined cow horse, reining, Western pleasure, trail, and Western riding.

Western tack The Western saddle descends from the medieval Spanish saddle. It was developed for sturdiness, comfort, and utility. It needed to handle the strain and stress of roping, be able to pack overnight gear, and keep the rider comfortable for many hours. The prominent Western saddle horn is designed to anchor the rope for cowboys working cattle. Western saddles feature a deep seat, which provides stability for sitting the horse when a cow jerks against a rope, and relative comfort while riding long distances. Stirrups are hung on wide fenders that protect the inside of the leg. (Australian stock saddles offer many of the same benefits to the rider, including protection for the inside of the leg.)

There are many variations on the standard Western saddle. Which one you choose depends on the event you're most interested in. In addition to the ranch or working saddle, specialized saddles are available for cutting, reining, roping, team penning, barrel racing, pleasure riding, horsemanship, or equitation.

The stock saddle is the type traditionally used by cowboys and livestock ranch hands. It has a longer horn

WESTERN SHOW ATTIRE

Western competitive attire differs from event to event, with show-ring riders wearing much more glitz and color than riders at other Western events. At rodeo games and working classes, attire is more low-key—jeans, chaps where appropriate, Western boots, a Western-style shirt, and a Western hat. Some competitors wear helmets; the Western-style safety helmet tends to be covered in tooled leather and somewhat resembles a polo helmet.

Western show saddles are usually tooled, and may be ornamented with silver and turquoise. The bridle and breastplate might also be decorated. Usually, the rider chooses colors for her shirt and chaps that enhance the horse's coat color.

Male riders generally wear a string tie with a shirt; they may wear a vest, but jackets are not worn to show. Women may wear bow ties, string ties, or rosettes at the closed collar of their show shirts. Some events call for jeans and Western boots; others call for chaps over jeans with shorter boots.

Gloves are not necessary, except in roping events where hand protection is desired. Boots are chosen to complement the rest of the outfit. For hacking and schooling, riders may wear jeans, chaps, and short boots, or they may wear jeans and Western boots, depending on their preference and what they are working on. Check rules of the competition, but here are some general guidelines.

Western Pleasure or Horsemanship
Vest or jacket optional; plain Wrangler jeans or Western pants; fitted chaps may be optional; neat, long-sleeved Western shirt; helmet or Western hat, preferably felt; cowboy or roper-style boots; necktie, scarf tied in square knot, or bolo; belt, gloves, and spurs optional

Western Showmanship
Coat or vest preferred; starched jeans or dress slacks; helmet or felt Western hat; no chaps or spurs; otherwise same as Western pleasure

Cutting
Batwing chaps; spurs; otherwise same as Western pleasure

Reining or Cow Horse
Shotgun chaps; spurs; otherwise same as Western pleasure

Mounted Games (Gymkhana or Rodeo)
Jeans; boots; Western shirt; helmet or Western hat; whip, bat, or quirt; shin guards worn under jeans; gloves

Roping
Jeans; boots; Western shirt; helmet or Western hat; cotton glove recommended for roping hand

WESTERN SADDLE

WESTERN BRIDLE

that allows for dallying ropes, when roping livestock, and a deeper seat that provides more stability and comfort for the long days of hard work in the saddle. The stirrups are usually much narrower than those found on the show styles of Western saddle, to enhance ease and speed of dismount.

Roping and team penning saddles have high horns and deep seats to absorb the shock of the cow hitting the end of the rope. Reining saddles have lower horns to stay out of the way of the reins. Barrel racing saddles are lightweight with deep seats and wide swells to keep the rider in place. Pleasure saddles tend to be richly decorated with tooling, fancy stitching, or silver medallions.

For fast work that requires many changes of direction and sudden stops, saddles generally have both a cinch and a flank cinch to provide added security. The cinch for a Western saddle is usually made of wool or mohair webbing, not leather, and the flank cinch is a leather strap.

BRIDLES Western bridles, also called headstalls, come in several types, but they generally have no nosebands. Some bridles have browbands that pass between the horse's ears instead of across the forehead; the one-ear bridle has a crownpiece and a browband that loops around only one ear.

Reins can be of three styles: open or split, closed, and roping. Most Western riders use open reins, which are long, separate straps that are not attached at the ends. Closed reins are connected with a 3-foot-long romal or quirt at the end. Roping reins are a continuous loop running from one side of the bit to the other.

➤ *See also bit; hackamore; saddle; tack*

West Nile virus

A disease present in parts of Africa, Asia, and Europe for more than half a century, which has migrated to the United States. Mosquitoes carry the virus from birds to other animals, including horses and humans. Only a small percentage of those infected actually show symptoms of illness, but the virus can be deadly. Affected horses become feverish and unable to control their muscles. An effective vaccination is available, and should be administered in the spring.

wethers A rarely used term for uterus.
➤ *See also breeding; foaling; gestation*

wheals
➤ *See hives/wheals/welts*

wheat and wheat bran A grain, not commonly fed to horses because of its cost; in wheat-growing areas where it is more affordable, it can make up part of the grain ration (no more than 20 percent). Wheat is high in protein and energy, but it isn't very bulky and should be mixed with other grains. It must be rolled or crushed to make it easier to chew and digest.

Wheat bran, the rough outer casing of the kernel, adds bulk to concentrated foods and has a laxative effect. A bran mash was once regarded as a nice pick-me-up for a tired or sick horse in winter and a constipation remedy, but it is not as good for horses as was once believed.
➤ *See also bran, bran mash; feeding and nutrition; weighing feed*

wheel horse, wheelers A wheel horse is the horse nearest the cart in tandem driving. Wheelers are the pair in a multiteam hitch nearest the carriage.

whiffletree/whippletree A pivoted horizontal crossbar to which the harness traces are attached. It is attached to the vehicle or implement which the draft animal is pulling. Doubletrees and singletrees are kinds of whiffletrees.
➤ *See doubletree; harness; singletree*

whinnying
➤ *See body language, of horses; vocalizing, of horse*

whip (as aid) One of the so-called secondary or artificial aids. In riding, a crop or a dressage whip can be an effective addition to the natural aids, which should always be used first. If a horse does not respond to the touch of the lower leg or to the voice, a tap with a whip can reinforce the desired response.

In longeing, the long whip keeps the horse from moving in toward the handler. A long whip can also help in teaching ground manners.

In driving, the whip is used to ask for forward movement, or to signal the horse to bend.
➤ *See also aids; crop; longe/lunge; protected contact*

whip (in driving) A term for a carriage driver.

whiskers The hairs on a horse's muzzle. Like cats, horses need those whiskers to feel their way in enclosed spaces (like a feed bucket). However, grooming requirements for most shows are for a clean-shaven muzzle, so most show riders trim the whiskers off their horses' muzzles and chins. If you're not showing your horse, trimming his whiskers is unnecessary. If you want to tidy him up, go ahead, but don't trim the whiskers too short.

white line The white border between the wall of the hoof and the sole of the foot, the junction of the sensitive and insensitive laminae.
➤ *See also hoof; white line disease*

white line disease (WLD) White line disease (WLD) is deterioration of the white line of the hoof caused by bacteria, yeast, or fungus. The line is filled with a white cheesy material and hollow air pockets. WLD is a potentially serious condition that can destroy the hoof laminae from the ground to the coronary pad. A farrier will clean out the affected hoof tissue, pack the hollow space with antiseptic, and put on a shoe with a pad to keep the medication in place. The hooves must be kept dry, and shoes reset regularly.
➤ *See also hoof*

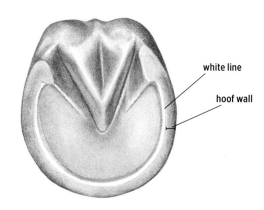

white line

hoof wall

"whoa" command

"Whoa" is a command for your horse to stop; some people pronounce it "ho." Your horse should learn the verbal cue as well as the rein and weight aids; this may enable you to stop him if you've fallen off, dropped the reins, or had an equipment malfunction. To avoid confusing your horse, use "Whoa" only to mean "halt," not as a general term meaning "Stand still" or "Stop doing that."

➤ *See also aids; leading; voice, as an aid*

wind

1. A description of a horse's lung capacity.

2. A natural hazard that can distract horses, increase nervousness, and contribute to a stimulus stack that leads the horse to misbehave. Wind creates noises that a horse may not know how to interpret—and remember, he hears more than we do. It also creates movement of trees, grasses, and debris that may be seen as a threat. Not all horses are bothered by wind, but in general it's best to avoid working a young or skittish animal on a windy day.

windbreaks, natural

Plantings of trees in a pasture that provide shelter from the wind and rain; canyons or gullies can also serve as windbreaks. A pasture with a grove of trees or patch of brush offers sufficient shelter for most horses with heavy winter coats.

windpuffs/wind galls

Soft, rounded swellings on the lower leg. Windpuffs are not sensitive to the touch and do not constitute an unsoundness. They do indicate stress and some injury to a nearby joint, which causes the tendon sheath to fill with synovial fluid.

windsucking

➤ *See cribbing; stereotypy; sucking wind*

winging in/winging out

➤ *See dishing; paddling*

winking

When mares in heat open and close the lips of the vulva to expose the clitoris and indicate readiness to mate.

➤ *See also breeding; estrus*

wisp, for grooming

➤ *See hay wisp*

withers

The bone structure at the top of the horse's shoulder, between his neck and his back. A horse needs well-defined withers to keep a saddle securely in place. **Shark, or shark-fin, withers** protrude sharply from the topline. **Wither pockets** are depressions in the muscle behind a horse's shoulder blade; they may be genetic or may result from excess saddle pressure.

➤ *See also conformation; mutton-withered*

wolf teeth

Often confused with canine teeth, wolf teeth are harder to see, as they sit farther back (in front of the upper premolars). Usually small with shallow roots, wolf teeth can interfere with the action of the bit, and many owners have them removed.

➤ *See also dental problems; teeth and age*

working cow horse

➤ *See reined cow horse*

working equitation/doma trabajo

A three- or four-phase competition developed in Europe in the 1990s from doma vaquera; it debuted in the United States in 2008. Competitors execute a dressage test, then an ease-of-handling phase, where horses navigate obstacles including bridges and barrel patterns and are judged on calmness, precision, maneuverability, style, and harmony. The speed phase, over the same obstacles, is judged on time only. In international team competitions at the advanced level, there is a fourth phase, the cow trial.

The sport is based on ranch skills in southern Europe, where cattle are quick and aggressive. Riders work with long poles, called garrochas, to prod the cattle and defend themselves from charges. Riders carry the garrocha during the ease-of-handling phase. Working equitation rules require culturally consistent attire and tack. Options include armed services or police uniforms (for members of these organizations), Western (including sidesaddle), English hunt seat or dressage, Spanish, Portuguese, or Charro. There is no penalty for using a safety helmet or vest.

Working equitation is becoming popular worldwide. Exciting for spectators as well as competitors, it offers challenge and variety for horses and riders. Having to work around obstacles can help a dressage horse understand the point of bending and flying changes, and challenges a rider's skills. The greatest challenge of all is creating the mental stability and flexibility that allows the horse to work at speed yet remain calm; this requires excellent horsemanship.

➤ *See also baroque horses; bridle horse; doma vaquera; dressage; Extreme Cowboy Race; versatility trail competitions*

working gait
In dressage, a gait that is free and easy, steady and elastic, but without the tightly controlled impulsion of a collected gait.

➤ *See also dressage*

working horse
In Western competition, working horse events include cutting, reining, and working cow horse. These events showcase the skills you and your horse would use when actually working with stock on a ranch.

➤ *See also Western riding; individual classes*

working hunter
A type of horse judged on his ability to negotiate a jump course.

➤ *See also English riding; hunter*

World Equestrian Games (WEG)
The international championship competition run by Fédération Equestre Internationale (FEI) every four years, midway between one Summer Olympics competition and the next. WEG lasts for two weeks and is held in rotating locations. Disciplines include combined driving, dressage, endurance riding, eventing, para-equestrian, reining, show jumping, and vaulting. The FEI regional disciplines of horseball and tent pegging hold their championships in other venues. WEG was held in Kentucky in 2010, the first time ever in the United States. As of 2015, the United States held fourth place in the WEG medal count, following Germany, Great Britain, and the Netherlands.

worming
Deworming a horse. The common term "worming" annoys grammar sticklers, since it implies the opposite of the procedure's actual goal, but it's what most people say in casual use.

➤ *See also deworming*

Team vaulting is one of the more unusual events showcased at the **World Equestrian Games,** held every four years.

XYZ

xylazine A popular tranquilizer for horses. Xylazine is a controlled substance, so it should be administered only by a licensed veterinarian. It can cause severe damage to muscle tissue if injected improperly. Beware of working around the hindquarters of horses on xylazine since they are known to kick aggressively, even if they've never been prone to kicking before.

yearling A foal who has passed his first birthday but not his second. All registered horses involved in racing (Thoroughbreds, Standardbreds, racing Arabians, and Quarter Horses) are given the same birthday—January 1 of the year they are born. For other breeds, the actual date of birth is used.
➤ *See also foaling; weanling*

yielding to pressure
➤ *See leg-yield; pressure and release/reward*

youth In most competitions, the youth division is for riders under age 18. However, each ruling organization has the right to organize and name its divisions however it chooses. One horse show may have a Junior Division for the youngest exhibitors (under 10 years), plus a Youth Division for exhibitors from 11 to 17 years. Another may have various Junior Divisions, without any mention of a "Youth" division. Check the rules of your organization before entering a show.

zebra A wild, boldly striped equine from the same genus and family (Equidae) as the horse. There are several branches of the zebra line, all native to Africa, including *Equus zebra* (mountain zebra), *Equus burchelli* (common or Burchell's zebra), and *Equus grevyi* (Grevy's zebra). Zebras can have stripes of black or dark brown and white or buff. All equids can interbreed to produce hybrids, which are normally sterile.

ZEBRA

The zebra's stripes are among the few features that truly distinguish it from the horse, since the two equines share many other traits:

- They live in herds, headed by a single stallion.

- Younger stallions will remain with their family herd until they are old enough to establish their own breeding herd. Aggression between stallions increases during breeding season.

- Females establish a pecking order with a lead female just below the stallion.

- The lead mare guides the herd when it is fleeing predators. The stallion is the rear guard.

- Gestation is a little less than one year.

- The female guards the foal when it is first born.

- Foals remain bonded to their mother until the next foal is born.

- Their natural diet is made up of available grasses, nonselectively grazed.

zebra stripes Faint stripes, similar to those on a zebra, that frequently appear on dun horses.

zorse A zorse, of course, is the offspring of a zebra stallion and a horse mare. Like mules, zebra hybrids are sterile.

Index

Page numbers in (parentheses) are for a main entry; *italics* indicate photographs or figures; **bold** indicates tables or charts.

EXPAND YOUR EQUINE KNOWLEDGE
WITH MORE STOREY BOOKS

by Cherry Hill
Detailed discussions illuminate how horses think, learn, respond to stimuli, and interpret human behavior. Explore everything that makes a horse tick — including their senses, pecking order, body language, and more — and gain a deeper understanding of the equine mind.

by Les Sellnow & Carol A. Butler
This informative guide to all things equine answers questions for both riders and nonriders about horse behavior, physiology, breed characteristics, training, sporting events, and the long-standing relationship between humans and horses.

by Allan J. Hamilton, MD
In these 100 essays exploring universal themes like leadership, motivation, and humility, the author — a celebrated neurosurgeon and veteran horse trainer — offers the horse as a metaphor for personal, professional, and spiritual growth.

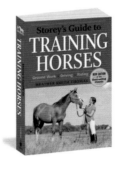

by Heather Smith Thomas
From start to finish, this is the definitive guide to developing a comprehensive, individualized training program for any type of horse, covering every aspect of handling, safety, training, and good horsemanship, both on and off the horse.

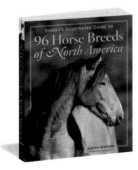

by Judith Dutson
This comprehensive encyclopedia is filled with in-depth profiles on the 96 horse breeds that call North America home. Stunning photos bring to life the spirit of these noble animals.